BEST PLACES TO STAY IN
AMERICA'S CITIES

Best Places to Stay in America's Cities

EDITED BY

Kenneth Hale-Wehmann

« »

THE HARVARD COMMON PRESS
A GAMBIT GUIDE
Harvard and Boston
Massachusetts

647.9473
B

The Harvard Common Press
535 Albany Street
Boston, Massachusetts 02118

Printed in the United States of America

Library of Congress Cataloging in Publication Data

Best places to stay in America's cities.

    ''A Gambit guide.''
    Includes index.
    1. Hotels, taverns, etc.—United States—
Directories.   I. Hale–Wehmann, Kenneth.
TX907.B457   1986   647'.947301   86-19369
ISBN 0-916782-81-6 (pbk.)

Cover design by Jackie Schuman
Text design by Joyce Weston

10 9 8 7 6 5 4 3 2 1

«CONTENTS»

v

«CONTRIBUTING» «WRITERS»

Faren Bachelis (*Sacramento*), Mario Borunda (*Honolulu*), Katharine A. Brady (*Louisville*), Maury M. Breecher (*Orlando, Tampa, St. Petersburg*), Bob Brooke (*Atlantic City, Cleveland, Detroit, Kansas City, Pittsburgh, San Juan*), The Burton Group—Marda Kaiser Burton, Becky Gillette, Carolyn Thornton, Mary Ann Wells—(*New Orleans*), Kate Butler (*Las Vegas*), Susan E. Chandler (*Chicago*), Elsa E. Cook (*St. Louis*), Pat Dalton (*Denver*), Joel Grossman (*Los Angeles*),& Kenneth Hale-Wehmann and Bruce Shaw (*Portland, Maine*), Martha Hodes (*Portland, Oregon; Seattle*), Ellen Hoffman (*Philadelphia*), Greg Jackson (*Cincinnati*), Gary Kaupman (*Atlanta*), Hank Kovell (*San Diego, Santa Barbara*), Stephen Lewis (*Santa Fe*), Scott Lively and Susan Lindsey (*Milwaukee, Minneapolis*), Robert Loupo (*Miami, Fort Lauderdale*), Kenneth Marks (*Madison*), John McCloud (*San Francisco*), Peter Rhein and Christina Tree (*Boston*), Gail Barber Rickey (*Austin, Dallas, Fort Worth, Houston, San Antonio*), Allen Silkowski (*New York City*), Teresa Turvey (*Oklahoma City*), Susan B. Whitlock (*Baltimore, Washington, D.C.*). With additional contributions from Marilyn McFarlane.

«INTRODUCTION»

For too long, people traveling to cities in the United States on business and pleasure have felt squeezed into staying at hotels whose biggest attraction was predictability. They all looked alike and offered the same impersonal services. The occasional maverick—distinctively appointed and staffed by people who pride themselves on going the extra mile to help guests feel at home—has been lost in the avalanche of advertising and guidebooks that focused only on the safe choices, the standard hotel fare.

Tastes have been changing, though, and it is becoming more common to find guesthouses and small, service-oriented hotels in urban areas. Now travelers have a guide to many styles of outstanding lodgings in *Best Places to Stay in America's Cities*.

Small hotels, guesthouses, bed and breakfasts, and exceptional larger hotels were chosen for this book because they provide guests with much more than simply a bed to sleep in. Whether furnished in European antiques or the latest Los Angeles designs, one thing nearly all of the Best Places pride themselves on is an aesthetically pleasing and comfortable environment, unlike the cookie-cutter approach to decorating that most chains take. These hoteliers may hang regional artwork on the walls, display a personal collection of Indian sculpture, or place a whimsical stuffed animal in every room.

But beyond decor and furnishings, perhaps the most significant offering of the Best Places is service. Many model their hospitality on the European tradition, employing a concierge who stands ready to recommend a restaurant, get tickets to a show, lend an umbrella—and what can't be provided from the hotel's own resources, the concierge will usually be able to provide from some other source.

Still other establishments, most often guesthouses or B&Bs, transplant country inn hospitality to city townhouses or Victorian mansions, pampering visitors with afternoon tea and cordials, breakfast in bed, fireplaces, and comfortable living rooms. Bathrooms may come stocked with fine toiletries, double-thick towels, built-in hairdryer and, for those with pressing business, a telephone.

Business travelers will find this new breed of hostelry a welcome—and not necessarily expensive—change from week after week of bland high-rise hotels. Many are equipped for business meetings and can provide teleconferencing, catering, and clerical services, all in refreshingly personable surroundings. All-suite hotels are included for travelers who need room to spread out or settle in. The book even covers resorts within city limits and country inns within a half hour of downtown.

In all, 250 hotels and inns in 40 urban areas were selected for *Best Places to Stay in America's Cities*. Seasoned and enthusiastic writers, many of them natives of the cities they covered, took a fresh look at each city's lodgings. They chose the most distinctive places to stay—not always the most famous or glamorous, not the ones with the biggest atriums, never simply the biggest. Their assignment was to unearth each city's unique lodgings. Some cities offer such a wealth of distinguished hotels that the final roster is presented with the understanding that omission from the book does not in any way constitute our disapproval of these fine hostelries. (Of course, inclusion in this book was not gained by a hotel making any kind of payment.)

Almost any guidebook to the entire United States that purports to be researched and written by one person is probably not telling the whole story. First, the writers of this book were given a list of leads to check out. In selecting, researching, and describing the hotels to be included in this book, the writers have been the final authority, since they knew their territory best. Far from making the result uneven, the range of writers has ensured this book's reliability and consistency.

To some, our choices may seem somewhat idiosyncratic and perhaps even obstinate. The establishments in this book are not ranked or rated according to any one set of criteria. In one city, perhaps we feature an upstart suite hotel and in another a vintage motor inn. We admit to a bias in creating this guide: we set out to recognize the diversity in style, cost, and size of lodgings in this country and to shed light on some of the best entries in a great variety of categories. This book, therefore, is not simply a guide to the most luxurious lodgings. Instead, we have created an anthology of fine lodgings of many different stripes.

« ATLANTA »

Atlanta Marriott Marquis
265 Peachtree Center Avenue
Atlanta, Georgia 30303
404/521-0000
Reservations 800/228-9290 (tollfree)

Singles $150
Doubles $170
Suites $275 and up

The Atlanta Marriott Marquis is the newest hotel to rise from the inner city gulch that once was home to the tarpaper-covered shacks of Atlanta's Buttermilk Bottoms. Gone are the shacks, the smells of fatback, collards, and kerosene. Here are the world's largest fabric sculpture, 25,500 plants, 5,433 doors and a host of other fascinating facts, figures, and facilities in Atlanta's newest, largest, and most spectacular lodging space.

The curvilinear but dull concrete exterior of John Portman's latest design could have been inspired by the buildings in *Blade Runner*. The facade is broken only by what appear to be two Parson's tables glued to the northern face of the 50-story tower on level 42. The effect is humorous and welcome.

The low, dark, and noisy motor entry area is mercifully brightened by the presence of a large inverted lavender cone bathed in white light. It's beginning to look more like *Close Encounters*.

If Steven Spielberg were staying in Atlanta, you would

1

probably find him in one of the 193 rooms or suites that comprise the six-floor concierge level atop the Marquis. Guests on these floors skip the long lines in the lobby, go directly to the special elevators that, in 30 seconds, will lift them to the private lobby 500 feet above the comings and goings of six convention groups and twice as many tour groups. If there does happen to be a wait to check in, they can sit on a sofa, nibble brazil nuts, sip wine, and watch all of Atlanta north to the Appalachian foothills go about its business while you wait. The atmosphere is very civil.

Ask for a room on the north side of the 42nd floor—the view is better and the lobby is accessible without having to ride the elevator. Concierge-level rooms are tastefully done in neo-oriental shapes and shades of tan, turquoise, and rose. The space is not overly large. There are chairs, perhaps a small sofa, a desk, and a clock radio. The color TV has cable and HBO, and offers additional current movies for a $5.95 charge. There is a small TV monitor in the marble-floored bath along with a telephone that reaches to the tub.

The ventilating system hums in a way seemingly inherent to large, new buildings. The Marquis offers some relief with full-size sliding glass doors that open just far enough to let the nonprocessed air in.

Morning brings thick towels, even thicker plush bathrobes, a *USA Today* at the door, and complimentary juice, fruit, coffee, and various breads in the lobby. The honor bar opens at 11 A.M. and closes at 11 P.M. Cocktail nibbles appear from 5 to 7 P.M. Complimentary cordials are served in guest rooms or the lobby after 8 P.M.

The lobby offers a TV attached to a VCR. The staff has tapes or you can bring your own. Room service is available 24 hours in your room or in the lobby just in case you want to munch nachos, have a drink, and watch a tape of *The Magnificent Seven* at 3 A.M. There is a small conference room complete with PC just off the lobby. If you need more private meeting space, one of the five suites will fill the bill.

The concierges will make dinner or entertainment reservations. It's a nice service, but don't expect suggestions outside the hotel and tourist mainstream. Ask a door or bell man if you are looking for local color. The concierges will also be happy to help with irons and boards, needles and thread, appointments at the hair salon and so on.

The public areas of the hotel are spacious, attractive, and as easy to navigate as areas this large can be. Functionally and aesthetically, they are the best Portman has done although the noise level inherent in his trademark atrium design remains. Guests can eat at five restaurants and drink at three bars. All are visual treats and staffed (as is the entire hotel) with pleasant if not terribly seasoned help. The descriptions and appearance of the food are better than the taste, especially at these prices.

The Marquis is a big, slick operation; its list of amenities seems endless. If your preference is for things on a grand scale and you need or want to stay downtown near the Atlanta Market Center and the offices of the captains of trade, industry, and government, it is the right place. The concierge-level service adds about $25 a night to the regular room rate, which is still a good value.

The Beverly Hills Inn
65 Sheridan Drive
Atlanta, Georgia 30305
404/233-8520

Singles $53
Doubles $62
Suites $80 and up
Weekly $290 for 1 or 2 persons

Despite its name, the Beverly Hills Inn is not a branch of some fancy Rodeo Drive lodging transported to Atlanta's poshest neighborhood, Buckhead. It is, rather, a converted three-story brick apartment house (built around 1927) on a quiet residential street just off Atlanta's famed Peachtree Road. While any sign of the peach trees themselves is long vanished, their road remains as the corridor from downtown to the near north suburbs; everything good and bad about the international city that Atlanta has become is in radiant evidence on Peachtree.

A visit to the Beverly Hills Inn is like coming to Atlanta to stay with your cousins, Bonnie and Lyle Kleinhans. You'll join Bonnie and the rest of your family (a large one from as close as around the corner—the kitchen is being redone—and as far as Berlin—here to supervise the opening of a new branch office) for fresh juice, sweet rolls, and coffee in the basement sunroom or its tiny adjacent garden. Bring a bottle of champagne to add to the juice so you can have mimosas, a tradition for leisurely morning meals in Atlanta. After breakfast wander up to the dark parlor where you can peruse magazines or books or pound out a bit of Chopin on the baby grand.

There is plenty of space for cars, but if you want to avoid dealing with Atlanta's frequently nightmarish traffic, you can leave it parked behind the house. The inn is within easy walking distance of two movie houses, a good health food grocery, churches, and an eclectic collection of shops, galleries and eateries varying in ethnicity from McDonalds to Grand China, where the hot and spicy whole fish is sublime.

The rooms have love seats, queen-size beds, a noncable TV and (in all but four cases) a small but complete kitchen. The four rooms without kitchens have an extra bed. Decor (Bonnie calls it "Period") varies from room to room, but is a mix of oriental patterns, chintz and unassuming modern and antique furniture. French doors open to tiny porches.

If you want to experience at least part of the Atlanta that its residents find so attractive, stay at the Beverly Hills Inn. Spend the money you save on afternoon tea, drinks, or dinner at the Ritz's excellent restaurant.

Try to reserve a month in advance. Seventy percent of the guests are repeats and referrals and that number is increasing every month.

Quality Inn Habersham Downtown
330 Peachtree Street
Atlanta, Georgia 30308
404/577-1980
Reservations 800/228-5151 (tollfree)

Singles, doubles $59–$67
Weekly $280

You need or want to stay in downtown Atlanta. You don't want to pay $100 plus to stay at one of the big names. At the 92-room Quality Inn Habersham, located just north of Peachtree Center, the rates are comparable to the chains (for a week they are downright cheap), but the hotel is much more hospitable.

The Habersham, renovated five years ago to be a European-style concierge hotel, didn't do enough business to keep the owners happy, so the concierge concept is gone. Replacing it, and bringing a more visible profile, is the Quality Inn affiliation.

The plain painted exterior is enlivened by trompe l'oeil window sills, shadows, and fancifully climbing vines. There is a small garden and some foliage around the concrete off-street entry. The registration area, lobby, and Habersham Club are done up in dark plaids and woods accented with hunt-themed lithos. These spaces offer nice foils to the city outside whether it is hot, cold, wet, or dry.

The Club, sporting a ten-seat restaurant and twice that many places in comfortable chairs and sofas, offers a continental breakfast, lunch, and dinner. Complimentary tea, coffee, and cookies are supplied all day, replaced by a cash bar at 5 P.M. This is a nice place to sit and read the paper (they provide the *Wall Street Journal* and Atlanta's dailies), organize your day, have a small business meeting, or meet your fellow guests.

The two elevators are noisy and are also used by room service and housekeeping, which can keep them busy. Rooms are priced according to elevation; the view from the lower three levels offers little more than concrete, brick, and a seedy park. The higher level's vistas are better but hardly breathtaking. The rooms are large, with closets big enough for a small party. The front corner rooms have loveseats; all rooms have either one or two beds, a couple of comfortable chairs, a desk, and a color cable TV with HBO. Beds are triple-sheeted and get turned down each night. Fresh juice and coffee are provided gratis in the morning on request. All rooms have small kitchenettes, but only when a guest stays for a week or more are utensils provided.

The blue, tan, and rose decor is much less institutional than similarly priced chains.

The staff is personable, not terribly professional, but friendly and willing to help when asked.

The advertised health spa is a small plain room with seven or eight pieces of muscle-teasing equipment scattered around. The single shower-tub-Jacuzzi in the next room will not suffice if six or eight decide to pump iron at once. The pool and other facilities at the Peachtree Plaza Hotel just down the street are available on a per-day basis.

There is adequate free parking if the uncontrolled lower level isn't occupied (as it frequently is) by nonguests' autos. Several lots lie within a block, but they are not free.

The block of Peachtree that the Habersham occupies is just starting to be renovated. Most of its buildings and people are somewhat unkempt. The nice park just up the street frequently doubles as a social club for the gentlemen on the street, but it is still a great place to sit and watch the city go about its business.

All the big hotels (Plaza, Marquis, Hilton, Ritz, Regency) along with their plethora of glitzy drinking and dining spots are within an easy walk, as are the Atlanta Market Center and Macy's. A rapid rail station is two blocks away. Ronnie's (a 24-hour deli-restaurant) stands a block away if you get a hankering for dill pickles or cheesecake and coffee at 4 A.M.

The Ritz Carlton Buckhead
3434 Peachtree Road
Atlanta, Georgia 30326
800/241-3333 (tollfree)
404/237-2700

Singles $115 and up
Doubles $135 and up

When General William Tecumseh Sherman marched through Atlanta, he leveled the city. One hundred years later Atlanta developers decided that imitation was truly the sincerest form of flattery and started the process again. One of the results of this mentality is a city without anything even resembling a grand old hotel.

What Atlanta does have is the Ritz Carlton Buckhead, built just two years ago. The Ritz Buckhead and its smaller brother downtown (at 181 Peachtree Street) look and feel like grand old hotels mashed into glass, steel, and brick frames.

The Ritz Buckhead is clearly the best all-around hotel in Atlanta (the physical plant and service at the downtown Ritz are equal). Still, the decor can seem incongruously grand for the surroundings. The brass-doored, oak-paneled elevators, lit by crystal chandeliers, have beautiful oriental rugs on their parquet floors. Trouble is, when your bellman, his glorious brass trolley, and you and your friend get in that elevator, you have it filled.

The halls, floored in beautiful wool replicas of the Ritz's carpets in Paris, are lined with more antiques, fresh flowers, and eighteenth-century art in discreet alcoves. The rooms, not over-large, benefit from large, non-opening bay windows. The pecan Chippendale and Hepplewhite reproductions, the Brunsweig & Fils fabrics, and the twice daily housekeeping look and feel like the real thing. The desk and bath are marble topped, the towels triple thick, the shower curtain is of white eyelet, and the smallish closet sports skirt, suit and satin-covered hangers. The TV has remote control, cable, and HBO. The person who cleans the room puts a book mark on today's page of the *TV Guide*. The clock radio is small and well styled. Throughout, it is obvious that attention has been paid.

Rooms with king beds have a love seat, while doubles have chairs. Both have entry areas with more pecan, Brunsweig & Fils, a chinoiserie mirror and a lacquer ice bucket. It really does feel like a lovely home.

The Dining Room is one of Atlanta's best restaurants. Chef Gunther Seeger, a man passionate about food, prepares a menu described by one local critic as "the cutting edge of Nouvelle Cuisine" and "kissed by sunlight." From simply perfect apple tart to simply exquisite celery or fresh oyster ravioli, patrons and critics offer raves for the taste,

7

look, and audacity of Seeger's food. Add a spectacular, if pricey, wine list, service difficult to fault, and piano music drifting up from the level below and this is a truly world-class dining room. Along with the piano, the lower level is home to a bar and the three-tiered Cafe, where dining is al fresco, weather permitting. Less spectacular in cuisine than the Dining Room, the Cafe presents as well prepared, well conceived, and good tasting breakfasts, lunches, and dinners as you will find in an Atlanta hotel. The decor is unaffectedly pleasant as is the service. Men are asked to wear jackets.

Expresso's, a ''deli'' near the banquet rooms, is open from 7 A.M. to 7 P.M. offering breakfast, lunch, and dessert items at very reasonable prices. The name, the atmosphere, and the pop-rock music are cutely inconsistent with the rest of this hotel.

There is an afternoon high tea, a Sunday tea with a string trio, dancing to the bands of Lester Lanin or Peter Duchin, a Sunday brunch buffet that comes on silver trays, and 24-hour room service.

Room pricing depends on the distance above ground. The 18th-floor club level (at $195) is only $20 more than its 17th- and 19th-floor neighbors, but is $80 more than a virtually identical room on level four or five. The complimentary breakfast, cookies, formal tea, cocktails, and cordials and chocolate truffles are a bargain for $20 if you use them; at $80 their value deserves question. The club-level staff is the most versatile and willing in town, but you could say the same thing about the folks that work in the rest of the hotel, too. The view (south to the city or north to the foothills) is spectacular from the upper floors.

The Buckhead location is in the midst of a business-hour traffic nightmare. A walk to the rapid rail station behind Lenox Square can lessen that annoyance. The downtown site sits atop the Peachtree Center rail station.

Shellmont Bed & Breakfast Lodge
821 Piedmont Avenue
Atlanta, Georgia 30308
404/872-9290

Single $65
Double $70
Carriage house $80–$90

In 1891 a Dr. Nicholson gave the small colonial revival mansion that is now the Shellmont to Mrs. Nicholson as a birthday present. Mrs Nicholson simply adored the design and abhorred the location—almost three miles north of the homes of her friends. Dr. Nicholson prevailed on his connections with the city fathers and the trolley line was extended to 10th Street so that Mrs. Nicholson and her friends might visit more easily. The migration to the north suburbs of Atlanta had begun.

Almost a century later the neighborhood (now called Midtown) surrounding the Shellmont is as close (save for two downtown condos and scattered artsy folk in old warehouses) as one can live to the "city" of Atlanta. If you like cities, with their attendant textures, architecture, and history, the Shellmont is the ideal place to stay in Atlanta. If, however, you are uncomfortable with the prospect of a district where not everything has been done over by upscale entrepreneurs, a district that is home to low-income people and people of various cultures and sexual orientations, it is best to make another choice.

Debbie and Ed McCord bought the Shellmont from descendants of Dr. and Mrs. Nicholson in 1982 just before a change in zoning laws that made it virtually impossible to have a guesthouse in Atlanta. We owe them thanks for their timing. The McCords have spent countless hours and more dollars than they care to discuss returning this lovely home to its original state. The two-tone green exterior accented with gold and the green and cream interior highlighted by stenciling are documented replicas of the original decor. The elegant stairway to the second level is fronted by a tufted banquette and backed by a simple but lovely wall of stained glass. The house is on the National Register and looks it.

The guest rooms, at the top of the stairs, are simple and spacious. The oriental carpet looks great on the heart pine floor. The huge lace-curtained windows fill the space with light and breezes. The tub is a clawfoot original and, at this writing, without a shower. A couple of small chairs, an AM-FM radio, a ceiling fan, and an air conditioner in the summer round out the rooms. There is a TV downstairs that guests are welcome to use.

Ed and Debbie will bring coffee and the paper upstairs half an hour before the complimentary breakfast of fruit, juice, croissants, and more coffee in the dining room. Guests are welcome to use the two parlors, library, and dining room for entertaining or relaxing—the McCords are willing to meet your needs. The guest rooms have fresh flowers and nightly chocolates, with a half bottle of wine waiting on arrival. There are several porches good for sitting and watching the neighborhood go about its daily routines.

The Carriage House offers two bedrooms and a kitchen, a TV, and a tiled tub with shower. It's not as grand as the main house, but it is attractive, comfortable, and very private. This is good for a family or for a couple to be alone, in the city, and still be able to meet other guests when they like.

Debbie and Ed obviously love antiques and old houses. They will be happy to direct you to things of that sort as well as their favorite restaurants and arts activities. You can walk to the Woodruff Arts Center, several legitimate theaters, one movie house (the largest screen in Atlanta), Piedmont Park, and restaurants from the modest but good Vietnamese Cha-Gio to the expense-account haute but inconsistent Abbey, spectacularly housed in an old church. The Mansion (across from and owned by the same folks as the Abbey) is probably the most ornate Victorian home still standing in Atlanta. Go there to gawk and have a drink but dine elsewhere, like the 1950s Mary Mac's Tearoom on Ponce de Leon or the neomodern Jake's Desserts at Midtown Plaza on Monroe.

You can walk to three major bus lines and Atlanta's efficient and attractive (if somewhat limited) rapid rail system. It is virtually impossible to hail a cab on Atlanta's streets (one must call) and the quality of the service once you get one may make you wish you had rented a car. The

McCords have a four-car garage that guests are welcome to use.

The Victorian Inns
192 Church Street
Marietta, Georgia 30060
404/426-1887

These two large, attractive guesthouses located north of the newly fashionable town square in Marietta are a great place to stay if you have business at Lockheed/Dobbins or near the I-75/I-285 interchange or if you want to explore north Georgia's Civil War or Indian historic areas. At $50 and up (with a private bath), these houses offer a nice alternative to the plethora of look-alike chains in the area. They even have meeting space for up to 75 people if you want to have a small conference.

The Waverly
2450 Galleria Parkway
Atlanta, Georgia 30339
800/325-5000 (tollfree)
404/953-4500

Singles $130
Doubles $145
Weekends $79 per night single or double
Suites $250 and up

If your trip to Atlanta requires that you stay on the north side of town along the strip of I-285 that PR people have dubbed the platinum triangle, chances are you will want to stay at the Waverly.

The folks from Stouffers (they are the managers) like to say that a visit to the Waverly is like being "a welcomed guest in a rich man's home." The rich man who owns this 14-story, 533-bedroom, $70 million home for folks away from home is Dallas developer Trammell Crow.

The Waverly and its surroundings could be Houston, Dallas, L.A., or any one of a dozen other urban sprawl cities spread across the U.S. The exterior of the Waverly is, in fact, virtually a half-scale replica of the Crow-owned Anatole in Dallas.

Six million dollars or so were lavished on art for this hotel, from the 24-foot-long brick murals that flank the entry, to the huge teak bells that hang in the atrium, to the 15-foot sculpture that looks like ice but isn't, to a delicate piece of jade in the museum-like garden court, to Atlanta fiber artist Susan Starr's tapestry in the 12th-floor elevator lobby. Much of the art is by Atlanta and Southeastern artists, a nice touch, as is the catalog of the collection available from the first-floor concierge.

The lobby and garden court are lush with marble, brass, flowers, art, and infinite detailing. There is a cozy mahogany library with over 2000 volumes, two spacious and comfortable bars, a health club with everything you'd expect plus two or three things you wouldn't, a garden area to stroll through day or night, a game room, and five restaurants.

The amenities and splendor of the Waverly's common areas are contrasted by rather ordinary sleeping quarters. The monochromatic beige walls, art, and bedspreads are slightly enlivened by rust carpeting and a love seat of the same color.

Baths are neither over-large nor over-sumptuous. TV's have cable, HBO, and in-house movies. There is 24-hour room service, and complimentary coffee and newspaper of your choice five minutes after your wake up call.

The 14th-floor is a club level, offering individual check-in, a slightly nicer bath spread, a terry cloth robe, fresh flowers, continental breakfast, pre-dinner wine and cheese, and post-dinner cordials and petit fours for an additional $35 per day per room.

«ATLANTIC CITY»

Admirals Quarters
Absecon Boulevard
Atlantic City, New Jersey 08401
800/833-3242 (tollfree)

Deluxe studios $100–$120
Two-bedroom suites $130–$150

The Admirals Quarters is one of the most accessible of the non-casino hotels in Atlantic City. Located in the new Marina Club on the boulevard near the Absecon Inlet, site of several casinos but near the traditional boardwalk area, this is one of the city's newest hotels.

This hotel-condominium operation is built in a spacious contemporary style with high-tech design and subtle colors. Its 51 units are divided into studio and two-bedroom units and were designed with business travelers in mind. However, with the opening of two more casinos in the inlet area, it is now catering to more affluent tourists.

Prices here are comparable to those in the casinos themselves, with guests getting a full apartment rather than just a hotel room. Included in the room rates are complimentary continental breakfast, free parking, free morning newspaper delivered to each room, turndown service with sweets, and 24-hour concierge service.

Valet parking is in a high-security area with closed-circuit television monitoring 24 hours a day. There is also luxury limousine service in the main Marina Club building, available to guests at half price.

The Admirals Quarters is the only Atlantic City hotel that will confirm a one-night stay instead of the required two-night minimum stay of other hotels. The units are stylishly decorated with pastel-colored fabrics and comfortable furnishings. All come with a fully equipped kitchen, color TV, and a balcony overlooking the inlet.

Guests with business may want to take advantage of the hotel's on-site secretarial service, open 12 hours daily, as well as recorded dictation 24 hours a day via in-house telephone.

A commissary is open in the Marina Club main building and other services, including the use of the health club and pool, are complimentary to guests. One of the hotel's high points is its convenience to the marina, for those who want to go fishing or just take an early evening boat ride up the inland waterway.

Several packages are available, including a "Surf and Turf" package with beach tags and free passes to Atlantic City Race Course. Another includes visits to Gardiner's Basin, a historic dockyard restoration, and elegant Smithville for shopping and dining. Transportation and meals are included.

The Madison House Hotel
123 South Illinois Ave.
Atlantic City, New Jersey 08401
609/345-1400

Standard rooms (single or double) $55 midweek, $75
   weekend
Luxury rooms $65 midweek, $90 weekend

The Madison House Hotel, built in 1929, has recently reopened, restored to its original elegance. An oasis of hospitality in this city of neon and glitter, it features a grandiose arched facade and formal entryway highlighted with Palladian windows. The 12-story Georgian brick building still has the crown molding, paneled wainscot, and piers of the original lobby and its three-tiered ceremonial staircase modeled after the one in Independence Hall in Philadelphia.

Situated across the street from the Sands Hotel and Casino

and a half block from the Boardwalk, it is close to all the major attractions, with convenient parking nearby.

The hotel has 206 rooms, 144 of which offer a view of the ocean. Each has been decorated in pastel colors with traditional furnishings and luxurious modern baths. Though evoking the 1920s, the hotel is modern in every respect and more luxurious overall than any of the casinos.

Accommodations are divided into two types: standard rooms with ocean or land views and luxury rooms with a spacious sitting area and mostly ocean views.

Guests dine in the Palladian Restaurant with its original oversized fireplace in an elegant, intimate setting.

The Palladian Restaurant was originally a public sitting room where notables gathered to discuss events of the day. The newly restored room tries to convey this atmosphere and offers a quiet place to enjoy the continental cuisine served here. Adjacent to the restaurant is a bar called Dolly's Lounge, named after Dolly Madison.

Sands Hotel and Casino
Indiana Avenue and Brighton Park
Atlantic City, New Jersey 08401
800/257-8580 (tollfree)

Singles $89
Doubles $129

This casino hotel is probably Atlantic City's most truly elegant. Located on fashionable Brighton Park across from Bally's Park Place and diagonally across from the Claridge, the Sands is one of the smallest, and since its beginning as the Brighton Hotel and Casino, it has been a favorite with discreet guests.

Like most of the casinos here, the best rooms, or "super suites," are reserved for the best customers, who are invited to the hotel on junkets. These feature lavish furnishings of traditional design as well as Jacuzzis and billiard tables. Since its opening, the Sands has been known for its excellent taste in decor and service.

The casino is more formal and European in atmosphere. Guests may dine in several outstanding restaurants. The best is Mes Amis, a beautiful paneled dining room that serves both traditional and nouvelle French dishes. Prices are close to $100 for two without wine, which can add up to half that amount to the bill. French as well as domestic wines are served in the traditional manner.

One of the features remaining from the original Brighton Casino is the cozy steak house that serves not only traditional cuts of steak but also one of the best Sunday brunches in the city.

The Sands' Food Court is a pleasant combination of eateries lining a brick walk that suggests a city block in old Atlantic City. Its mainstay is the Carnegie Delicatessen, named for the famous one of the same name on New York's Eighth Avenue. This 24-hour deli serves hefty sandwiches at prices that suggest they be split between two people.

Rooms here are magnificent, with old world luxury and modern appointments. Rich Queen Anne and Chippendale reproductions help to give this place its elegant air. Baths are large and luxurious, with phone and hair dryer included. Each room has a sitting area, and the suites feel like small houses or condominiums.

A casino would not be complete without some sort of entertainment. The Copa Room at the Sands features major stars at reasonable ticket prices.

The casino also provides parking for 500 cars and valet service.

«AUSTIN»

Bed & Breakfast Texas Style
Ruth Wilson
4224 West Red Bird Lane
Dallas, Texas 75237
214/298-5433 and 298-8586

Singles $30–$40
Doubles $35–$45

Operated by the statewide enterprise Bed & Breakfast Texas Style, headquartered in Dallas, this bed and breakfast agency is small but offers an appealing range of choices. At this writing, there are four participating host families, with another home due to reopen as an overnight lodging after renovation of the guest quarters.

As in her hometown of Dallas, Bed & Breakfast Texas Style director Ruth Wilson does an excellent job of matching guests with hosts, pairing them according to mutual interests and backgrounds as well as compatible personalities.

South of downtown Austin, Jim and Nelda Haynes live in a comfortable home set on two acres. Nelda, who is a nurse, grew up on a farm in Texas, and while she and her husband, a professor at the University of Texas, enjoy city life, they have created a minifarm at their doorstep. There are goats, sheep, chickens, ducks, and rabbits as well as a pond with catfish. Elephant ears grow along the creek that feeds the pond, and the property is dotted with fig trees, peach trees, and berries.

Guests stay in an attractive room with double bed, decorated with pink and lace. Separated from the other sleeping areas of the house, the room has its own stereo, refrigerator, and coffee maker as well as a private bath with shower. Nelda offers a choice of a full or continental breakfast (continental breakfast on Sundays). The den and the outside patio are conducive to relaxing and visiting with the congenial hosts. Rates are $40 single, $45 double.

Farther south, within the planned community of Onion Creek, is the sparkling-fresh condominium of Gloria Walton. A talented artisan, Gloria has decorated her home to reflect her personality—warm and gracious. The guest room has two twin beds and is well decorated as well as comfortable. The furniture is modern, the carpeting is plush, the atmosphere is welcoming. Its private bathroom has homey touches, such as candles and sweet-smelling soaps.

An especially hospitable host, Gloria enjoys cooking and pampering her guests. Since she works full time during the week, she serves her largest breakfasts on weekends.

Guests have use of a pool at no charge and tennis courts for a nominal fee.

To the northwest is the home of the Kavanagh family, a polished contemporary home in the North Oaks residential area. Guests are invited to make themselves at home throughout the house, which is tastefully and comfortably furnished.

The upstairs guest room has a twin-size brass bed and a desk. Decorated in blues and browns, it features plush carpeting, a ceiling fan, and a telephone. A guest room with a queen-size bed is also available on request. The private bath is cheerful, decorated in yellows and greens. Rates are $25 single, $30 single.

Ingrid Kavanagh, a native of West Germany, has a background in hotel management, and is now a real estate agent. Both qualifications make her an especially helpful host. Breakfast, a full meal served in the candlelit dining room, is a special occasion.

West of downtown is Cliffside, the home of Fran and Bill Hornung. Situated high above Barton Creek, it has the feel of a secluded retreat, although downtown Austin is only five miles away. The driveway leading to the ranch-style home is lined with low-growing cedar, typical of the Texas hill country. Guests can sit on the patio of the main house and see the pink dome of the State Capitol to one side, with the heavily wooded banks of the creek below.

Trails from the Hornung home lead down wooded slopes, and guests can hike along the creekside. Bill will tell them where to find the mysterious Barton Creek Corrals, recently listed in the National Register of Historic Places. While the origin of the low stone walls has not yet been deciphered, Bill has done extensive research into the subject, helping to stimulate local interest in the ruins.

While the creek bed is dry during part of the year, guests can enjoy tubing in the creek during the spring and early summer. At night Bill feeds raccoons and an occasional fox near his back door, and deer frequently wander through the property.

The guest room, separated from the main house by a carport, has a double bed (actually a pull-out couch), dining table, and a private bathroom. Equipped with a minikitchen, it has a toaster, crockpot, and coffee maker. The hosts will stock the kitchen with breakfast food of guests' choice.

The Driskell Hotel
6th and Brazos Streets
Austin, Texas 78767
800/252-9367 (tollfree from within Texas)
800/531-5043 (tollfree from rest of U.S.)
512/474-5911

Singles $89–$109
Doubles $99–$119
Suites $125–$675

When the Driskell Hotel welcomed its first guests in 1836, it was the grandest lodging in the Southwest. In more recent times, Lincoln Hotels purchased the historic hostelry, restoring it to its position of grandeur. Now both a state and national historic landmark, the hotel has a history intertwined with that of Texas—from being the site of the first phone call ever made out of the capital city to hosting inaugural balls.

Situated in the heart of Austin, the 183-room Driskell is an architectural treasure, with its immense arched entranceway, richly ornamented balconies, and a column-studded lobby. A bust of the hotel's builder, cattle baron Colonel Jesse Driskell, is perched on top of one exterior wall and stares southward; busts of his two sons look to the east and west.

Reflecting its link to cattle trail days, the hotel has a feeling of openness and space. Behind the registration desk is an expansive painting of the Texas range. Overlooking the lobby is a massive bronze sculpture specially commissioned for the hotel. *The Widow Maker* is a 4000-pound bronze depicting a mounted cowboy trying to save his compatriot from being dragged to death by his horse.

At the Driskell, guests have no doubt that they are in Texas. Portraits of the state's governors line the walls of the handsome lobby bar. Outside the LBJ Suite on the fifth floor is an intriguing array of photographs of the president who hailed from the Lone Star State—and who frequently made the Driskell his headquarters throughout his political career.

Guest rooms in the Driskell are arranged in two connecting buildings: the 100-year-old original hotel with high ceilings and an assortment of room configurations, and the 50-year-old tower with lower ceilings and a more uniform room design. Rooms in both of the buildings are spacious. Baths in the tower rooms are especially convenient, having an adjacent dressing area with vanity and basin.

Tastefully decorated, all of the rooms have touches of grandeur, from border designs on the walls to crystal drawer pulls on the period furniture. Rooms have two double beds, one queen-size, or a king-size. Tower rooms have their own thermostats, while those in the original hotel do not.

The Driskell Dining Room serves new American cuisine in a romantically decorated room with a white carved ceiling, mirrors, and elegant table settings. Specialties have a Southwestern flavor, ranging from duck to channel bass, pheasant to wild boar.

Guests have use of health club facilities located across

the street from the hotel. The Supreme Court Racquetball Club & Fitness Center features a fitness area with Universal and Nautilus equipment, five racquetball courts, lap pool, hot tub, and sauna.

The hotel's meeting facilities include the Crystal Ballroom and nine smaller rooms. On display in the Maximilian Room are large gold-leaf mirrors given by Maximilian to his bride, the Empress Carlotta of Belgium.

Within the hotel are a gift shop, men's boutique, and art gallery, as well as an airline ticket office. The concierge arranges such services as babysitters or secretarial help.

The Driskell has complimentary van service between the hotel and Robert Mueller Airport. Valet parking is $6 per night. Guests should allow extra time when calling for their cars, for service tends to be slow.

Located a few blocks from the state capitol and the University of Texas, the Driskell fronts onto Sixth Street—a lively entertainment area with restaurants, bars, and specialty shops.

La Mansion Hotel
6505 I-35 North
(at Highway 290)
Austin, Texas 78752
800/292-7300 (tollfree from within Texas)
800/531-7208 (tollfree from rest of U.S.)
512/454-3737

Singles $85–$125
Doubles $100–$140
Suites $140 and up
Children under 18 free

A Spanish hacienda set on the northern edge of the state's capital city, La Mansion offers quiet charm. The 350-room hotel, a member of Preferred Hotels Worldwide, opened in mid-1984.

Guests drive up to the stately white portico of the Spanish colonial mansion where they are greeted by hospitable doormen. The lobby with its distinctive Mexican decor has a feeling of openness and space. A carved credenza circa 1800, 18th-century Spanish chairs, and Aubusson tapestries add to the feeling of authenticity.

Beyond the lobby is the hotel's focal point—a multilevel inner courtyard with waterfalls, fountains, and a shell-shaped pool. Nearly half of the guest rooms open onto this peaceful courtyard, a seeming sanctuary from the bustling city beyond.

Guest rooms are spacious and comfortably furnished, with a choice of two double or one king-size bed. Some have french doors opening onto small balconies. All have dressing areas adjacent to the bath. Bathrooms have telephones and are stocked with toiletries.

The sixth floor, designated as the Premier Floor, has two styles of suites and a range of special services. Guests are pampered with continental breakfast in the mornings, and cocktails are served in the private lobby in the late afternoon. Rooms on this floor have extra touches, from fresh flowers to bathrobes. Of interest to business travelers are the executive boardrooms on this floor, allowing them to conduct meetings in personalized surroundings.

A service-oriented hotel, La Mansion seems to exude a spirit of caring, and the 300 employees are well-trained at their individual tasks. The concierge will arrange babysitting services on request, and the hotel in general is well suited to families. Standard service includes valet parking, 24-hour room service, and bedtime turndown.

On the second floor is a fitness room with a sauna and exercise equipment, including treadmill, stationary bicycle, and free weights. The landscaped pool within the outdoor courtyard has a whirlpool spa.

La Mansion's most distinctive dining area is La Talavera Restaurant, featuring a display of 18th-century Talavera pottery collected by the hotel's owner. To complement the museum-quality collection, the hotel commissioned hand-thrown copies of the pottery for its everyday service in the restaurant, resulting in an eye-catching table setting. Dedicated to fine dining, La Talavera serves classical and contemporary cuisine, utilizing a separate kitchen for its service.

Las Ventanas has an informal atmosphere, serving Southwestern specialties. Rio Brazos is a cozy bar with a stone fireplace, a dance floor, and live entertainment nightly. Most of the public areas, especially the restaurants and the elegant lobby bar, overlook the courtyard.

Meeting space in La Mansion is considerable, with more than 18,000 square feet of function space and the city's largest ballroom. Meeting rooms are especially well lighted and pleasantly decorated.

A gift shop, newsstand, and American Airlines reservation desk are located off the lobby.

Situated about four miles from Mueller Municipal Airport, La Mansion provides complimentary transportation to the airport as well as to downtown Austin. And on top of the hotel is a heliport available to guests.

While valet parking is available, guests also have the convenience of free parking in the garage adjoining the hotel.

Stephen F. Austin Hotel
701 Congress Avenue
(at 7th Street)
Austin, Texas 78701
800/252-3025 (tollfree from within Texas)
800/531-5048 (tollfree from rest of U.S.)
512/476-1061

Singles $80–$120
Doubles $95–$135
Suites $150–$500

The newly restored Stephen F. Austin Hotel in downtown Austin is elegant in decor and hospitable in service. A 60-year-old lodging, it has a residential feel, with the lobby and adjoining bar arranged like a spacious living room. Classical music, Persian rugs, antique furnishings, fresh flowers, and works of art combine to create an atmosphere of warmth.

Guests have their choice of 178 rooms, designated as traditional, junior traditional, junior suites, and large junior suites. Decorated in rich colors, they are comfortably arranged and exquisitely decorated. The highlight of each room is its custom-designed canopied bed, with yards of draped fabric and an intricately tucked covering overhead. (For guests who prefer rooms without canopy beds, there are more contemporary rooms available.) Special touches such as doorbells, luxuriant plants, and turndown service with chocolates add to the feeling of warmth.

Both the junior traditional and junior suites are highly recommended, worth the additional price over that of the traditional rooms, which are fairly small.

French doors separate the living and sleeping areas in the one and two bedroom suites. The living room has a writing desk, comfortable seating, television in an armoire (no TV in the bedroom of the suites), and separate bathroom.

Bathrooms are large, with dressing room–style lighting, brass fixtures, and lots of fluffy towels. Junior suites have a shower but no tub; large junior suites have a tub with shower and an adjoining dressing area.

The Remington Dining Room, which serves continental cuisine, is named for the Frederic Remington bronzes showcased in the restaurant. A serpentine seating arrangement weaves through the center of the dining room. The adjoining Crystal Room is especially inviting, with crystal sculptures and mirrored walls.

The Austin Garden Room is casual and cheery, decorated with lattice-work and floral colors. The restaurant serves three meals a day, with a weekday lunch buffet and a lavish Sunday brunch—served to the accompaniment of harp music.

Afternoon tea is served in the lobby lounge.

Meeting and banquet rooms are on the mezzanine floor, an aesthetically pleasing area with oriental sculptures, plush seating, and an exterior balcony overlooking Seventh Street.

Hotel guests have use of the facilities of the Supreme Court Racquetball Club & Fitness Center one block away. The club has Universal and Nautilus equipment, exercise classes, racquetball courts, lap pool, steam room, hot tub, and saunas.

A service-oriented hotel, the Stephen F. Austin has a concierge who will arrange rental cars (available on the property), secretarial services, and babysitters, and field other requests. Valet parking, costing $5 per night, is particularly courteous and efficient, with attendants priding themselves on having cars waiting by the time guests reach the curbside. Complimentary van service to surrounding areas, including the airport, is offered from 7 A.M. to 10:30 P.M.

Newspapers and sundries are available at the bell desk in the lobby.

Situated a few blocks from the Capitol, the Stephen F. Austin is also close to major business and recreational highlights of the city. Old Pecan Street/Sixth Street entertainment and specialty shops are one block away.

Wyndham Hotel Southpark
4140 Governor's Row
(I-35 and Ben White Boulevard)
Austin, Texas 78744
512/448-2222
800/822-4200 (tollfree from rest of U.S.)
800/252-4545 (tollfree from within Texas)

Singles $82–$110
Doubles $92–$120
Suites $182–$600

South of downtown Austin is Wyndham Hotel Southpark, a 315-room hotel with outstanding recreational features, a relaxing environment, and a hospitable staff. Situated approximately ten minutes south of the central business district and 15 minutes from Robert Mueller Airport, the hotel offers travelers—both business and leisure—an alternative to downtown hotels.

Opened in mid-1983, the hotel is contemporary in design, with a sleekly furnished lobby. Adjoining the lobby is the Texas-size pool and recreation area, probably the best among Austin hotels. The oblong pool, spanned with a bridge leading into the fitness center, curves into the enclosed center itself—giving guests a choice of indoor or outdoor swimming.

Inside the center is an attractive deck area with whirlpool, weight and exercise room with Universal equipment, stationary bicycles and treadmill, sauna, locker rooms, and video game room. Outside is a sports court for basketball or volleyball, shuffleboard court, and jogging track encircling the hotel property.

Guest rooms in the 14-story hotel are available in four configurations: rooms with two double beds, one king bed, king bed and balcony, and concierge-floor accommodations. Furnishings are luxurious and modern—comfortable seating, rich fabrics, plush carpeting, and colorful art work. All rooms have color televisions with in-house movies and digital clock radios. Warmly decorated bathrooms have wide vanities and a host of toiletries.

Executive suites have a parlor with conference table, sitting area with foldout bed, and a choice of one or two connecting bedrooms. Both the Presidential and the Governor's suites have a large parlor and two bedrooms; the Presidential has a Jacuzzi.

Lodging on the concierge floor ($110 single, $120 double) includes such extras as complimentary continental breakfast, hors d'oeuvres, and newspapers.

Guests park in the Wyndham Southpark's outdoor lot at no charge. (No valet parking is available.) Van transportation between the hotel and Robert Mueller Airport is complimentary. The hotel is staffed with a concierge, laundry service is available, and a gift and sundry shop is on the premises.

Onion Creek Grill, a casual dining room, serves all three meals. In addition to steak and seafood dishes, its menu features many moderately priced selections including pizza and pasta. (*Fajita* pizza is one of its specialties.) Sweetwaters is a popular lounge, with nightly entertainment. The Lobby Bar, with comfortable couches and piano music, is good for relaxing.

Well suited for meetings and group functions, the Wyndham Southpark has a large ballroom and 13 meeting rooms.

The hotel is part of Southpark Executive Center, a planned, mixed-use development.

Complementing its hotel in south Austin, Wyndham Hotels is opening Wyndham Hotel Northwest Austin, a 479-room luxury hotel, in the fall of 1986.

26

«BALTIMORE»

The Admiral Fell Inn
888 South Broadway
Baltimore, Maryland 21231
800/292-4667 (tollfree)
301/522-7377

Singles $80–$105
Doubles $90–$115
Suites $135

In a world where almost all new hotels are furnished in subdued colors, the bold colors and echoing spaces of the Admiral Fell Inn make a big splash. Dark greens and reds jar each other and compete for attention in the inn's lobby, sitting room, and library, and the polished hardwood floor and dark furniture hold their own. Outside the business district and beyond the Inner Harbor, the Admiral Fell Inn, opened in June 1985, offers a different model of the contemporary American bed and breakfast.

Originally a boarding house for sailors, at another time a vinegar bottling plant, the inn on the corner at Fell's Point has a number of intriguing architectural features. Most noticeable is the central air shaft, which serves as a small atrium on the first floor and onto which the hallways of the upper floors open. The guest rooms have been carved out of three buildings in a variety of shapes and sizes, with sitting areas added on every floor. Happily, this is one renovated hotel that had the foresight and the means to include access for the disabled: a courtyard entrance, elevators, wide corridors, and three specially equipped rooms are all part of the layout.

The open feel of the public rooms is striking. To the right as one enters, the lobby boasts a huge working fireplace and a grandfather clock. To the left, a second sitting area looks out to Shakespeare Street and the docks, where a number of tugs are tied. Behind this, the library offers a somewhat more closed setting. Continental breakfast is served here in the morning, and coffee left on all day. In the afternoon, an honor bar takes the place of the morning's muffins. Behind the hotel desk on the other side is a small anteroom where local artwork is displayed at no cost to the artists.

The 37 guest rooms are each named after a famous Baltimore resident—a plaque inside the room tells who the individual was. Color schemes vary imaginatively, and wallpapers, drapes, and upholstery play off each other. The furniture is mostly reproductions: high canopied beds covered with white lace, a writing desk and easy chair, and a large armoire containing a color television. The bathrooms are painted a dark sea green, with cream-colored towels.

Every room has its own thermostat and at least one phone. The honeymoon suite features a full living room with fireplace and mantel, and a whirlpool tub in the bathroom.

Though the Fell's Point neighborhood is beginning to fill up with specialty shops, it hasn't lost its distinction from the rest of the city. The inn's owners are contemplating building an observatory deck on the roof, to look out over the harbor and the nearby markets. A below-stairs restaurant, under construction when visited, will seat 30 and serve new American cuisine to compete with nearby Little Italy's European fare; the inn's pub will serve light snacks to both guests and stragglers from the street.

The Admiral Fell Inn provides many services offered by other hotels: complimentary valet parking, daily newspaper, concierge service, and passes to an athletic club. It also offers what others can't—its charming location outside the city where there's salt in the air and space to turn about. Whether one drives, uses the inn's free van service, or takes the summertime ferry from the Inner Harbor, Fell's Point deserves a visit.

Note to travelers: don't ask how the Admiral Fell Inn; the staff has heard it before.

The Belvedere
1 East Chase Street
Baltimore, Maryland 21202
800/692-2700 (tollfree)
301/332-1000

Singles $70–$77
Doubles $80–$87
Suites $80–$180

Midway between Pennsylvania Station and the waterfront, the Belvedere is an imposing structure with an elaborately decorated brick and stone facade. The inside does not disappoint: the enormous square lobby, with marble floors and maroon loveseats, sets the tone for the rest of the hotel. A chandelier and numerous lamps reflected in mirrors on the ceiling and the four marble posts make the area irresistibly light and sparkly.

In the tradition of a grand hotel, the Belvedere seems to have almost as many entertainment areas as guest rooms. Of these, two are outstanding. The John Eager Howard Room, on the first floor, offers formal dining for breakfast, lunch, and dinner. Dominated by a portrait of John Eager Howard over a massive fireplace and mantel, the dining area is dark and distinguished, with richly upholstered benches and Empire chairs. The soaring ceiling makes possible the huge rectangular windows and surrounding murals, recently restored with the help and expert advice of the woman who painted them in 1933. A baby grand piano polishes off the room—it's played every evening during dinner hours.

Twelve stories above is the 13th Floor Lounge, a cocktail bar with gorgeous views to the south and north. From 5 P.M. to 2 A.M. live music attracts a varied crowd to this former cloakroom; semiformal attire is reflected in the mirrors along one wall and the plate glass windows that lean out into the night.

The Belvedere is the kind of hotel that still has everything one needed in the past—not one, but two ballrooms grace its upper floors—but has been equipped for the modern world as well. When it was converted into apartments in the 1970s, ramps were added for the disabled, and the lower levels were leased out to a variety of businesses. Now the Shops Belvedere offer most anything one could want, including the Midtown Y athletic club, to which all guests gain complimentary passes, and a Japanese restaurant, in case the Owl Bar's Cajun cooking doesn't hit the spot.

Room options at the hotel are as various as the entertainment and service areas. The smallest and least expensive, simply called the guest room, offers two double beds, an easy chair, writing desk, and huge closet, with the standard color television. Next up, the efficiency adds a sofa, dining table, and kitchenette. Each successive category contains more space and furniture than the last, up to the corporate suite, which has a full living room with corner (nonworking) fireplace, a large bathroom with ample storage space, half bath, and a two-oven kitchen. (All kitchens are stocked with dishes for four; guests may request more.) The decor of the rooms fits basic hotel standards. Each room has a brass knocker and peephole surveying the wide corridors with their tacky flowered carpeting.

Despite its size—180 rooms, with 250 staff—the Belvedere's clientele runs more to individual corporate travelers than to groups. Occasionally, smaller executive board meetings will be held here, 12 blocks from Baltimore's major convention hotels. In addition to the ballrooms, the hotel has three large conference rooms and a number of smaller "breakout" rooms. Its caterers are the third largest in town. Group rates are negotiable.

The Belvedere takes its role as a part of the Baltimore community seriously. In addition to countless weddings and bar and bat mitzvahs, it has hosted all the performers coming in for shows at the Lyric Opera House and Mechanic Theater for decades. A recent innovation is tours of the Belvedere for area senior citizens, who often find the hotel's past intertwined with their own.

The Peabody Court
612 Cathedral Street
Baltimore, Maryland 21201
800/732-5301 (tollfree)
301/727-7101

Singles $105–$145
Doubles $125–$165
Suites $255–$450

When it comes to luxury accommodations, nobody does it better than the Peabody Court. From the gloved doormen to the heated towel racks, from the coded, two-line conference phones in every room to the eleven-chef rooftop gourmet restaurant, the Peabody Court's elegance exceeds even that of the European hotels it takes as its models.

Renovated at extraordinary cost—close to $10 million—the hotel was meticulously planned over three years. Nothing was left out, and no second-bests accepted; all of the public areas and suites are filled with antiques and originals. Moreover, the most modern technologies were employed. The lighting of the pink marble lobby exemplifies the dual approach: its main ornament is a six-foot antique crystal chandelier; the lighting, however, is adjusted automatically by computer to ease the traveler's transition from the outside in.

The hotel's magnificence is not contained in its showiest rooms; it spills over into each and every guest room. With seven color schemes, the rooms offer variations on the theme of luxury. Textures are delightful, whether those of the marble-topped beside tables, the embossed leather writing desk, or the sumptuous drapes and upholsteries. The bathrooms, done in Italian marble, offer more conveniences: full-length and over-sink mirrors, a full complement of amenities, a makeup/mustache mirror and built-in hair dryer in the sink area; and a retractable clothes line, heated rack for the extra-soft towels, and Jacuzzi whirlpool (in 65 percent of the rooms) for the tub.

Each room has its own wet bar and prestocked minifridge, both on the honor system. Color televisions are secreted in the armoires and feature in-room movies as well as local channels. The rooms are opened with a computerized card, and have individual doorbells.

The hotel's two restaurants make meals events. La Brasserie, the less formal of the two, was the only room not gutted when the renovation process began. Its wood floors, dark paneling, and green marbleized pilasters are perfectly accentuated by the painting of the original molding, by the regal drapes, and by the framed photographs of Peabody Conservatory graduates. On the mezzanine, La Brasserie can be reached from either the main lobby, via a winding marble staircase in a tapestried stairwell, or from Monument Street, on the side of the hotel.

Atop the Peabody Court, the Conservatory offers indisputably the best views of Baltimore from its unbroken plate glass window-walls. In the dining area, air and temperature controls for each table assure comfort. The patterned pink and green wall- to-wall carpeting is complemented by the upholstered chairs and by the intricate painted ironwork overhead. Plants and flowers also contribute to the atmosphere of this exquisite French restaurant, which has been booked solid since the hotel's opening in April 1985. The piano lounge, surrounding the marble-topped bar, focuses on an original painting of dancers and panpipers, specifically commissioned for the room.

The hotel's services are as complete as its decor. Twenty-four-hour room and butler service, valet parking, limousine service, 24-hour concierge service, and electronic security controls make stays for all guests enjoyable and hassle-free. The Peabody Court also caters to the meeting groups that are half of its clientele with such offerings as an electronic paging system, complete audiovisual capabilities in meeting rooms, computer hookups in every room, and satellite downlink services. Its eight meeting rooms are divided by soundproof, collapsible walls, making larger spaces possible.

The Shirley House
205 West Madison Street
Baltimore, Maryland 21201
301/728-6550

Singles $60–$70
Doubles $75–$85

"Who the heck was Shirley?" Bob Black hasn't found the answer to this question after two years of careful research into the history of his property, which originally opened as a hotel in 1880. But he's found out much else about the building, and put it to use in his careful restoration process. Black's humor and earnestness suffuse the Shirley House's latest incarnation as an urban inn, making it the homiest lodgings in Baltimore.

The sitting room, or front parlor, is the focus of the hotel. Guests trip out of the 17 rooms for their continental breakfast here in the morning, and stop off for a glass of wine before retiring in the evening. The enormous bay window looks out on a side street of Baltimore's Mount Vernon neighborhood, and is perfect for a good read (a full bookcase stands nearby) or a tete-a-tete. The rest of the room lends itself to gatherings of more than two—around a coffee table in front of the magnificent heath, or around the small breakfast table. The soft pinks and fine fabrics, combined with personal attention from the owner and manager, keep visitors as warm as the blazing fire in winter.

The guest rooms, accessible by either the grand, finely carved oak staircase in the center of the inn or the restored elevator (big enough for two) at the back, are spacious units with ten-foot ceilings and wall-to-wall carpeting. Connecting doors make for a variety of rooming options: the standard suite with kitchenette, suite with parlor, and bedroom with kitchenette can be mixed and matched to suit individual and group needs.

The furnishings, all imported antiques, are complemented by Victorian wallpapers. All rooms have color televisions in the armoires and conference telephones, and the kitchenettes are equipped with mugs for the complimentary coffee, tea, and hot chocolate. (Guests may request additional kitchen equipment.)

But Bob Black's care for his hotel and guests goes beyond furniture and supplies. When he found that the hotel's brick front, though decorated, was a little too low-key to attract notice, he asked a friend to design a self-lit stained-glass sign. He commissioned two murals to go on either wall of the front entrance, one depicting the women of 1880, one the men. And to bring in new people and raise the neighborhood's awareness of his project, he sponsored an art show in his first year.

Rules and regulations at the Shirley are never harsh and seldom strict. Pets are not allowed, but cribs are available for children. Check-out is at the convenience of the guest; if there is an overlap of visitors, luggage will be stored in the Shirley Suite, the inn's extra-large first-floor unit. (This suite is also used for board meetings and small group conferences.) Breakfast hours—normally 7–11 A.M. Monday through Saturday and 7 A.M.–12:30 P.M. Sunday—are flexible at either end, and those who miss the meal are welcome to have coffee at any time of day from the Thermoses kept in the parlor.

Finally, Black has leased spaces in a nearby parking garage to offer free parking to his guests. And for those who still don't think they're getting their money's worth, he automatically lowers rates during quiet months. Lease rates are available for stays of a month or more.

Once an all-female dorm for the Maryland Institute of Art, the Shirley has proved especially attractive to women in all its incarnations. But the effortless taste, warmth, and security of this tiny hotel will be enjoyed by all travelers with the time and inclination to stop by and see for themselves.

Society Hill Hotel
58 West Biddle Street
Baltimore, Maryland 21201
301/837-3630

Singles $65–$80
Doubles $85–$95

The Society Hill Hotel puts the hospitality back in the hospitality industry. With three properties in the Baltimore area, the SHH sets out to capture travelers of taste from very different arenas—government, the corporate world, academia, and medicine. But each guesthouse, with its limited number of rooms and abundance of special services, is sure to attract as many wedding parties and honeymooners as business guests.

The original Society Hill Hotel in Baltimore is tiny, having only fifteen rooms. Each one, however, is a miniature masterpiece. All of the furniture is antique, and of exquisite beauty and quality. The decor is Victorian throughout, and the wallpapers, bed covers, and drapes are richly patterned and gorgeously matched. The larger rooms have sitting areas with oriental rugs over the wall- to-wall carpeting. Nothing here is ramshackle: in every glance one sees the care and effort taken to make this hotel outstanding.

The amenities also are well thought out. Fresh flowers grace the bedrooms, conveniently outfitted with individual thermostats, push-button phones, and color televisions; the bathrooms have scented soaps from London, makeup/mustache mirrors, built-in hair dryers, and brass and porcelain fixtures. All rooms have private baths; some of the smaller rooms have shower stalls rather than tubs. All rooms also have doorbells and peepholes.

Along with the room come generous services. Breakfast served to the room tops the list; complimentary parking and free local phone calls are also built in. There is no charge for extra persons. The innkeeper provides full concierge service, and as of summer 1986, the hotel will have shuttle service to the Inner Harbor.

The hotel restaurant and bar, through which guests must enter to register, is bright and sparkling clean, with tiled floors and white brick walls. At the back is a tiny atrium, with inlaid marble tables and plush Victorian chairs. The menu is inventive and eclectic. At the bar, a jazz pianist entertains guests nightly. Like the rooms, the entertainment areas have been thoughtfully decorated piece by piece.

The SHH on West Biddle Street is a narrow, three-story townhouse on the corner with a decorative brownstone front. Guests are given keys to the heavy, wooden front door when they register, as well as keys to their own rooms. The location, very near Pennsylvania Station, has the advantages of three major cultural centers nearby: the Meyerhoff Symphony Hall, the Lyric Opera House, and the Theater Project.

The Society Hill property at Johns Hopkins University is if anything more beautifully appointed than its older sibling, and has a few meeting rooms for small groups and boards, in addition to a sitting/reading room for guests. The third property, at Government House (not opened at this writing), promises to be as distinctive as the first two.

The Tremont Hotel
8 East Pleasant Street
Baltimore, Maryland 21202
301/727-2222

Singles $85–$105
Doubles $110–135

At two years, the Tremont ranks as one of the oldest modern hotels in Baltimore. Yet it needn't fear the fast-paced hotel boom. Ahead of its time when built, it still has an edge on the market for corporate travel.

The lobby of the Tremont has a dark, compact feel to it. Through two sets of brass-and-glass doors one escapes Baltimore's business district into a kind of private business club. To the left is a small sitting area with comfy leather chairs, a low wooden table, and atop its polished surface a hefty volume on Matisse—all backed by black oriental screens. To the right, the bar called Celebrities is lighter, with numerous small tables looking out on the street, and autographed pictures of the Tremont's more famous guests adorning the walls.

The staff at the reception desk opposite the entrance are courteous without being stuffy. Behind them the hotel's formal restaurant, 8 East, serves international cuisine to up to fifty persons in a romantic oriental-and-pink decor.

Of the sixty suites at the Tremont, over half are full-fledged executive suites, the rest the smaller corporate suites. The latter, mostly on the lower floors, combine bedroom and sitting area with one queen bed and a pullout sofa. The brass standing and table lamps and the large mirrors around the room add some flash to the otherwise subtle, tastefully decorated rooms. Muted oranges and grays predominate, and the art and wall hangings, mostly by local artists, blend in nicely.

The executive suites on the upper floors add to all this room to roam and breathtaking views of the city from the full-view plate glass windows. Every executive suite has a bathroom with entrances from both the bedroom and the living room, convenient for those who need to hold meetings in their suites. The bedrooms, with two queen beds and a remote-controlled TV (there is another TV in the living room armoire), are enormous and comfortable.

But the kitchens in all suites show the hotel to its best advantage. Equipped with a medium-size refrigerator, gas stove, toaster oven, and microwave, the kitchens are ultra-modern. The automatic drip coffeemaker, coffee grinder, and jar of fresh beans delivered daily may even top the comforts of home.

Extras keep piling up at the Tremont: heavy, soft robes at night along with turndown service that includes chocolate and a cordial; room service; two in-house movies every month; newspaper of one's choice delivered to the door each morning; access to the outdoor pool at the Tremont Plaza Hotel, a few blocks away, and to the downtown athletic club; and a basket of snacks, sweets, and drinks pre-stocked in the kitchen. The hotel has a courtesy van for special groups and occasions; parking is provided in the hotel lot for $7 daily with in and out privileges.

The executive suites provide ample space for small, informal meetings. For larger groups, the hotel has three function rooms, two attached to guest suites, the third in the lower lobby, with a capacity of seventy persons.

The Tremont caters to busy businesspersons. Its efficiency, cleanliness, and up-to-date facilities provide all they could want, and more.

«BOSTON»

The Boston-Cambridge Embassy Suites Hotel
400 Soldiers Field Road
Boston, Massachusetts 02134
800/362-2779 (tollfree)
617/783-0090

$110–$600 including full breakfast and afternoon
  cocktails

This hotel is an outstanding representative of the new breed of all-suite lodgings. And the suites cost no more than most luxury single rooms in Boston. The lobby presents an expansive flower arrangement on a round table, white marble stairs, brass elevator doors, palms in huge pots, and a very long escalator going up to a second level in an atrium the height of the building. Green seems to be the predominant color throughout the hotel, with countertops and bar tops being malachite green.

The 310 guest rooms make the hotel special. They are nicely planned to allow businesspeople to entertain or live comfortably for an extended visit. The suite is also perfect for a family on a weekend getaway since special weekend rates are available and the sofa in the living room folds out into a bed. The amenities are fairly standard; however, the closet doors are mirrored and the telephone in the living room is a speakerphone. Bedroom furnishings have a lacquered look. Headboards have padded floral prints. The bed is very comfortable and a second sheet is used for a blanket cover.

A nice swimming pool is available on the first floor.

The hotel is on a bend of the Charles River so some rooms have an interesting view of both Cambridge and Boston. Several top-floor suites are bi-level, with the bedroom overlooking the living room. They are very romantic and often serve as honeymoon suites.

Free self-parking simply adds to the overall good value of this hotel.

The Bostonian
Faneuil Hall Marketplace
Boston, Massachusetts 02109
800/343-0922 (tollfree)
617/523-3600

$140–$450

The Bostonian is a new hotel that incorporates two historic buildings into a predominantly modern structure. Located across from Faneuil Hall Marketplace, the hotel was added onto part of the Haymarket. It has blended in well with its neighbors. Businesspeople during the week and families on weekends love the festive atmosphere of the Haymarket with its hawking vegetable vendors.

The red brick building has a European-style porte cochere entrance, consisting of a circular cobblestone driveway around a courtyard. The centerpiece of the courtyard is a fountain and a stainless steel sculpture, *The Spirit of Boston*, by artist David Lee Brown. The sculpture rises from an adaptation, in granite, of an early 18th-century map of Boston, detailing the city when the harbor extended to where the hotel now stands.

The lobby is designed only for guests, who are treated to solicitous service. Other visitors have a separate entrance to such public spaces as the bar and restaurant. Traditional and contemporary elements have been combined to create an intimate feeling found only in small private clubs and guesthouses. Registration and cashier functions are shielded as much as possible. A roaring fire and bowls of apples welcome guests in the winter. Doormen wear distinctive uniforms with Russian fur hats. Luggage is taken directly to rooms, never to the lobby.

An exposed glass elevator connects the public lobby with the nationally acclaimed Season Restaurant on the rooftop. The restaurant is also enclosed in glass, with a lighted stainless steel ceiling arched with laminated wood beams, and affords a broad view of Faneuil Hall Marketplace. The food served is some of the best in Boston. The manager takes a personal interest in a rather extensive all-American wine cellar.

Four different color schemes and two types of furnishings are used for the guest rooms. The rooms in the newly constructed sections of the hotel are decorated in a contemporary style, while a more traditional approach is taken in the rooms in the totally renovated historic sections. Room no. 734 has real beams in the ceiling, a water view, and French reproduction antique furniture. Suite no. 735 has a two-story room with fireplace, and is decorated in warm brown colors.

Bathroom amenities are extensive, and worthy of note because they are unusual: small packets of Woolite, Roger Gallet products, silk sachets, and of course a terry cloth bathrobe.

Most rooms have french windows opening onto small balconies with wrought-iron railings and flower boxes that are kept full of seasonal plantings year round. Most suites have Jacuzzi tubs and many rooms have oversized oval tubs.

The atrium lounge is a great place for people watching and is a local gathering spot for the young moneyed class.

The Charles Hotel at Harvard Square
One Bennett Street
Cambridge, Massachusetts 02138
800/882-1818 (tollfree)
617/864-1200

$125–$400 double occupancy

Built of brick to match Harvard buildings and Cambridge sidewalks, the Charles fits in well with its surroundings. The medium-rise hotel (with 300 rooms and suites) has many large windows to let in views of the river, Harvard, and its own square, a bricked plaza with a cafe, street vendors, and a cluster of shops. Inside, walls are punctuated with paintings of Cambridge and with exquisite quilts. The spare, modern lines of public rooms set off New England antiques.

Guest rooms all feature down quilts and come equipped with three telephones and two cable TVs (one in the bathroom and one in a tasteful armoire that also includes a desk and honor bar). Baths have terry cloth bathrobes and scales. Some rooms are equipped with computer modems (computers may also be rented). An elaborate spa offers pool, solarium, Jacuzzi, sauna, splash pool, exercise room, hair and skin salon, massage, and cafe.

Opened in January 1985, the Charles caters largely to Harvard University's visiting VIPs. Guests also have easy access to Boston via the subway station in Harvard Square. Cambridge shops, restaurants, sights, and street life are attractions in themselves. The hotel's two restaurants, the bright, informal Courtyard Cafe (outside tables in warm weather) and the haute expensive Rarities, have already earned a strong local following. The Regattabar, featuring top jazz groups, is very popular.

The Copley Plaza

138 St. James Avenue
Boston, Massachusetts 02116
800/225-7654 (tollfree)
617/267-5300

$135–$190 double occupancy
Suites $250–$700

The Copley Plaza was built in 1912 by the same architect who designed the Plaza in New York. The hotels were also furnished identically, to the extent that you still find the same gilt-armed, petit point–covered chairs in both lobbies.

The lobby at the Copley Plaza is a space worth stepping into, even for those not staying here. A high, cloud-studded sky crowns ornate ceiling designs, and the walls are marble.

In contrast to newer hotels, the front desk here is a massive, wooden presence and the lobby is vast, with wide halls leading off to a choice of restaurants, shops, and meeting rooms. Few hotels still offer so many amenities: a shoeshine stand and jeweler as well as barber and newsstand. Obviously a convention space (the ratio is 60 percent individual guests to 40 percent group business), this is also a place for intimate meetings.

The obvious place to meet is beneath the large crystal chandelier, on the grand, round settee. From here you can choose to take a few steps into the pink and green Tea Court, or to lunch in the Edwardian townhouse atmosphere of Copley's. This dining room, with its mix of art and books, is about as Bostonian as any public room in Boston. You can also sink into the shadows of deep leather wing chairs in the wood-paneled Plaza Bar, or the book-lined Library Bar.

Singles tend to gather around the Copley Bar, another magnificent paneled room with green-hooded lights and gleaming brass. The formal dining room is the Cafe Plaza, a confection of glass, gilt, crystal, and white napery. All are frequented by Bostonians. Sunday brunch at Copley's is particularly extravagant and popular.

The Copley Plaza, like most grand dames, is a period piece. Now owned by its wealthy neighbor, the John Hancock insurance company, it is constantly being refurbished, but rarely is a stick of furniture changed. In the guest rooms as well as public rooms you find gilded, finely tooled furniture, the height of fashion in 1912. The TVs are hidden in armoires and the large closets are faced in glass. Price differences hinge largely on the view, either out over Copley Square, or not. Although there are daily rates, packages are usually a better bargain.

Four Seasons Hotel
200 Boylston Street
Boston, Massachusetts 02116
800/268-6282 (tollfree)
617/338-4400

$140–$950

This hotel is designed to cater to the rich and famous. It is prepared to shelter or spotlight its guests according to their whim. No expense has been spared to provide the highest-quality surroundings and service.

The most striking aspect of the lobby in this new building is the feeling of openness, yet at the same time a sense of comfort that usually comes with smaller, more cozy spaces. Large windows permit a view completely through the building from one block to the other. A giant brass and crystal chandelier hangs in the porte cochere. Marble floors, oil portraits, reproduction antique furniture, and warm, indirect lighting create the Four Seasons mood.

A grand staircase looks out over the Public Garden to the acclaimed Aujourd'hui restaurant. All the restaurants offer an alternative menu for the calorie conscious. The 288 guest rooms are reached from a large reception room off the elevators. In the hallways there is never the sign of a linen cart, since the service is provided in small baskets carried by the housekeepers.

The rooms called Four Seasons rooms are suitelike in that they are divided by attractive, louvered, sliding doors that separate bedroom from living room. Refrigerators in each room are stocked with ample snacks and beverages. Bathrooms have oversized tubs, beveled marble sink tops, hair dryers, excellent lighting, and wallpaper that looks like it was hand-painted.

The swimming pool is perhaps the most beautiful in Boston. Located on the eighth floor and overlooking the Public Garden, it is surrounded by plants, chairs, and tables, and food service is available. Health spa services are in adjoining rooms.

Shoes are shined if left at the door in the evening. Afternoon tea is served properly—loose. The overall style of the hotel is refined, yet not formal. A coat and tie in the dining room might make men feel more comfortable, but it is not required.

Hotel Meridien
250 Franklin Street
Boston, Massachusetts 02110
617/451-1900

$160–$190 double occupancy
Suites $260–$800

The Hotel Meridien combines the grandeur of a great 1920s building with 1980s touches like a six-story atrium and sloping glass walls in many guest rooms. Despite its size, it conveys the ambience of a small hotel.

This is Boston's former Federal Reserve Bank building, a Renaissance Revival granite and limestone structure modeled on a Roman palazzo. When it reopened in 1981 as the Meridien, three stories, with a glass mansard roof, had been added. There was also a new 41-story office building next door, served by a large garage.

Whether they park in the garage or come through the front door, guests enter a low-ceilinged, low-key lobby. The magnificent public space is on the floor above. Here the former ''members' court'' with its vaulted, gold leaf–edged ceiling is now the Julien Restaurant. Espaliered vines climb the walls. One has the sense of dining in a very elegant courtyard, one with upholstered wingback chairs. The fare is a mixture of nouvelle and traditional French fare.

There are unexpected levels to the hotel's public space. The former mezzanine has been enhanced by the soaring atrium beneath which is the Cafe Fleuri, a smaller dining area used for morning croissants, Sunday brunch, and light dinners. On still another level the former reception room for the bank's governors is now the Julien Lounge. This is a truly luxurious bar with coffered ceilings and two N. C. Wyeth murals on paneled walls.

The guest rooms, by contrast, are light and modern. Because most have been carved from former office space, they come in more than 150 different sizes and shapes. Colors are light, furniture is contemporary, and there are niceties like live plants, minibars, sofas, radios, bathroom scales, and bathroom telephones. In the evening, beds are turned and French mints are left along with tomorrow's weather forecast.

Guests can enjoy Le Club Meridien, a third-floor sports facility with a four-foot-deep lap pool, a Jacuzzi, aerobic exercise equipment, and a sauna.

The Meridien stands at the heart of Boston's financial district; midweek, 95 percent of its clients are here on business. On weekends, when packages include free parking and breakfast in bed, tourists increase to 50 percent. The hotel is a short walk from Faneuil Hall Marketplace, the waterfront, and shops.

The Meridien has an unusually large staff (235 for 328 rooms) and you can't help but notice. The French management is very apparent, from the moment you are greeted with "bonjour." But there is nothing stuffy about the Meridien. Service is unusually friendly.

The Parker House
60 School Street
Boston, Massachusetts 02107
800/225-4545 (tollfree)
617/227-8600

$158–$205 double occupancy

The lobby at the Parker House is a classic grand hotel lobby right out of the movies. In fact it fits the definition so perfectly that it is frequently used as a set for advertisements and television and movie productions. The huge, elaborately detailed brass elevator doors are focal points. The pattern in the carpet reflects the pattern in the carved coffered ceiling. Centered on the carpet is a giant round marble table with a huge flower decoration that is kept fresh and beautiful.

The grandeur of the lobby suits the history of a hotel that has been in continuous operation for 130 years, making it the oldest in Boston. Charles Dickens stayed in room no. 338. Saturday Literary Club meetings were held in the hotel; that group's magazine, the *Atlantic Monthly*, lives on. In the dining room, scrod, Boston cream pie and Parker House rolls were invented. The present chef, Joseph Ribas, is a modest man who does not like publicity, but it should be known that many chefs at other Boston restaurants had their start at Parker's Restaurant.

The 541 bedrooms are tiny but elegant and very comfortable. Real blanket covers are used, and the amenities are ample considering the price of the room. There are two types of color schemes in the oddly shaped rooms: mint green or rose with a contrast of taupe. Silent valets are nice touches. Beds are turned down at night and a chocolate is placed on the pillow. Extra pillows are double tucked on the beds in the European fashion.

Proper dress is requested in the dining room in keeping with a more formal atmosphere. The hotel offers bargain weekend deals and executive plans.

The Ritz-Carlton Boston
15 Arlington Street
Boston, Massachusetts 02117
800/241-3333 (tollfree)
617/536-5700

Rooms $140–$205 single occupancy, $160–$225 double occupancy.
One-bedroom suites $270–$400
Two-bedroom and premier suites available at higher rates

"We are not merely surrounded by traditions, we have become one," says the Ritz's promotional material. It's true. Despite the spate of new luxury hotels, the Ritz remains the place to stay in Boston.

The 16-story hotel was built in 1927 and a new addition, which includes 52 private condominiums, was completed in 1981. From within the hotel it is extremely difficult to tell the difference between the two. New rooms have the same careful detailing that distinguish the old. The only visible difference is in the bathrooms; those in the new wing are roomier and modern, and the old ones (newly refaced in Vermont marble) have porcelain fixtures from the 1920s.

The most handsome rooms are the suites with elegant mirror-topped mantels (there are 42 working fireplaces), furnished with fine antique breakfronts, desks, and sofas.

All rooms are large and equipped with closets that lock. All have their own refrigerator and honor bar. Most have fine views, either of the Boston Public Garden or looking off across the rooftops of Newbury Street. There are a total of 346 rooms and 41 suites.

The elevator is staffed by a white-gloved operator, and many of the hotel's 460 employees have been here more than ten years (a few have been here since the '20s).

The Dining Room is very formal with tall mullioned windows overlooking the Public Garden and a menu of continental cuisine. The lounge (no windows) is a gathering place rather like a drawing room, popular for tea. Downstairs on the entry floor, the Cafe is a less formal place for breakfast and lunch (like grilled baby flounder with lemon butter and champagne by the glass). The Ritz Bar, a popular Boston meeting spot, has recently acquired the look of a richly paneled club, complete with fireplace.

The Ritz offers such welcome extras as ice skates (to use on the pond across the street) and a chauffered limousine to make morning rush-hour appointments.

Terrace Townehouse
60 Chandler Street
Boston, Massachusetts 02116
617/350-6520

Rooms $70–90
Apartment $350 per week

This brand-new bed and breakfast is in a brick townhouse on a tree-lined street in the South End of Boston, only a few blocks from Copley Square. The owners, Bob and Gloria Belknap, have meticulously restored the house to its original elegance. The small entrance is finished with a black-and-white marble floor, and there are wide hardwood floors throughout. The hall and stairwell are painted a striking peach color, accented with antique French prints, white woodwork, and brass sconces.

Among the four guest rooms, the China Trade Room has an Asian motif, using Clarence House and Pierre Deux prints. The walls are a bright, cheery yellow, and furniture

48

is antique wicker. Antique botanical prints decorate the walls, while dhurries cover the hardwood floors. The room has the comforts of a luxury hotel, and the cozy feeling of a private home.

Another guest room called the Drawing Room has the feeling of an English club, with dark brown woodwork and warm brown colors. A white Chinese-style screen is used for a headboard on the very comfortable king-size bed.

Rooms have their own private telephone lines. The apartment on the ground floor has a fireplace and a small bedroom. Gloria was a caterer in California before she came to Boston, so the full breakfasts and afternoon teas, included in the room rates, are special. The Belknaps welcome well-behaved children in the apartment, and will accept pets with advance notice.

« CHICAGO »

Ambassador East
1301 North State Street
Chicago, Illinois 60610
312/787-7200

Rooms with king-size beds $150–$170
Rooms with queen-size beds $140–$160
Suites $190 and up

Set among tree-lined streets just west of Chicago's Gold Coast, the Ambassador East Hotel provides elegant living just steps away from the city's hottest night spots. Home to the legendary Pump Room restaurant, the Ambassador East was built in the Roaring Twenties and restored to its original grandeur in 1977.

Suites are large and feature two lounging couches with large throw pillows and art deco furnishings along crisp, clean lines. Decorated in pale shades of blue and gray, the rooms offer a variety of multimedia artwork that looks like it wasn't commissioned as hotel art. The king-size beds provide a wonderful night's sleep for guests who appreciate down comforters and king-size down pillows.

A marble-topped desk next to the bed is set with two brandy snifters and individual bottles of cognac, while a credenza offers fluted glasses and bottled spring water from the French Alps. A basket of fruit and chocolates also awaits guests.

Bathrooms have an old-fashioned air because of marble floors and showers, but feature modern amenities like large mirrors and Soehnle scales. Complimentary shampoo, bath gel, and shower caps are provided as well. Other unexpected touches include complimentary shoeshines and daily weather forecasts that are slipped under the door with the morning newspaper. The hotel also has a special program for Japanese guests that includes translation services, kimonos, and a Japanese bilingual newspaper.

Guests step into a Victorian-style lobby boasting large Chinese screens, 18-foot ceilings, and a striking green marble floor. Parking is a bit of a problem because the hotel lot fills up early. Guests with cars can park them in several lots close by; however, charges may range from $12 to $20 for overnight parking. Cabs are the best way to negotiate this part of the city.

The Ambassador East is within easy walking distance of Chicago's famous strip of bars along Rush Street. The intersection of Rush and Division streets features bars of all varieties, from sports bars to rock bars to quiet bars conducive to conversation. The street is filled with people all evening, and many out-of-town visitors find it easy to mingle in Rush Street's carnival atmosphere. The hotel is also close to Michigan Avenue's Magnificient Mile and the beaches along Lake Michigan.

The Barclay Chicago Hotel
166 East Superior
Chicago, Illinois 60611
312/787-6000

Singles $120–$170
Doubles $140–$190

The Barclay is a hotel designed with the hardworking business traveler in mind. Because it was an apartment building before its renovation in 1981, each of the 120 rooms is a suite complete with a full kitchen. The suites are arranged with only six to a floor, lending an intimate atmosphere to the corridors.

Rooms have a homey feeling because of their comfortable couches, dining room tables, and breakfronts, complete with a few books. Although the furniture is unexceptional, the high ceilings and large picture windows do much to compensate. Rooms with a completely separate bedroom retain the feel of a small apartment, and come complete with a console color television in the living room and a portable color TV in the bedroom.

The large bathrooms offer a magnifying mirror, heat lamp, and built-in hair dryer.

The living areas in all the Barclay's rooms are suitable for informal gatherings and meetings. The hotel staff is willing to stock the full-sized refrigerator upon request, making the hotel perfect for transferred executives searching for a home or others planning a prolonged stay in the city.

The hotel also provides limousine service on request, and guests can use the McClurg Court Center, the sports facility of a highrise apartment building several blocks away. The Barclay has a small outdoor swimming pool on the 29th floor that is open during Chicago's rather short summer season.

Barclay guests can visit the Bookmark Lounge in the lobby for a casual drink and chat, although they shouldn't expect much interesting browsing among the too few and rather obscure titles lining the walls. The hotel also hosts a Benihana's restaurant, offering the chain's usual Japanese fare.

Guests of the Barclay can partake of the continental cuisine offered by the Barclay Club on the seventh floor. The private club is only available to its individual and corporate members—and guests of the Barclay. The Barclay Club prides itself on its offerings of fresh seafood and tableside cooking, and is open seven days a week for breakfast, lunch, and dinner.

The Barclay has three fully equipped conference rooms for meetings of up to 50 people and has just finished its version of a corporate boardroom, complete with leather chairs and oval table.

The hotel is located just steps away from Chicago's Magnificent Mile and its selection of opulent stores such as Neiman Marcus and Saks Fifth Avenue.

The Drake Hotel
140 East Walton
Chicago, Illinois
312/787-2200

Singles $115–$180
Doubles $130–$185

If you are looking for a Chicago tradition rather than a place to stay, it has to be the Drake. Sitting atop Michigan Avenue's "Magnificent Mile," it is renowned for its Cape Cod Room restaurant and lavish trappings, which include nice little touches like sofas in the elevators and wet bars in its rooms.

The hotel has just celebrated its 65th anniversary. One gets the impression that some things haven't changed in all that time—indeed, have recently come back into fashion. Visitors are greeted by a sumptuous lobby with a 25-foot ceiling, and do not get past the bell captain carrying their own bags.

Rooms face Lake Michigan on the north and Michigan Avenue on the west, and are decorated in understated Victorian style, mixing a variety of prints with white wainscoting and a hint of the oriental in the artwork.

An alcove shelters a desk equipped with writing materials, a reading lamp, and a telephone, which makes the room feel less like a place only to sleep. A wet bar comes stocked with everything from the latest Beaujolais to Tattinger champagne—all for a specified price that will be added to the bill. An unexpected touch is the real crystal provided to drink the variety of beverages, from champagne flutes to wine glasses. Fresh fruit is laid out in wicker baskets, and fresh flowers adorn the bathroom. The invisible staff makes sure to turn down beds, lay out terry robes, and leave chocolates beckoning on pillows.

A walk-in closet equipped with a bureau provides plenty of room for clothes and packages, and an armoire hides a color television, with cable and pay movies.

While Drake bathrooms are not opulent, they do have homey touches like cloth shower curtains and wicker hampers for towels. Wooden shades and brass accessories lend to the feeling that one is visiting a home rather than a hotel.

The hotel offers a number of diverting activities including high tea at 3 P.M. in the Palm Court. A lower level arcade boasts a variety of designer clothing shops, as well as art galleries, gift shops, and florists. The Drake has two fine restaurants, the Oak Terrace Room and the Cape Cod Room. The latter features some of the city's best seafood.

Leaving the Drake, avid shoppers can quickly reach Oak Street, one of the city's most chic thoroughfares, and Watertower Place, Chicago's upscale answer to suburban shopping malls.

Mayfair Regent
181 East Lake Shore Drive
Chicago, Illinois
312/787-8500

Singles $160–$180
Doubles $180–$200
All rooms $99 Friday and Saturday

For the traveler who wants to be pampered and greeted by name, Chicago's Mayfair Regent is the appropriate setting. No standing in line at a desk waiting to check in here. Guests are escorted to a settee where they are asked to sign their name once.

Upon entering rooms decorated in shades of peach, guests are greeted by Japanese style tea, and are provided with comfortable robes and slippers. In its attempt to anticipate the needs of visitors to the Windy City, the Regent even provides umbrellas, which can be purchased if so desired.

The Regent has been under its current management for only five years and was extensively remodeled and refurbished at the time it was purchased. A lobby bar resembles an elegant sitting room in Louis XV style, complete with a roaring fire, grand piano, and attentive service. Visitors can feel comfortable writing letters there or conducting business while sipping tea or wine.

The hotel strives to make its foreign visitors feel comfortable, and many hotel employees are European. Most of them are at least trilingual and one employee speaks Japanese. The lobby provides two racks of newspapers, one for Chicago papers and the other for foreign, and foreign exchange rates for major currencies are posted daily at the reservation desk. But all visitors, from guest conductors of the Chicago Symphony Orchestra to travel-weary businesspersons, are treated with special care. The hotel staff meets every morning to review the guest roster for the day, and notes are kept about regular visitors' preferences. The staff is even willing to rearrange furniture or provide special reading lamps.

Rooms to the north face Lake Michigan and Lake Shore Drive, an impressive view by day or night. The decor is French provincial and comfortable. A modest refrigerator-bar is hidden in a nightstand and is ready to meet most nighttime cravings, whether for fruit juice or champagne. The chocolates left on pillows are noteworthy because they come from Huwyler's, a Swiss chocolatier on Michigan Avenue, and they are anything but milk chocolate.

Bathrooms are decorated in marble and feature modern amenities like a telephone and bath sheets. A variety of Neutrogena soaps and shampoos are provided in wicker baskets, and the bathroom mirror is lit with dressing room lights. A fresh flower is another nice touch.

Ciel Bleu, considered one of Chicago's best French restaurants, is located on the Regent's 19th floor and provides a clear view of the lake. Excellent service and delicious French cuisine and wine make for a memorable, albeit expensive, dinner. Reservations are required.

Park Hyatt
800 North Michigan Avenue
Chicago, Illinois
312/280-2222

Singles $170
Doubles $195

There's one Hyatt hotel that doesn't have the chain's trademark lobby waterfalls and bubble-like glass elevators. It is the Park Hyatt, an unpretentious-looking hotel on Chicago's Michigan Avenue that prides itself on luxury accommodations and personalized service.

Don't be fooled by the Park Hyatt's ugly 1950s version of chunky concrete architecture. It is more than compensated for by the hotel's well-appointed rooms and elegant dining.

Rooms and suites are decorated in a mixture of dark woods, marble, and chrome. Among the eclectic elements in the decor, the oriental tone predominates. A large lacquered cabinet hides a well-stocked bar and refrigerator that can be opened only with a room key. A full assortment of liquors is offered, as well as Tattinger champagne and imported beers. The supply is restocked daily, and charges are added to the bill.

Desks come equipped with a full complement of stationery, and the color television is arranged on a swivel to allow viewing from the sitting area or the bed.

The spacious bathroom contains everything even the most forgetful guest could want, including hand lotion, talc, Gucci soap, a sewing kit, and a pair of dark socks. A scale is provided, and bottled spring water is set out for brushing teeth.

The ice bucket is filled by the hotel staff, and the bed is turned down with a rose bud and chocolates left on the pillows. Terry robes and a bowl of fruit also await guests. Other nice touches include copies of *USA Today* in the evening and the *Wall Street Journal* waiting outside the door in the morning.

The staff, from the doorman to the concierge, is extremely courteous and willing to help.

The hotel faces Chicago's historic Water Tower, a landmark that provided the name for the nearby Water Tower Place, which is a must for avid shoppers. The old Water Tower is surrounded by a small park where horse-drawn carriages line up waiting for customers.

The hotel's restaurant, the Park Hyatt, overlooks the nostalgic scene of the lighted park and antique carriages. Meals are traditionally French, and not inexpensive, while the service is stately but not overbearing.

A typical offering might include soft-shelled crabs as an

appetizer, swordfish with lemon sauce as an entree, and praline souffle for dessert. An extensive wine list is available, and entrees run between $17 and $25.

The Raphael
201 East Delaware
Chicago, Illinois 60611
312/943-5000

Singles, doubles $76–$104
Suites $104–$131

From its etched glass doors to its high-beamed ceilings, the Raphael lives up to its ideal of being Chicago's "elegant little hotel."

Its 170 rooms are distinctive for their Spanish-style decor carried out in stucco walls, wood beams, and warm colors. High-backed chairs and tables are all done in dark wood, as are the rest of the comfortable furnishings. A credenza hides drawers, and an end table disguises a refrigerator stocked with mixers, champagne, and beer. A selection of liqueurs is provided as is a variety of snacks for a rather high price that will be added to the bill.

A full-size couch faces a large hexagonal coffee table that comes complete with the latest issue of the *New Yorker* magazine and *Chicago Scene*, which lists restaurants and entertainment in the city.

Twenty-four-hour room service is available, and a typical continental breakfast can be ordered for $5.50. The menu runs the gamut from eggs benedict to a bottle of Tattinger Blanc de Blanc. Laundry service is available five days a week, and charges run from $1.50 for a pair of socks to $3.50 for shirts.

Rooms have individual controls for heat and air conditioning, and suites come complete with two phones. A safe for valuables is found in the closet of every room. The safe operates like an airport locker that locks when the key is removed.

Bathrooms are quite small and rather old-fashioned, but are very clean.

A copy of the *Wall Street Journal* is delivered in the

morning, and a basket of fruit, cheese, and Godiva chocolates awaits guests upon arrival.

The hotel features the Raphael restaurant, which offers a continental menu, soft lights, flowers, and comfortable booths. The setting is casual and the food moderately priced. The Raphael also has a bar with small tables that is decorated in quiet shades of rust and brown.

Valet parking is available, although one should call ahead because service is sometimes slow.

The Raphael is located just off Michigan Avenue amid some of the city's best shopping and a few blocks away from Chicago's huge business district. Public transportation by bus or subway is very accessible.

The Whitehall Hotel
105 East Delaware
Chicago, Illinois
312/944-6300

Singles $145–$190
Doubles $170–$215

The Whitehall is one of Chicago's smaller elegant hotels located centrally amid some of the city's best nightlife and shopping. Its colonial facade gives way to a cozy wood-paneled lobby where guests are surrounded by paintings of the English countryside and greeted by an attentive hotel staff.

Rooms are large and spacious with high ceilings accented by Victorian border prints in patterns of hunter green and cream. An elaborate print bedspread picks up the green shades of the carpet, while floor-length curtains frame large bay windows. Several comfortably overstuffed chairs create the atmosphere of a sitting room.

Beds are turned down for guests returning from dinner, and terry robes and chocolates are laid out. The color television is equipped with cable stations such as Home Box Office and ESPN, the sports network. A nightstand hides a stocked refrigerator.

Some rooms come equipped with three telephones, one of which is located in the bathroom. A phone on the desk has two separate lines and a card explains how to set up a conference call. The desk also provides a book about Chicago, complete with a map and listing of museums, restaurants, and entertainment.

Every room has its own thermostat control, and closets come complete with electric shoe buffers and plenty of wooden hangers. Dry cleaning and laundry services are available to guests.

In the bathroom, sandalwood-scented shampoo and soaps are provided along with shower cap, all in a wicker basket.

The hotel restaurant is the Whitehall Club, which is open only to hotel guests and club members. The Whitehall's bar provides a quiet conversational setting for those tired of blaring music.

Within easy walk of the Whitehall are Michigan Avenue's Magnificent Mile and its offering of Neiman Marcus, Saks Fifth Avenue, Bonwit Teller, and I. Magnin. In the other direction is Rush Street's collection of bars and restaurants, which offers everything from Chicago-style pizza to fancy French cuisine.

Many of the hotel's guests say they return whenever they are in the city because of its understated elegance and quiet atmosphere.

«CINCINNATI»

The Golden Lamb
27 South Broadway
Lebanon, Ohio 45036
513/932-5065

$44–$60 double occupancy

The first guests to stay at the Golden Lamb arrived by horseback. The state of Ohio was barely a few months old in 1803 when the state legislature granted Jonas Seaman a license to open a public house in Lebanon. Horses soon gave way to stagecoaches, stagecoaches to trains, and then trains to cars but still the guests continue to arrive at Ohio's oldest and most famous inn. As Ohio grew, the Golden Lamb grew along with it. The original log structure was quickly replaced by a sturdier brick building, and many additions have been added over the years.

During the nearly two centuries of its existence, the Golden Lamb has seen its share of American history and has played host to many who shaped that history. The state of Ohio figured prominently in 19th-century America. Ten U.S. presidents have stayed at the Golden Lamb, along with Henry Clay and many of Ohio's governors. Mark Twain stayed at the inn when he was performing at the Lebanon Opera House and Charles Dickens stayed overnight during his 1842 American tour. Dickens is said to have complained bitterly to his fellow guests about the rigors of travel and the accommodations available to him in the United States.

Guests who stay at the Golden Lamb today have no reason

to complain about the accommodations. A stay at the inn provides a refreshing alternative to the hotels and motels in the area. The ambience of the inn is vintage 19th century but with all the conveniences of the 20th. The inn has 19 rooms, each furnished in period antiques and named for a famous guest. All rooms are equipped with telephone, air conditioning, private bath, and television. Even if it is not possible to stay overnight, a visit to the inn is well worth the time. Rooms not rented are left open for display to the inn's guests and diners, and visitors are encouraged to wander through the halls and peek in the rooms. The Golden Lamb also has an impressive collection of Shaker furniture, some of which is displayed in two rooms on the fourth floor.

The Golden Lamb is almost as famous for its dining as for its history. A total of nine dining rooms, all furnished in antiques, offer diners hearty classic American fare in an old-fashioned atmosphere. The restaurant is open every day of the year except Christmas. Lunch is served Monday–Saturday, 11 A.M. to 3 P.M. Dinner is served Monday–Thursday 5–9 P.M. and Friday and Saturday 5–10 P.M. On Sundays the inn serves breakfast from 8 to 10 P.M. and dinner from noon to 8 P.M. Continental breakfast is included in the room rates.

The Black Horse Tavern is open seven days a week and offers a special selection of native Ohio wines in addition to domestic and imported vintages.

The Hampshire House Hotel
30 Tri-County Parkway
Cincinnati, Ohio 45246
513/772-5440

Singles $70
Doubles $80
Special weekend rates available

The Hampshire House Hotel is located in the heart of Cincinnati's corporate corridor and serves as a conference center for many of the corporations headquartered in the area. The hotel is approximately a half hour from downtown and 35 minutes from the airport. Although much of the hotel's clientele is business and conference related, this is not a large convention hotel. However, the 151-room hotel does offer many of the executive services common to a larger hotel.

Hotel meeting rooms can accommodate up to 70 persons each and the hotel's theater has 126 fixed seats with desk tops and a projection room. All guest rooms have desktop work space. Four executive suites are available, each with a giant bed, a foldout couch, a large tub, separate shower area, a phone in the bathroom, a meeting room, and a wet bar. Complimentary coffee and newspapers are delivered to rooms each morning. Room service is available from 7 A.M. to 11 P.M., as well as valet laundry and dry cleaning.

The hotel has a swimming pool, sauna, and whirlpool located beneath a high atrium in the middle of the hotel. The atrium can also serve as a reception or banquet area, with food provided by the hotel restaurant, Checquer's. The Hampshire House provides complimentary passes to nearby tennis courts and health clubs and a courtesy van is available to take guests to any of the large shopping malls or restaurants in the immediate area.

The Vernon Manor Hotel
400 Oak Street
Cincinnati, Ohio 45219
513/281-3300

Rooms $38–$69

Cincinnati's Vernon Manor Hotel harks back to a past age of hostelry, to a time when hotels were not anonymous high rises but integral parts of their neighborhoods. Built in 1924 to resemble an English country manor, the stately hotel perfectly complemented the older mansions that surrounded it in this southwest Cincinnati neighborhood. The neighborhood has changed dramatically over the years and few of the estates remain intact, but the Vernon Manor has changed very little. It is still a neighborhood hotel, and it is still committed to the personalized and friendly service that is expected from a smaller hotel.

The hotel's neighbors are the University of Cincinnati

and many of the city's medical centers. Four major hospitals and numerous medical offices are nearby. But visitors to the university and to the medical area are attracted not only by the hotel's convenient location but also by the hotel's very relaxed and quiet atmosphere.

Renovation of the hotel began in the mid-1970s and most of the rooms have been redone since then. The hotel offers a variety of room sizes, from spartan minisingles to lavish two-bedroom suites. The minisingles are very small (approximately 10 by 15 feet). The regular rooms are good-sized, tastefully furnished, and have a dining table and chairs. The suites would qualify as luxury apartments in most cities: two huge bedrooms with oversized beds, two baths, a living room, a kitchen, and a dining room/meeting room.

The hotel has two dining rooms. Cardigan's Cafe serves meals from 7 A.M. to 10 P.M. The Forum Room, which offers more formal dining, is open from 11A.M. to 10P.M. The hotel bar, Beagle's Lounge, open from 11 A.M. to 2 A.M., serves Sunday brunch and provides nightly entertainment.

The hotel has facilities to accommodate meetings and receptions of up to 250 people. The hotel provides free passes to the Friars' Club, a nearby health club that features a pool, racquetball, basketball courts, and weights.

«CLEVELAND»

The Bond Court Hotel
777 St. Clair Avenue N.E.
Cleveland, Ohio 44113
216/771-7600

Singles $84
Doubles $100

This sleek contemporary highrise hotel is located adjacent to the Cleveland Convention Center. An executive hotel, the Bond Court features three floors of special rooms with concierge service.

The newest of the downtown hotels, the Bond Court features luxurious accommodations with lake or city views. Each of the 486 rooms and 45 suites features 24-hour room service, free in-room movies and cable news stations, luxurious marble and tile baths, and ultramodern furnishings.

Catering to the VIP client, the hotel offers limousine service and the best suites in the city. For a real treat, a penthouse suite at the Bond Court for the weekend will certainly perk up a heavy workload. Continental breakfast and hors d'oeuvres are complimentary on the executive levels.

The hotel is presently undergoing a $22 million renovation and will be connected directly to the Convention Center by tunnels. Though in the thick of the action, it is surprisingly quiet.

Guests may dine at one of two eateries. Le Bistro Restaurant offers continental cuisine with gourmet touches and is small and richly decorated. An informal coffee shop has been carved out of a corner of the once-larger formal dining room. There is also the Continental Lounge, serving lunch and cocktails only. Le Bistro Nightclub and the Continental Lounge have live entertainment five or six nights a week.

Though the hotel doesn't have its own health club, facilities are available free to guests across the street. These include two indoor tennis courts, as well as an indoor pool, Nautilus equipment, and fitness center.

Hollenden House Hotel
6th Street and Superior Avenue
Cleveland, Ohio 44114
216/621-0700

Singles $90
Doubles $120

Though the Hollenden House is a contemporary concrete and steel block, this hotel offers some of the best hospitality in Cleveland. Located along the city's main thoroughfare, it is convenient for strolling or for taking care of business.

This 510-room property is really for executives and as such offers many luxury amenities for a reasonable downtown price. Especially good are the weekend packages, when the hotel tries to fill the void left by its business travelers.

The upper three floors—200 rooms—are designated executive rooms. These feature a more spacious room arrangement, fluffier towels, phone in the bath, and a work area. Regular rooms feature first-run movies and windows that open, though all are air-conditioned.

Guests are not at a loss for a place to eat. The hotel has five dining places plus room service. The best is the four-star Hollenden Tavern, winner of two national awards for excellence and popular with local citizens. Menu selections are varied, featuring wine and brandy sauces served with French and Italian dishes.

There is also an informal coffeeshop serving all three meals. One of the most unusual dining areas is the poolside Club Bistro. Here, guests may dine on everything from steak to salads while sipping cocktails from the poolside bar.

A very popular local spot is the hotel's piano bar, which also serves light lunches in the afternoons. Sandwiches are available in the cozy Sixth Street Bar, a lounge in pub style, with memorabilia of Cleveland's past.

If guests wish to relax, a masseur is available in the hotel's health club, or they can take advantage of the indoor pool and sauna.

Inn on the Square
24 Public Square
Cleveland, Ohio 44113
216/696-5600

Singles $105–$125
Doubles $120–$140

Every U.S. city has its landmark hotel and Cleveland is no exception. The Inn on the Square, built in 1918, was given a new lease on life as part of the Terminal Tower Complex in the center of the business district. This beautiful neoclassical hotel features 14 stories of elegant accommodations.

As part of the renovation, a former courtyard was covered over to produce a dramatic atrium with indoor pool, cocktail area, bar, and plenty of trees and flowers, which are badly needed during the cold winters. In addition, this became the lobby, featuring the city's most urbane bar and lounge.

The Terminal Tower Complex consists of a magnificent old railroad station skyscraper that has been transformed into a flowing art nouveau–style mall with shops and restaurants. Guests staying at the hotel do not even have to go outside in winter, as the whole facility is connected to the hotel.

Rooms are large and elegant, all 501 of them. Each has its own temperature control, color TV with cable movies, and luxurious furnishings. Since Cleveland is more popular as a business travelers' destination, the hotel caters to them in the many amenities featured, such as complimentary morning coffee and newspaper.

Restaurants in the hotel are some of the best in the city. The French Connection, an elegant affair serving provincial

French cuisine with special regional dishes influenced by French Canada across the lake, is the top of the line. A Brasserie Coffee Shop serves meals all day long and is more casual, although just as French in its offerings.

For lighter fare, head to Mowrey's Lounge for either lunch or evening entertainment. Buffets are sometimes held by the pool in the atrium.

The hotel is as nostalgic as any in the Midwest and offers a comfortable stay.

«DALLAS»
«FORT WORTH»

The Adolphus Hotel
1321 Commerce Street
(at Akard Street)
Dallas, Texas 75202
800/441-0574 (tollfree from within Texas)
800/221-9083 (tollfree from rest of U.S.)

Singles $136–$174
Doubles $151–$189
Suites $350–$1,000

Occupying an entire city block in downtown Dallas, the 21-story Adolphus is a grand and glorious hotel. Now a registered historical landmark, it was built in 1912 by Adolphus Busch, the St. Louis beer baron. The hotel's exterior design is an extravagance of ornamentation—sculptures, bas-relief figures, gargoyles, heraldic characters, even a beer bottle–shaped corner turret.

In 1981 the hotel's interior was totally renovated, transformed into a 437-room luxury hotel decorated with an amazing collection of antiques from Europe and Asia as well as the U.S. Public areas have a museumlike quality, with such treasures as two large 1661 Flemish tapestries, a six-foot early 19th-century portrait of Napoleon in ermine coronation robes, and a carved English Regency oak table. So extensive is the collection, with more than 200 pieces, that the hotel distributes a 22-page guidebook describing the lamps, engravings, clocks, carvings, furnishings, tapestries and paintings that adorn the Adolphus.

One of the most unusual pieces is the "signature" lobby chandelier, one of a pair purchased by Busch at the 1904 Louisiana Purchase Exposition in St. Louis. Ornamented with eagles and hops, the chandeliers caught Busch's fancy since they symbolized the trademark of the Anheuser-Busch brewery. The matching piece hangs in the Clydesdale stables in St. Louis.

The hotel's centerpiece is the richly ornamented French Room, a dining room with vaulted ceiling, columned walls, and rococo murals. On the ceiling, cherubs holding garlands of flowers fly beneath a pale blue sky. The carpet of 59 colors was handmade in Hong Kong.

From the 18th- and 19th-century grandeur in the hotel's public areas, guests go to tastefully decorated rooms with modern-day comfort and convenience. Arranged in 31 configurations, they are designated as standard, superior (with sitting area), and deluxe (with sitting and dining area). With their original high ceilings, the rooms are spacious and warm yet elegant, with reproduction antique furniture (mostly Queen Anne and Chippendale), matching draperies and bedspreads, and touches of lace.

Most of the rooms have queen- or king-size beds, and many have refrigerators, multiple phones, and televisions enclosed in armoires. All rooms have goosedown comforters and terry cloth robes. Standard room features include thermostats and clock radios.

Junior suites have two baths, an expansive sitting area, and a large terrace. Skylight suites on the 19th floor—ideal for entertaining—are unusually appealing, with slanting glass exterior walls, a large wet bar, and Asian accents intermixed with reproduction period furniture. Rates for the skylight suites are $350.

The penthouse, accessible by private elevator, was once the residence of Adolphus Busch himself. Its hardwood floors have been retained, and the apartmentlike suite is decorated with deep greens, mirrors, and art objects. The antique canopy bed has an accompanying stool to make climbing into the elevated bed easier. There's even a baby grand piano. The elegant den is comfortable and inviting.

Services in the Adolphus are comprehensive. The concierge desk is staffed around the clock. Room service is offered 24 hours a day. Babysitters and a house physician are available on request. The staff of approximately 350 has multilingual capabilities including French, German, Spanish, Chinese, and Italian.

On the premises are a barber and beauty salon and a gift shop. Valet parking costs $7.50.

The French Room features classical and nouvelle cuisine, serving dinner only. The Grille, decorated to resemble an English men's club, serves continental fare and is open all day. The Palm Bar is open for lunch and for cocktails Monday through Friday. An elaborate afternoon tea service is featured in the lobby bar on weekdays.

Adjoining the hotel is the Clark Hatch Physical Fitness Center, a well-equipped facility with weight room, whirlpool, sauna, and steam room. Exercise equipment is extensive—variable resistance weights, free weights, treadmill, stationary bike, and rowing machine.

Bed and Breakfast Texas Style
Ruth Wilson
4224 West Red Bird Lane
Dallas, Texas 75237
214/298-5433 and 298-8586

Singles $20–$45
Doubles $25–$50

Bed and Breakfast Texas Style offers a diversity of lodging choices. Travelers contact Ruth Wilson—a gracious host who strongly promotes bed and breakfast statewide—and explain their personal needs and preferences. In the Dallas—Fort Worth area Wilson offers a choice of more than 20 homes, ranging from condominiums to ranch homes.

In a centrally located residential area of Dallas are two popular bed and breakfast homes. The Iris on Swiss Avenue is an early 1900s two-story home with a wide porch at the front of the house and a pool out back. Decorated with antiques, the home is comfortable and inviting.

Guests have a choice of four bedrooms, with the king-size bedroom renting for $50 and the rooms with double beds priced at $45. The private guest bath has a tub but no shower.

Hospitable host Doris Bowman enjoys her guests, offering to take them shopping or to the airport if they wish. Many of her guests are professional people on business trips or attending conventions. The historic neighborhood in which the Iris is located lends itself to long walks.

Bowman likes serving big breakfasts, from egg and ham casserole and fresh fruit to her own specialities such as pumpkin custard. She requests that guests not smoke, and she does not accept small children or pets.

Across the tree-shaded boulevard from the Iris is the Rose, the home of Cathy Davis. Her guest room has a double bed with a handmade rose quilt, an antique armoire, and a private bath. The rate is $45 single, $50 double. A garage apartment is also available for $150 per week. The host serves breakfast continental style, with the menu chosen according to guests' preferences. As in the Iris, the Rose does not accept small children or pets, but smokers are welcome.

One of the largest bed and breakfast homes in the area is the Hacienda, a sprawling ranch home built in the 1930s with rooms available for meetings as well as three bedrooms for overnight guests.

Ruth Wilson is adept at matching guests with people of complementary interests and personalities. Reservation deposits of $20 are paid to her in advance; the balance of the fee is paid to the bed and breakfast hosts.

The Mandalay Four Seasons Hotel
221 East Las Colinas Boulevard
Irving, Texas 75039
800/268-6282 (tollfree)
800/462-1150 (tollfree from New York State)
214/556-0800

Singles $135–$165
Doubles $160–$190
Suites $325–$1,000

In the gentle hills of North Texas is an idyllic new town called Las Colinas. A sparkling gem set apart from the rest of the Dallas–Fort Worth metroplex, it was created by a wealthy rancher who didn't want encroaching development to erase the beauty of his land.

Set amid the office towers, residential villages, and green space is the Mandalay Four Seasons Hotel, a gracious and distinctive hostelry. So masterful is its design and so accommodating is its service that although the Mandalay has 424 guest rooms in its 27 stories, it does not have the feel of a large hotel.

The low-ceilinged multilevel lobby is sophisticated but unintimidating, decorated with sumptuous furnishings and softened with a profusion of greenery.

The 96 Four Seasons rooms, each with bay windows that open onto private balconies, are quite spacious—more akin to suites than to standard hotel rooms. Situated at the four corners of the building, the rooms are triangular in shape, allowing for nontypical use of space. The bathrooms, which are particularly luxurious, are divided from the sitting areas by an interior wall. The king-size bed is recessed into an alcove, creating a feeling of separation from the sitting and work areas.

Rooms designated as moderate, with two twin beds, and superior rooms, with king-size beds, are also well designed, with traditionally styled furniture and rich fabrics.

All rooms have remote-control televisions with 52 cable channels (including 24-hour movie and sports channels), digital clock radios, and telephone extensions in the bathroom. There are terry cloth bathrobes, round-the-clock room service, complimentary shoeshine, and turndown service.

The Mandalay's well-trained staff of approximately 450 extends efficient and friendly service. A concierge fulfills special guest requests, rooms have twice-daily housekeeping, and valet parking is complimentary.

Within the hotel, guests have several dining choices. The gourmet restaurant, Enjolie, is an epicurean's delight. Not only is the menu expansive, but meals are served in an elegant setting. Cafe D'Or, overlooking a poolside courtyard as well as Lake Carolyn, serves American cuisine and is open all day. Rhapsody, an informal restaurant and lounge area, serves Tex-Mex and Italian dishes as well as light meals.

On the lobby level in a tropical garden setting, Les Jardins serves light meals at lunchtime, tea in the afternoons, and hors d'oeuvres in the evenings. Apertif, also serving light lunches, has a wine and champagne bar.

To accommodate guests who are weight conscious or who have dietary restrictions, the hotel's restaurants offer an alternative cuisine, which has gourmet-quality offerings with reduced calorie, cholesterol, and sodium content.

One of the focal points of the hotel is its attractive outdoor pool, fronting onto Lake Carolyn. In addition, guests at the Mandalay have a multitude of other recreational options. On the premises is a fitness facility with Jacuzzi, saunas, exercise equipment, and massage room. Jogging trails wind along the shores of the lake.

One of the most pleasurable aspects of staying at the Mandalay is strolling outside its doors and following the picturesque Mandalay Canal to the 20-plus shops that line its banks. Spanish in atmosphere, the canal is a miniature San Antonio Riverwalk, with cobblestone lanes, a bell tower, and a covered bridge spanning the waterway. Water taxis stop at the hotel's miniwharf, and guests can climb aboard for sightseeing or for riding to several business destinations.

Complementing the Mandalay Four Seasons is the 315-room Las Colinas Inn and Conference Center, also a Four Seasons Hotel, which opened in mid-1986. Adjoined to the Four Seasons Fitness Resort and Spa, the hotel has comprehensive, state-of-the-art conference facilities. Guests at either of the Four Seasons facilities may charge to their room the cost of services and meals at the other hotel, or at a lavish, affiliated fitness and spa complex nearby.

The Mandalay Four Seasons is approximately 12 minutes from D/FW International Airport, 15 minutes from downtown Dallas, and 40 minutes from downtown Fort Worth. Texas Stadium is nearby.

Weekend packages are frequently featured at the Mandalay. Some are geared to sports, such as tennis or golf, while others are designed as getaways.

The Mansion on Turtle Creek

2821 Turtle Creek Boulevard
(at Gillespie Street)
Dallas, Texas 75219
800/442-3408 (tollfree from within Texas)
800/527-5432 (tollfree from rest of U.S.)
214/559-2100

Singles $165–$205
Doubles $190–$230
Suites $500–$750

Checking into the Mansion on Turtle Creek is entering a world of quiet opulence, with an attentive staff who treats each registrant as an honored guest. Indeed it is a mansion, set on a terraced hillside in one of Dallas's most prestigious residential areas.

Once it was the home of millionaire Sheppard King, who built the 16th-century-style Italianate structure, with its imaginative spires, turret, and cupola, in 1925. In 1981 Rosewood Hotels restored the original building, converting it into an exceptionally fine restaurant and constructing an adjacent hotel tower to complement the mansion.

A hotel of rare charm, the 143-room Mansion has a residential feel. The concierge wears a suit, not a uniform. There are no shops off the lobby, no hints of commercialism. Instead, there's soft music, fresh flowers, and a bevy of employees to satisfy every whim.

Courteous attendants greet guests as they drive into the bricked courtyard, accented with a marble fountain brought by the Kings from Europe. Entering through a high rotunda with arched windows, visitors walk into a small lobby resembling a fine living room, accented with such furnishings as antique mirrors and an English Chippendale breakfront filled with porcelains.

Beginning at a guest's initial registration, his or her profile is recorded, with personal preferences noted such as choice of room and services requested. On return visits these preferences are acted upon, whether it means serving a certain wine or reserving theater tickets. The 350 staff members, many of whom are young, strive to make guests feel at home—taking time to talk and extend unaffected hospitality.

Guest rooms are exquisite. Decorated in peach, gold, or beige, they have a four-poster bed with ruffled pillow shams, overstuffed chair with ottoman, loveseat, butler tray table with an array of good magazines, armoire with concealed television, and French doors that open onto a small balcony.

Bathrooms are not only luxurious but pleasing to the eye. Decorated with marble and brass, they have curved vanities, large tubside trays filled with personal care accessories, and telephones. A separate vanity outside the bathroom has dressing room–style lighting and added amenities. And there's a terrycloth robe provided for each guest.

The 14 suites range from those designated as executive, with canopy beds, built-in bar, and balconies off the living and dining areas, to terrace suites, with a large bathroom and separate shower room, kitchen, built-in bar, and terrace with a skyline view of Dallas.

Room-service meals are promptly and beautifully served, accompanied by fresh flowers and a newspaper at breakfast. In addition to round-the-clock room service, the Mansion has bedtime turndown with imported chocolates, and complimentary shoeshine.

Concierge service is all-encompassing, from arranging hot-air ballooning to tickets for sporting events. While staying at the Mansion each guest is given a special treat, chosen according to how often they have visited. Perhaps it's a tray of milk and cookies at bedtime, or hot spiced tea.

Valet parking, at a cost of $8.50 per night, is efficient. No self-parking is available. Limousine service can be arranged through the concierge.

One of the highlights of staying at the Mansion is dining at its top-rated restaurant, an architectural treasure as well as a culinary delight. Much of the grandeur of the original King mansion has been retained in the restoration. The building's features are distinctive: a dramatic staircase with wrought-iron railing that ascends two floors, arched entranceways, and a profusion of marble.

Many of the components of today's structure were collected by the King family, who designed their home around them. The ceiling of the main dining room is formed of 2400 separate pieces of enameled and inlaid wood. There's a set of stained-glass windows depicting British barons signing the Magna Carta, a 16th-century German stone mantel, and two pairs of early 19th-century Spanish cathedral doors with hand-carved helmeted faces.

The food served in the restaurant does justice to its rich surroundings. Nouvelle American with a Southwestern flair, dishes are imaginative, well prepared, and attractively presented. Service is polished and personalized but unpretentious.

While the menu changes several times a year, some of its highlights are New Zealand venison, pheasant, and Dover sole, in addition to more standard offerings of beef, veal, and lamb. Most of the menus feature at least one pumpkin dish—whether it's pumpkin muffins or quail served in a fried pumpkin crepe. (Pumpkin is a personal favorite of Rosewood Hotels owner Caroline Hunt Schoelkopf.)

The Mansion serves an elaborate brunch on Saturdays and Sundays. Complementing its service in the main restaurant, the hotel serves breakfast, lunch, and afternoon tea in the Promenade, a cheerfully decorated room with arched windows.

Situated approximately five minutes from downtown Dallas and 30 minutes from D/FW International Airport, the Mansion on Turtle Creek is a short drive from several shopping and business areas, including the Galleria and NorthPark.

The Melrose Hotel
3015 Oak Lawn
Dallas, Texas 75219
800/MELROSE (tollfree from within Texas)
800/527-1488 (tollfree from rest of U.S.)
214/521-5151

Singles $95–$105
Doubles $115–$125
Suites $195–$250

The Melrose is a gracious home, stately and proud. Originally opened in 1924 as a residential apartment house, the building underwent a $20 million renovation in 1982, resulting in a 185-room hotel with classic charm. The staff of 125 is eager to please, offering personalized service.

Throughout the hotel are reminders of its heritage: high ceilings, large windows, brass elevators, and classical architecture. Guest rooms, designed in 27 different styles, are airy and cheerfully decorated. All have separate sitting areas. Comfortably furnished with overstuffed chairs, they have such accessories as marble-topped dressing tables and ceiling fans. Guests have a choice of a king- or twin-size beds. Bathrooms are large and feature old-style fixtures with modern-day efficiency.

Offering a range of suites, the Melrose has executive and king junior suites. The Presidential Suite, with approximately 850 square feet, has an especially appealing large sitting area, dining room, and bedroom.

The VIP key-access floor provides a continental breakfast buffet, afternoon cocktails, and even milk and cookies at bedtime, as well as preregistration and express check-out. And a newspaper is delivered each morning to the guest's door.

The Library is a handsome restaurant and bar, and its menu features such delights as Pulitzer Prize Prime Rib Sandwich and Editorial Eggs Cocotte, with choices from the Final Chapter pastry shop for dessert.

The Garden Court, cosmopolitan in its decor, serves three meals daily, with such dinner selections as beef tournedos, quail stuffed with crabmeat, and grilled baby salmon.

Specializing in accommodating small meetings, the Melrose has a 2000-square-foot ballroom and five meeting rooms. Its boardroom is well designed for business conferences.

Conveniently located for business travelers, the Melrose is near the central business district, Dallas Market Center, and Infomart. The hotel offers complimentary limousine service to nearby Love Field as well as to downtown Dallas and Market Center. Airport shuttle service via the Link is available to D/FW International Airport, approximately 25 minutes from the hotel. Parking at the Melrose is free.

Stockyards Hotel
Main Street and Exchange Avenue
Fort Worth, Texas 76106
817/625-6427

Singles $75–$125
Doubles $85–$135
Suites $200–$350

When visitors walk through the doors of the Stockyards Hotel, they can imagine being in the world of affluent cattlemen in the early 1900s who traveled to Fort Worth to deal at the livestock markets. Dating back to 1907, the hotel was transformed in 1983 from a dilapidated building into a luxury hotel with 52 guest rooms. Not intended as a historical reproduction, the hotel is inventive and vivacious, recapturing the spirit of the time it portrays.

Not only is the Stockyards Hotel an imaginative reflection of the city's heritage, but it offers a fun-filled atmosphere and an escape from the commonplace. Fronting onto Exchange Avenue, it is situated in the midst of the Stockyards National Historic District. Western shops, restaurants, and saloons line the streets in the area which was once the cattle center of the Southwest, today supporting a thriving cattle-auction business. Nearby is Billy Bob's Texas, "the world's largest honky tonk," with a Texas-size dance floor, an indoor rodeo, Western shop, restaurants, and a host of bar stations. Within a few blocks are other entertainment centers with names like Pickin' Parlour and Filthy McNasty's. Downtown Fort Worth is several miles to the south.

The lobby of the hotel is decorated in "cattle baron baroque," with Chesterfield leather sofas, carved-wood chairs covered with animal skins, bronze sculptures, Western paintings, even a mirror framed in doeskin and topped with antlers.

A grand oak staircase leads to the two guest floors. Rooms are decorated in a choice of motifs: Indian, Western, Mountain Man, and Victorian. A delightful departure from traditional design, each room has its own personality, accented with such unusual touches as shutters made of 200-year-old wormwood originally used in Mexican haciendas, or cow skulls decorated with feathers.

Natural materials—slate, limestone, wood, animal skins—are dominant in the decor. Western rooms are decorated with wooden rockers and tables made of cedar branches bound with rawhide and topped with fossil-patterned limestone. The Indian theme is carried out with Navaho print bedspreads and tables formed of earthenware vases topped with slate. Mountain Man suites have a deerskin headboard, hide-covered chairs, and a ram's skull chandelier. Bedskirts have a plaid design, reflecting the Scottish heritage of the mountain men. Victorian rooms offer white wicker furniture, chintz fabrics, lace curtains, and fringed lamps.

Guest rooms have king-size beds and baths with chain-pull waterclosets. Wardrobes replace closets, and conceal televisions. Nightly turndown service includes a gold nugget candy and a copy of a cowboy's prayer placed on the pillows (''Give me a saddle and a blanket for a bed / Out where the stars shine and twinkle overhead . . .'').

The Bonnie and Clyde suite, once frequented by the infamous twosome, has an assortment of memorabilia mounted on the walls: Bonnie Parker's gun, newspaper clippings of the pair's escapades, photographs, and a letter testifying to their presence in the hotel.

The Celebrity Suite, priced at $350, has a living area with fireplace and antique furnishings, private deck with hot tub, and its own private entrance.

Downstairs is Booger Red's Saloon, named for a tough bronco buster who charmed audiences with his antics at the turn of the century. Patrons sit at the bar on saddles mounted on bar stools while a belt-driven multiple ceiling fan whirs overhead.

The adjacent restaurant specializes in home-style cooking with a Southwestern flavor. Naturally, steak has a prominent place on the lunch and dinner menus. Breakfast can be hearty, with names of combination meals such as ''cow hand'' and ''the dude.''

The North Side Room and the Niles City Room are designed for small meetings and are adjoined by a redwood deck overlooking a creek.

The Stockyards Hotel has valet parking, with an overnight charge of $4.

«DENVER»

Accommodations Plus
4155 East Jewell Avenue, Suite 505
Denver, Colorado 80222
303/785-7143
Reservations 800/621-8385, ext. 465 (tollfree)

One-bedroom suites $35–$49
Two-bedroom suites $50–$59
Three-bedroom suites $57–$69
$100 security deposit on check-in, refunded in full at
    check-out
Four-Day minimum stay
Corporate and long-term rates available

For Western wide, open spaces, these 645- to 1145-square-foot suites are larger and less expensive than most hotel rooms. All are tastefully furnished and fully equipped with everything from a popcorn popper to a colander.

Accommodations Plus multiplied its properties by opening five newly constructed buildings in 1986 in addition to four earlier properties. The total pretty well covers the suburban areas of metro Denver—east, west, southeast, southwest, and north. Most are close to particular office and commercial areas. A car would be essential for most locations, but is generally necessary for getting around Denver anyway (and the money saved on accommodations should cover car rental rates).

Only one of these pseudo-hotels is near downtown: Parkway Center with 100 suites in a 12-story mid-rise. Here, services rival other downtown accommodations, with 24-hour security, complimentary continental breakfast, and free shuttle service in the downtown area. Valet service even extends to alterations and shoe repair as well as dry cleaning and laundry at a nearby shopping center, which also has a major supermarket.

Extras vary at the other eight locations, but all include housekeeping, free parking, laundry facilities, and iron and ironing board. Various buildings may offer fireplaces, indoor and outdoor pools, racquetball or tennis courts, volleyball courts, exercise rooms, saunas or hot tubs, and billiard rooms.

Guests have free use of International Athletic Club facilities in downtown Denver or southeast Aurora, which include an elevated jogging track with banked turns and cushioned surface, a supervised nursery, and a dining room.

Bed and Breakfast Rocky Mountains
Box 804
Colorado Springs, Colorado 80901
303/630-3433

Bed and Breakfast Colorado
Box 20596
Denver, Colorado 80228
303/333-3340

These are reservations agencies for bed and breakfast inns and host homes in Colorado, including Denver. Neither appear to be very efficiently operated (both were closed during the busy two-week Christmas holiday season, but the Colorado Springs agency had at least emergency telephone coverage). Bed and Breakfast Rocky Mountains charges $3 for a directory with approximately 100 listings in five states but only half a dozen in Denver, priced from $17 to $55 double. Bed and Breakfast Colorado charges $2 for six typed pages highlighting accommodations, including six B&Bs in Denver costing from $24 single to $50 double. Neither lists specific addresses since reservations are to be made through the agency.

Cambridge Club
1560 Sherman Street
Denver, Colorado 80203
303/831-1252

Rooms and suites $110–$265 Monday–Thursday
(business travelers' rates lower), $69–$89 Friday–
Sunday.
No tipping (ten percent service charge is included in
rates)

A half block to the north, the gold dome of the Colorado
State Capitol building glitters like a shiny medallion on the
Denver skyline, and less than six blocks away the Denver
Mint stores the second-largest horde of gold bullion in the
United States (after Fort Knox). The guest services at the
Cambridge Club are 24-karat also, symbolized by the gold
coat of arms on the business cards. With a British name
and a French restaurant, it revives the traditions of small
European hotels, billing itself as "a tiny hotel in the grand
manner." A $4 million restoration of the structure, which
had alternated between being a hotel and an apartment building, was completed in November 1982.

Panels of leaded glass lend elegance to the entrance. Each
of the 27 rooms is decorated in a different style with appropriate art, antiques, accessories, and colored or patterned
linens. Choices range from English traditional with a canopy
bed to ultramodern with a platform bed, with oriental, art
deco, and contemporary in between. The dark green Hunt
Suite features a chair fashioned of antlers, an antique desk,
and a bookcase with a full set of World Book encyclopedias
along with an eclectic selection of other volumes.

Accessible via a locked elevator or a stairway hidden in
the hall paneling, the suites average 900 square feet in size
and always sport fresh flowers and fruit. Butler pantries
include a refrigerator, a sink, and a microwave (on request),
along with a complimentary stock of nuts, snacks, Perrier
water, soft drinks, and fruit juices. Complimentary liquor
and other items will be added on request. For late night
cravings, cognac and Swiss truffles are provided when the
bed is turned down, although any order from milk and

cookies to herb tea will be substituted. A complimentary continental breakfast featuring a different type of croissant baked fresh each day is provided along with fresh-squeezed orange juice, but again any request will be honored including room service for a full breakfast. Individual guest records are maintained and consulted so that special requests need be stated only once.

A hospitality suite offers complimentary liquor and snacks while affording an opportunity to mingle with other guests, who may include oilmen, opera performers, business executives, lawyers, and celebrities. Ten percent of the guests hail from tony Aspen, Colorado. Varied special functions for all guests are scheduled in the hospitality suit, such as evening wine and cheese parties and afternoon teas.

Lunch and dinner are offered in the adjoining Le Profil, a deluxe four-star restaurant that celebrated its 30th birthday in 1985 and was among few places in Denver where one could appear in formal dress a quarter of a century ago without risking laughter from other customers. Dinner entrees cost $16 to $24.

Room service is available round the clock (a hamburger costs $9.50). The management says they'll bring anything from Chinese take-out food to a Cadbury bar at 3 A.M.

Amenities include overnight shoe shine, valet quick steam press, packing, and unpacking. The concierge staff is trained for extras, from obtaining theater tickets to renting a tuxedo to chartering a jet.

For local gadding about, a chauffeured Lincoln town car is available free anywhere in the downtown area, or for a fee to and from the airport; it's often used in the winter to jump-start guests' own cars. No parking lot is adjacent, but valet parking is available for an extra charge. A horse-drawn carriage may be ordered for downtown forays. Bus service is nearby but limited and often inconvenient for transportation outside of the downtown area.

For an additional $10, guests may use the facilities of the downtown International Athletic Club. For those who'd rather walk for their health, several attractions are within half a mile, such as the Denver Art Museum, the Colorado Heritage Museum, the Denver Public Library, and the City and County Building.

Fairmont Hotel
1750 Welton Street
Denver, Colorado 80202
303/295-1200
Reservations 800/527-4724 (tollfree)
800/492-6622 (tollfree from Texas)

Singles $120–$175
Doubles $145–$200
Suites $175–$925

The Fairmont is a great place to see lots of red while preparing to spend lots of green, entering through the plush burgundy-colored lobby. Sister hotel to the famed older Fairmonts in San Francisco and New Orleans, this one was built in 1979 on 17th Street in the heart of the downtown Denver business district.

The Fairmont boasts that no two of its 535 guest rooms and 27 suites are decorated alike, but all include down pillows and Irish linen handtowels.

The Fairmont is not so much for the upwardly mobile as for those who have already made it, seeking 1940s splendor at 1980s prices. The Moulin Rouge alternates weekly bookings of such groups as the Modernaires, the Limelighters, and the Ink Spots with such performers as country-and-western Doug Kershaw and jazz pianist McCoy Tyner.

The Moulin Rouge offers nightclub entertainment, dancing to the big band sound of Dick Hammergren's Orchestra, dinner, and cocktails. The buffet brunch table adorned with elaborate ice sculptures is an event on Sundays and holidays at $16 for adults and $8 for children.

The Marquis Restaurant, winner of a Travel/Holiday Fine Dining Award, seats eighty for lunch and dinner at tables bedecked by hand-woven lace tablecloths and Royal Doulton china atop a silver base plate. The ceiling is of Belgian crystal set in brass. A brass rack from floor to ceiling displays vintage wines. The Marquis Lounge is mellow with melodies from a piano bar.

McGuire's Restaurant is open 24 hours a day. Selections range from Cajun and creole fare to a fitness menu endorsed by the American Heart Association. Complimentary hors d'oeuvres tempt during Happy Hour from 4:30 to 7:30 weekdays.

Continental breakfast, light lunch, cocktails, and evening piano serenades are available in the Lobby Terrace. Room service hustles 24 hours a day.

Atop the 26-story hotel is an outdoor athletic facility with swimming pool, jogging track, and tennis court open only from Memorial Day to Labor Day. This spot is for persons who don't mind having their heads in Denver's notorious brown cloud of smog, second-worst in the United States (after Los Angeles). Fitness need not be lost, however, because a half-block stroll leads to the indoor, full-facility International Athletic Club available to the Fairmont's guests.

Many Mansions
1313 Steele Street
Denver, Colorado 80206
303/355-1313

One-bedroom suites $79.50
Two-bedroom suites $98–$118
Seven-day minimum stay required

Many Mansions isn't really very many and isn't really a mansion. But this engaging, converted apartment building offers 24 one-bedroom suites and 12 two-bedroom suites, all airy and spacious (from 750 to 1150 square feet). Every living room and bedroom has its own balcony.

On the eighth floor, in the Penthouse Clubroom, guests mingle for the complimentary full breakfast amid tropical decor of pineapple, lime, and tangerine tones. From the balcony is a view of the downtown Denver skyline dwarfed against the violet-blue backdrop of towering Rocky Mountains. After breakfast, the Penthouse Clubroom can host private conferences or parties for up to 25 persons.

A complimentary limousine whisks guests from this central-east location to downtown (ten to fifteen minutes) or to the popular Cherry Creek shopping area (five minutes). The

University of Colorado Health Sciences Center is nearby, as are several other major hospitals.

Returning home that evening may mean cooking dinner, but some comfort may be taken from the fact that Many Mansions' staff will do the grocery shopping at no additional service charge and will wash the dishes the next morning. Kitchens are fully equipped, with the exception of microwave ovens. Catering may be arranged. The highly regarded French cuisine of the Normandy is nearby, but no other restaurants are within easy walking distance.

The hotel provides saunas on the eighth floor, and facilities of the Cherry Creek Sporting Club are available, but no transportation is provided.

Usually, getting around Denver with ease involves having your own car, so thankfully free underground parking is available. Bus service is two blocks away but not convenient except to limited areas.

Guests may use laundry facilities on the premises, and overnight shoeshine is available. The staff will arrange any type of reservation on request.

Many Mansions must be doing something right since it opened in 1982, because the average stay is six weeks. The hotel is popular with low-profile celebrities and foreign visitors, and once hosted an entire delegation from China.

«DETROIT»

The Dearborn Inn
20301 Oakwood Boulevard
Dearborn, Michigan 48123
313/271-2700

Singles $75–$83
Doubles $85–$93

The Dearborn Inn, America's first airport hotel, is far from that. Built in 1931 by Henry Ford, it offers a leisurely step back in time. Consisting of an inn and five colonial houses, each a replica of a famous house in the United States, it has an atmosphere of graciousness and elegance that is completely different from any other establishment near Detroit.

More like Williamsburg on a small scale, the inn covers 25 acres ten miles west of Detroit and ten miles from the airport. Visitors are often taken aback when stepping into the lobby, with its high ceiling, large area rugs, comfortable array of chairs and tables, well-stocked bookshelves, and airy windows.

For history buffs, this place offers the opportunity to browse among the historic rooms or spend the night in replicas of houses where Edgar Allan Poe, Walt Whitman, and Patrick Henry lived.

The Early American Dining Room serves a gourmet feast, including roast duck and honey-basted rack of pork served by candlelight. Guests might also try the delicious Michigan bean soup in the cozy, pine-paneled Ten Eyck Tavern, pattered after an inn of 1826 vintage.

For camaraderie, the copper-topped bar can't be beat. Many repeat guests return to mingle with friends here.

Most of the inn's furnishings are exact replicas of work selected by the Fords. Rooms are decorated with blanket chests, three-legged milking stools in baths, brass candlesticks over fireplaces, English shaving mirrors, Dutch doors, brass or pencil-poster beds, and reproduction lighting fixtures.

There are three types of accommodations: rooms in the main inn, rooms in colonial homes (which number from one to fourteen in each home), and rooms in the newer motorhouse, which is more like a motel. All are spacious and furnished in early American style and feature fireplaces and cozy baths, as well as colonial fabrics and patterns.

In the warmer months, guests can use the two tennis courts or the outdoor heated pool. Arrangements have been made with the Dearborn Athletic Club for guests to use facilities for $3 per person. Arrangements can also be made to play golf nearby.

Weekends are especially inviting. A delicious Sunday brunch is served and activities are geared to leisurely walks and events on the grounds.

The Mayflower Hotel
827 West Ann Arbor Trail
  (at Main Street)
Plymouth, Michigan 48170
313/453-1620

Singles $61–$66
Doubles $71–$79

The Mayflower Hotel is a 100-room, historic, family-owned and -operated hotel on the outskirts of Detroit. What makes the hotel unique is that it is actually a large bed and breakfast.

Since its founding in 1927, the Mayflower has operated as an English-style inn featuring full breakfast for overnight guests. Elegant and comfortable surroundings and an excellent reputation for good food and service have made it one of the best in the area.

Located 25 minutes from Detroit and in the heart of villagelike Plymouth, the hotel is within walking distance of 150 shops and lies on the town square. This is the site of many of the town's festivals and events throughout the year.

Rooms, though small, are simply decorated and are equipped with color TV, queen-size, double, or twin beds, and individually controlled heating and cooling. Newer rooms in an adjacent wing all have refrigerators and there are 20 deluxe rooms equipped with whirlpool baths and king-size beds.

Three fine restaurants and an English-style pub give the hotel an excellent reputation for dining. Both the traditional dining room and the newer nautical-motif steakhouse feature Norwegian cooking and steaks. The pub features entertainment on weekends.

Sunday Brunch at the Mayflower Meeting Room is an event that is both popular and well worth the price.

Several packages are available on weekends. One takes in the Greenfield Village and Henry Ford Museum and includes champagne on arrival, Sunday brunch, and a deluxe room.

The Pontchartrain Hotel
Two Washington Boulevard
Detroit, Michigan 48226
313/965-0200

Singles $115–$125
Doubles $125–$135

In the heart of downtown Detroit, a landmark hotel has been reborn. The Pontchartrain Hotel has recently completed a $14 million renovation, making it the most outstanding hotel in the city.

The hotel now has an up-to-date feeling, from its oak-paneled lobby, imported Italian marble floors, and cozy fireplace to the soft pastel decor that gives the place its elegance.

A glass solarium lets guests have a beautiful view of the

river from the lobby lounge while creating a greenhouse effect that is a welcome treat in winter. Elegant millwork, wicker furnishings, and plants help to create a light, airy feeling.

A quiet, intimate bar in a corner of the lobby shows off a rich mix of mahogany, imported tapestry fabrics, marble, and brass. The focal point of the room is the off-white imported marble U-shaped bar.

The main dining room serves light American cuisine in an atmosphere of off-white lacquer millwork and light-colored furniture accentuated with bright colors. The entire feeling is one of elegance but not formality.

Guests can also dine in a lively open garden court lounge while listening to piano music, or they might want to watch sports on a large-screen TV in the paneled bar.

All the rooms have a warmth that is reflected in their neutral colors, fine furnishings, and luxurious decor. Each features a queen-size, double, or king-size bed, luxurious marble bath, and color TV. The extras are meant to suit executives from the major automobile companies, who are the Pontchartrain's main customers.

Over the 20 years since the hotel's construction, Detroit has come to regard the Pontchartrain as its premier hotel. All guests receive turndown service, complimentary continental breakfast, and complimentary morning paper. A concierge is on duty six days a week.

The renovations included a new health and fitness center with sauna and exercise room. There is also complimentary limousine service within the downtown area and out to the automobile plants.

«HONOLULU»

The New Otani–Kaimana Beach Hotel
2863 Kalakaua Avenue
Honolulu, Hawaii 96815
808/923-1555
Reservations 800/421-8795 (tollfree)
800/252-0197 (tollfree from California) 800/665-8818
  (tollfree from Canada)

Rooms $54–$170
Apartments $71–$100
Suites $230–$240

On the easternmost end of Waikiki, at the base of Diamond Head Crater, lies a cluster of buildings that includes hotels, apartments, and private beach clubs. Separated from the main part of Waikiki by Kapiolani Park, the cluster seems unusually isolated.

The nine-story Kaimana Beach Hotel is adjacent to Kapiolani Park, which encompasses sandy beaches, jogging trails, a golf driving range, the Honolulu Zoo, and the Waikiki Shell (an outdoor concert arena). The Kaimana was the first hotel built on this end of the beach, and it is the only building with an unobstructed view of the ocean and the mountains, including Diamond Head Crater.

Separated from central Waikiki, the hotel is quieter and less touristy than those along the main drag. Though some may miss the restaurants, movie theaters, and other tourist attractions downtown, the quiet location, fine hospitality, and lower prices of the hotel will compensate.

All guest rooms are located on the third through ninth floors, with an atrium extending up the middle of the building. Because of the atrium there are no rooms directly across from each other and each room has access to a beautiful view of land or sea.

The rooms are categorized by three specific views. Mountain view rooms (*Mauka* in local dialect) offer an exquisite look over Diamond Head Crater and the Koolau Mountains. Ocean view rooms provide a westward (*Ewa*) view across the park, up the Waikiki shore, over west Oahu, and of potentially spectacular sunsets. Ocean front rooms (*Makai*) afford a fabulous 180-degree view of the ocean and the shoreline.

All rooms in the Kaimana are fully air-conditioned, have a color TV with cable, radio, refrigerator, and lanai (patio). Rooms with mountain views are less expensive than similar rooms with ocean views or on the ocean front. Rooms offer more space and quality than similarly priced rooms in central Waikiki. The daily trade winds blow through the large sliding glass doors to cool the rooms.

The warm hospitality of the Kaimana's staff is one of its more pleasant features. The staff is not large, but then neither is the hotel, and their graciousness overcomes any problems that might arise. The hotel makes available concierge services, room service, a travel desk, babysitting referral, and three meeting rooms, the largest of which can accommodate 150 people.

The Kaimana houses two very good restaurants and a lounge with a premier view. The Hau Tree Lanai serves breakfast, lunch, and dinner. This is the same hau tree that Robert Louis Stevenson sat under and wrote about during his visits to Hawaii almost a hundred years ago. Miyako's is a popular Japanese restaurant that serves dinner only. It offers tatami rooms for traditional Japanese dining or Western-style seating, but the tatami rooms generally offer much better views. The Sunset Lounge, next to the Hau Tree Lanai, is available for cocktails and is privy to one of the most gorgeous views of the sunset.

The Garden Apartments are studio and one-bedroom suites located on the mountain-view side of the hotel. The rooms are larger than similarly priced ones in the hotel, and have kitchenettes that are fully supplied with utensils. Monthly rates are available.

The Kaimana's hospitality, location, unique building, and its range of rates are not surpassed anywhere in Honolulu.

The Royal Hawaiian Hotel
2259 Kalakaua Avenue
Honolulu, Hawaii 96815
808/923-7311

Dec.–March: Rooms $115–$160, suites $190 and up
April–Nov: Rooms $105–$150, suites $180 and up

In 1927 the luxurious Royal Hawaiian Hotel opened its doors to the rich, famous, and titled. The six-story Moorish-style building was painted a luminous coral pink, hence its nickname, the Pink Palace of the Pacific. The hotel was built on a beautiful palm grove in Waikiki with a grand view of the shoreline, Diamond Head Crater, and the Pacific.

The site had served as a summer retreat for Hawaiian royalty. The hotel's size, location, and bright color made it the dominant landmark along the Waikiki shoreline. Moreover, its elegance, excellent facilities, and the tropical weather combined to make it one of the finest and most distinctive resorts in the United States.

Its elegance faded and its popularity decreased during the Great Depression. The Navy leased the hotel during World War II and used it as a place for R&R. Soon after the war, development of Waikiki increased dramatically, so that today, the once regal Royal is dwarfed by highrise hotels and shopping malls.

Stepping onto the Royal's grounds is like returning to the Waikiki of 60 years ago and finding an oasis in paradise. It is one of the few hotels in Waikiki that still has courtyards filled with flowers, palms, banyan trees, and bamboo. The grounds and buildings are impeccably tidy and well kept.

Visitors enter the hotel and are greeted with the ocean view from the lobby. The contrast between the pink and maroon motif in the lobby and the bright blue water makes a memorable view.

The Royal is now made up of two buildings, the 384-room main building (the old hotel) and the 192-room tower, built in 1969. The tower is a modern, highrise luxury hotel with great facilities, fine views, and advantages not found in the main building. But the history, uniqueness, and beauty of the old hotel makes it a more intriguing place to stay.

Four types of rooms are available in the main building: the standard garden; deluxe garden; ocean view rooms; and a few prestigous one-bedroom suites. Each room is entered through an intricately carved Nara wood door, thick and fire-proofed, and is decorated in French provincial furniture. Rooms are equipped with air conditioning, color television (cable extra), small refrigerator, clock radio, and an electronic safe (at extra cost, but the safe at the main desk is free of charge). The bathrooms are fully stocked with toiletries, and there is twice daily towel service. The standard rooms have either twin beds or one king-size bed with charming headboards, and an occasional canopied bed. The comfortable chairs and writing desk, complete with hotel stationery, make the rooms quite pleasant.

Deluxe rooms have two double beds or one king-size with a seating area overlooking the gardens or the ocean. These rooms are more spacious, with high ceilings, and encompass a wider view than the standard room.

The suites each have three rooms: one bedroom (with king-size bed and TV), a sitting room with TV, and a dining area. Each suite has one large bathroom, walk-in closets, and the three suites have Jacuzzis. Exquisite views are included.

The hotel is generously staffed and a warm aloha spirit is pervasive. The Royal offers complete amenities including room service, a travel center, cable office, 20 specialty shops, nurse and physician service, babysitting, a shuttle service to a championship golf course, and, naturally, the beachfront area on Waikiki Beach.

The Sheraton Corporation operates the Royal and four other hotels in Waikiki. Guests at any one of the five hotels can use the facilities and restaurants of the other Sheraton hotels and charge expenses to their room.

Restaurants in the Royal include the Monarch Room, which features entertainment and gourmet dining. The more moderately priced Surf Room serves breakfast, lunch, and dinner and has a grand view of Waikiki. The snack bar near the freshwater pool is open during the day. The famous Mai Tai Bar still provides shade and drinks on the beach.

The Sheraton Moana Hotel
2365 Kalakaua Avenue
Honolulu, Hawaii 96815
808/922-3111
800/325-3535
Eastern Canada-800/268-9393
Western Canada-800/268-9330

Dec. 21–March: $65–$140 single or double
April–Dec. 20: $60–$130 single or double

The Moana Hotel was Waikiki's first resort hotel. The 237-room main building was built in 1901 and wings were added in 1918, creating the present H-shaped building. The Ocean Lanai, added in 1952, is adjacent to the Moana on the Diamond Head side. The historic main building is much more intriguing and atmospheric. It is the main building that is affectionately referred to as the First Lady of Waikiki.

Located in the heart of Waikiki, the Moana presents one side to the ocean and the other to busy Kalakaua Avenue, the main street. Having first crack at the Waikiki beachfront, the Moana occupies one of the most pleasant and scenic spots on the shore. Guests can scan a lovely panorama from its restaurants, beach, and courtyard.

The six-story colonial-style building presents a placid exterior when contrasted with the surrounding modern hotels. It maintains a classic South Seas touch, much of it due to the famous banyan tree courtyard that sits facing the Pacific. The tree overshadows the courtyard's restaurant and cocktail lounge. "Hawaii Calls," the popular radio program of the '40s, originated here and was broadcast across the nation until 1978.

The age of the hotel is more apparent once in the guest rooms, which tend to be small and dark. The view from many of the rooms in the main building is rather limited, which has been further hindered by the tremendous development surrounding the hotel. Kalakaua Avenue is a very busy street about 22 hours a day so the rooms on this side of the hotel can be noisy. But the rooms are clean, nicely furnished, and all have lovely tropical ceiling fans (no air conditioning). The decor is Victorian with brass beds, marble top end tables, glass lamps, and cherrywood writing desks, although some rooms have rosewood furniture and lanais. All have a bathtub as well as a shower, a color TV, daily housekeeping, and a full complement of toiletries.

The Moana is one of five Waikiki hotels operated by the Sheraton Corporation. Guests at the Moana can enjoy the restaurants, entertainment features, and other activities at any one of the five hotels and charge the expenses to their rooms. The Moana offers the Captain's Galley Restaurant and Lounge, for dining at the water's edge. The Paisan Pizzeria is open for lunch, dinner, and take-out, while the Ice Cream Terrace on the beach provides light snacks, ice cream, and cold drinks during the day.

The hotel has a private sunbathing area and its own beach club that makes chairs and towels available and refers people to other nearby rental agencies for water sports equipment. The surfing directly in front of the hotel is generally serene enough for beginning surfers. The reef protecting the inner beach provides an excellent and safe swimming area.

Other hotel facilities and amenities include a Travel and Entertainment Center, room service, beauty salon and barber shop, gift shop, babysitting service; 24-hour bell service, parking nearby, and shuttle service to a championship golf course (Makaha West).

A major renovation is scheduled to begin in 1987. The exterior will not be changed but the interior and guest rooms are to be modernized. Upon completion it will be a super-luxury hotel with luxurious prices.

«HOUSTON»

Bed & Breakfast Society of Houston
Marguerite Swanson
921 Heights Boulevard
Houston, Texas 77008
713/868-4654

Singles $25–$30
Doubles $35–$40

An especially well-managed organization, Bed & Breakfast Society of Houston has a diversity of offerings spread over the city. Travelers contact Marguerite Swanson, who is adept at matching guests with appropriate hosts.

Her own home, a beautifully restored Victorian house in the Heights residential area, sets the tone for the society. From the moment guests enter, they know that their visit will be special. Once an antique dealer, Marguerite has decorated her home with turn-of-the-century treasures, from china dolls to a player piano. One of the guest rooms is a confection of blue, with lace curtains and a white iron double bed topped with a cozy comforter.

Swanson's warm personality is reflected throughout the room: fresh flowers, scented linens, towels with hand-embroidered borders, a basket of fruit. Inside the antique wardrobe are Victorian nightgowns, and hanging on the wall is a bonnet bedecked with flowers.

A second bedroom has an antique single bed set beneath bay windows and covered with a hand-crocheted bedspread.

The guest bath has a clawfoot tub, a washstand converted into a lavatory, and brass fixtures.

Breakfast is an important feature of all stays at Houston bed and breakfast homes. In the Swanson household, guests have a choice of breakfast in bed, the country-style kitchen, or the Victorian dining room. And breakfast is always hearty, including hot bread and fresh fruit.

Choices of other bed and breakfast homes range from those in historic neighborhoods to ones in the suburbs. In the Montrose area, Mary Kathryn Hitt has a three-story home with a second-floor apartment that she opens for guests. Decorated with lace and bows, the home is a cheerful retreat from modernity. Its wrap-around front porch has white wicker furniture, and guests are welcome to sit and visit. An excellent cook, Hitt is also a convivial host who can entertain her guests with stories about Houston and its local personalities.

Southeast of downtown is the stunning contemporary home of the Karolyn Bratton family. One of their guest lodgings is a romantically decorated garage apartment. In southwest Houston, Pat Thomas, a personable host and excellent cook, welcomes guests to her suburban home with backyard swimming pool. A home in Spring Branch to the west of downtown, decorated with country accents and lots of quilts, has an inviting backyard well suited for relaxing.

A rapidly growing organization, Bed & Breakfast Society of Houston has listings in surrounding farm communities, as well as in neighborhoods convenient to Houston airports, Texas Medical Center, the Galleria, the Astrodome, and downtown. Marguerite Swanson keeps close tabs on the participating homes, making sure that a high level of quality is maintained. Fees are paid directly to her in advance, an arrangement that further enhances the feeling that guests are visiting in the home of new-found friends.

La Colombe d'Or
3410 Montrose Boulevard
Houston, Texas 77006
713/524-7999

Singles, doubles $150–$200
Penthouse $400

Once the home of a wealthy Houston family, the yellow brick house of Montrose plays host to visitors from around the world. With five suites on the second floor and a third-floor penthouse, the inn has an atmosphere of intimacy. Visitors are treated like house guests—there is no formal check-in procedure, and fresh coffee is often perking on a hall table.

Set on a mid-town residential lot, it has a welcoming front porch characteristic of its age. The mahogany staircase and decorated ceilings are part of the original design of the 1920s home. Owner Steve Zimmerman has gathered an eclectic mix of antiques to complement his Houston treasure, including a brass lectern from a church in Italy, an onyx chandelier made in Europe, and works of art from around the world. The dimly lit bar—originally the residence's dining room—now has architectural components from France, Germany, Italy, England, and Scotland.

La Colombe d'Or has an extremely fine restaurant, specializing in French cuisine with an emphasis on seafood. Serving both lunch and dinner, the restaurant is popular with local residents as well as hotel guests. The dining area, decorated in soft pinks and mauves, is sophisticated and inviting. Guests are invited to retire to the Library for cognac and liqueurs after dinner.

The inn's accommodations are spacious and comfortable. Suites have a bedroom with king-size bed, sitting area, bath, and large private dining room—ideal for entertaining. Named for well-known painters, each suite is distinctive in its decor. The Renoir, which is the smallest, is especially appealing. Its dining area is separated from the bedroom with interior columns and draped fabric, yet its theme is Asian, with a carved screen for a headboard, oriental rugs and chest, and a glass-topped dining table.

The Cezanne Suite, once the master bedroom, is boldly decorated in bright green and orange. The Degas Suite is contemporary in design, highlighted by a glass headboard with padded inset, and an airy dining room with an upper border of hand-painted geese. Its balcony overlooks Montrose Boulevard.

Amenities in the guest suites include terry cloth robes, clock radios, and ceiling fans. Bathrooms in the regular suites have the home's original lavatories, including brass faucets. Some of the bathrooms have showers in addition to tubs.

The spacious penthouse features a luxurious bathroom with an elevated Jacuzzi tub, contrasted with the antique furnishings in the bedroom, dining area, and sitting room.

Since the inn's guest list is small, the staff can offer extremely personal service—from notifying guests who are dining in the restaurant of phone calls to catering to personal preferences. (Some frequent guests even request that their favorite suite be rearranged, and their wishes are promptly granted.) Upon check-in, fruit and wine are sent to the room, and complimentary continental breakfast is served bedside each morning.

While staff members at La Colombe d'Or sometimes wear more than one hat (approximately 20 people operate the inn and restaurant), there is someone available around the clock to extend services. A concierge is on duty during part of the afternoon and evening, with the general manager doubling as the receptionist or bellman when needed.

The inn is approximately five minutes from downtown Houston and within easy access of Texas Medical Center, the Galleria, and such cultural attractions as the Museum of Fine Arts, Alley Theater, and Jones Hall. The University of St. Thomas is one block away.

Parking is free. The concierge will arrange transportation between the inn and either airport upon request.

Inn on the Park
Four Riverway
(off Woodway, one block west of West Loop 610 North)
Houston, Texas 77056
800/828-1188 (tollfree)
713/871-8181

Singles $120–$175
Doubles $145–$200
Suites $375 and up

A tranquil oasis within the bustling city, Inn on the Park is within a few minutes of a host of office addresses. In contrast to the metropolis surrounding it, the hotel has a parklike setting, with the heavily timbered banks of Buffalo Bayou on its eastern perimeter and a reflection pond set among weeping willow trees to the west. Guests drive onto the grounds from a busy city street, unexpectedly discovering a fine lodging spread over rolling terrain, yet nestled among highrises.

The entrance of the hotel bespeaks graciousness and warmth, with affable doormen extending a welcome. (Guests often do a double take when they see the lifelike statue by J. Seward Johnson, famed for his realistic human portrayals.)

The Palm Court Lounge, a lush tropical garden just inside the door, sets the tone of the inn. Its decor is elegant yet comfortable, and seating areas are arranged to create a sense of privacy. There's a calmly flowing waterfall, soft piano music, and a view of the hotel's pools, fountains, and reflection pond.

The colors of the garden are repeated throughout the public areas, with a profusion of green marble in the lobby, accented with an eclectic mix of Asian screens, modern paintings, and even a grandfather clock. Indeed, the entire hotel takes on a gardenlike atmosphere, simultaneously bringing the outdoors inside with a myriad of plants while affording ample views of the exterior's landscaped grounds.

The 383 guest rooms—all of which are spacious—offer a view of either the bayou or the hotel's grounds. Furnishings are modern in design and luxurious in quality. Rooms designated as moderate have two twin beds; all others have one king-size bed, with deluxe rooms having slightly more floor space than the superior units. All rooms feature overstuffed chairs, remote-control color television, digital clock radio, telephone in the bathroom, and terry cloth robes. TVs are concealed in armoires. Minibars are stocked with soft drinks, fruit juices, and snack food.

Suites range from comfortable one-bedroom units having a living room and separate bedroom to the two-bedroom Riverway Suite with 2200 square feet of space including a fireplace, balcony, and butler pantry for serving private parties.

Service in the hotel is personable and expansive, from complimentary shoeshine to 24-hour room service. The concierge is especially helpful, delighting in arranging the unusual as well as in fulfilling simple requests.

While the hotel has meeting space accommodating groups of up to 850, with ten conference rooms in addition to the Grand Salon, the property is designed so that several events can occur simultaneously without being noticed by the individual traveler.

A good choice for a weekend retreat as well as for business travel, Inn on the Park is geared to recreation. Its two large pools are heated—they even feature underwater music. Next to the bayou are four outdoor tennis courts, situated on top of the parking garage.

The health club has exercise equipment (treadmill, exercise bike, rowing machine, dumbbells, multi-use weight machine), mats for exercising (with optional instruction on video cassette), and a whirlpool. The locker rooms have saunas and are stocked with a range of grooming accessories including hair dryers.

Bicycles are available, with trails easily accessible in nearby Memorial Park for both bikers and joggers. And the grounds of Inn on the Park are well suited for strolling. Two black swans glide across the pond, yet if visitors get too close, their docile nature quickly disappears. Staff members explain that the swans, which have proven to be prolific breeders, are suspicious of intruders since the young swans are frequently "given up for adoption."

Dining at Inn on the Park is especially pleasant. Cafe on the Green overlooks the pool and pond area. Open daily from 6:30 A.M. to midnight, the cafe serves a bounteous brunch (highlighted by delectable pastries) on Sundays. La

Reserve is an outstanding gourmet restaurant serving French, American, and regional dishes. A five-star restaurant, it is the only Houston restaurant that features the eight-course *menu de degustation* on a regular basis.

Downstairs is the Black Swan, a pub named in honor of the hotel's two mascots. Specializing in serving over 100 brands of beer, it serves British-style lunches with an American flair. At night there is live music for dancing and listening.

Guests may park in a covered garage at no cost. Valet parking costs $8 for overnight. The hotel provides courtesy limousine service to nearby Galleria shopping and to Post Oak Airline Terminal (where bus transportation is available to both Intercontinental and Hobby airports).

Downtown Houston lies approximately ten miles to the west of the hotel. Transportation time to Intercontinental Airport averages 45 minutes, and to Hobby Airport 25 minutes.

The Lancaster Hotel
701 Texas Avenue
(at Louisiana)
Houston, Texas 77002
800/392-5566 (tollfree from within Texas)
800/231-0336 (tollfree from rest of U.S.)
713/228-9500

Singles $125–$150
Doubles $150–$175
Suites $275 and up

More like a fine home than a hotel, the 93-room Lancaster Hotel is warm, comfortable, and refined. The combination of its personable atmosphere and prestigious downtown address makes this lodging attractive to business travelers as well as weekend vacationers. Situated within the central business district, the Lancaster is also at the cultural heart of the city—next door to Alley Theatre, across the street from Jones Hall, and within a few blocks of the Music Hall and Albert Thomas Convention Center.

A small luxury inn, the Lancaster's trademark is its personalized service. From the doorman who meets each guest at the curbside to the ever-helpful concierge, the 106 staff members take personal pride in the hotel. Throughout the lodging are touches that convey a spirit of attentiveness: newspapers at the door each morning, an umbrella in the room, turndown service that is more than perfunctory.

The lobby of the Lancaster is small and intimate, with fine period furnishings, fresh floral arrangements, and paintings connoting the English theme. A curved staircase with brass railings leads to the second-floor private dining and conference rooms. Elevators with handsome brass doors are equally handsome on the interior, decorated with mirrors and polished woodwork.

Built in 1926 as the Auditorium Hotel, this building with a Renaissance-style facade has a colorful history. According to local folklore, Clark Gable stayed there early in his career, and when he found himself short on cash, the management held his trunk ransom until he could pay his bill. In 1928 delegates attending the National Democratic Convention crowded into the Auditorium Hotel, holding caucuses in its rooms. During World War II, the hotel basement housed the Stage Canteen, a social center for servicemen, and Gene Autry rode horseback down the stairs to the club when he was the night's headliner.

In late 1982 the once-grand hotel underwent a multi-million-dollar transformation, becoming a top-rated luxury hotel as well as a Texas Historical Landmark. While the Lancaster's rooms reflect their historical flavor, their sumptuousness far surpasses any luxury that guests at the Auditorium ever experienced.

Guest rooms are arranged on the upper ten floors, with no more than nine rooms per floor. As in the lobby, their decor has a British flavor, with imported English fabrics and wallpaper, framed prints depicting the English countryside, overstuffed chairs with foot stools, and finely carved poster beds. Brass fixtures and hardware enhance the feeling of quality. Televisions are concealed in armoires.

Rooms are designed for comfort and convenience, having such amenities as three to four phones (including one in the bathroom), digital clock radio, remote-control television, terry cloth robes, and a range of toiletries. Suites are especially luxurious without losing their air of coziness.

Bathrooms have distinctive white marble decor, wraparound mirrors in the dressing areas, and fresh flowers. The towel racks, even the curtain rods, are made of brass.

For dining, the 58-seat Lancaster Grille serves three meals a day and late-night fare. Conveying the tone of a British polo club, the restaurant is decorated with 19th-century oil paintings displayed on hunter-green walls. The menu features continental and American cuisine. Service is personable yet unobtrusive.

For recreation and exercise, guests have access to the Texas Club one and a half blocks from the hotel. The private membership club has a rooftop swimming pool, Nautilus equipment, squash and racquetball courts, basketball gym, and aerobics classes. Jogging trails along the banks of Buffalo Bayou begin four blocks from the hotel.

The Lancaster offers complimentary downtown limousine service on request, round-the-clock room service, and complimentary shoeshines. Same-day laundry service is offered Monday through Saturday, and pressing is available day or night. Of special interest to business travelers, the hotel has portable cellular telephones available for lease, and some of the guest rooms can be equipped with computer systems.

Theater packages and getaway weekends are often available at the Lancaster.

The Remington on Post Oak Park
1919 Briar Oaks Lane
Houston, Texas 77027
800/392-4659 (tollfree from within Texas)
800/231–9802 (tollfree from rest of U.S.)
713/840-7600

Singles $135–$195
Doubles $155–$210
Suites $390 and up

One of the most expensive hotels ever built in the U.S., the Remington is a gleaming palace, combining sophisticated taste with warmth and hospitality. Throughout the hotel there is an atmosphere of intimacy, making the Remington more akin to an elegant residence than a traditional hotel. Instead of large public areas, there are small skylighted rotundas, arched corridors decorated with greenery and fine furnishings, and alcoves with comfortable seating.

Most importantly, each visitor is treated as an honored guest, with personal preferences given notice and attention. The 350 employees are attuned to pleasing guests, from calling them by name to fulfilling their requests promptly and cheerfully. Standard services include valet parking, 24-hour room service, and complimentary transportation to nearby shopping and business areas.

The hotel's decor is a mix of marble floors and bleached oak walls softened with dhurrie carpets, original works of art, and a profusion of flowers. The theme is contemporary, tempered with such treasures as pre-Hispanic pottery, Chinese screens, and antique mirrors.

The living room is the gathering place for tea. With an exterior fountain as its focal point and harp music in the background, it creates a tone of refinement characteristic of the entire hotel. Nearby is the handsome bar, decorated to resemble an English men's club with couches and a fireplace.

The 221 guest rooms, available with one king-size or two twin beds, are comfortable and aesthetically pleasing. Deluxe rooms are especially large, with bay windows and separate sitting areas. Baths are warmly decorated with richly colored marble vanity tops and brass fixtures.

Attention to detail is the keynote: a choice of goosedown or synthetic pillows, terry cloth robes, digital clock radios, three telephones including one in the bath. Remote-control televisions are concealed inside large armoires. When guests enter their room upon check-in they feel as if they are expected—the thermostat has been set, lights are on, the radio is playing soft music.

Suites have canopied beds, expansive wet bars with refrigerators, and large bathtubs with Jacuzzi jets. The Presidential Suite (priced at $1500) has a living room and two bedrooms, with such extras as a baby grand piano, wide-screen TV, fully equipped kitchen, and sunken marble bath-tub.

The second-floor pool is a tranquil hideaway. Heavily landscaped, it features fountains and statuary in addition to a half–Olympic size pool.

Guests also have access to the extensive health and rec-reational facilities (tennis, racquetball, exercise equipment, jogging track) at the nearby Houstonian Hotel and Confer-ence Center. Complimentary transportation is provided via limousine.

Catering to an upscale clientele, the Remington has sev-eral distinctive specialty shops on its premises. Here is the only complete outlet in the U.S. for the work of designer Carlos Falchi, featuring leather goods (purses to luggage), desk accessories, and costume jewelry. Adjacent to the pool area is the Payot Club, which carries the Payot line of beauty care products and offers such services as manicures, pedi-cures, facials, hairstyling, massage, and body wraps. Down-stairs, a gourmet shop features a full line of caviar.

Dining at the Remington has several distinctive person-alities. There is the formal Garden Room with etched glass and antique tapestries, the airy Conservatory with wicker seating, and the handsome Bar and Grill with dark woods, western sculptures, and English paintings. The cuisine is new American, with an emphasis on using fresh ingredients. The kitchen staff does everything from smoking salmon to making sausage, baking bread to dipping chocolate.

Meeting space at the Remington is well planned, stylishly blending into the overall decor. The skylighted prefunction space adjacent to the ballroom features a huge marble bar, beveled glass, and works of art. The boardroom has tele-conferencing, telex, facsimile, and closed-circuit television capabilities. Secretarial services are available on request in this ''out-of-town office.''

Situated within Post Oak Park off Loop 610 West, the Remington is a few blocks from the Galleria, with easy access to several business areas including downtown. Intercontinental Airport is approximately 45 minutes to the north; Hobby Airport is about 25 minutes south. Transportation to both airports is available by limousine and helicopter (a heliport is located a few blocks from the hotel). The Remington's overnight valet parking costs $8.

«KANSAS CITY»

Embassy on the Park Hotel
1215 Wyandotte Street
Kansas City, Missouri
816/471-1333

Singles $55–$85
Doubles $70–$110

This small, classy hotel is the choice of discriminating people who visit the city. Intimate and charming, its Romanesque architecture features a brick and stone facade dressed up with green awnings, flags, and brass planters.

The inviting lobby is small and elegant, with more green and brass accents, a circular sitting area, and black and gold marble pillars rising to the balcony. Old world ambience is the key, even though it is located in one of the most progressive cities in the Midwest.

Dining facilities include a small intimate New York–style cafe with lunch specials and deli sandwiches. In the evening, this becomes a continental restaurant with singing waiters, candlelight, and piano music. One of the best restaurants in the city, it is usually full and features a menu with regional as well as international dishes.

A lounge with a cozy library motif serves cocktails and offers a respite away from the hustle of the city.

Accommodations are traditional in styling, with beautifully coordinated interiors, plush carpeting, and very spacious baths. Each room receives a complimentary morning newspaper with coffee via room service, turndown service, luxury bathroom amenities, and color cable TV.

There is covered parking adjacent to the hotel but no exercise facilities. All bedrooms feature either double, king-size, or queen-size beds, though a few are smaller than normal. All 210 rooms are impeccably maintained and service is of the highest caliber. Concierge service is available during the day.

The Phillips House
12th and Baltimore Streets
Kansas City, Missouri
816/221-7000

Singles $58–$95
Doubles $68–$107

The Phillips House is an older restored downtown hotel that qualifies for Grand Dame status. Dignified and European in character, it caters to the luxury set, including executives.

Rated locally as one of the two best in town, this is a popular meeting place and is one of the tallest of the older hotels at 20 stories. Its interior is an art deco masterpiece with lots of gilding, painted decoration, and a statue of a golden woman flanked by a double staircase under crystal chandeliers.

Rooms were renovated a few years ago so that now all are suites with traditional wood furnishings, plush carpeting, coordinated fabrics, sitting areas with sofas and chairs, and spacious luxury baths. The top two floors are reserved as an executive floor, with private access, a bar, and continental breakfast.

Guests dine in the popular beef restaurant located in the basement, which, though expensive, is elegant and true to the period. Cuisine is inconsistent and, therefore, it is not rated as highly as it once was. There is also a cafe that features soups, salads, and sandwiches. A jazz trio performs there in the evenings. Another mezzanine lounge is open at cocktail hour.

Service is attentive and friendly, with a staff that has been on the books for a long period. Management tries to make sure that every guest gets the best attention.

Though there are no athletic facilities on the premises, health clubs are located nearby and the location of the hotel makes it ideal for shopping and sightseeing downtown. There are parking facilities and laundry and valet service.

Raphael Hotel
325 Ward Parkway
Kansas City, Missouri 64112
816/756-3800

Singles $65–$83
Doubles $70–$92

The Raphael is an elegant small all-suite hotel on the posh Country Club Plaza with its shops and restaurants. Formerly an apartment building, it was converted some years ago to this 124-room facility. Posh and old-style European in atmosphere, it makes a good alternative to the more modern hotels nearby.

Most accommodations are suites, though small, and feature original woodwork, small luxurious baths with dressing areas, traditional decor and furnishings, and color cable TV.

This and the Alameda are the only hotels on the plaza. The lobby is small and charming, with intimate decor and friendly atmosphere.

A modern, friendly restaurant serves excellent food throughout the day, and a lounge on the main level offers a cocktail hour in the afternoons. In addition, there is a roof restaurant with fine views of the neighboring Alameda Plaza Hotel, as well as a coffee shop with more moderate prices.

Through an arrangement with the Alameda Plaza Hotel, guests at the Raphael have full use of the two swimming pools on the Alameda's garden terrace. Guests also receive a complimentary morning newspaper and coffee with their wakeup call.

«LAS VEGAS»

Alexis Park
375 East Harmon
(between Las Vegas Boulevard and Paradise Road)
Las Vegas, Nevada 89109
800/223-0888 (tollfree)
702/796-3300

Suites $85–$1100

The Alexis Park, a nongaming luxury hotel built in 1983, is Las Vegas's finest full-service resort. Only minutes from the dazzle of the Las Vegas Strip, Alexis Park offers an ambience of elegant serenity unmatched by other Nevada hotels. The resort has 500 spacious suites, each artfully decorated, on 18 acres of beautifully landscaped grounds. With 17,000 square feet of convention and meeting space, indoor and outdoor recreational facilities, fine restaurants and lounge, gift shop and salon, concierge, and free limousine service, the Alexis Park stands ready to satisfy the needs of its guests, vacationers and business travelers alike.

There are ten different floor plans for the two- and three-room suites offered at Alexis Park. Individually decorated in contemporary or provincial styles, some in subdued colors, some dramatically modern, the rooms provide both tasteful decor and relaxed living. All suites have a fully stocked European bar with a refrigerator, and at least one color TV with free movies; some suites add the luxury of a gas-lit fireplace and Jacuzzi tub. Atriums in slate-tiled bathrooms, one-of-a-kind furnishings, original wall hangings, one- and two-level designs and similar unique touches lend an aura of distinction to small business conferences or social gatherings. Arranged in fourteen two-story building complexes, connected by meandering pathways and covered walks, the suites at Alexis Park provide quiet accommodations and privacy.

The Alexis Park has two fine restaurants: the Pegasus Gourmet Room, with an excellent dinner menu and impeccable service; and the more moderately priced Cafiñao Garden Cafe, where breakfast, lunch, and dinner are served by an efficient and friendly staff in a cheerful atmosphere of pink and red flowers. The cafe offers a champagne brunch on Sundays. There are three cabana bar and grills providing food and drink service near the swimming pools, and 24-hour room service is always available. The Pisces Lounge, just off the hotel lobby, opens at 5 every evening for nighttime libation and entertainment. Catering service for business meetings and parties is also available, and the garden gazebo makes a particularly lovely setting for weddings. For ESP corporate club members, the Alexis Park hosts a complimentary continental breakfast and cocktail hour every day in one of its suites set aside for this purpose.

The Alexis Park has two championship tennis courts, three outdoor swimming pools with heated spas, a nine-hole putting green, and a fitness and aerobic center open daily from 7 A.M. to 8 P.M. The center, available at no additional cost, is equipped with Universal weight machines, rowing machines, unisex hair salon (open Tuesday through Saturday), toiletries and towels, and steam and sauna rooms. These recreational facilities are set in a landscape of rolling lawns, flower beds, palm trees, and rock gardens with small streams and waterfalls. Arrangements can easily be made for golfers to play on their choice of several nearby championship courses.

The Alexis Park resort is centrally located, close to the airport, the Las Vegas Convention Center, major shopping malls, and the Strip casinos. Hotel guests are provided free limousine service for travel to any location in the general area. A concierge is available in the lobby or by phone from the suites. The concierges are an excellent source of information about the Las Vegas area and can arrange for tours to more distant attractions.

Other services at the Alexis Park that distinguish this luxury hotel from many of its competitors are free safe deposits for valuables, phones conveniently placed near seating areas in the lobby, special touches such as rapid check-out, and a full complement of staff who are gracious, efficient, and informed.

The Boulder Dam Hotel
1305 Arizona Street
(between Nevada Highway and Hotel Plaza)
Boulder City, Nevada 89005
702/293-1808

Rooms $27.50–$37.50
Suites $65

First opened in 1933 and recently restored to its earlier, gracious style, the Boulder Dam Hotel offers a charming alternative to contemporary hotels and highway motels. Located centrally in Boulder City, a city built to support the construction of Hoover (née Boulder) Dam, the 59-room hotel is steeped in history. As far as possible, the original decor has been retained; and the suites and many of the rooms have been redecorated in the fashion of the 1930s. With Las Vegas only 25 miles away, the recreation and scenic beauty of Lake Mead close at hand, and the heritage surrounding the building of Hoover Dam right at its doorstep, the Boulder Dam Hotel is a good choice for both business and pleasure travelers.

The hotel has a small, sharp staff. The service is extremely gracious and personable. Newcomers are made to feel at home; returning guests are welcomed like family. Beyond the customary kinds of assistance, the guest at Boulder Dam Hotel will get tips about good fishing holes, personal insights on the history of the area, or a dining room waitress following into the lobby to keep the cups of coffee full and steaming.

The hotel lobby, once the gathering place of Hollywood celebrities, politicians, and royalty, is a delightful room with original oak paneling and light fixtures, brick fireplace, green velvet winged chairs, rolltop desk, and heavy tie-back curtains framing multipaned windows. The furniture is arranged to promote conversation; a large scrapbook of clippings about the hotel rests on the coffee table inviting guests' perusal.

The downstairs Spillway Lounge boasts sepia-toned old photographs of the building of Hoover Dam. It is rustically decorated in floor-to-ceiling rock veneer and comfortable wooden tables and chairs. While gambling in Boulder City remains illegal today, liquor was legalized in 1969. Guests of the hotel will enjoy meeting local residents who saddle up to the bar from time to time for libation and conversation.

The Celebrity Dining Room, built in 1935, is set up with tables for four, dressed in white tablecloths. The restaurant continues the style of the lobby with tie-back drapes, similar lighting, and sections of period wallpaper trimmed in wood. Breakfast, lunch, and dinner are served in this main room or the adjoining Garden Room, which is decorated with white wrought-iron tables, original brick flooring, hanging baskets of cascading plants, wine cabinet, and a wall of windows overlooking the outside patio. The patio, usually bathed in sunshine, is used for relaxing, parties, and weddings as in earlier days.

The bedrooms and suites are reached by the original wooden staircase that overlooks the lobby or by a newly installed elevator. Three types of accommodations are available: plain rooms (not redecorated), restyled rooms, and suites. The refurbished rooms have simple decor with tiny rose-patterned wallpaper, draw-back white lace curtains, and embroidered blanket coverings over white and brass metal beds. An AM-FM clock radio sits on the bedside table, a color TV in the corner cabinet. The bathrooms have tubs or showers; many use the original tiling and fixtures, which were unusual comforts for hotels in the '30s. The suites are similarly dressed in the period styles, though more spacious and with more luxurious furnishings.

The hotel's neighborhood has many contemporary amenities—drugstores, banks, gift shops, markets, library —all within walking distance. Guests of the hotel will need their own transportation for longer travel as Boulder City has no public bus system or taxis.

The Boulder Dam Hotel is of Southern plantation architectural style, with white block bricks, green shutters, and two-story white pillars. Once a lodging of worldwide reputation and considered the finest in southern Nevada, the hotel began losing business during World War II and eventually succumbed to Las Vegas hotels. In 1980 the hotel was purchased by a Nevada senator interested in helping the hotel make a comeback. The present owners have continued a program of restoration. Present plans include completing room refurbishing, building an outdoor swimming pool, and developing downstairs meeting rooms for small workshops and conferences.

The Golden Nugget
129 East Fremont Street
(at Carson Avenue)
P.O. Box 610
Las Vegas, Nevada 89125
800/634-3454 (tollfree)
702/385-7111

Rooms $54–$70
Suites $90–$750

The Golden Nugget, a recently remodeled luxury hotel and casino located in downtown Las Vegas, is a dramatic trendsetter among gaming establishments. Ringed by a sidewalk of white granite inlaid with brass strips and more than sixty palm trees growing in planter beds, the Golden Nugget stands apart in elegant simplicity from its neon-lit neighbors as the only hotel without its name displayed in flickering bulbs. Unlike other casino hotels, where entrance is through garish casinos, the Golden Nugget receives guests through a white portico and gently leads them down to the registration desk over marble floors carpeted with custom-designed orange and rose runners. Behind the desk, reaching the full length of its white marble counter, is a hand-painted mural, a scene of graceful birds in delicate pink and white. This elegant entrance lighted by overhead chandeliers and accented in brass, is the first introduction to one of Las Vegas's most opulent and luxurious hotels.

First opened in 1946, the Golden Nugget has been extensively reconstructed and remodeled since 1972 by its present owners. In 1977, a new 17-story hotel was opened; by 1984, the Spa Suite Tower was completed. With the addition of a second new tower and expanded grounds (under construction when visited), the Golden Nugget will offer a total of 1485 spacious bedrooms and suites, six major restaurants, two showrooms, health spa, swimming pool and Jacuzzi, several cocktail lounges, over 14,000 square feet of meeting space and more than 30,000 square feet of casino games.

Once Victorian in style, the new accommodations are decorated in contemporary colors of plum and peach, blues and greens, and fabric textures of chintz, leather, and raw silk. Furnishings are in wood and wicker, with accents of brass, glass, and stone. Woven basket lamps, wall mirrors, shell wall sconces with indirect lighting, flowers and plants, and other decorations lend a comfortable air to the rooms. The one and two-bedroom suites, distinguished in decor, have been designed with great care given to even the smallest detail. All accommodations have cable TV with movies and sports programs; the suites have stereo equipment for which tapes are available through the VIP desk. The suites also have entrance halls, deluxe bathrooms, and wet bars.

An exclusive section of the Spa Suite Tower, reached only through use of a computer key card, is dedicated to lavish suites for VIP guests. These suites have large entrances with hall closets and half baths, expansive living rooms, unique luxurious furnishings, two-story windows with electronic control of shades and drapes, spiral staircases leading to second-tier elegant bedrooms and bath areas, steam showers, and Jacuzzi tubs. Enormous pieces of art adorn the walls; chandeliers hang from high ceilings. Remote-control television, fully stocked wet bars, stereo systems, shoe polisher, padded walls, padded hangers in the closets, and many other amenities add to the high-style living.

The Golden Nugget has several fine restaurants. Lillie Langtry's on the first floor, a longtime favorite of both locals and guests, serves excellent Cantonese cuisine every evening from 5 P.M. until midnight. Elaine's, a 94-seat gourmet dining room, and Stefano's, a 70-seat Italian restaurant reached through a charming streetlike scene, are new restaurants located on the second floor of the Spa Suite Tower. These restaurants open in the early evening for dinner. The popular buffet, open daily, serves an elaborate yet moderately priced breakfast, lunch, and dinner buffet and a Sunday champagne brunch. Zachariah's is a 24-hour cafe entered through the casino. It serves a variety of menu selections, as will the new 500-seat cafe overlooking the swimming pool which opens with the completion of the second tower. There is also a snack bar in the Keno lounge. Twenty-four-hour room service and special catering services are also available.

The Golden Nugget has a beautifully designed, luxurious spa available to guests for a $15 fee per use. Entrance to the spa is through a large courtroom fashioned after the Garden Room of the Frick Museum in New York City. Spa services and facilities include spa clothing, towels and toiletries, complimentary beverages, sauna, steam rooms, whirlpools, and use of weight and exercise machines, lockers, and lounge. Also available are fitness instruction, float tanks, massage, and a full-service beauty salon. Hand-painted murals, plants, rolled towels as part of the wall decor, custom tiling, and other elements of design blend together to create a rich and restful spa environment.

The ornate casino includes blackjack tables, crap tables, roulette wheels, poker tables, a big six wheel, baccarat, keno lounge, and nearly 700 video and traditional slot machines set in brass covers.

The Theater Ballroom on the third level is a special event showroom featuring stars like Frank Sinatra, Kenny Rogers, and Willie Nelson. On the main level, the extravagantly styled Cabaret, used for headliners, is decorated with illuminated brass palm trees, floor to ceiling glass walls and a specially lit ceiling of "stars."

The Golden Nugget is located in the heart of the downtown section of Las Vegas—the famous "Glitter Gulch" area—along with other hotels, casinos, restaurants, government buildings, banks, professional offices, and retail stores. The Nugget provides a limousine service for VIP guests, and participants in city-wide conventions can use free shuttles from the Nugget to meeting sites and other convention hotels. For other guests, a car or taxi is needed for convenient in-town travel. The hotel's bell captain will assist guests in selecting tours to more distant attractions.

Although a large establishment, the service provided by the Golden Nugget staff, commensurate with the elegance of the hotel environment, is gracious, personable, and efficient.

The Sheffield Inn
3970 South Paradise Road
(between Flamingo Road and Desert Inn Road)
Las Vegas, Nevada 89109
800/632-4040 (Tollfree)
702/796-9000

Suites $75–$150

Among the newest of Las Vegas hotels, the Sheffield Inn offers visitors to southern Nevada a quiet alternative to the neon and glitter of casino accommodations. At prices comparable to single rooms in other quality hotels, the inn's 171 suites provide a pleasant homey atmosphere, including comfortable living areas, kitchenettes, and private balconies. For the business traveler, the living rooms adapt well to product displays, small-group conferences, and entertaining. Larger groups of up to 150 persons can be accommodated in downstairs meeting rooms. The inn is conveniently located close to the airport, the Las Vegas Convention Center, and the excitement of the Strip.

Three types of suites are offered: petites, one-bedroom, and two-bedroom (accommodating two, four, and six persons respectively). All include a wet bar, refrigerator, microwave oven, cable TV with sports and movie channels, and outside balconies. Although the hallways are plain and relatively narrow, the suites are spacious and attractively decorated in soft colors and French country furnishings with polished wood counters and cabinetry, American of Martinsville furniture, and mirrored walls. Either queen-size or king-size beds are available; there are no rooms with two beds. Larger suites have two bathrooms; all suites have a Jacuzzi tub large enough for two people.

The Sheffield Inn has no restaurant or public bar. Fast-food services and nearby delicatessens will make food deliveries; and many gourmet and moderately priced restaurants are within a mile radius of the inn. The closest food market is about five blocks away.

The small, hardworking staff takes pride in providing personalized service to its guests. A complimentary continental breakfast is served every morning in the inn's Fireside Room, and the manager hosts a cocktail hour for guests on Saturday evenings. Convention and tour information is available in the reception area. The staff will direct guests to shopping malls, tourist attractions, and other points of interest. Show tickets, babysitting, dry cleaning services, and catering for parties can all be arranged at the inn. Underground parking, European-style sauna, outdoor swimming pool, Jacuzzi spa, and patio round out the amenities.

Guests who are participants in large conventions receive free shuttles between the inn, other major hotels, and convention meetings. Otherwise, a car or taxi is necessary for travel within the Las Vegas area. It's around one mile from the inn to the Las Vegas Strip casinos and about six miles to downtown Las Vegas ("Glitter Gulch"). The inn will reimburse its guests for the cost of their arrival taxi ride from the airport.

When visited in early 1986, there was considerable road

and building construction in the vicinity of the Sheffield Inn, and plans for the completion of the inn itself were not firm. Additional rooms, a restaurant, and tennis courts were being considered. However, the Sheffield's incomplete rear grounds and nearby construction activity were not disturbing to the restful atmosphere within the inn.

« LOS ANGELES »

Anaheim Country Inn
856 South Walnut
Anaheim, California 92802
714/778-0150

Singles, doubles $40–$75

The Anaheim Country Inn is a Queen Anne Victorian bed and breakfast with nine guest rooms spread out over three-quarters of an acre in a quiet residential neighborhood located one mile from both Disneyland and the Anaheim Convention Center. Built in 1910 by a former Anaheim mayor who farmed avocados, oranges, and lima beans on the surrounding property, the inn offers nonsmokers traveling without young children an alternative to the local motel row. On occasion, businesses have rented out the entire house while working at the Convention Center.

The house has pine floors, beveled glass windows that throw prismatic shadows on the staircase toward evening, and an old clock that chimes on the hour. The furnishings are mostly turn of the century, though not strictly Victorian, with each room decorated according to a different theme. The Rose Room features wallpaper with roses and lace curtains, in recognition of the fact that the original owners had extensive plantings of roses (only a few rose plants are in the front yard, with nine avocado trees in the backyard —the feel is distinctly suburban California).

The Garden Room looks out on the backyard, and is the only room with a private bath. The room has a poster bed and a walnut burl furniture group. Three other downstairs rooms share one bath, while the five upstairs rooms share another bath. Not all baths have showers to go with the clawfoot tubs. Guests needing a shower should take care to make arrangements with the owners to be near one of the two baths that has a shower.

The upstairs Mayor's Room has a queen-size bed and shares a large family-style bathroom. The Mayor's Room is decorated with hunting pictures and has a decoy duck on the desk next to a bottle of sherry, which, with glasses, is provided in all rooms for those desiring a nightcap. Baskets of fruit are also provided. There are late afternoon appetizers, too.

Anyone wishing to watch the fireworks at Disneyland without leaving the premises might consider renting the small upstairs Sun Room or soaking in the hydrospa under the backyard gazebo. The backyard area also has a laundry room (available without charge) and horseshoes. The parking is in back next to the old carriage garage, where a caretaker lives.

Anaheim's elected officials have been slow in adjusting to the bed and breakfast movement, fearing, in the words of one, that it would attract transients. As a result, Anaheim is one of the few area cities with special bed and breakfast ordinances that, among other things, limit the stays at bed and breakfasts.

The breakfast is the cook's choice and is full course. As a concession to city ordinance, the original kitchen and tiles had to be removed and replaced with the stainless steel sinks and refrigerators required of restaurants. Guests have access to the refrigerator, but are prohibited from using the stove.

Bed and Breakfast of Los Angeles
32074 Waterside Lane
Westlake Village, California 91361
818/889-7325 and 889-8870

Singles, doubles $20–$60

Bed and Breakfast of Los Angeles is a service agency that places visitors in private homes, near where guests' business or pleasure dictates, at reasonable prices. The agency, which is in its fourth year of business, personally inspects all lodgings and strives to make compatible matches for guests. The accommodations are quite varied and can range from exclusive use of a condo, apartment, or guesthouse to sharing a family's home. In most instances, the guests are provided use of linens and a light breakfast (fruit, roll, beverage).

In many instances, use of pools, spas, and nearby hiking trails is included. If something very specific is needed, such as an accommodation near a family reunion in Van Nuys, then the agency's directory of homes may be consulted. The directory, which is available for a first-class postage stamp, breaks Los Angeles down into five areas; central, south, east, west, and north.

The directory descriptions include with whom, if anyone, the accommodations would be shared, whether bath is shared or private, special privileges, and a brief description of the lodgings.

Those needing to be near Cal Tech in Pasadena might choose from among an Irish country inn with antiques, lace, and leaded glass, an older home in a quiet neighborhood where children are welcomed and Yiddish is spoken, or a hilltop home with views, patio, and spa. Beverly Hills, Hollywood, downtown, Westwood, Santa Monica, Studio City, Venice, the beach towns, and the San Fernando Valley are all represented.

Casa Laguna Inn
2510 South Pacific Coast Highway
Laguna Beach, California 92651
714/494-2996

Singles, doubles $56–$85
Suites $71–$135

Casa Laguna Inn is a 20-room Spanish Mission Revival –style bed and breakfast villa overlooking the Pacific Ocean in the artsy Orange County town of Laguna Beach. Built in the 1930s, the villa was split in two by the construction of the Pacific Coast Highway. The villa was recently acquired by a pair of hospitable entrepreneurs who renovated the stuccoed arches, terra-cotta roof tiles, wrought-iron fixtures, decorative tiles, and gardens into a delightful bed and breakfast.

There are six courtyard bedrooms opening onto patios and gardens planted with palms, bougainvilleas, bananas, ferns, and flowers. Eight balcony bedrooms with louvered windows look out over the Pacific Ocean, red-tiled roofs, and villa courtyards. The two one-bedroom suites come with private patios, while the two two-bedroom suites have private balconies. One-bedroom suites include a bedroom, a living room with a pullout sofa bed, dining room, kitchen, and bathroom. All rooms have showers, baths, color televisions, and a blend of antique and modern furnishings.

A heated pool with sundeck and poolside furniture may be used 24 hours a day. Behind the pool is a cottage with private sundeck that is elevated from the pool level. The cottage is the most expensive rental and includes a spacious living room, dining room, kitchen, master bedroom with leaded glass, fireplace, sitting room, and attached patio greenhouse area.

Late afternoons, the inn serves up wine, tea, cheese, crackers, and other appetizers, along with musical entertainment to guests desiring to drop by the large Mission House occupied by the owners at the base of the hillside. The tables, chairs, and sofas of the Mission House living and dining rooms are a comfortable blend of the old and new that is best described as a relaxed, California casual. A fireplace adds warmth to an atmosphere that is conducive to chatting with your fellow guests, many of whom are southern Californians indulging in a brief escape.

A large continental breakfast is served in the Mission House from 8:30 to 10 in the morning, though the hosts have been known to leave unattended pots of coffee on the white wrought-iron patio tables after that time. The bell-tower opposite the pool area is a pleasant place to sip coffee and catch the cool breezes blowing in off the Pacific Ocean.

Every July and August, Laguna offers up its Festival of Arts and Pageant of Masters (where real people pose to re-create works of art such as Leonardo da Vinci's *Last Supper*).

Winter is a pleasant, less crowded time to visit the shops, galleries, restaurants, and the recently renovated Laguna Beach Museum of Art. The inn has a library stocked with travel materials, and free parking is offered behind the inn.

Eastlake Inn
1442 Kellam Avenue
Los Angeles, California 90026
213/250-1620

Singles, doubles $45–$90
Suites $125

The Eastlake Inn offers guests a choice among six rooms and two suites in an 1887 Victorian house overlooking downtown Los Angeles from the hills of Angelino Heights, where the suburbanization of Los Angeles first started. The bed and breakfast is in a historic preservation district containing the largest concentration of Queen Anne and Eastlake-style Victorian homes in Los Angeles. Through the efforts of a strong neighborhood association, Carroll Avenue and the streets surrounding the Eastlake Inn are being returned to their turn-of-the-century Victorian look, with utility cables being buried underground and fancy horse-and-buggy hitches being returned to their proper, if anachronistic, places along the streets.

The two owners, who live nearby in Carroll Avenue Victorians that may be toured, and a live-in staff member offer very personalized service. Help with sightseeing and restaurant selection is generously provided. Celebration of special events is a specialty of the house. Besides the weddings, anniversaries, and birthdays celebrated here, the owners have created a number of special weekend adventures and events. For example, there are detective mystery weekends, hot air balloon flights, limousine tours of the best chocolate and ice cream places in L.A., guided horse trail rides to Mexican restaurants, private chamber music concerts, Halloween celebrations, groundhog gambols, and Valentine weekends.

The living room, dining room (where a breakfast of sweet rolls, muffins, croissants, jams, fresh fruit juices, fresh-ground coffees and herb teas are served), and bedrooms are all furnished to the period. The inn retains much of its original flashed-glass windows etched with scenes of flowers, girls, dogs, and Grecian urns. The floors retain the original softwoods, and there are ceiling fans. Ornamentation such as gilded cupids may surprise you while looking up at the ceiling while reclining on the comfortable antique beds.

The bedrooms are all spacious and include sitting areas that may be furnished with fainting couches. There is ample closet, dresser, and desk space. The six upper-story bedrooms share four bathrooms that include clawfoot tubs, showers, brass fixtures, and medicine cabinets stocked with sundries. Chenille robes are provided for comfort, along with other amenities such as wine, sherry, candies, fresh fruit, flowers, and a daily newspaper. Beds are turned down before guests retire for the night.

The Eastlake Inn was built in 1887 as a grand duplex for two young widows who shared the kitchen, dining room, and downstairs parlors. The upstairs was divided by a large double hallway for privacy, with each half having almost mirror-image accommodations (with a slight asymmetry to avoid boredom). The almost mirror-image bedrooms are the North Star and Moonrise, Sunset and Sunrise, Tom Thumb and Thumbellina. The downstairs parlor is used as Planaria's Suite and shares an upstairs bathroom. The more spacious downstairs suite, known as Murray's Suite, has a separate sitting room, parlor, bedroom, and bathroom that looks out on the garden lemon tree.

A variety of good views of the city are offered from the upstairs rooms. A good walking tour of the historic Victorian neighborhood is available at no extra cost, and includes the haunted house used in Alfred Hitchcock's *Psycho*. The old cable tramline that connected Angelino Heights to downtown Los Angeles via Temple Street is now gone, but downtown is only a five-minute car ride away. Parking is free at the front entrance of the inn.

Popular destinations for visitors include the many nearby restaurants (at least 100 representing most ethnic cuisines), the Ahmanson Theater, the Music Center, Chinatown, and

Little Tokyo. The hosts have a collection of restaurant menus for guests to peruse before going out on the town. Also in the neighborhood is Echo Park Lake, the city's first reservoir park, built in 1868, and home to Egyptian water lotus plants that bloom in April, as well as the Pacific Asian Festival and dragon boat races in July. Major Los Angeles freeways are only a few short minutes away—it was through a wrong turn searching for a freeway 15 years ago that the owners discovered this historic neighborhood and began the preservation and restoration effort that is so visible today.

Figueroa Hotel
939 South Figueroa Street
Los Angeles, California 90015
800/331-5151 (tollfree from within California)
800/421-9092 (tollfree from rest of U.S.)
213/627-8971

Singles, doubles $48–$64
Suites $75–$90

Built as a YWCA in 1926, the 12-story, 280-room Figueroa was the first highrise structure in downtown Los Angeles. In 1957, Los Angeles rescinded its 150-foot height limit and a new crop of skyscrapers sprang up, dwarfing the Figueroa to the east, though the hotel's rooftop sign is still visible from the Harbor Freeway on the north and the Santa Monica Freeway on the west. The Figueroa, which has been completely renovated over the last several years, is located one block from the Convention Center.

A large mural commemorating the 1984 Olympic Games graces the northern side of an otherwise ordinary exterior. Entering the Figueroa's early California–style tiled lobby, one is greeted by skylights, ornate ceiling beams in muted earth colors, hanging black wrought-iron lighting fixtures, excellently maintained antique furniture, and a tile wall map of early California. Service personnel are courteous and provide guests with a map of downtown (which includes bus routes) when they register at the front desk.

Rooms are spacious and equipped with color television, air conditioning, direct-dial telephones, tables, chairs, desks, lamps, dressers, and comfortable new mattresses on the beds. Most of the furnishings were purchased from the Hilton Hotel Equipment Corporation. There are 200 free safe deposit boxes for guests at the front desk, and a coin laundry is available within the Figueroa.

At the lobby level, there are two restaurants and a bar. The Figueroa Street Cafe serves inexpensive, simple breakfasts, lunches, and dinners. Dinners are served to the strains of classical music in the simple yet elegant Music Room. In summer, poolside bar service is offered by the Figueroa Street Bar.

The Music Room also offers service overlooking the pool, which is in a garden setting of palms, citrus, and hibiscus surrounded by wrought iron. A Jacuzzi is located in a back corner of the pool area.

Free parking is offered behind the Figueroa. Direct bus service to Los Angeles International Airport is available from the front door of the Figueroa. Gray Line tour buses also stop at the front door. Across the street from the front door is the historic Variety Arts Theater. Down the street to the east is the original Pantry restaurant, in operation 24 hours a day since the 1930s Depression. Providing good value for the dollar keeps the Figueroa's occupancy rate among the highest in Los Angeles.

Hotel Bel-Air
701 Stone Canyon Road
Los Angeles, California 90077
213/472-1211

Singles, doubles $180–$305
Suites $450–$1250

The Hotel Bel-Air has just completed extensive renovation and an expansion from 66 to 92 rooms on its lush 11.5-acre grounds. The original Spanish Mission–style architecture created in the 1920s has been faithfully maintained by the new owners, Rosewood Hotels of Dallas. Rosewood Hotels, the creation of a daughter of the H. L. Hunt oil fortune, outbid Wall Street arbitrageur and Beverly Hills Hotel owner Ivan Boedsky to acquire this Southern California real estate gem that has been a romantic getaway since the early 1940s.

Privacy and luxury are offered to those willing to pay the price. The grounds encompass numerous courtyards and fountains, along with extensive plantings of palms, redwoods, azaleas, camellias, petunias, and numerous other flowering shrubs and trees. The atmosphere is one of year-round flowers and fragrances. Also prominent is a large swimming pool outfitted with chairs, chaise lounges, tables covered with white-canvas umbrellas, and generous plantings of banana and palm trees against the background of chaparral-covered hills.

The room interiors have been completely redecorated. Five different designers were employed, and the result is that each of the 33 suites and 59 rooms in the one- and two-story buildings is different. Cords of oak wood are provided for the fireplaces, which are made of Italian marbles that echo the marbles used in the bathroom and table counters. Large French ceramic tile squares impart an earthy brown color to the interior and patio floors. Suites with private patios often have tiled outdoor Jacuzzis. Whether the sofas and chairs in the spacious rooms are rattan and white fabric or pink florals, the feeling is one of relaxed country living.

Hotel Bel-Air has banquet rooms, a public bar (jackets are required after 5 P.M.), and a restaurant serving California cuisine. Sorrel, cilantro, and other herbs from the herb garden find their way into the restaurant seasonings and sauces. Fifteen-minute room-service delivery of restaurant dishes is offered. Meals may also be taken on an outdoor terrace or poolside. In summer, fish is barbecued with mesquite by the pool.

There is a high staff-to-guest ratio. For example, there are 12 full-time gardeners and a resident florist to make sure that all rooms are supplied with fresh flowers, and the hotel has even purchased its own nursery to supply the flowers. Attention to detail shows up everywhere.

Maid service is twice daily, and dried fruit baskets are part of the VIP treatment. Laundry delivered by the overnight service is returned neatly bundled in white paper, tied with a red ribbon, and placed in a wicker basket. Extra rolls of toilet paper and facial tissue are gift-wrapped and placed in a closet. Alarm clocks, radios, televisions, and stereos are standard room features, as are large throw rugs, a telephone per room (including the bathroom), bathroom scales, an icemaker, and refrigerators stocked with wine, beer, and mineral water.

The hotel is located adjacent to Beverly Hills just north of Westwood, UCLA, and Sunset Boulevard. There is valet parking in front of the hotel and self-parking available on the hillside across the street. The pink and white Mission-style hotel is reached by walking across a canopy-covered bridge that extends from the valet parking area to the lobby and crosses over a small pond frequented by a family of swans.

Hotel Shangri-La
1301 Ocean Avenue
Santa Monica, California 90401
213/394-2791

Singles, doubles $65–$75
Suites $80–$160

The 55-room Shangri-La resembles a seven-story high oceangoing liner with its sleek Streamline Moderne facade anchored across the street from the cliffs of Palisades Park, overlooking the Pacific Ocean. Reflecting the futuristic imagery of a nation emerging from the Depression when it was completed in 1939, the Shangri-La's sleek lines converge on a curved glass-block entrance that points out over the ocean in the direction of Malibu. The more modern Cafe Casino and Lawrence Welk Champagne Tower apartments on the adjacent block echo the nautical shapes.

Current management has pursued a restoration policy that includes furnishing many of the rooms with art deco door knobs, light fixtures, desks, tables, and sofas. Color televisions, telephones, and fully equipped kitchens are part of most rooms. Rooms tend to be spacious and quiet, with a one-bedroom suite facing the ocean renting for $90 to two people and including bedroom, living room, kitchen, and bathroom. Suites not directly facing the ocean, which may still offer a view of the ocean and palm tree–lined Palisades Park, rent for about $10 less. All the kitchen utensils needed for a prolonged stay will be provided by management, though there are many restaurants in the area and complimentary continental breakfasts with newspapers are provided.

The hotel's outside entrance is guarded by a pair of cement lions. The lobby is art deco style and includes a comfortable couch along with indoor palms and other plants. Near the elevator is some of the original gray deco glass. At lobby level, there is a large courtyard patio with tables, chairs, and umbrellas.

Guests step from the elevator or the navy blue staircase that curves around white walls onto an interior balcony that overlooks the patio and provides views of Santa Monica. All the rooms open onto this interior balcony and have curved deco lines.

Across the street at 1400 Ocean Avenue in Palisades Park is the Santa Monica Visitors Information Center. Information can be obtained about the new red trolleys that offer 50-cent fares to Venice's trendy Main Street shops and eateries and drop-offs near the rollerskating madness of the Venice Beach boardwalk. Within walking distance of the Shangri-La is the Santa Monica pier, complete with its game arcades, palm reader, fish and chips, and the restored antique wooden carousel used in the movie *The Sting*. Convenient bus lines offer service to other areas of Los Angeles.

The New Otani Hotel & Garden
120 South Los Angeles Street
Los Angeles, California 90012
800/252-0197 (tollfree from within California)
800/421-8795 (tollfree from rest of continental U.S.)
213/629-1200

Singles, doubles $98–$135
Suites $200–$675

The triangular 21-story, 448-room New Otani, with its half-acre ''garden in the sky,'' anchors the Little Tokyo section of downtown Los Angeles, just blocks from City Hall. Built in the 1970s, the New Otani spearheaded the ongoing redevelopment of downtown into an area once again frequented and lived in. The Japanese garden on the fourth level, built atop the parking garage, is a haven of tranquillity in the downtown hustle and bustle and an echo of the 400-year-old Japanese garden at the New Otani in Tokyo.

A ride up the elevator in the New Otani is likely to have its share of brief case–carrying businesspeople conversing in Japanese. The New Otani exemplifies the Pacific Rim, where Japanese and Western cultures meet, and nowhere is this more evident than on the 18th, 19th, and 20th floors. Stepping into these rooms through a short entryway, one first sees a typical Western-style living room. Taking off one's shoes, according to Japanese custom, it is then but a short step up from the Western-style room onto the softly matted floors of the tatami room.

These hybrid Western-Japanese suites are available to guests as part of the ''Japanese Experience'' ($279–$349 per couple, the lower price offering a Western-style bed instead of the floor-level Japanese futon sleeping mat). The Japanese Experience includes a visit to the hotel's Sunwa Health Spa, with sauna, herb-scented Jacuzzi bath, and shiatsu (fingertip massage), along with a multicourse dinner at the hotel's Thousand Cranes restaurant and a Japanese breakfast.

The Thousand Cranes restaurant and the Genji Bar, both of which feature musical entertainment on certain nights, look out on the small waterfalls, pools of water, plants, and rocks of the garden. Yonetaro Otani, founder of the Otani empire, had the red rocks, which are found only on the island of Sado in central Japan, in his personal rock collection. The red rocks and the ''shakkei'' (borrowed scenery) of the downtown Los Angeles skyline were incorporated into the garden by artist Sentaru Iwaki. The seven Zen principles of asymmetry, simplicity, calm, naturalness, austerity, subtlety, and unworldliness are blended into this miniature version of the ten-acre garden of the New Otani Tokyo.

Simplicity, naturalness, and subtlety show up in all the rooms. Finding beauty in simplicity seems to be the motto underlying the decor. Rooms that have the most Japanese atmosphere (the 18th to 20th floors) leave the wood unpainted on the window sills to expose the natural grain and have shoji window screens akin to rice paper to "tenderize" the light. The New Otani is currently working with a group of New York designers to upgrade all the rooms to more fully reflect the Japanese influence.

Most of the rooms come with good views across downtown, and many also overlook the garden. Three rooms are designed specially to accommodate the disabled. The staff is personable and courteous, and may indulge in such courtesies as leaving a yukata kimono on the bed and having the music playing on arrival on a stereo system that has speakers extending into the bathroom.

A typical Western room is moderate to large in size and has a lamp table next to the bed with built-in controls for the room light, foot light, and radio. (The off control for the music is spelled out only in Japanese characters.) Small digital alarm clocks are also provided. The staff turns down the bed and provides a small box of candies in the evening. There is an extra charge of $5.95 for using the special movie channel on the television sets provided with every room.

Rooms have phones in the main room as well as on the bathroom wall. The refrigerator beneath the bathroom sink is supplied with juice, soft drinks, and mineral waters that are paid for ($1–$2.25) on an honor basis. The hotel also provides small boxes of mild, scented soap, a comb, razor, toothbrush, moisturizing cream, bath and shower gel, conditioning shampoo, bath cap, water glasses, and ice bucket (there is an ice cube tray in the freezer). Most bathrooms have a hand-held shower used in the tub, though the more luxurious units have Jacuzzi tubs.

Banquet rooms accommodate from 25 to 500 people and may be divided with gold foil screens from Japan. The Japanese art is new era and includes a mural-size ceramic depicting nature scenes, a new-era Ikebana flower arrangement called *Cosmic Spark*, and abstractions. The mezzanine and lobby levels have numerous shops and restaurants, and much more is available in Little Tokyo.

It is a short walk to City Hall and the court buildings of downtown Los Angeles. The hotel is also very close to the Pacific Stock Exchange (which has a trading observation area), the Japanese Cultural and Community Center, the Higashi Hongwangji Buddhist Temple (with its blue tile roof and dragons standing guard), the Broadway district (historic theaters and low-cost shopping), the hectic Grand Central Market, the Bradbury Building (whose cast-iron elevators and stairs played an eerie role in the movie *Blade-runner*), and other downtown sights.

The New Otani runs a courtesy downtown minibus on weekday mornings. Rapid Transit District and direct bus service to Los Angeles International Airport is also available. Overnight parking at the New Otani costs about $6.

Le Parc Hotel
733 North West Knoll Drive
West Hollywood, California 90069
800/252-2152 (tollfree from within California)
800/252-2152 (tollfree from rest of U.S.)
213/855-8888

Suites $120–$200

The modern, four-story, 154-room Le Parc Hotel in West Hollywood is a former luxury apartment building turned hotel deluxe by the owners of L'Ermitage in Beverly Hills. Situated between Melrose Avenue and Santa Monica Boulevard, one block west of La Cienega Boulevard, on a narrow residential street lined with parked cars, apartment buildings, and Spanish-style houses, Le Parc is recognized from the street by the international flags waving from the rooftop tennis courts.

The rooms are either one-bedroom suites or executive suites, and include kitchenette, dining area, and dressing area adjacent to the bathroom. Executive suites feature a sunken living room separated from the sleeping area by an unobtrusive hardwood- topped black wrought-iron railing and a floor-to-ceiling drapery that may be drawn for additional privacy.

Televisions and telephones are found in both the living room and the bedroom. A digital AM-FM radio alarm clock is found on one of the bedside end tables, with additional music built into the television consoles. The cable-equipped televisions rest atop a dresser in the bedroom and within a larger oak storage unit in the living room.

Contemporary, comfortably upholstered sofa and chair are grouped with lamps, potted green plants, and oak coffee table across from the fireplace in the living room. Adjacent to the living room is a dinette set next to a sliding glass door that opens onto a private balcony. The kitchenette includes a wet bar, double stainless steel sink, cutting board, wine rack, and full-size refrigerator. A special key opens the cocktail cabinet, with its array of snacks ranging from mixed nuts and potato chips to wine, beer, liquor, champagne, mixed cocktails, mineral water, and soda. Guests may tally their own tabs or let management take inventory.

On the third floor, across from the well-equipped executive exercise room with its weight machine, rowing machine, massager, exercise bicycle, sauna, and view of the Hollywood Hills, is the intimate Cafe Le Parc (reserved for the exclusive use of hotel guests). Accompanying the morning newspaper left outside each room is a letter from Cafe Le Parc chef Jean-Marc announcing the special daily creations of Provençal cuisine. There is 24-hour room service and poolside roof garden service from 7 A.M. to 10:30 P.M.

The roof garden's heated swimming pool has an inner perimeter of orange tiles topped with turquoise, and is surrounded with olive chaise lounges, chairs, and glass tables. Beyond the planters of trees, shrubs, cacti, and flowers are panoramic views of the Los Angeles area. To the north are the Hollywood Hills. The building at the base of these hills with bands of purple, blue, yellow, orange, and red is another L'Ermitage hotel, Le Mondrian on Sunset Boulevard, which has interior and exterior design by kinetic artist Yaacov Agam. Farther to the east, with the San Gabriel Mountains in the background, is the dome of the Griffith Observatory in Griffith Park. The cluster of skyscrapers that is downtown Los Angeles also stands out. To the west is the multistory blue glass Pacific Design Center, which is only blocks away on Melrose Avenue. The view to the south of the ''Blue Whale'' includes the tiled dome of the Beverly Hills City Hall, the towers of Century City, and Marina del Rey.

Hidden from the swimming pool level by green plants is

an upper deck with more seating, gazebo, piped in soft rock music, and a blue-tiled Jacuzzi. A plant-lined rooftop bridge leads from the upper deck to the tennis courts. Guests are invited to reserve court time (the lights stay on until 10 P.M.) or leave requests for tennis partners. The spacious courts have spectator benches and chairs along with private dining nooks.

A mirrored elevator lined with hardwoods takes guests from the rooftop back down to the modern lobby. Complimentary transportation by chauffeured limousine is offered within specific areas of Hollywood and Beverly Hills. There is complimentary valet parking as well as self-parking (the room key opens the underground parking garage gates).

La Cienega Boulevard, a block to the west of Le Parc, has numerous galleries and a reputation as restaurant row, while the billboard-lined Sunset Strip is only about a mile north of Le Parc. Melrose Avenue, which borders Le Parc, is known for its areas of avant garde and new wave. Located just down the street on North West Knoll Drive is an African art museum. The Los Angeles County Art Museum and the Rancho La Brea Tar Pits Museum are both within a few miles of Le Parc.

Sovereign Hotel
205 Washington Avenue
Santa Monica, California 90403
213/395-9921

Singles, doubles $30–$65
Suites $65–$110

Designed by Julia Morgan, architect of the Hearst Castle in San Simeon, the Sovereign has occupied a choice corner in a residential neighborhood blocks from the beach for over fifty years. The 83-room multistory Spanish-style building has undergone a number of recent ownership changes, with the current management beginning a renovation program limited both by cash flow and by the fact that the long-term tenants occupying half of the rooms are protected by strict Santa Monica rent control laws designed for apartment buildings (the neon sign out front still flashes Sovereign Hotel and Apartments).

The rooms vary widely in character and condition, as the one room at a time renovation continues. But it is hard to find better prices in this quiet residential neighborhood north of Wilshire Boulevard, one and a half blocks from the Sheraton Miramar (where the current manager previously worked) and two blocks from the cliffs of Palisades Park that look out over the Pacific Ocean. Many of the rooms come with balconies and good views of the ocean and nearby palm tree–lined streets.

An old elevator pulled from the roof and lined with hardwoods takes guests up the five stories of this majestic whitewashed building. Sometimes temperamental, as is the prerogative of a relic nicknamed Aunt Nellie by residents, the elevator nonetheless reliably takes guests to rooms that may be furnished with antique, modern, art deco, or an eclectic mixture of furniture styles. The doors with brass knockers are outfitted with peepholes. Iron gratings are common throughout the building, as are half-century-old light fixtures. Many rooms also have kitchens, with management offering discounts for stays of a week or more.

There is a rooftop garden suite as well as a master suite with a panoramic view of Santa Monica. All rooms have tubs, showers, and television sets. The telephone system operates through the front desk switchboard, which is run by a very friendly staff.

The lobby is tastefully furnished with antiques, such as an old dark wood smoking table with carved bears, which echoes the large chime clock that has carved wood bears crawling up the carved wood trees along its side. The lobby and accompanying outside lawn and garden areas are elevated from street level and provide convenient places for sunning. The management has recently introduced a weekend bed and breakfast plan including fresh fruit.

Airport buses are available from the nearby Sheraton and Huntley hotels. The Huntley has a glass elevator up to its rooftop restaurant, which is worth riding for the view and the late afternoon happy hour. Santa Monica and Rapid Transit District buses are easily accessible from here.

Sportsmen's Lodge Hotel
12825 Ventura Boulevard
(at Coldwater Canyon)
Studio City, California 91604
800/821-1625 (tollfree from within California)
800/821-8511 (tollfree from rest of U.S.)
800/341-6363 (tollfree from Canada)
818/769-4700

Singles, doubles $65–$85
Suites $115–$155

The 196-room Sportsmen's Lodge Hotel, one of the first hotels in the San Fernando Valley when it was built in 1962, is situated on six acres along with ponds, swans, and redwoods just north of that suburban concrete channel known as the Los Angeles River. It all started with a hot dog stand at the corner of Ventura Boulevard and Coldwater Canyon. There were lakes here, and people would take rowboats out to catch the trout. In 1946, the Sportsmen's Lodge Restaurant, which is still here, came into being to cook the trout. Then the lake was filled to build the hotel, leaving the ponds that are now home to swans, ducks, and carp (trout are no longer stocked, as the hotel got tired of requests to ship people's catches cross country).

The hotel still retains the country feel that marks it as being of the era before houses replaced crops and orchards in the San Fernando Valley. However, the rooms are as modern as any, having recently been renovated with new carpets, drapes, and decor. Don't be surprised to find plaids or floral wallpaper (in the bathroom). Radios, color televisions, and telephones are standard, as is room service and a 24-hour front desk staffed with helpful personnel, including some who remember when the hotel first opened. Staff at the Sportsmen's Lodge Restaurant, which serves continental cuisine in a location overlooking the bridges, ponds, and wildlife, has worked here an average of 15 years.

The hotel also has a coffee shop overlooking its Olympic-size pool. Ground-floor rooms facing the pool come with lanais. The four upper floors facing the pool come with balconies. Rooms facing the pool cost $10 more than their counterparts not facing the pool. The hotel also has a Jacuzzi and an exercise room with a rowing machine and a life cycle.

Adjacent to the large pool and sundeck area, a gazebo enclosing a barbecue was under construction at this writing. This area, which is lushly shaded by redwood trees and other vegetation, will be available for outdoor receptions and cocktail parties. The hotel has numerous banquet and conference rooms, many of which look out on the refreshing surroundings.

Amenities include complimentary afternoon tea, courtesy limousines to the Burbank and Van Nuys airports, and free transportation to the connecting buses for Los Angeles International Airport. Within walking distance, there are facilities for golf, tennis, and bowling. The hotel is near the Griffith Park Equestrian Center, the L.A. Zoo, NBC Studio Tours, Universal Studios, and the Hollywood Bowl. Nearby Ventura Boulevard offers a variety of shops, boutiques, restaurants, and delis. Plenty of free parking is available. Major RTD bus lines operating along Ventura Boulevard carry passengers to other parts of the Los Angeles area.

«LOUISVILLE»

Breckinridge Inn
Breckinridge Lane and Watterson Expressway
Louisville, Kentucky 40220
502/456-5050

Singles $45
Doubles $52

The Breckinridge Inn is situated out of the mainstream of Louisville hotels, both in location and size, but it turns both differences into benefits. The location away from downtown is welcome for those tired of the noise and bustle of the city. And its 123 rooms are a point of pride. This is obviously not the place for a large convention, but the clientele, mostly businesspeople, routinely come back for the family-style hospitality and southern comfort found here.

The low prices may also play a role in the hotel's continued popularity with return visitors. In addition to regular rooms, the hotel also has five minisuites. The rooms are tidy and spacious, tastefully decorated in early American decor. Each room contains a triplex, two chairs, a round table, and beds.

The hotel is not short on facilities. In addition to an indoor and an outdoor pool, there is a health club, color and cable television in the rooms, room service, Jeremiah Sweeney's Lounge/Restaurant, and a beauty shop, barber shop, and gift shop. This hidden spot has much to offer.

The Galt House and The Galt House East
4th Avenue at the River
Louisville, Kentucky 40202
502/589-3300

Old Galt: singles $55 and up, doubles $75, suites $200
Galt East: singles $67 and up, doubles $92, suites $375–
$450

The Galt House Hotels form an incredible complex on the river. Once the new Galt House East is complete, the two hotels combined will house 1300 guest rooms and suites. In addition to new rooms, the Galt House East is planned to include a revolving rooftop restaurant, a rooftop helicopter landing pad, and tennis courts. Not only are the hotels reasonably priced, but their location provides many rooms with a beautiful river view. There is also easy access to downtown Louisville.

Much of the Galt Hotels' business comes from conventions, with numerous ballrooms, meeting halls, and restaurants to show for it. The Grand Ballroom contains 30,000 square feet and can seat 5000. There are eight more meeting rooms on the same floor, which can hold 50 to 500 people each.

The fact that both buildings are highrises of at least 15 stories does not detract from the comfort found within. Each and every suite in the Old Galt has a balcony. Thirteen two-bedroom parlor suites are available, all with river views. The decor inside the rooms is heavy on velour, with many rooms done in red, the owner's favorite color.

The Galt Houses are strong on extras, too. An indoor shopping center at the Galt House East makes for added convenience. Many bars and restaurants are found in both wings of the hotel complex. A barber shop and beauty salon are another feature of the hotels. A large staff works to keep room service open from 6 A.M. to 11:30 P.M. daily.

The hotel complex is quite convenient to many attractions. Across the street is the Actor's Theater, and the hotels are only yards away from the Belle of Louisville. Belvedere Park and the Kentucky Center for the Arts are not far away.

As Louisville's only river-view hotel complex, the Galt Houses are worth looking into.

The Seelbach
500 Fourth Avenue
Louisville, Kentucky 40202
800/626-2032 (tollfree) 502/585-3200

Singles $72–$92
Doubles $95–$115

The Seelbach is a study in elegance. In the heart of downtown, the location is prime, while the rooms are luxuriously peaceful. The Seelbach is one of about 57 hotels in the Preferred Hotels association. It has been open only three years, yet had already experienced a 70-year history, beginning in 1905 and ending in 1975. The pinnacle of its fame was in the 1920s, when F. Scott Fitzgerald chose the place as the scene for Daisy's wedding in *The Great Gatsby*. The Seelbach renovations, which allowed the hotel to reopen in April 1982, were under the guidance of Roger Davis. Davis is a Louisville native, Hollywood actor, and entrepreneur who, with the support of the Atlanta Metropolitan Life Insurance Company, successfully completed the $24 million restoration of the hotel to its former magnificence.

The Seelbach has 322 guest rooms, each containing four-poster mahogany beds and an armoire housing a color TV with cable. A marble bath and brass fixtures complete the effect. Plush carpeting and drapes give the room a sense of warmth and comfort. Perfect for a weekend getaway, the hotel also houses a grand ballroom, where fashion shows and business meetings are held.

The hotel has an attentive staff that will hurry to carry your baggage, park your car, and see to your comfort. Twenty-four-hour room service is available, as well as overnight shoeshines. A small gift shop, a wonderful restaurant (the Oak Room), a cafe, and the Old Seelbach Bar add to the charm of the hotel. A courtesy van to the airport, currency exchange, and an airline ticket office in the building are also available.

The hotel is directly across the street from the Galleria, the center of Louisville's office and retail space, consisting of 90 shops. It is a block from the Macauley Theatre, the Commonwealth Convention Center, and only a few blocks from the Kentucky Center for the Arts, Historic Main Street, and the Natural History Museum.

«MADISON»

The Collins House
704 East Gorham Street
Madison, Wisconsin 53703
608/255-4230

$55–$75

Recently opened six blocks from Capitol Square is the city's first bed and breakfast. The resident proprietors, a husband and wife team, have opened their establishment in a lakeside home built in 1911 for a lumber baron. Like the Mansion Hill Inn, this house is listed in the National Register of Historic Places, and is an example of the prairie style of architecture.

The mahogany-paneled living room and the oak-paneled library on the first floor are open for lounging; a VCR is set up in one, with a selection of classic movies in a videotape library. Quality continental breakfasts are served on weekends, full breakfasts weekdays. Full catering services are available with notice. All four rooms have a private bath.

The Mansion Hill Inn
424 North Pinckney Street
Madison, Wisconsin 53703
608/255-3999

$70–$170

Opened in November 1985, the Mansion Hill Inn is the first small hotel in Madison, designed to add to this city's stock of larger, chain, or otherwise expectable hotels used by an expanding business and academic trade.

The Mansion Hill Inn underwent extensive renovations during the summer of 1985 by the Alexander Group, one of Madison's first preservationist developers. Overlooking Lake Mendota, the mansion was the city's most ambitious residence of the 1880s, built of Mississippi limestone, Carrara marble, and Swedish cast iron by architect August Kutzock and Italian craftsmen after they completed the state's first capitol building.

On the corner of Gilman and Pinkney streets three blocks from Capitol Square, in the quietest of downtown's four corners, the inn is the premier of a quartet of fine limestone homes listed in the National Register of Historic Places as Mansion Hill. The parlor is quite lavish, and decorated with the same care as the ten private rooms. The grand staircase, which curves around two sides of the center hallway, might present an obstacle to those using a crutch or cane.

The renovation staff has fashioned each of the ten rooms after a particular style appropriate to very high Victoriana. The staff's excitement with refurnishing this mansion (as well as an apparent open budget) can be appreciated with quick glimpses of the Japonesque Suite or the Turkish Nook for the exotic, the Craftsman or the Baron for the practical, or the Lillie Langtry or the Carrie Pierce for the romantic. The tops of the antique bedside tables and armoires bear a discreetly modern finish—no worry about putting down coffee cups. Amenities include cable TVs hidden in the armoire in most rooms, whirlpool baths or steam showers in all rooms, and all the expected (though unusually lavish) foaming bath gels, soaps, and shampoos. Continental breakfast is complimentary and other meals can be catered if requested.

The Craftsman and Garden rooms are below street grade overlooking a minuscule garden and are the only rooms accessible to wheelchairs. Under the skylights just below the belvedere are the Japonesque and Carrie Pierce rooms.

These four rooms are small in comparison to the other six, but all ten are filled with the dreams of decorators. Although each of the ten rooms is filled with light from arched or bay windows or the skylights, the views from most are limited, especially in the rooms at the back. Eight rooms have a balcony or veranda, and all have either a whirlpool or a steam shower. Valet parking and a major domo round out the services.

«MIAMI, FORT» «LAUDERDALE»

Bed and Breakfast Company
P.O. Box 262
South Miami, Florida 33242
305/661-3270

May–Dec. 15: Singles $20–$38, doubles $24–$44
Dec. 16–April: Singles $24–$44, doubles $32–$65
Rates based on three-night minimum, with a $5 per night
   surcharge for one or two nights

Bed and Breakfast Company offers visitors to its Florida locations reasonable rates, comfortable accommodations, and hospitality. All host homes are carefully selected and offer a wide variety of styles to choose from: everything from lush oceanside homes to a yacht, a "treehouse" and a cottage.

Host families may provide as much attention as guests desire—from giving a personal tour of the city to allowing visitors to come and go with barely a sign. Breakfast is included in all rates.

Multilingual host families are available, with French, German, and Spanish the major second languages.

Bed and Breakfast Company has host facilities in most South Florida locations, including both east and west coasts, and almost all of the Florida Keys. There are also locations in central and northern Florida, including Tampa, Melbourne, Palm Coast, Orlando, Gainesville, and the Panhandle.

The Fontainebleu Hilton Resort
4441 Collins Avenue
Miami Beach, Florida 33140
305/538-2000

Singles $135–$195
Parlor and one bedroom $295–$420
Parlor and two bedroom $420–$570
Extra person $15

The grande dame is back: The Fontainebleu, through an eight-year, $50 million renovation program coupled with Hilton Hotels Corporation management, has shed its manqué image. It now offers a fresh tropical fantasy, with luxurious dining and sophisticated entertainment—all qualities that made the 1224-room hotel world famous in the '50s and early '60s.

Miami Beach itself has undergone major changes in the last decade. One of the most remarkable changes is the beach itself. It has been rebuilt to restore its eroded width, and now is a beautifully expansive space of white sand and surf, nothing like the small strip of sand that so many remember from 15 or 20 years ago. The recently completed boardwalk, 25 city blocks long, provides a delightful means for strolling the oceanfront. Renovation of the art deco structures, both residential and commercial, has brought many young, affluent South Florida professionals to Miami Beach to live, work, and play.

The Fontainebleu's tropical fantasies include the newly designed $8.5 million free-form, half-acre swimming pool in the style of a rock grotto, complete with an artificial mountain that has waterfalls cascading down its exterior and a hidden "Lagoon Saloon" nestled inside. The Dining Galleries, an elegant old world collection of three connected eateries (one formerly the famous Gigi Room of the 1950s), offer superb food and service. The galleries have become one of the outstanding restaurants of South Florida, frequented by many locals.

The hotel offers a self-contained resort for the leisure, business, or convention traveler. On its 18 acres, there are seven tennis courts, 33 cabanas, and 12 restaurants and lounges. And because of Miami's new international flavor, the hotel's worldly guests will find an International Hospitality Center with a full staff of hosts fluent in six languages, as well as a currency exchange, the largest on Miami Beach, with currencies of 120 countries.

The Miami International Airport is 18 minutes away. The hotel is easily accessible by automobile, with a major causeway, 195, connecting I-95 to Miami Beach, just three blocks from the hotel.

Business and meeting facilities are currently being enlarged through a $15 million project. The expansion will include a 27,000-square-foot International Ballroom (in addition to the already existing Grand Ballroom, which accommodates 5000). There will be seven major break-out rooms, convention planning offices, and an executive boardroom and dining room. The public space expansion will bring the total amount of meeting space to 175,000 square feet, one of the largest in the Southeast.

The Grand Bay Hotel
2669 South Bayshore Drive
Coconut Grove, Florida 33133
800/327-2788 (tollfree)
305/858-9699

Singles $120–$600
Doubles $135–$600

The recently opened Grand Bay Hotel offers the finest in deluxe accommodations in Miami. The 200-room structure, overlooking Coconut Grove's picturesque marina, combines the best of all worlds: the confidence and refinement of polished wood, brass, and leather merging with the breezy, colorful, relaxed, and spacious feeling of South Florida, creating an aura of casual elegance.

The business or leisure traveler immediately becomes aware of the poised efficiency at every turn, from check-in, to queries posed to staff, to effortless check-out.

The rooms are beautifully furnished, all with scenic terrace views of Biscayne Bay, minibars, and baths furnished with telephones and hair dryers.

The Grand Cafe offers superb continental food and local seafood specialties (don't miss the she-crab soup; it is consistently delicious). The Ciga Bar, across from the Cafe, is a prestigious gathering spot for Miami's young executives. The lobby lounge presents tea, canapes, and aperitifs each afternoon and evening complemented by piano music. Regine's Nightclub is located atop the hotel and is open to registered guests.

The hotel's amenities include a large private swimming pool, Jacuzzi, and complete health facilities for men and women.

The Grand Bay also offers excellent meeting facilities and custom catering for gatherings of up to 250, and provides telex and secretarial service.

The hotel is conveniently located 15 minutes from Miami International Airport and eight minutes from downtown.

The Hotel Carlyle
1250 Ocean Drive
Miami Beach, Florida 33139
800/327-6306 (tollfree from U.S. except Florida)
305/535-2135

Standard rooms $55
Oceanview rooms $75
Oceanfront rooms $80

Twenty blocks south of the "big splash" hotels of Miami Beach is the delightful refreshing 65-room Hotel Carlyle, one of the many fine examples of art deco architecture in the area currently being restored. The Carlyle, facing the Atlantic, is located in the Art Deco District, one of the nation's youngest districts entered on the National Register of Historic Places. In the Art Deco District, a mile-square area of hotels, apartments, and homes built in the '30s and early '40s, the visitor can marvel at the abundance of sprightly, fanciful, pastel-draped varieties of art deco architectural styles.

The Carlyle immediately creates an inescapable mood. The sounds and scents of the beautifully restored beach filter past the wide wrap-around veranda, with the turquoise At-

lantic and swaying palms completing the daydreamscape.
The sun melts tension. A hotel combo plays jazz and reggae.
A wristwatch becomes at worst nagging, at best useless.
Stylish upscale tourists and business professionals mix well
with the artists, writers, and actors who are regular patrons
of the hotel's bar and restaurant. The mood is at once elegant
and laid-back, youthful and creative, whimsical and ambitious.

The hotel is also planning to accommodate business meetings, with boardrooms and executive services.

Walking tours of the Art Deco District are available.
Tennis, handball, and shuffleboard are easily accessible at
Flamingo Park, four blocks away. And of course, the 350-
foot-long beach beckons both day and night.

The hotel is 20 minutes from the Miami International
Airport, and is easily reached by automobile, exiting the
395 causeway connecting I-95 to Miami Beach.

Hotel Place St. Michele
162 Alcazar
at Ponce de Leon Boulevard
Coral Gables, Florida 33134
305/444-1666

Singles $65
Doubles $75
Suites $110

The Hotel Place St. Michele, located in the heart of historic Coral Gables, is a charming 30-room European-style
inn that offers welcome relief from the press of Miami's
urban noise and pace. The hotel, originally built around
1926 in Spanish Mediterranian style, has been beautifully
restored and refurbished, with great attention to architectural
detail and authenticity.

The hotel rooms, lobby, and dining areas are furnished
with European and American antiques and paintings, and
create a pleasantly and unexpectedly genteel mood in Miami's
cityscape. Continental breakfast of coffee, fresh-squeezed
juice, and croissants is included in room tariff.

The Restaurant St. Michele, located off the hotel lobby,

offers delightful French cuisine in an elegant and relaxed setting. And the Charcuterie, also located off the lobby, offers a variety of light salads and sandwiches.

The hotel is conveniently located within walking distance of the Miracle Mile shops, theaters, galleries, and boutiques, and is approximately ten minutes from Miami International Airport and downtown Miami.

Business meetings can be arranged, and the hotel is currently remodeling one section of its cafe to accommodate a full-service bar.

The Marriott Harbor Beach Resort
3030 Holiday Drive (Off A1A)
Fort Lauderdale, Florida 33316
800/228-9290 (tollfree)
305/525-4000

Dec. 22–April 12: Standard rooms $160, coastal view
    rooms $175–$190, oceanview rooms $205–$220
April 13–Dec. 21: Standard rooms $90–$115, coastal
    view rooms $100–$135, oceanview rooms $120–$155

The world-famous Fort Lauderdale Beach has a new excuse for a party: the opening of the new Marriott Harbor Beach Resort, a 645-room facility located on 16 acres of oceanfront property. Each room has a water view and balcony, and there are 36 oceanview suites.

The resort complex offers excellent amenities for the leisure or business traveler or the conventioner. Access to the hotel is convenient: The Fort Lauderdale/Hollywood International Airport is a ten-minute drive; I-95 is five minutes away.

Meeting and banquet facilities offer 30,000 square feet of meeting space with a 24-hour Convention Service Department. There are a total of 27 meeting rooms available, which include a 15,000-square-foot grand ballroom, two boardrooms, and breakout meeting rooms. For the convenience of each type of traveler, the hotel complex is well designed so that traffic patterns of large groups of conventioners do not interfere with those of leisure or business travelers.

The resort features an expansive 1100 feet of white sand beach. Hobie Cats, windsurfers, and Sunfish sailboats can be rented at the beach. Sport fishing and ocean sailing can be arranged at the marina, which is three minutes away. The famous Bonaventure Country Club Golf Courses are available to registered guests.

The Cabana Club of 50 oceanfront cabanas is also available for registered guests. The cabanas feature chaises, chairs, showers, wet bar, and three whirlpools. An 8000-square-foot free-form swimming pool boasts a 12-foot cascading waterfall. Five tennis courts, health club with Universal equipment for men and women, as well as locker and shower facilities complement the saunas and massage service available.

Fort Lauderdale attractions located minutes from the resort include the chic Las Olas Boulevard shops and restaurants; the Galleria Mall, a collection of the finest stores on Florida's Gold Coast; riverboat cruising and dining; and the Museum of Art.

The resort offers a variety of restaurants. The Oceanview is perfect for casual dining; Sheffield's, reflecting its Tudor decor, specializes in beef, veal, and lamb. The guest will find in the Seabreeze Grille one of South Florida's finest selections of fresh seafood. Its mesquite-grilled swordfish is a delightful example of one of the house specialties.

Lounges include the Oyster Bar, the Lobby Bar, and separate beachside and poolside bars.

The Mayfair House
3000 Florida Avenue
Coconut Grove, Florida 33133
800/341-0809 (tollfree from within Florida)
800/443-4555 (tollfree from rest of U.S.)
305/441-0000

Singles, doubles $140–$800

The Mayfair House, located in the heart of downtown Coconut Grove, offers a self-contained world of luxuriously romantic fantasy. The ingredients are corridors with swirls of walls, original Tiffany stained glass, custom-designed dining chairs with six-foot-high backs, abstract architectural ornamentation (both inside and out), art nouveau etched-glass dividers, accompanying TV and telephone in each bathroom, and antique English pianos in 50 of the suites.

There is a hint of excess and sometimes the sacrifice of substance for style: The key chains for each room key are solid brass scrolls, but their weight and bulk make them unwieldy and impractical for most suit or pant pockets.

The continental breakfast (included in the room rate), made to order and served in your room's own dining area, dispels any misgivings one might have. The breakfast (with morning paper) consists of fresh juices, fruit bowl, assorted breads, danish, jams, jellies, marmalades, and a fresh pot of coffee or tea.

Hotel registration entitles guests to temporary member-ship to Ensign Bitters Grill and Ensign Bitters Club, the hotel restaurant and nightclub respectively. Complimentary limousine service is provided within a limited area. The hotel also offers rooftop pool and sundeck and 24-hour room service, which includes in-suite catering for private dining.

The hotel consists of 185 suites, each different in shape, decor, and size, and each opening onto a private veranda with Japanese hot tub, tropical garden, and dining area.

Twenty-seven suites have separate dining rooms for for-mal board meetings and business entertaining. A separate executive conference center has various meeting rooms and a wide range of audiovisual equipment. The Mayfair Ball-room, with its strikingly electric decor, may be subdivided into three areas for small or large groups. The ballroom can accommodate up to 700 theater style.

Hotel guests need never fear boredom. The hotel is an integral architectural unit of the World of Mayfair, a com-plex that includes six restaurants, four sidewalk cafes, the hotel's retail bakery shop, and over 100 shops and bou-tiques. Strolling through the Mayfair complex and observing the architecture alone can occupy a guest for hours.

Visitors also enjoy the Coconut Grove day and night life, which includes everything from latter-day hippies, to the blatantly yup/gup-scale, to new wavey punkers. It's all a few feet outside the lobby door. Coconut Grove has become the one and only gathering spot for an otherwise uncohesive Miami.

The Silver Sands Motel
301 Ocean Drive
Key Biscayne, Florida 33149
305/361-5441

Efficiency Apartments $62–$125
Oceanfront patio apartment and duplex cottages $125–$180
Rates vary by season; weekly rates available for both efficiency apartments and patio apartment and duplex cottages

Although Key Biscayne has undergone drastic building development over the past ten years, the island still possesses one unchanging landmark: the Silver Sands Motel. If you long for the Florida of the 1950s, with fan-back, wooden-slat lawn chairs on carpets of St. Augustine grass, pink flamingo yard ornaments with gentle surf sounds and breezes, look no further than the Silver Sands.

The motel, whose construction began in 1956, was the first oceanfront motel on Key Biscayne, and now, 30 years later, is the last one left on the key. It has been owned by the same family since 1960.

The efficiency apartments and oceanside cottages are clean and simple, providing refrigerator, stove, and color TV.

Enjoying the Silver Sands and Key Biscayne is easy. The hotel has a private beach, private pool, and its own Sandbar Restaurant, another landmark for natives of the Miami area. The restaurant consistently offers good food at reasonable prices, with indoor or outdoor dining overlooking the beach and the Atlantic. The adjoining Sonesta Tennis Courts are available for a small fee; golf is available at the Key Biscayne Golf Course nearby.

The Eagle's Nest Lounge offers an upstairs open-air bar (surprisingly, one of Miami's few) overlooking the ocean, and provides nightly entertainment featuring local musicians. Another bar is located poolside, and the restaurant contains a glass-enclosed bar featuring that '50s conversation novelty, a rainmaker. Be sure to ask for a demonstration.

The Rickenbacker Causeway, which was completed in the late '40s, has recently been expanded, greatly enhancing access on and off the island.

«MILWAUKEE»

Astor Hotel
924 East Juneau Avenue
(at Astor Street)
Milwaukee, Wisconsin 53202
800/242-0355 (tollfree from within Wisconsin)
800/558-0200 (tollfree from rest of U.S.)
414/271-4220

Singles $53
Doubles $61
Studios $70–$78
Suites $82–$110

Built in the 1920s, this eight-story brick and limestone edifice lies in a residential neighborhood a few blocks from Lake Michigan. A dome with stained-glass windows highlights the vast lobby, whose French classical architecture dates to 1941. Pictures of Astor's famous guests line the walls in two corners of the lobby, which also contains a small selection of books. The hotel, on the National Register of Historic Places, has offered both apartments and transient rooms since the 1920s. Studio apartments with one, two, and three bedrooms are available on a permanent or nightly basis. Come to the Astor to relax: The tranquillity found here is duplicated nowhere else in Milwaukee.

The recently redecorated rooms have been furnished as apartments. Overnight guests in the affordable parlor suites enjoy all the comforts of home including a kitchen with stove and refrigerator, dining table, loveseat, chairs, a desk, queen-size bed, television, and telephone. Large plants enhance the rust or pastel tones in the rooms. Although the rooms have air conditioning, some guests like to open the windows to savor the fresh air from Lake Michigan. Amenities include fancy toiletries placed in a basket. The color televisions have HBO. Each guest receives a morning newspaper delivered to the room.

Guest services include a bellman and a beauty shop. Nantucket Shores, the Astor's restaurant, has a fabulous salad bar and promises prompt service. The restaurant is open for breakfast, lunch, and dinner. The Astor also provides room service.

Guests may use the exclusive Downtown Club, a short jog away, for $3. The club has a running track, swimming pool, whirlpool, and steam and sauna rooms.

The Marc Plaza
509 West Wisconsin Avenue
(at North 5th Street)
Milwaukee, Wisconsin 53203
800/558-7708 (tollfree)
414/271-7250

Singles $70–$80
Doubles $85–$95
Suites $90–$160

This 550-room hotel may lack some of the individual attention that makes the Pfister so attractive but guests thoroughly enjoy the Marc Plaza and its convenient location in downtown Milwaukee. The Marcus Corporation owns both the Marc Plaza and the Pfister. Ben Marcus purchased the Marc Plaza in 1972, then called the Sheraton Schroeder, and began extensive renovations. More recently, the lobby has been refinished in its original art deco style.

The tower, encompassing the 20th through 24th floors, provides the best rooms in the Marc Plaza. For a slightly higher price, guests receive better accommodations and an array of services. Only guests with proper keys can take the elevator to the 20th to 24th floors. A complimentary cocktail hour from 5 to 6 P.M. in the 20th-floor lounge is followed by a cash bar from 6 to 9 P.M. In the morning, the hotel offers a complimentary continental breakfast in the lounge for all tower guests, who also have the services of a concierge. A freshly cut flower and a candy dish greet guests in the tower rooms, which have electric shoeshines and remote-control color televisions with satellite movies.

The other rooms in the hotel which have been recently renovated have queen-size or two twin beds, a television, a desk, and three chairs. These renovated rooms look crisp and modern.

Facilities include a pool, sauna, and exercise equipment in a glass-covered room. Within the hotel are a newsstand, a flower shop, a hair salon, a women's boutique, an auto rental firm, and a shoe repair shop. Guests may also use the same-day laundry and valet service. Horse and carriage rides leave from the hotel Monday through Saturday evenings. The Marc Plaza also has a concierge in the lobby. There is a fee for parking.

Le Bistro serves French cuisine in the lower level of the hotel. (Complete dinners cost over $20, and a la carte luncheons and dinners usually cost under $30. A coffee shop, the Cafe Plaza, offers more simple fare for breakfast, lunch, and dinner. The Bombay Bicycle Club has nightly jazz and like the lobby, an art deco style.

The Marc Plaza's convention facilities can accommodate from 20 to 2000. Offices are available for guests.

Pfister Hotel
424 East Wisconsin Avenue
(at Milwaukee Street)
Milwaukee, Wisconsin 53202
800/558-8222 (tollfree)
414/273-8222

Singles $70–$80
Doubles $85–$95
Suites $95–$220

Charles Pfister's special greeting, ''Salve,'' offering a heartfelt welcome and an assurance of a safe visit, has adorned the two ends of the grand lobby of the Pfister Hotel for over a century. The staff gives this greeting a personal touch by being efficient and friendly, as well as enthusiastic about their hotel. The beauty of the woodwork appears most becomingly in the front desk, though intricate designs abound in the lobby. Original 19th-century paintings hang throughout the public areas of the hotel. The collection of paintings in the Pfister belonged to Charles Pfister and is the largest collection of 19th-century art found in a hotel anywhere in the world.

The addition of an uninspiring 23-story tower behind the original building in 1966 provided the Pfister with more parking space, more rooms, a club, and a swimming pool. Though the newer rooms tend to be uniform in size as well as furnishings, none of the exquisitely decorated rooms in the original hotel are alike. Individual rooms in the older section of the hotel offer such features as brass beds, step-up bathrooms, and beautiful views of Lake Michigan.

Dance above Milwaukee in La Playa on the 23rd floor of the tower. The glass-walled club offers superb views of the city as well as live entertainment. The rose-lighted swimming pool and exercise center next to the club also has glass walls.

The richly decorated Cafe Rouge serves luncheons during the week and a champagne brunch on Sunday. The award-winning English Room on the lower level of the hotel has continental cuisine. Three adjoining restaurants at street level, the Greenery, La Veranda, and Cafe Ole offer more casual dining and cocktails. The Pfister also has room service.

The unparalleled meeting facilities at the Pfister include the Grand Ballroom, Hall of Presidents, King's Row, and the spectacular Imperial Ballroom with a ceiling 32 feet high. The Pfister can accommodate from 20 to 2000 people for a meeting.

The Pfister has its own television channel in guest rooms. The channel supplies information about the hotel, restaurants, and services. There is a barber shop, beauty salon, gift shop, men's clothing shop, and a concierge to assist with any other need. The seventh floor of the hotel holds all the conference and banquet facilities and connects the tower with the older part of the hotel.

Washington House Inn
W62 N573 Washington Avenue
(at Center Street)
Cedarburg, Wisconsin 53012
414/375-3550

Singles, doubles $49–$89

The Washington House was built in 1886. The hotel operated until the 1920s, when it was converted into offices and apartments. The historic building was restored and reopened as the Washington House Inn in September 1984, and is the best choice for travelers who want to stay in Milwaukee's outlying area.

The Washington House serves an unbeatable breakfast. In this Victorian-style bed and breakfast, the cook begins preparing muffins, breads, and cakes at 5 o'clock each morning, using recipes from a historic Cedarburg cookbook. Freshly squeezed orange juice, fruit, tea, and coffee are part of the continental breakfast served from 7 to 10 A.M. in the Gathering Room. An afternoon social hour, held in the same room from 5 to 6 P.M., allows guests time to become acquainted and relax. Refreshments include white wine from the Stonemill Winery and cheese and crackers from a local cheese shop. Although somewhat bare, the large room has an intricate reproduction tin ceiling and has been well restored.

Each guest room at the inn has a specially built armoire with color television (HBO), clock radio, and pullout desk. Rooms also have down comforters, telephones, a highback chair, a smaller chair, and a dresser. Twelve of the fifteen rooms have whirlpool baths. Two rooms have beautiful stained-glass windows. The inn has an elevator. An iron and ironing board are available from the innkeeper and the inn provides an overnight dry cleaning service. Amenities include mints on a brass tray in each room and Neutrogena soaps and shampoos. Guests also have access to the sauna on the lower level.

The inn is located thirty minutes north of Milwaukee. Take Highway 57 to downtown Cedarburg, a national historic district with many restored buildings. Ask for a copy of the Walking Tour and take a stroll through town.

«MINNEAPOLIS»

Hotel Sofitel
5601 West 78th Street
(I-494 and Normandale Avenue)
Bloomington, Minnesota
612/835-1900

Singles $78
Doubles $90
Suites $170–$370

The Hotel Sofitel attracts corporate conventions with its concern for the business traveler. The three French restaurants and the School of French Culinary Skills in the hotel attest to the Sofitel's commitment to fine cuisine. The Paris-based chain has only two other hotels in the United States.

Every room has a sitting area that includes a loveseat and two chairs, which lends itself, to small informal meetings. Rooms also contain a king-size, queen-size, or two double brass beds, a desk, and color TV. The comfortable furniture has a European flair. All the rooms are pleasantly decorated in pastel shades. Each room has a freshly cut flower, and the baths are stocked with fine toiletries.

Cafe La Terrase evokes images of the classic sidewalk cafe. The restaurant and bar has a relaxed atmosphere and specializes in snacks and light meals, such as cheeses, soups, or eight different salads. A few traditional entrees, such as steak, chicken, and seafood are also available. La Terrase opens at 11 A.M. and closes at 3 P.M.

Chez Colette, a lively brasserie, offers a fine array of

regional specialties including quail, duckling, and lobster. Though the lights are low, this isn't the place for a quiet dinner, as the atmosphere is boisterous. The menu also includes a healthy sampling of hors d'oeuvres, salads, fish, and cheeses. Chez Colette is open for breakfast, lunch, and dinner.

Dine in elegance at Le Cafe Royal. Entree prices range from $17 to $22. The Sofitel's most refined restaurant is open for lunch and dinner every day except Sunday. For those without the time for Le Cafe Royal's cuisine, the Sofitel has box lunches for $4.50.

An airport limo leaves the Sofitel every half hour between 5:50 A.M. and 6:20 P.M. A concierge is available to help guests. The health club has a swimming pool, sauna, whirlpool, and bodybuilding equipment. The club opens at 7:00 A.M. and closes at 10:00 P.M. The Sofitel operates a massage service by appointment only.

The Grand Ballroom holds a thousand people, and eight parlors each hold approximately 50 people. The Sofitel lies just off I-494 in Bloomington, 20 minutes south of downtown Minneapolis.

Lowell Inn
102 North Second Street
Stillwater, Minnesota 55082
612/439-1100

Singles, doubles $69–$89
Suites $109–$119

Nelle and Arthur Palmer opened the Lowell Inn on Christmas Day, 1930. They began the commitment to making guests truly feel at home which is carried on by Arthur Jr., his wife Maureen, and their nine children. The Palmers and the rest of the staff have a strong devotion to the 21-room inn, which is 45 minutes northeast of downtown St. Paul. Many of the guests have been returning to the Lowell for years.

The Williamsburg theme seen throughout the hotel has a French twist in the guest rooms. Most of the furnishings in the hotel were collected by Nelle Palmer. Reproductions and antiques give individually decorated rooms a plush appearance and a slightly cluttered but homey feel. A ceramic cat rests at the foot of each bed. The Palmers also place a small complimentary bottle of wine in each room. A brush, hand mirror, and bottle of perfume rest on a table. A phone, a sleek and unobtrusive AM-FM radio, and air conditioning are the only modern conveniences. The rooms have no TVs. The three-story inn does not have an elevator nor does it have room service.

Partake of a full-course fondue dinner in the Matterhorn Room. Wood carvings by Swiss masters and stained glass make a warm setting for Lowell's unique dining experience. The fixed-price meal includes four wines, escargot, salad, Fondue Bourguignonne, and dessert. Guests dip pieces of beef and shrimp in one or more of the six sauces. The Palmers have served this extravagaza in the Matterhorn for over twenty-five years.

The Garden Room, with its spring-fed trout pond, makes guests feel at home in nature. Brick walls and polished agate tables help create a relaxed atmosphere. The George Washington Room epitomizes the Colonial Williamsburg theme which creates such a pleasant aura around the Lowell. Waitresses in period costumes serve drinks on silver trays. A collection of Sheffield silver service rests above the fireplace and portraits of George and Martha Washington hang on the walls. The wine cellar has a fine selection of California wines.

Minnesota's first city has dozens of antique and craft shops in restored buildings near the hotel. Make reservations several months in advance, especially for weekend visits.

Nicollet Island Inn
95 Merriam Street
(at Hennepin Avenue)
Minneapolis, Minnesota 55401
612/623-7741

Singles $76, $88, $100
Doubles $88, $100, $112

The simplest of the Nicollet's three classes of rooms has a queen-size bed with old-fashioned comforters, an armoire with color TV, a wing chair, and a writing desk. The intermediate rooms are slightly larger than these. The deluxe rooms have canopy beds and a few other comforts, such as Jacuzzi baths and views of the Mississippi River. All 24 rooms have been individually decorated with Victorian-era antiques and reproductions.

Each guest receives a complimentary beverage and a bedtime chocolate in addition to a continental breakfast and one of several newspapers.

The refined Victorian decor complements the River Room, the inn's restaurant that wraps around the inn on the ground level. Enjoy traditional American fare in a cheery setting. The River Room serves breakfast, lunch, and dinner. Reservations are recommended for the 200-seat restaurant.

The John Tapper Pub, in the lower level, has live jazz during happy hour from five to nine. On pleasant days, drinks are served on the patio next to the English garden.

Nicollet Island, conveniently located between Minneapolis' bustling downtown and Riverplace, an exquisite new mall decorated with brass and mirrors, has good views of the Mississippi River and the Minneapolis skyline. Unlike other inns, the Nicollet has not always housed travelers. The Island Sash and Door Company built the limestone structure in 1893. The Salvation Army used the building from 1913 to 1972. After an extensive renovation, the Nicollet Island Inn opened with a competent and friendly staff. The inn correctly retained its rough exterior appearance but the interior has a splendid new look. Even the small elevator has style: the glass sides permit inspection of the refurbished stories.

The Nicollet has a ballroom that holds 150 people and can be divided into three rooms. Another room holds 32 people. The inn has a meeting and banquet planning service. Room rates drop during the weekends as most clientele are businesspeople.

«NEW ORLEANS»

When booking New Orleans rooms, remember: For special events, such as Sugar and Super bowls, Jazz Festival, and Mardi Gras, room rates go up at least 10 percent and sometimes more. At those times most hotels also require a minimum stay of three nights. Also, French Quarter parking is at a premium, and is often an extra charge. If you are driving, this could add as much as $5–$11 to your daily tab.

——————— BED AND BREAKFAST ———————

There are two B&B listing services in New Orleans. They say they can find travelers rooms, suites, and apartments anywhere in the city. Accommodations and rates range from modest to deluxe, and all lodgings have been inspected.

Bed & Breakfast, Inc.
1236 Decatur
New Orleans, Louisiana 70116
504/525-4670

New Orleans Bed & Breakfast
P.O. Box 8163
New Orleans, Louisiana 70182
504/949-6705 and 949-4570

---------------- GUEST HOUSES ----------------

For lodgings with local color, the New Orleans guest house is unmatched anywhere. Some of the city's most sumptuous accommodations (with prices to match) and also some of its best bargains can be found tucked away behind the old walls of the French Quarter and in splendid uptown mansions near the streetcar line.

Very European in their traditions, and in fact consistently sought out by the European traveler, these hidden treasures usually have just a few rooms and offer an intimate, personal view of what it's like to live in the exotic city.

Often there are special amenities offered, such as complimentary breakfast or afternoon sherry. What's even better, hosts go to great pains to give the traveler a real sense of place.

Decor and rates vary widely, not only from place to place, but also from room to room. When making reservations it is necessary to question your host carefully as to type of beds, private baths, stairs, tub or shower—all those little details that may surprise you later, but pleasantly distinguish such accomodations from standardized hotels.

In an attempt to include as many of these little gems as possible in a limited space, little more than a listing follows, with just a few details to whet your appetite.

French Quarter

The first three listings offer all the conveniences of a deluxe hotel, but in the atmosphere of a luxurious home filled with exquisite period furnishings. Services include complimentary continental breakfast and morning paper, room service, valet parking, designer soaps, robes, hairdryers, and personalized attention from an attentive staff.

Soniat House
1133 Chartres Street
New Orleans, Louisiana 70116
504/522-0570
$90–$200

This place is so charming and noncommercial that you'll feel you're staying in a private home. From this quiet, residential end of the Quarter, an easy stroll puts you in the thick of things, but you are out of the way of the noisier revels. Rodney and Frances Smith have done a million-dollar restoration that is a labor of love. There are 24 rooms and suites, some with Jacuzzis. Some have balconies over the street; some are located around the central courtyard.

Hotel Maison De Ville
727 Toulouse
New Orleans, Louisiana 70130
800/634-1600 (tollfree)
504/561-5858

Rooms $110–$145
Cottages $275–$350

There are two superb four-star facilities here: the main hotel, a restored double townhouse located a step away from Bourbon Street madness; and the Audubon Cottages on a quieter street two blocks away, at 509 Dauphine.

The 14 antique-filled rooms include one in which Tennessee Williams completed *A Streetcar Named Desire*. One of the seven cottages was once occupied by John James Audubon. The secluded cottages all have their own walled courtyards and surround a patio swimming pool that serves all hotel guests.

Grenoble House
329 Dauphine Street
New Orleans, Louisiana 70112
504/522-1331

Suites $125–$300

Three meticulously restored townhouses display a delicate marriage of classic New Orleans architecture and sophisticated modern convenience. Seventeen suites contain a tasteful blend of antiques and contemporary furnishings, and each has a fully equipped kitchen that even includes a microwave. For noncooks who want to dine in, the famous

Arnaud's, located just around the corner, delivers an elegant repast.

The heated swimming pool with whirlpool spa is adjacent to an outdoor cabana with barbecue grill. This four-star property specializes in catering to a guest's every whim.

A Hotel—The Frenchmen
417 Frenchmen
New Orleans, Louisiana 70116
800/131-1781 (tollfree)
504/948-2166

$60–$95

A courtyard pool with Jacuzzi, rooftop patio, off-street parking, complimentary American-style full breakfast served either in your room or poolside, and home-cooked snacks and lunches make this pretty hotel a delight. Located near the French Market, the Frenchmen is in a quieter border area of the Quarter, yet is just a stroll from the action.

The hotel has 24-hour concierge service and gives guests lots of personal attention. It is also known for never raising rates for its 25 rooms, no matter what special event is taking place in the city.

La Mothe House
621 Esplanade
New Orleans, Louisiana 70116
800/567-5858 (tollfree)
504/947-1161

Rooms $75–$85
Suites $100–$155

On wide, tree-shaded Esplanade Street on the eastern boundary of the Quarter, Lamothe House offers all the Old South enchantment one could wish for, with its lavish 19th-century antiques and complimentary Creole "little breakfast" served in an opulent dining room setting.

Flagstoned courtyard, courtesy parking, room telephones, morning paper, afternoon coffee and soft drinks, 24-hour concierge, color TV, plus pleasant little attentions from the staff (such as a homemade praline on your pillow) make this one of the city's nicest values.

Dauzat House
337 Burgundy
New Orleans, Louisiana 70130
504/524-2075

$90–$250

There are just four suites here, but each is attractively different: one with a wrap-around balcony, one with its own Jacuzzi, and two former slave quarters with spiral staircases. Each suite has its special legends and decor and is furnished with antiques collected over many years by the owner.

Each suite has an all-electric kitchen provisioned each night with homemade amaretti, coffee, tea, jellies, and croissants. The enclosed courtyard contains a heated pool. No deluxe hotel services here, because the guests who come here treasure their privacy.

Dorothy Dauzat and son Donald also have six similar guesthouses scattered throughout the Quarter.

Cornstalk Hotel
915 Royal
New Orleans, Louisiana 70116
504/523-1515

$65–$95

Historic and visually arresting, this Victorian house smack in the middle of the Quarter is fronted by a rare old cast-iron cornstalk fence, one of only three in the city. Crystal chandeliers, towering ceilings, and stained-glass windows set off period furnishings to perfection. A complimentary continental breakfast is served wherever you choose: room, patio or upstairs gallery.

Lafitte Guest House
1003 Bourbon Street
New Orleans, Louisiana
800/331-7971 (tollfree)

$65–$105

The 14 rooms have lush Victorian decor, and some are located beside a pretty enclosed courtyard. A typical Victorian parlor welcomes guests, along with a complimentary carafe of wine on the first evening. Also complimentary is the delicious continental breakfast.

A special attraction of the Lafitte is its convenient Bourbon Street location, just across the street from Lafitte's Blacksmith Shop, which dates from 1772 and has live piano music until 2 A.M.

Maison Chartres
508 Chartres Street
New Orleans, Louisiana 70130
800/457-2386 (tollfree)
504/529-2172

$65–$85

A carefully preserved historic building, this guesthouse has a gemlike pool in a beautiful courtyard and three floors with 16 rooms, seven with balconies overlooking the pool or busy Chartres Street. It is conveniently located just two blocks from Jackson Square and next door to one of the city's oldest bar-restaurants, the Napoleon House.

Free continental breakfast is included in the rates.

French Quarter Maisonettes
1130 Chartres Street
New Orleans, Louisiana 70116
504/524-9918

$36–$42 for one or two

Besides the nice guest quarters surrounding a courtyard, the attraction here is the ''chatelaine,'' Mrs. Underwood, a charming lady of a certain age who welcomes her well-traveled clientele year after year to what has to be one of the best values in the Quarter.

It is a casual sort of place: the resident cats have their own spiral staircase; and Jesse, the houseman for 28 years, helps take good care of the guests. No phones in the seven maisonettes, but there are down pillows and good beds. No breakfast, but there is a tiny convenient kitchenette. You pay extra (about $5.50 per day) for parking in a nearby garage.

623 Ursalines
New Orleans, Louisiana 70116
504/529-5489

$44–$48 for one or two

The guest house called 623 Ursalines could trade places with Mrs. Underwood's place, and often does; as she usually sends them her overflow and vice versa. The buildings are similar, the number of rooms is the same, and the hosts even admit to copying her successful formula.

Uptown

The following guest houses are near the historic St. Charles streetcar line. Just an inexpensive cab or streetcar ride away from the Quarter, they offer a different but equally engaging view of life in New Orleans, set within broad vistas and Victorian architecture and furnishings. Uptown also has its share of lively restaurants, nightclubs, and shops.

Josephine Guest House
1450 Josephine
New Orleans, Louisiana
504/524-6261

$50–$90

This beautiful Italianate mansion with its fabulous antiques and hospitable hosts is without a doubt one of the city's best finds. An ebony bed made for the Hapsburgs is a honeymooners' delight. Fresh breads, a steaming pot of coffee on a breakfast tray, modern bathrooms, pristine luxury, all reveal today's graceful New Orleans life-style that echoes the splendor of a past era.

This elegant gem is located just one block from St. Charles

Avenue, the Ponchartrain Hotel, and the new Eiffel Tower Restaurant.

Terrell Guest House
1441 Magazine Street
New Orleans, Louisiana 70130
504/524-9859

$50–$75

Old, historic, and junky, Magazine Street is loaded with antique and funky furniture shops, and this lovely old building is in a run-down area now being gentrified. The 11 guest rooms are richly furnished with period antiques, oriental carpets, and gaslight chandeliers.

Complimentary continental breakfast in the dining room and evening cocktails in the parlor or courtyard add to the lure of an Old South ambience. Guests are four blocks from the streetcar line, but would need their own automobiles in this area.

The Columns Hotel
3811 St. Charles Avenue
New Orleans, Louisiana 70115
504/899-9308

$30–$85

One of the city's best known B&B operations, the Columns was once used to film the movie *Pretty Baby*, the story of a Storyville bordello. These days the opulent Victorian home turned seedy boarding house turned picturesque B&B packs the locals in daily for a gourmet buffet lunch, intimate dinners, and a 4:30–6:30 happy hour in its stunning, high-ceilinged bar. Another opportunity to mingle with the locals is the popular Sunday champagne brunch.

Stunning architecturally, the building contains antiques, stained glass, original woodwork, and a magnificent staircase. Its 15 rooms are being renovated and the process is about half done, reflected by the wide swing in rates. Six rooms have private baths; the others share.

Parkview Guest House
7004 St. Charles Avenue
New Orleans, Louisiana 70118
504/861-7564

$40–$65

Built in 1884 as a hotel for the World Cotton Exchange Exposition, this light-filled Victorian structure has 25 rooms, balconies and verandas, wonderful colored-glass windows, and the requisite antiques. It is adjacent to Audubon Park and Tulane and Loyola universities. Some of the rooms share baths. There is an airy dining room where you help yourself to the complimentary continental breakfast.

St. Charles Guest House
1748 Prytania Street
New Orleans, Lousiana 70130
504/523-6556

$30–$40

Clean and basic describe the St. Charles Guest House. Because it fills a need for an inexpensive haven with plenty of hospitality rather than deluxe creature comforts, it is also a good value. For those who are on a budget, or want to save their money to spend on other New Orleans enticements, this homey European-style operation with 26 rooms fills the bill.

A free continental breakfast, a pool and patio, and the nearby streetcar line are extra attractions.

———————— HOTELS ————————

Avenue Plaza Hotel
2111 St. Charles Avenue
New Orleans, Louisiana 70140
800/535-8575 (tollfree)
504/566-1212

Singles $80–$125
Doubles $90–$150
Suites $200–$400

For a pampered stay, the Avenue Plaza offers the ultimate
escape with its newly opened European Health Spa. The
entire second floor has been taken over and reconstructed
to feature space for exercise classes, tanning treatments,
massage, herbal wraps, shampoo and sets, makeup and beauty
treatments, and a health food bar. Access to wet area facilities costs $12 and includes the Eucalyptus Room, Scan-
dinavian sauna, Turkish steam bath, whirlpool, cardiovascular
equipment room, and Universal fitness area. A physical
screening to determine guests' current level of fitness is
conducted by a licensed physician. An extra charge is made
for massages, facials, loofah treatment, and other special
programs. Package plans include various aspects of the spa
in the price of the room. Guests can also use the weights
and stationary bike, sauna, and whirlpool on the rooftop
level free of charge.

The Avenue Plaza, which opened as a hotel in 1982, was
originally an apartment building, so that each room—singles
and suites—comes with kitchen facilities, including some
microwave ovens, coffee makers, wet bar, and large refrigerator. Suites are cozy and tastefully decorated in either
traditional or art deco styles. Air conditioning is via window
units. Revamped baths reflect the simplicity of the 1950s
style. Special corporate rates appeal to business travelers.

Sipping wine coolers beside the patio pool gives guests
a sense of neighborhood since St. Charles Avenue residences are just on the other side of the crepe myrtle trees
and ivy-covered fences. Also unique to Avenue Plaza is an
1850s antebellum home, which was moved to the site for
small meetings and wedding receptions. Period antiques
grace the high-ceilinged rooms, and guests can view a wall
of late 1800s graffiti left intact on the top floor.

Other features include a cozy bar-lounge off of the small
lobby with piano music in the evening, and Giovanni's on
the Avenue dining room, with Italian cuisine. Parking is on

site and free of charge. Twenty-four-hour room service and a concierge handle special requests.

Dauphine Orleans Hotel
415 Dauphine Street
New Orleans, Louisiana 70112
800/521-7111 (tollfree)
504/586-1800

Singles $75
Doubles $85

A bordello has been converted into a bar and lounge for this New Orleans hotel. Red lights, memorabilia, and the bar's name (Bagnio, which is translated in New Orleans as sporting house) are all that remain of the old incarnation.

The red light district of Storyville was legal in New Orleans until 1917, and legendary madames and their girls entertained tourists and the sporting gentry here. Now Storyville has vanished into history. Most of the bordellos have been demolished—Bagnio's is the exception that will allow the visitor a glimpse into the city's indiscreet past.

A meeting room and guest room within the hotel complex were once the home of John James Audubon when he was working on his Birds of America series of paintings.

The 109 rooms and 11 suites come with complimentary continental breakfast from 7 A.M. to 11 A.M., morning paper delivered to each door, goodnight treats and turndown service, valet parking (rarely free in New Orleans), a welcome cocktail, in room movies, hors d'oeuvres at cocktail time, and hotel guest transportation (in a restored Filipino jitney) within the French Quarter.

Ice is provided already bagged for guests on every floor. All rooms have clocks, color TVs, telephones, and minibar refrigerators stocked with soft drinks and snacks. There is a hot tub tucked away in one of the many courtyards and patios that lace through the hotel complex in maze fashion.

Children 12 and under stay free.

Three blocks from Canal Street, the Dauphine Orleans caters to the corporate traveler as well as the tourist. The hotel has no restaurant, but all the world-famous French

Quarter restaurants and cafes are just a few blocks away, as are the antique shops and art galleries on Royal Street, and the heart of the Quarter, Jackson Square and St. Louis Cathedral.

De la Poste
316 Chartres Street
New Orleans, Louisiana 70130
800/448-4927 (tollfree)
504/581-1200

Singles $84
Doubles $95

New Orleans brides taking their walk down the aisle in an outdoor setting often choose the courtyard of this unique motor hotel in the French Quarter. The stairs curving out from the second-story sun deck into the courtyard ooze romance. The simple French provincial architecture is a delight.

One unique aspect of the hotel is that parking is free to guests, and in fact is inside and on the premises: a rare situation in the Quarter. Telephone calls are also free, another rarity.

Old world charm and new world convenience are blended together here. The hotel is quiet and relaxing, with an air of semitropical luxury. Chez Helene is the chef and the name of the restaurant and cafe on the premises. Soul food is Chez Helene's speciality.

There are 100 spacious rooms, each with color TV and AM-FM radio. The rooms are furnished in French provincial. Bellmen are on duty 24 hours a day. Security is a top priority of management: access to the guest rooms and courtyard cannot be gained through the lobby or restaurant, and guests and visitors are monitored. The employees are friendly, with babysitting being assigned to parents of employees. Everybody knows everybody and no one is treated as a stranger.

There are sundecks and pools, and private courtyards for individual rooms and suites. The Bacchus Den Lounge offers the spirit of Mardi Gras year round.

For friendliness, cleanliness, service, a sense of the multicultural flavors of New Orleans, the comfort of informality and convenience for the automobile traveler, De la Poste is the best bargain in the French Quarter.

The Fairmont Hotel
University Place
New Orleans, Louisiana 70140
800/527-4727 (tollfree)

Singles $115–$160
Doubles $140–$185

The Fairmont Hotel is, quite simply, the ultimate in Old South luxury hotels. For old-fashioned elegance tastefully meshed with all the modern conveniences, this is the place to be.

The hotel is a block off Canal Street away from the French Quarter, which means it's quieter than most Quarter hotels. This is a large hotel: 14 stories high and a block wide; 750 rooms, including 50 suites, half of which have been completely renovated recently; 19 meeting rooms; four ballrooms, including one that can seat 4500 people; several restaurants and lounges; a heated outdoor pool and two tennis courts on the fourth floor; and a number of shops.

A revolving door leads into a lobby with 30-foot-high ceilings, antique chandeliers, large gold-leaf mirrors (decorated with real gold), huge golden columns, and Italian marble floors. Off the lobby is the famous and venerable Blue Room supper club, which hosts big-name entertainers such as Stevie Wonder and B. B. King, and a big band to provide a romantic evening of dining and dancing.

The Fairmont's restaurant, the Sazerac, is considered to be the ultimate in formal gourmet dining. The presentation of the meal is very impressive—as much a show as the entertainment in the Blue Room. The Sazerac features French, continental, and Creole cuisine. The hotel also has less expensive restaurants: Bailey's (open 24 hours a day) and Fairmont Court.

A number of luxuries are standard in the Fairmont rooms: twice-daily housekeeping plus turndown service; triple-sheeted beds with down pillows; electric shoe buffers; an alarm clock; Irish linen hand towels; a bathroom scale; bathrobes on request; high ceilings that make the rooms seem very spacious; window views of the city; and 24-hour room service.

The staff at the Fairmont is friendly and helpful, and many have been with the hotel for a very long time. More than 100 employees have been there longer than ten years, thirty more than 25 years.

Everything at the Fairmont is done with a great deal of style; even competitors have high praise for this historic hotel.

Place d'Armes Hotel
625 St. Ann Street
New Orleans, Louisiana 70116
800/535-7791
504/524-4531 (toll free)

Singles, doubles $69

There are bits and pieces of Europe all over New Orleans, most of them in the old world style showing colonial French and Spanish influence.

Modern European touches are rare, but do exist at the Place d'Armes. Much like a nice, moderately elegant pension in Italy or France, this hotel greets visitors with quiet courtyards, fountains, the soothing sound of rippling water, and swimming pools.

Breakfast of French pastry and coffee is included in the price of the room and served in a pleasantly appointed breakfast room.

The front lobby is small, as is the staff. But the guest is made to feel especially welcome, and the staff can arrange any service or tour on request. Southern hospitality dictates that any request of a guest be filled, and it is always done with charm and graciousness.

Less than a block from Jackson Square in the heart of the French Quarter, the 74 rooms (including eight suites) are in several different buildings including 18th- and 19th-century slave quarters and the "priests' house" for the fathers of St. Louis Cathedral. The lobby and administrative offices are "new" but built to conform with the architecture and style of the other buildings it unites.

There is valet parking for a fee. The hotel has an arrangement with a beauty salon around the corner, where guests have a priority status even without an appointment. Restaurants, shops, and top attractions are within walking distance.

The Pontchartrain Hotel
2031 St. Charles Avenue
New Orleans, Louisiana 70140
800/952-8092 (toll free)
504/524-0581

Singles $95 and up
Doubles $105 and up
Suites $150–$450

Few hotels ever achieve the legendary status of the Pontchartrain. Named on all the poshest lists as one of the world's top elegant hotels, the Pontchartrain is bound to surprise a first-time visitor.

It is a small hotel, so small in fact that the wide angle views magazines have used are deceptive. The entrance and lobby are faux marble. The breakfast room just inside the front entrance has a nook lined with blue patterned tiles, but the room itself is paneled in light blond wood and furnished with enough Formica to give the illusion of stepping into a bus station in mid-America circa 1955. Nevertheless, this is the "in" spot for local politicians and civic leaders to gather for morning coffee, breakfast, and debate. The Bayou Bar and the Caribbean Room (the hotel's world-famous restaurant) are covered with murals by local artists. A pianist plays nightly in the bar.

In truth, this is a hotel charm built. Family owned and operated, with each visitor being treated as a favorite guest, the hotel has been popular since it opened in 1927. Many guests are permanent residents and the Crescent City's most colorful characters. (For example, the oldest living carnival

queen and the richest grande dames of the city's social and
financial circles live here full time.)

The management claims that no two rooms in the hotel
are the same. Each is generously sprinkled with antiques
and art. Doormen and elevator operators are on duty 24
hours a day. The front desk can arrange to fulfill any guest's
request. Third-generation owner-operator Honore Aschaf-
fenburg says, "We will stand on our heads if that's what
our guests want."

The 100 rooms and baths are some of the smallest in the
city. Employees have been with the hotel in many cases for
over 30 years and reflect the philosophy of the owners that
"hotels are more than bricks and mortar."

Room service operates from about 7 A.M. to about 11
P.M. There is valet parking for a fee. The hotel is located
in the Garden District, the old American sector of the Creole
city, and is neighbor to some of the poshest antebellum
mansions in New Orleans.

The Saint Charles Street electric streetcar passes right in
front of the hotel, giving easy and picturesque access to
downtown and the French Quarter in about 20 minutes.

Prytania Park Hotel
1525 Prytania Street
New Orleans, Louisiana 70130
800/862-1984 (tollfree)
504/524-0427

Singles $39–$49
Doubles $49–$59
Deluxe/junior suites $59–$69

Efficiency and European-style guest rooms of the Prytania
Park Hotel are clustered in a neighborhood of wrought
iron–decorated mansions and New Orleans–style shotgun
houses of the Lower Garden District. Guests get to know
the friendly staff easily in this limited-service guesthouse,
since the desk clerk will likely help with the luggage as well
as check guests in. Even though there's no concierge, the
staff cheerfully assist guests with special requests.

In the Victorian House, the original 13 rooms have recently been redecorated with burnished pine "rice-carved" beds and armoires and pastel-hued fabrics. The house dates from the 1850s, and all but one room have nonfunctioning fireplaces. Brick walls, high ceilings, ceiling fans, and balconies add to the sense of life in an earlier, lazier era. The emphasis here is on a room designed to take the harshness off the hustling world beyond the Prytania Street address.

In the newer 49-room section, rooms feature mahogany wall units with European pulldown double beds designed by the owner, Alvin Halpern, who also owns the Home Furnishings Shop. This allows maximum living space during the day and a restful area at night. Each room has a refrigerator, microwave, desk, and eating area. Deluxe rooms feature a second-story loft bedroom with queen-size bed reached by a spiral staircase. Several rooms have standard beds permanently in place.

A complimentary European-style breakfast is available in the small lobby, with trays to encourage guests to enjoy the fresh pastries in the patio or take them to their rooms. A small commissary has a selection of light meals and snacks to purchase and prepare in guest rooms. The Prytania Park is located a block from the St. Charles streetcar, 12 blocks from the central business district, and 15 blocks from the French Quarter. Off-street parking is free.

This pristine, attractive hotel is one of the best values in New Orleans accommodations. It is charming and has every convenience.

Quality Inn Maison St. Charles
1319 St. Charles Avenue
New Orleans, Louisiana 70130
800/228-5151 (tollfree)

Singles, doubles $49 (each extra person $5)
Suite executives $59

Don't let the Quality Inn in front of Maison St. Charles's name fool you. The Maison St. Charles is located in the Uptown section of New Orleans on part of the old Bienville plantation, and includes five pre–Civil War buildings that have been renovated for guests.

The staff likes to call the Maison St. Charles the best-kept secret in New Orleans, and is quick to do a little celebrity guest name dropping to show this is a place even the rich and famous choose as a hideaway while visiting the Crescent City. Since this is a bit off the beaten path, you avoid the noise and rowdiness of the French Quarter, except when you purposefully seek it out.

Although not in the French Quarter, the hotel is on the streetcar route. Sixty cents brings visitors to the French Quarter in minutes, or, by going in the opposite direction, to see the Garden District and visit the world-class Audubon Zoo. The 150-year-old streetcar system runs 24 hours a day, so there's no worry about being stranded after hours.

Some of Maison St. Charles's offerings are a swimming pool surrounded by a lush, tropical courtyard, a heated whirlpool, airport limousine service, oversized beds, concierge service, antique furnishings in some rooms, suites with 14-foot ceilings and hanging chandeliers, tour arrangements, and banquet facilities for up to 300 guests. There is also an 1850s-style restaurant and lounge called Beauregards.

The bed and breakfast rate of $49 includes a continental breakfast, streetcar ride, and free parking. ''Suite executives'' are in the restored antebellum houses, and include (in addition to the above) a cocktail on arrival, morning newspapers, and extras such as champagne and cheese and cracker trays in the room.

The Maison St. Charles is also on the Mardi Gras parade route, and crowds here aren't as large as in the central business district and French Quarter. As with all hotels in New Orleans, rates are higher for Mardi Gras and other special events, and you need to make reservations many months in advance.

You can't beat the rates at the Maison St. Charles, and you're likely to be pleasantly surprised you can get accommodations this nice in New Orleans without spending a lot more.

Le Richelieu
1234 Chartres Street
New Orleans, Louisiana 70116
800/535-9653 (tollfree)

Singles $60–$75
Doubles $70–$80
Additional guests $10

If you want to take advantage of the famed nightlife of the French Quarter, and then retreat to a place quiet enough for a decent rest, check into the reasonably priced Le Richelieu motor inn on Chartres Street.

The historic four-story Le Richelieu is located only a few blocks from Bourbon Street, the French Market, and Jackson Square—far enough away for rest and quiet when you need it, yet within walking distance of the action the French Quarter is famous for. And you won't have to sacrifice charm and comfort for a moderately priced room.

The Greek Revival Le Richelieu was renovated into a hotel in 1964 from two historic buildings, a macaroni factory, and five mid-19th-century rowhouses. The lobby features a French interior, antique chandeliers and black and white marble floor tiles. No two of the 88 rooms in the hotel are exactly alike, and each room has brass ceiling fans, large mirrors, refrigerators, and art and furnishings individually selected. All of the rooms have windows with a view, and many have access to a balcony on the second and third floors overlooking either the street or the hotel's pool and courtyard.

The hotel's restaurant doesn't try to compete with the many fine (and expensive) restaurants in the Quarter, but it does provide an informal low-cost meal—hamburgers, crepes, sandwiches, soup and salad—for the convenience of guests.

The hotel has a friendly, family atmosphere, and is more casual than most in the area. The staff is helpful; their motto is that every staff member is a concierge—willing to help in any way possible, by suggesting a restaurant and making reservations, arranging tours, babysitting, performing room service, valet or laundry service, or fulfilling other requests.

Since this is a small hotel, it can accommodate meetings

of only up to 20 people. The hotel has the advantage of free parking on the premises, which is rare in the French Quarter. A deposit of the first night's rental is required to hold reservations.

Royal Orleans
621 St. Louis Street
New Orleans, Louisiana 70140
800/843-6664 (tollfree)
504/529-5333

Rooms $95–$165 single occupancy, $158–$190 double occupancy
Suites $195–$395 single occupancy, $438–553 double occupancy

Staying in the French Quarter at the Royal Orleans is like being part of the heartbeat of the city. The cozy Esplanade Lounge, removed from the reception area, is where New Orleanians gather for after-dinner drinks and dessert, or to listen to piano music. Locals refer to the hotel as the Royal "O." In the afternoon, cups of Twinings tea or coffee are served with English scones or finger sandwiches. Locals don't think of the club-style Rib Room as a hotel restaurant. Beside the bar you'll see wine cubbyholes with brass nameplates: local wine connoisseurs store their vintage stock here.

Part of the reason for the Orleans's appeal is the efficient yet down-home service of the ample staff. Most have been with the hotel for at least 15 years, and some go as far back as the '60s, when the hotel first opened its doors. Since that time, four times its original cost has been poured into the hotel to keep it in the grand style of the Old Saint Louis Hotel, which originally occupied the site. The gold-leaf mirror in the lobby passage is actually from the Old Saint Louis, on permanent loan from the Louisiana State Museum.

Now an Omni Classic, the Royal Orleans has rooms and suites with a phone in the bath, consistent turndown service, and Jacuzzis and steam baths in some suites. A fitness room with exercise equipment and aerobics classes are available. The hotel has a rooftop pool in a lush garden setting with a Casablanca-style patio bar. An observation deck with telescope is one flight above. By the way, you're likely to rub elbows with locals around the pool in summer, since many maintain lockers and pool privileges at the hotel. An on-site garage offers valet parking for an additional charge.

A few rooms have access to an inner courtyard. Others have balconies overlooking the French Quarter streets. From the skylit breakfast room of the Cafe Royale to an evening meal in the roof-level La Riviera (during seasonal operation), the hotel is self-contained, with laundry service, shops, barber and beauty shops, and babysitting services. Yet one only has to open the inner shutters of the room to hear the echo of horses' hooves, a reminder of the thriving French Quarter life just outside.

The Royal Sonesta
300 Bourbon Street
New Orleans, Louisiana 70140
800/343-7170 (tollfree)

Singles $95–$145
Doubles $105–$155
Suites $195–$500

One thing's for sure. If you stay at the Royal Sonesta, you won't forget what city you're in, because the Sonesta *is* New Orleans. It features inviting, tropical landscaping in an outstanding courtyard, Creole and French cuisine presented with impressive flair at Beque's restaurant, and hand-painted tiles of Mardi Gras Crewes that decorate the Mystick Den Lounge.

The Royal Sonesta has one of the most prestigious addresses in New Orleans, right next to all the party action Bourbon Street is famous for. Venture outside of the hotel, and you are immediately surrounded by live music flowing from Bourbon Street hotspots. Join the high-spirited crowds strolling the street (which is closed to motor traffic), and dine at the best of restaurants. In fact, there are so many fine restaurants in the area, it's nearly impossible to make a bad choice.

Every room at the Sonesta has a view, either of the street

scene or of the courtyard, fountain, and pool area. Most rooms have double french doors framed by full-length shutters opening out onto a balcony framed by traditional lace wrought-iron rails.

Staff at the Royal Sonesta are quick to assist guests in need of advice, information, or services. Many staff members have been with the hotel since it was opened about 17 years ago, and are very knowledgeable about the city. The staff, which includes a concierge, will arrange tours and limousine service, recommend restaurants or nightclubs, exchange foreign currency, cash personal checks, and provide translation services for foreign guests. Other services include babysitting, one-day valet service, and 24-hour room service.

There are a number of nice extras in the Sonesta's rooms: comfortable bathrobes; down pillows (and mixture of hard and soft); a mint placed on the pillow as part of the turndown service; complimentary nuts, fruit, and wine for special guests; a choice of queen, king or two double beds; and complimentary *Wall Street Journals* and local newspapers (on request).

There are several restaurants with a range of prices, a cabaret, oyster bar, the Mystick Den Lounge, a tobacco shop, flower shop, gem shop, and more.

Although the Sonesta has 500 rooms, the hotel is arranged in such a fashion that it doesn't feel that large. The hotel takes up an entire city block, built around one of the largest courtyards in the city. The plant life in the courtyard is so dense that it's quite easy to find a lovely spot all to yourself. On those rare occasions when temperatures drop below freezing, the entire courtyard is covered by a huge canopy to prevent frost damage to the plants.

And during those long, hot Southern summers, the hotel's large pool is the center attraction, a great place to sunbathe or just cool off while enjoying the scenery.

The Saint Louis
730 Bienville Street
New Orleans, Louisiana 70140
800/535-9111 (tollfree)

Singles $95–$135
Doubles $105–$150
Extra person $10

The charm of old New Orleans is recalled at the Saint Louis, a small luxury hotel in the French Quarter. The Saint Louis is a relatively new brick and stucco hotel built around a lovely small courtyard that is particularly appealing at night, when the fountain is lit, and light filters out from the hotel restaurant's fan windows into the yard. The brick courtyard is so romantic that many local couples choose to be married there.

The hotel has 68 rooms, and two fine French restaurants, the Louis XVI, and the Savoir Faire. The hotel's decor is French all the way, from the imported parquet floor in the lobby to the period furniture and bidets in the rooms. About a third of the rooms have balconies (very popular during Mardi Gras), either on the street or the courtyard. Some of the hotel's suites actually have their own private courtyard.

The Saint Louis has a good location on Rue Bienville between Bourbon and Royal. There are no shops in the hotel, but it is within walking distance of all the many specialty shops, antique stores, and fashion houses that are found in the French Quarter.

There is a concierge to provide personal service, and tours are available twice a day. Typists, stenographers, and translators can be hired, and a house physician is on call at all times. Babysitting and one-day valet service are available. You can receive complimentary newspapers on request. There are meeting facilities for small groups.

The Saint Louis is considered a quiet hotel—by French Quarter standards—that specializes in personalized service.

Windsor Court Hotel
300 Gravier Street
(at Tchoupitoulas)
New Orleans, Louisiana 70140
800/262-2662 (tollfree)
504/523-6000

Suites $125–$175

Discreetly luxurious are the best words to describe the Windsor Court, one of the finest hotels to have been built in the United States in the last decade and a must in any listing of grand hotels. When New Orleanian James Julius Coleman Jr. built this classy new addition to the New Orleans hotel scene in 1984, he was out to provide travelers with the very best of everything, with more than a hint of England thrown in for good measure.

The place is so very English, for example, that paintings of Windsor Castle are everywhere, and of an afternoon both hotel guests and high-style locals indulge in the gracious British custom of high tea, complete with imported teas, scones, clotted cream, and chamber music.

Dining in the Grill Room is also an experience reminiscent of London—say the Connaught—although Creole dishes join continental for that necessary, and delectable, bow to New Orleans. A magnificent Lalique table in the foyer, subtle shades of peach and green, Edwardian-era country scenes, an extensive wine list, and tuxedoed waiters set the scene.

Conveniently located just off the river and adjacent to the New Orleans business district, across Canal Street from the French Quarter, the Windsor Court provides wonderful views of the big Mississippi, which meanders through the heart of the city, as well as the convenience of valet parking and a complete health facility with a 75-foot pool featuring piped-in underwater music.

Although the hotel is within walking distance of the Quarter, late at night, cabs are plentiful and preferable to walking alone around lower Canal Street.

This masterful blend of Old World elegance and contemporary design was actually built around a million-dollar collection of artworks from the 17th, 18th, and 19th centuries—paintings, sculpture, and tapestries that could grace any museum. Each of its 330 spacious suites contains princely furnishings, huge closets, and marble baths, and features every amenity known to hotels, such as turndown service, terry cloth robes, hair dryers, English soaps and shampoos, even chocolates in the fridge.

The stylish hostelry gives extraordinarily good value for

the money spent. With its exquisite appointments and its impeccably dressed and suavely polished staff, the Windsor Court goes that extra mile to pamper and delight its guests. This elegant, mid-sized European-style hotel has set new standards of excellence in a city where European-style elegance has been in fashion for centuries.

«NEW YORK CITY»

To include all of the hotels in New York that have been called "best" would have made this chapter the length of a book. To include only those usually mentioned as New York's superlative hostelries—such as the Carlyle, the Waldorf-Astoria, the St. Regis, and the Pierre, to name only four—would have eliminated many of the smaller or more modest establishments that are by far the best of their class. Indeed, New York's low-profile hotels of whatever price range often provide travelers with a very memorable stay, perhaps for the very reason that they are not legends—yet.

Room rates in New York are among the highest in the United States: A room for $90 is considered by many a bargain. About half of the establishments in this chapter fall below the $100 per night mark, while the other half start at $100 and go up. A couple of ways to beat the high prices are to stay outside the midtown area, in neighborhoods such as the Upper West Side, and to consider staying in a bed and breakfast listed with one of the agencies covered here. As always, keep in mind that some rates may have risen since researched. When budgeting a trip to New York City, travelers should remember to add 8.25 percent sales tax and $2 per day per room occupancy tax to the rates listed in this chapter.

BED AND BREAKFAST

The B&B Group (New Yorkers At Home)
301 East 60th Street
New York, New York 10022
212/838-7015, Monday–Thursday only, 9 A.M.–4 P.M.

Urban Ventures, Inc.
Box 426
New York, New York 10024
212/594-5650

New World Bed and Breakfast, Ltd.
150 Fifth Avenue
New York, New York 10011
800/443-3800 (tollfree)
212/675-5600

Hosts & Guests, Inc.
Box 6798, FDR Station
New York, New York 10150
212/874-4308, Monday–Saturday only, 9–11 A.M.
    and 4–7 P.M.

Singles $40 and up
Doubles $55 and up

Even most New Yorkers don't know that one of the best ways to beat the high cost of the city's hotels is to book a room through a B&B agency. This is not for everybody, however. Travelers who would not feel comfortable in a stranger's apartment (there are always vestiges of the owner) and those looking for service should look elsewhere. In many cases, business travelers should also probably look elsewhere. But anyone looking to save on accommodations might consider going the B&B route. Since accommodations and hosts vary widely, certain guidelines should be followed. It is important to remember that this is not like staying at a hotel. In choosing B&B, travelers have to put up with what New Yorkers have to put up with.

Location is of primary importance. Out-of- towners might not feel comfortable in newly gentrified areas that New Yorkers take for granted. Though usually safe, these areas may be ragged around the edges. Before committing to a B&B arrangement, travelers should question the agency on the neighborhood and remember that the agency is talking from a New York standpoint.

Next in importance is safety. New Yorkers develop a sixth sense about potential danger which out of towners might not have. Travelers should make sure they have agreed to an arrangement where they will feel and be safe. This might mean requesting a building with a doorman, an elevator operator, or the like, especially if the neighborhood is borderline.

Other things to consider are privacy (whether or not the owner—and his or her children—are on the premises), smoking or nonsmoking, private or shared bath, telephone, television, pets, and—a must in the summer—air conditioning.

Agencies have supposedly inspected all apartments thoroughly, so they should be able to answer any questions.

A good example of a B&B is an apartment on West 88th Street, a block and a half from Central Park West, listed with the B&B Group and other agencies. It may also be reserved by contacting the owner, who occupies the upstairs section, directly at 800/367-3003 or 212/867-7318. This would be best for the adventurous traveler who would enjoy a neighborhood away from midtown that is in the process of gentrifying. The owner is a young woman who runs a cooking class in the upstairs section of this apartment in a beautifully renovated brownstone. Past three sets of locked doors, the clean ground floor bedroom and adjoining bath are a real gem—more inviting than the majority of hotel rooms costing three times the $55 single or $65 double tariff.

A standout element is cherry wood wainscoting in the bedroom and hall area, carved cherry molding, and a nonworking fireplace with a cherry mantle. Other aspects of the cozy room are oak doors, wall-to-wall carpeting, white walls hung with a watercolor of the brownstone and another of the kitchen, a queen-size bed, a walnut vanity table with mirror, and a rocking chair decked out with pillows and teddy bears. A bookcase is full of readable material.

A telephone and answering machine can be used by guests. There is also a Sony color T.V. and electric blanket. However, there is no air conditioning. The bathroom features brown Mexican tiles in the bath-shower and a vanity sink with mirror.

Breakfast is either served by the host or set up for self service. This might consist of cranberry bread, or lemon walnut bread, or perhaps eggs and coffee and herbal teas. The host also provides information on nearby Columbus Avenue restaurants in the heart of the Upper West Side renaissance. In addition, maps and guidebooks and inside information on sightseeing are provided.

The procedure for booking a B&B is similar among the agencies. At the B&B Group travelers choose from a list of available apartments. It is best to phone to inquire about availability. Otherwise, at least seven choices in order of priority should be given. The minimum stay is two nights, and reservations should be made at least three weeks in advance.

A deposit is required for each night of stay. In some cases the full amount is required in advance. Upon receipt of payment, travelers receive the name and address of their host, who should be called before arrival to confirm time. Guests are required to fill out a short questionnaire, which is forwarded to the host.

There are substantial charges for cancellations and changes, making it difficult to change accommodations if, once seen, they are not to a guest's liking.

HOTELS

The Drake
440 Park Avenue
(at 56th Street)
New York, New York 10022
800/372-5369 (tollfree)
212/421-0900

Singles $160–$190
Doubles $180–$210
Suites $365–$575

The Swiss are among the world's greatest hoteliers, so
it's no surprise that since 1981, when Swissotel purchased
the Drake, this aging Park Avenue dowager has shown
welcome signs of Swiss savoir faire. A hefty refurbishing
brought the lobby burnished wood, brass lamps, and an
Alpine-size clock that chimes. All of this sets a quaint,
innlike tone, making this 640-room, 49-suite establishment
seem a lot smaller than it really is.

The Swiss connection also gives reason for such Helvetian
niceties as Birchermuesli and Bundnerfleisch on the breakfast menu, as well as rosti and air-dried meats from the
Grison Alps available from a 24-hour room service. A large
bowl of Swiss chocolates is strategically placed on the check-
in counter, attracting chocoholics from every stratum of the
Drake clientele which ranges from celebrities on the Phil
Donahue show to business people to elderly travelers.

Six types of accommodations are offered, including three
categories of rooms of increasing size, and junior, one-,
and two-bedroom suites.

The rooms—somewhat larger than the average New York
City hotel room, since the building was constructed in 1926
as residential—are being transformed from an acceptable
but standard hotel look to something more homelike. Rooms
are currently in either green and white or earth tones.
Printed curtains match printed bedspreads. Walls are hung
with tasteful Asian art. Desk space and lighting are sufficient
for working. The best part of the decor is a live plant
in every room, tended by the hotel's own in-house plant
specialist.

All guest rooms have refrigerators, 24-hour cable TV,
rental movies, digital AM-FM alarm clock radios, direct-
dial phones with message signal and call waiting, full-length
mirrors, ample closet space, and satin and wood hangers
that are not attached to the closet. Refrigerators are discreetly hidden in wooden cabinets.

For the nightly turn down service, someone freshens the

room and deposits a bar of Swiss Cailler chocolate on pillows.

Tile baths in muted tones of yellow and green feature a radio speaker and a second telephone. Complimentary amenities include Neutrogena soap, special face cloths, bath foam, a sewing kit, shoe polisher, and shower cap.

Suites are already residential in look and feel, and include an in-room safe, hair dryers in the bath, and, in six instances, terraces with neighborhood views. The best suites to ask for are the outstanding 2020, and numbers 529 and 522.

All rooms have Thermapane windows for noise control and energy conservation—something other hotels in midtown should take note of.

The lobby, which was actually redone by internationally known architect-designer Adam Tihany, leads into intimate seating at Cafe Suisse, which serves Swiss and continental snacks and provides a wine and champagne bar. Here, to accompanying piano music, guests can order 12 different kinds of champagne ranging from Pommery Extra Dry to Louis Roederer Cristal Brut, by the glass.

At one far end of the lobby is an extravagant new French restaurant where Louis Outhier, chef at the acclaimed L'Oasis in La Napoule, acts as a consultant.

Also new to the lobby area is a Swiss chocolate shop. A lobby newsstand sells domestic and foreign publications.

Special guest services at the Drake include a concierge, shoeshine service, 24-hour valet parking, complimentary morning limousine service to Wall Street, free access to the tony Atrium Health Club, and a free baggage check-in at the hotel for guests departing JFK on Swissair.

In addition, each guest receives a copy of what must be the world's most esoteric in-hotel magazine, with high quality photographs and articles on various Swiss regions.

The Drake is at the geographic heart of Manhattan, close to Trump Tower, Fifth Avenue, and many corporate headquarters.

The Excelsior Hotel
45 West 81st Street
(between Central Park West and Columbus Avenue)
New York, New York 10024
212/362-9200

Singles $56
Doubles $66
Suites $92–$145

The 300-room Excelsior, built in the mid-twenties, is primarily recommended by price and location—the prices start at a little over a welcome $50 per night.

Excelsior management stresses that this is a "family" hotel, meaning that none of the hanky panky or lunatic fringe sometimes connected with an inexpensive hotel in New York exists here. In fact, the clientele consists of professors from nearby Columbia University, curators from the Museum of Natural History (located right across the street) and youthful visitors from France, Germany, Italy, and America's hinterlands.

Located only a half block from Columbus Avenue, the main artery of the Upper West Side, the Excelsior is near inventive boutiques, hot new restaurants, and expensive co-ops.

The sunken lobby looks out over a park connected to the Museum of Natural History and a bus shelter that provides a quick link to the Upper East Side and the Metropolitan Museum of Art.

Wood paneling (nobody knows what wood), a ceiling with decorative molding, and a wall display of clocks showing the time in New York, Moscow, Geneva, London, Tel Aviv, Tokyo, Paris, and Buenos Aires are the predominant design elements.

Just off the lobby is a typical New York coffeeshop with pleasant help and real coffeeshop prices—rare in connection with a hotel.

At these prices in New York, travelers shouldn't expect much in the way of room decor, but rooms are surprisingly nice in a motel-modern kind of way. More than half the rooms have been renovated and most of the others are in various stages of renovation (some might have such flaws as cracks in the ceiling or slightly peeling wallpaper).

The single/double rooms have walls covered with patterned wallpaper that blends well with curtains and bedspreads in a blue floral pattern, and new carpeting in a sculpted blue pattern. Beds, a dresser with built-in desk, and a night table are in a matching wood set with the beds sporting cane backing.

The bathroom is standard, with white and blue tile floors, a medicine cabinet, the same wallpaper as in the room, and mustard towels and a matching mustard shower curtain. The bathtub is slightly more substantial than tubs found in newer hotels.

Two-room suites come with a kitchenette, and the hotel supplies pots and pans. The living room includes a desk, TV, blue pullout couch, end tables with brass lamps, and a coffee table. There is also a dining table with two chairs.

Rooms are air conditioned in summer, and all have color TV, but are not hooked up for cable.

Travelers should request rooms that are renovated or that overlook the museum (or both) when making reservations. Because of the low price and good location, it is advisable to make reservations well in advance.

Golden Tulip Barbizon
140 East 63rd Street
(at Lexington Avenue)
New York, New York 10021
800/223-1020 and 800/522-5669 (tollfree)
212/838-5700

Singles $85–$145
Doubles $135–$165
Suites $200–$300

The Barbizon, a New York landmark near another New York landmark—Bloomingdale's—is a good place to stay for a small but attractive $85 single in spiffy surroundings. All accommodations, in fact, offer very good value for such a high-rent neighborhood.

This 342-room, 10-suite hotel arrived on the New York

scene in 1927. However, even now, many New Yorkers don't associate its name with its real namesake: France's Barbizon school of painters. Moreover, there are probably still a few who don't know it was transformed from a residence for women, where the likes of Grace Kelly, Gene Tierney, and many others first bedded down in New York, into a first-class hotel.

Perhaps because of its location in an area catering to the design, decoration, art, and antique crowd, this is one of the new breed of hotels where much attention has been given to avoid cliches in hotel design. The Barbizon is listed on the National Register of Historic Places.

Existing details of the lobby have been retained by award-winning interior designer Judith Stockman. Contemporary additions incorporate colors and lighting effects that inspired the Barbizon school of painters. Skylights draw in natural daylight, which plays off pink marble and sandstone columns. A trompe l'oeil work of art by Richard Haas graces the lobby ceiling.

Overlooking the lobby, from a floor above, is the Barbizon Restaurant. A special $14.95 table d'hote lunch offers exceedingly good value by New York standards. The restaurant's Dover sole is one of the city's best renditions of this entree.

One of several special event rooms, the adjacent Rousseau Room is a 1700-square-foot space accommodating up to 200. Dark oak paneling, coffered ceilings, stained-glass windows devoted to each of the Barbizon painters, a large pipe organ, and a fireplace have been restored to their original beauty.

Guest rooms, which are more attractive than some higher-priced hotels, feature "bee"-patterned bedspreads. Based on traditional French designs, they were created by Milton Glaser, America's premier graphic artist. (Glaser also created the distinctive signage seen around the hotel.)

Room chairs are functional versions of French antiques with patterned fabrics in peach and melon. Desk space is adequate yet unobtrusive. The single telephone does not stretch as far as the bed in many cases.

Cabinets for storing clothes have been ingeniously built

into closets with white louvered doors. This is extremely important in the very compact $85 petite, where space is at a premium. Coat hangers are attached to the closet.

Stylish French art posters hang from the walls. Window treatments, featuring narrow-slatted venetian blinds or white shutters, allow for natural lighting and windows that actually open.

Bathrooms, some with magnifying mirrors, feature wall-size mirrors, massage shower heads, make-up lights, and tile floors. (The $85 petite provides only a shower.)

Room service, operating from 6:30 A.M. to 11:45 P.M. daily, charges saner prices than many New York hotels, including such offerings as a platter of Holland cheeses with fruit. Wake-up calls are on time, and a complimentary newspaper is delivered with breakfast if ordered.

Adjacent to the lobby, in addition to the flower shop, jewelry shop and newsstand, is a bar where piano music is played in the evening.

Cafe Barbizon serves breakfast (yogurt, cereals, croissants) and light meals until midnight. A hot breakfast is served at the Barbizon Restaurant.

Gramercy Park Hotel
2 Lexington Avenue
(at 21st Street)
800/221-4083 (tollfree from outside New York State)
212/475-4320

Singles $85–$90
Doubles $90–$95
Suites $115–$125

The 500-room Gramercy Park Hotel's rates, and access to New York's most lovely park, are what recommend it.

Gramercy Park is a quiet residential area where some of the most elegant brownstones in New York surround a private square, London-style. This area offers a pleasant alternative to midtown, and guests are given the same privilege as residents: use of a key to enter the park.

The warm, L-shaped lobby, fresh from having its pine paneling stripped back to its original beauty, is the hotel's strong point. Comfortable chairs sit under crystal chandeliers on geometric-pattern carpeting.

Off the lobby, the restaurant, also with crystal chandeliers, and a maitre d' in black tie, is more formal looking than customary for this type of hotel. The hours are from 7:30 A.M. to 10:30 P.M., with selections ranging from Chateaubriand to Jell-o. There is also room service operating during the same hours.

The Gramercy Park Hotel Bar, open until 1 A.M. and offering a piano player in the evening, is sometimes frequented by neighborhood residents as well as hotel guests.

Rooms at the Gramercy Park, though clean and good-sized, are not always in mint condition (blinds slightly askew, scrapes in a bath tub). All rooms have a safe in the closet, air conditioning (units are stored in closets during winter months), and television, and some have small refrigerators, which can be requested if needed and absent. Furniture—the requisite king-size bed, night tables, desk, sitting chairs, and dressers—is chunky and sometimes marble topped. New brown wall-to-wall carpeting and brass lamps brighten things up a bit.

At less than the price of a room at most uptown hotels, suites offer the luxury of an extra room. Some suites have fireplaces (nonworking) and kitchenettes. A family suite offers two double beds and a fold-out couch in the living room.

Travelers should request rooms overlooking Gramercy Park.

For some curious reason, the Gramercy Park attracts rock groups, middle management from the insurance industry (offices located nearby), and vacation travelers. Guests at the hotel can arrange for nearby, 24-hour parking for $10 a day—a bargain in New York.

Hotel Algonquin
59 West 44th Street
(between Fifth Avenue and Avenue of the Americas)
New York, New York 10036
212/840-6800

Singles $92–$114
Doubles $95–$114
Suites $182–$428

Providing a copy of the *New Yorker* for every guest room and steeped in civility without being stuffy, the Algonquin is decidedly the thinking person's hotel. Long as oasis for the literati (and Broadway gliterati), the hotel maintains rates that are surprisingly sensible for a place of so much substance.

Needless to say, the Algonquin is a New York landmark. It's here that Alexander Woolcott, Robert Benchley, George S. Kaufman, Dorothy Parker, and others formed the Algonquin Round Table and became the arbiters of the '20s and '30s. It's here that Lerner and Loewe wrote much of *My Fair Lady*, Tallulah Bankhead first lived in New York, and Angela Lansbury stayed while starring in *Mame*.

Built in 1902, and with fewer than 190 rooms, the Algonquin is virtually equidistant between Brooks Brothers and most Broadway shows. Here on a dreary but safe stretch of West 44th Street, the mood changes dramatically upon entering the dark paneled, slightly dated lobby.

Actually, it is more like an English club than a lobby, with a grandfather's clock, a galaxy of smart table lamps, and couches and clusters of chairs around tables outfitted with a bell for summoning martinis.

A magazine stand with esoteric titles and a theater ticket service are set in the lobby's southwest corner, and Hamlet III, the resident cat who recently appeared in a revival of *You Can't Take It With You*, can be found at various points throughout.

The adjacent Rose Room (where the Round Table actually met), appropriately done up in rose and white, is the creation of set designer Oliver Smith, who also designed special summer slip covers for the lobby.

The Rose Room vies with the paneled Oak Room and Chinese Room for in-hotel dining. Tea is served in the Oak Room, which later in the evening becomes a classy supper club with fabled chanteuses or chanteurs interpreting Gershwin, Porter, and Sondheim two shows a night, five nights a week.

Another bar, the Blue Room (although it hasn't been blue for years), stays open late and boasts drawings by James Thurber and Thornton Wilder.

One of the pleasures of life at the Algonquin comes from the lack of computers, mechanical cheerfulness, and other dehumanizing devices. It is one of the few hotels where reservations are actually kept on a card. After each stay, a guest's preferences are noted for future reference.

The bellman has been there for so long that he has devised his own theory about the relationship of the amount of guests' luggage to the seasons. And owner Ben Bodne once said that the day a budget required self-service elevators is the day he would sell the Algonquin.

Cozy rooms and hallways have been spruced up by Claire Fraser, a designer friend of managing director Andrew Anspach who normally works on residences in New York and Palm Beach. A typical room features chic, dark-colored walls with contrasting white trim, curtains from Clarence House or Liberty of London with fabric valences, a brass bed, mahogany chest of drawers with a built-in desk, a print or two depicting the lively arts, large mirrors, and wall-to-wall carpeting. Radios and TV's are concealed in wood cabinets.

Baths have newly installed tubs, crisp black and white tiles circa 1948, and black and white printed wallpaper extending over the ceiling.

The Regency-style Playbill Suite is decorated with 56 *Playbill* covers relating to over 50 years of Broadway productions in which celebrated Algonquin guests played a role. Suites of varying size can accommodate one to six persons.

All hotel services, including a somewhat creaky room service that operates during normal waking hours, are provided. After 5 P.M. Friday, garage parking directly opposite the entrance is complimentary for a minimum two-night visit until 5 P.M. Sunday or 10 A.M. Monday.

Check-out time is a very civilized 3 P.M.

Hotel Empire
Broadway at 63rd Street
New York, New York 10023
800/221-6509 and 800/223-9868 (tollfree)
212/265-7400

Singles $70–$95
Doubles $85–$110
Family Rooms $90–$110 (up to four persons)
No charge for children under 14 sharing room with
    parents

Special rates for students, faculty, government, military,
    and clergy.

Location and price have always been the main attraction
of this 500-room hotel originally built as a residential struc-
ture in the late 1920s. Although a reasonable room rate in
New York so often brings a whole pack of undesirable
elements—depressing neighborhood, crime, or worse—the
Empire's location, directly across the street from Lincoln
Center, and at the gateway to the upwardly mobile Upper
West Side, happily avoids all that.

Except for an approximate 10 percent increase in room
rates, none of this will change when a massive overhaul is
completed by autumn 1986. And guests will get a shiny
new room, to boot.

The new lobby, now complete with real trees, marble
floors and benches, mauve carpeting, and art deco lighting
fixtures, harkens changes still to come.

Some hotels just renovate the lobby and forget about the
rooms, but this will not be the case at the Empire. Although
the clean but tatty rooms have been sufficient enough to
attract the likes of the Berlin Philharmonic, numerous bus
tours, and others, new wallpaper, new furniture, new carpeting, new curtains with new matching bedspreads, and
additional items will transform existing accommodations
into something more light and airy.

Even more attention will be given to floors where rooms
will be rented at higher rates to primarily business travelers.
Features will include queen-size beds, colonial furniture,

tasteful matching drapes and bedspreads, a wooden desk, a wing chair with table, a luggage bench and a color TV concealed in an armoire.

Also planned for the "new" Empire are a guest services rep who will provide some of the services of a concierge, valet dry cleaning, and a gift shop in the lobby.

Rooms already come with air conditioning and color TV. Family rooms, two connecting twins, provide especially good value at pre-renovation rates of $90 to $110.

The lobby provides access to a coffee shop, but just outside the main entrance to the hotel is a separate entrance to O'Neals Balloon restaurant, which is a real New Yorker haunt appropriate before or after Lincoln Center.

Hotel Empire is one block from the New York Coliseum and close to Central Park. Valet parking is available.

Hotel Kitano
66 Park Avenue
(at 38th Street)
New York, New York 10016
212/685-0022

Singles $90–$105
Doubles $110–$120
Suites $170

The 93-room Hotel Kitano is, perhaps, New York's most singular hotel. It is the city's only Japanese managed hotel—the current general manager is an alumnus of the distinguished Imperial Hotel in Tokyo. Although 70 percent of its clientele is Japanese (the brochure states, "Even those in New York for the first time can feel as comfortable and safe as they would in Japan"), close proximity to the garment district, good service, and prices that hover around the $100 a night level explain its high rate of occupancy and popularity with business travelers from the occident.

The heavily mirrored lobby with comfortable leatherlike chairs and matching rug could be more of an Asian haven, but there are some nice touches such as a gurgling fountain splashing over Japanese tiles, beautiful Shogetsu floral arrangements, and oriental rugs. Other lobby elements include a gift shop that sells many of the items a traveler would find at an airport duty-free shop.

The most outstanding feature of the Kitano is the two tatami suites with low Japanese-style seating, Japanese tile bathroom, and Western bedroom. Arrangements can also be made for sleeping on the floor. Additional design features include a shoji screen effect, more Japanese floral arrangements, and Japanese art.

Other rooms are considerably less distinguished, but corner rooms have kitchenettes and some rooms provide views of the Empire State Building. A smallish $95 single with white walls and standard hotel furniture—queen-size bed, two blue chairs, a chest of drawers, coffee table, brass lamps, brownish rug, and Panasonic TV—lacks a writing desk. More cheerful doubles employ coordinated fabrics in colors such as turquoise and salmon.

Numbered lithographs deck the halls, and two of the ten suites, considerably more inviting than the rooms, have terraces.

Additional Japanese touches are Shiseido soap, and for a charge, a drink called Lipovitan in the minibar along with other soft drinks. Lipovitan is a therapeutic vitamin drink that tastes like medicine and is popular with Japanese executives for quick energy. In addition, from the front desk guests may request use of a yukata, a cool cotton robe popular in Japan.

Although there is no room service, a Japanese breakfast of rice, soup, fish, and tea is available in the Hakubai restaurant. Entered from the lobby, the Hakubai, with its tranquil interior garden, is modeled after an Osaka original. Open seven days a week, service is provided by kimono-clad waitresses. Guests deposit their shoes at the entrance.

Hotel Parker Meridien
118 West 57th Street
(between Avenue of the Americas and Seventh Avenue)
New York, New York 10019
800/442-5917 (tollfree from within New York State)
800/223-9918 (tollfree from rest of U.S.)

Singles $165–$225
Doubles $185–$245
Suites $265–$525

The 700-room Parker Meridien is one of only eight hotels in Manhattan sporting a swimming pool—and the only one whose pool overlooks Central Park. This, in addition to a plush fitness club and proximity to the deal-making enclaves of the Russian Tea Room, must explain its myriad guests from California, and why New York's Mayor Koch calls it the "L.A. Lounge."

All guests receive free membership (excluding court fees and aerobics classes) at the Meridien's Club La Raquette. Features of this in-hotel facility include eight climate-controlled racquetball, handball and squash courts, all in excellent condition, aerobics and fitness classes, a complete Nautilus circuit, life cycles, stationary bicycles, motorized treadmills, slant boards, rowing machines, whirlpools, saunas, and carpeted locker rooms.

Up on the roof, the 40-by-20-foot glass-enclosed heated pool overlooks the park, and one flight above, on the 42nd floor, there is a professional jogging track (30 laps equal a mile).

Rooms and suites, the more expensive of which also offer views of the park, are compact but adequately designed. Features include all-marble baths, custom cabinetry with an ingenious swivel TV arrangement in some rooms, mirrored dressing areas, a desk, coffee table, seating area, wall-mounted lighting, and limited edition lithographs by artists working in France. Special amenities include Hermes soap and Sassoon shampoo.

The standard guest room, available with twin or king-size bed, comes in gray, brown, or green interpretations with matching grid-patterned bedspread and curtains, full mirror, comfortable velveteen chair, and a small writing desk with chair upholstered in a tweed fabric.

Reaching from 56th Street to 57th Street, the lobby is a design tour de force—perhaps too stagey for some tastes. In the style of high Roman revival, the ceiling is lifted the equivalent of six floors height to form an atrium with skylight, supported by arched columns. At the end of a long passage stretching from 56th Street, a ceiling painting in medieval colors gives the impression of mosaics.

A flight up from the lobby is the formal dining room, Maurice, named after Maurice Chevalier. The room was conceived as a modern, more elegant version of the classic French brasserie in rich colors taken from Asian porcelains. Noted French chef Alain Senderens devised a nouvelle cuisine menu for every meal including breakfast, which offers the most extravagant morning entree in town—soft boiled eggs served with Beluga caviar. Food is gastronomic, at astronomical prices.

The oak-paneled Le Patio, directly off the lobby, serves more informal meals, including a first-rate weekend buffet brunch in full view of the room's 17th-century tapestry from Flanders and 18th-century mounted Aubusson. There is also 24-hour room service.

Le Montparnasse bar runs into Le Patio and boasts etched-on-glass drawings depicting works by French impressionists.

Also in the lobby area is a newsstand that sells periodicals from around the world, and a concierge service.

Although the Meridien uses the more fashionable sounding 57th Street address, the actual address for arriving by taxi with luggage is West 56th Street between Sixth and Seventh avenues.

Hotel Plaza Athenee
37 East 64th Street
(between Madison and Park)
New York, New York
800/223-5672 (tollfree from outside New York)
212/734-9100

Singles $195–$300
Doubles $220–$325
Suites $500–$1500

The Plaza Athenee, a New York version of the Paris original, successfully simulates tradition even though it has been here only since fall 1984. It is one of the best places to stay for travelers who like the impression of old world elegance, but with shiny new trappings.

There are 160 rooms, of which 34 are suites, in shades of peach and mushroom, mid-green and coral, and mauve and beige. The same brass clock that graces every guest room at the Paris Plaza Athenee has been placed on the wall of each room of the New York hotel. (The hotel's ornate logo echoes a flowing detail from these French-made clocks.) Framed architectural drawings hang from the walls and there are touches of the French Directoire style throughout.

Furnishings come from top-of-the-line sources. Fabrics are from Switzerland's Zumstag, with patterned black-out shades matching drapes. Desks and cabinets for remote-control television are from Baker. Navan carpets are imported from Ireland, terry cloth bathrobes are from Porthault, complimentary toiletries by Nina Ricci, and there are Teraillon scales.

Beds have upholstered velvet headboards, and all rooms have at least one comfortable love seat. Many accommodations come with wet bars, including a refrigerator. Safes have been built into closets, and tie racks are attached to the closet doors.

Rooms are stocked with two small bottles of French Evian water, and chocolate truffles made on the premises are placed in rooms for arriving guests.

Bathrooms have walls and floors made of rose Aurora marble from Portugal, and include hair dryers, lighted makeup/shaving mirrors, and a chest of Lucite trays for storing.

Eight suites come with dining rooms, and eight suites have terraces with Upper East Side views. From the upper floors, guests look out over the roofs of many select townhouses. In addition, all suites have telephones (with two lines) and real greenery.

Special services include room service with, as in Europe, an actual pantry on some floors, and concierge service until 11:30 P.M.

An elevator lined with leather leads to the lobby, designed by noted interior designer Valerian Rhybar. Pastoral scenes painted by a California artist cover the walls, and the marble floors of the lobby are on two levels, separated by a faux stone balustrade.

The dining room, reached by passing through a clubby anteroom, is named Le Regence, after the restaurant in the Paris hotel. There are large mirrored panels and a profusion of turquoise, and the ceiling is painted with a cloudscape. Seafood is the specialty, with a special $24.50 *menu minceur* at lunch for the calorie conscious. Evening dining is by candlelight.

It is wise that the owners do not purport to be a clone of the Paris Plaza Athenee, because the small scale of the rooms and public spaces, and lack of lobby life, does not convey the aura of a grand French hotel.

Incentra Village House
32 Eighth Avenue
New York, New York 10014
212/206-0007

Singles $60
Doubles $70

Many people come to New York specifically to enjoy Greenwich Village, with its vibrant nightlife, unique shops, and palpable sense of history. But the Village is not exactly hotel row, so the opening in 1980 of the Incentra was greeted enthusiastically. Situated in two adjacent 1841 townhouses on the northern side of the Village, the Incentra offers easy access to surrounding sights, charming lodgings, and re- markably reasonable rates.

Perhaps the best recommendation for the Incentra is that New Yorkers entertaining visitors and unable to put them up in their own apartments will often point them toward the discreetly marked door of the Incentra. The clientele of the Incentra runs the gamut from gay people who come to be near the Village social life to parents of neighborhood res- idents to visitors from Canada and abroad. Owner Gaylord Hofteyser, manager Lee Huttick, and staff keep a low profile yet provide a gracious welcome, and are always ready to recommend sights, restaurants, and activities.

There are 11 rooms in all (three of which are not in the townhouses themselves, but are nearby and feature all of the same services). All rooms have private baths, nine have kitchens (stocked with basic utensils and such appliances as a blender and toaster), and seven have fireplaces (management prefers that guests use artificial logs, which are sold in the variety store on the corner).

Each room has been individually decorated according to a theme. The India Room features Bengali modern paintings. The Dakota features a pleasing Great Plains motif, with antiques, old photos, a rag rug, and brass bed. Its skylight is painted on the outside in a floral design. The Dakota's kitchen and bath are on a separate level from the bedroom.

The most ample lodgings are found in the Bishop Room, actually a three-level apartment. The living area has a fireplace and pullout couch, along with a roomy double closet. The kitchen and smallish bath lie down a short set of stairs, and a loft just big enough for a double bed and night table is situated above. The Bishop would be fine for two couples who don't mind togetherness for a short stay, and is perfect for one or two persons' extended stay. (The Bishop goes for $75 single, $80 double.)

Downstairs, off the entrance hall, is a reception area and living room sparingly furnished with art objects from India, oil lamps, old oak furniture, and a grand piano.

The Incentra enjoys a 50 percent repeat business. Weekends are generally booked well in advance.

The Lowell
28 East 63rd Street
New York, New York 10021
212/838-1400

Junior suites $240–$260
One-bedroom suites $300–$340
Lowell suites $400
Two-bedroom suites $400–$440

The Lowell, with only 60 suites, takes being a small hotel seriously. For a price, but not out of line with what other hotels are charging, travelers can enjoy this genre at its very best.

Benefits will be most appreciated by the well traveled: no lines at the registration guest, no tour groups, no conventioneers, no signs in the lobby, no dehumanizing atriums, no revolving restaurants. What's more, there are all the little things that only a small hotel can do really well, like filling a guest's kitchen before arrival, arranging for in-room shopping, supplying forgotten articles such as a hair dryer, or iron, or even loaning an ironing board (in addition to offering one-day valet service). Moreover, the hotel operator will temporarily suspend telephone service and arrange for messages to be slid under the door for real privacy. And room service, upon notice, can arrange for a small in-room dinner party, while the concierge sends up a log for the working fireplace.

The Lowell has been an apartment-hotel for long or short stays since 1928, with such personages as Zelda and Scott Fitzgerald, T. S. Eliot, William Randolph Hearst, Jean Cocteau, and others staying there. And that was before a recent $25 million renovation.

On the other side of a spruced up art deco facade, the boutique-size lobby, not really for sitting, sets a tone of exclusivity with luxurious trappings and a team of concierges in cutaway morning coats and striped trousers.

Except for the entrance through an art deco doorway to the adjoining Post House restaurant, there is not a hint of commercialism. The lobby is in French Empire style, apart from several remnants of the Lowell's art deco heritage, including an Edgar Brandt console.

Walls are covered in pale, Empire gray silk, complementing faux marble wainscoting and pilasters. The marble floor is covered with a carpet copied from an original that once graced Empress Josephine's bedroom. Other notable items are an Empire console table, French bronze lamps with ormolu mounts and a chiaroscuro classical wall mural behind the concierge desk. Yellow silk from Scalamandre covers Empire-style settees and armchairs.

In contrast to most hotels, the Lowell's restaurant, the Pembroke Room, is located on the second floor. This evokes a feeling of privacy, further enforced by the room's diminutive size and well-spaced tables. Crystal sconces, mirrored walls, ivory wainscoting, Chinese porcelains, burnished mahogany, and chairs covered in striped satin complete the rarefied atmosphere. The Pembroke Room serves breakfast, lunch, and tea, as well as New York's only traditional English breakfast on Sundays.

The Lowell is best represented by its one-bedroom suite. The comfortable overall effect, greatly enhanced by a working fireplace (also available in two-bedroom suites, but not in smaller accommodations), is more impressive than any single element of the decor. Bedrooms feature somewhat plain, straight-lined black lacquer cabinet furniture and an enormous bed. The living-dining area includes shelves filled with books, and such homey objects as a heavy metal ''decoy'' duck, real plants, and Chinese lamps. Suites feature separate dining areas. Unusually solid casement windows, covered with solid blue cotton curtains, may be opened.

Since the Pembroke Room is closed for dinner, a meal ordered from room service, served on the dining room table with a white table cloth and accompanying candle, makes for a relaxing evening's entertainment.

Another option is to prepare a meal in the spotless white kitchen. The kitchen is stocked with china, crystal, silverware, appliances, electric range with oven, dishwasher, and full-sized refrigerator.

Good-sized baths feature brass art deco fixtures, large mirrors, marble walls with veining in tones of brown and beige, and white terry cloth robes. Complimentary toiletries and a basket of potpourri are provided. There is a phone extension within reach of the tub.

Smaller accommodations have similar furnishings, but no fireplace. All accommodations have a kitchen and dining room table.

The Mayfair Regent
610 Park Avenue
(at 65th Street)
New York, New York 10021
800/545-4000 (tollfree)
212/288-0800

Singles, Doubles $170–$230
Junior suites $270
Parlor and one bedroom $290–$330
Parlor and two bedrooms $460–$800

The Mayfair Regent is not the most expensive New York hotel, but it does attract the most expensive-looking clientele. Its glowing, columned, lobby-lounge—the city's most beautiful—provides a glimpse of New York at its most stylish. In fact, the afternoon parade of habitués and hotel guests on their way to the super-chic Le Cirque or tea in the Mayfair's own lobby reveals faces regularly seen in *W* and *Town & Country*.

The lobby, with its colorings of sienna, ochre, and terra-cotta, and its high, decorative ceilings, mirrors, arch-topped columns, ducal fire place, lavish floral arrangements, and sunken palm-filled lounge, resembles one of the grand hotels of Venice. But with only 80 rooms and 119 suites, it is more of a baby grand.

The staff, roughly one person for every room, is professional without being stuffy. Upon check-in, guests are discreetly sized up so that they will be given the best accommodations, color-wise and style-wise, in their price category. There are rooms that are more on the masculine side, and others that are more feminine in look. After checking in, guests are escorted by an assistant manager to their room, reached by elevators manned by attendants in snappy gray uniforms with white goves.

Comfortable rooms and suites, quite spacious, with high ceilings and walk-in closets, sometimes exhibit a certain old guard snub at interior design. Each is somewhat different, and wall colors in such palpable shades as dusky salmon and tones of pink, teamed with good lighting effects, are more distinctive than the furniture. The standard single, located in the hotel's most quiet section, features a queen-size bed, writing desk, comfortable chair, dresser, television, and radio—all sturdy and built to last.

Baths, the same throughout, have marble floors, a scale, and wallpapered ceilings. Extra-large mirrors feature vanity lights. Extras include terry cloth robes, Neutrogena shampoo and soap, shell-shaped Crabtree & Evelyn soaps, Vitabath and lingerie soap in special Mayfair Regent wrappings, a small sewing kit, a shower cap, and a shoe cloth.

Suites and some rooms have butler pantries with refrigerators and sinks. Several suites have wood-burning fireplaces.

The large, two-bedroom Presidential Suite features a working fireplace, large windows overlooking Park Avenue, and three color televisions with remote control.

Special services include hand-delivered telephone messages and 24-hour room service including several selections from Le Cirque and afternoon tea. An evening turndown service provides a choice of full-size soaps, hand delivered in a basket. Secretarial services are available along with translation and telex services. Valet service includes laundering, dry cleaning, alterations, and a complimentary shoeshine. A guest's requests are recorded for future visits. Complimentary umbrellas are available for loan.

The Mayfair Regent's tea, served in the lobby lounge, offers four herbal teas, five English teas, finger sandwiches, and scones with clotted cream and jam. Of all the teas now being offered in New York, this attracts the creme de la creme.

Le Cirque, reached through a special entrance off the lobby, is the most fashionable restaurant in town for lunch. Guests wishing to make lunch reservations may do so when making reservations for accommodations.

Bruno Brunelli, the Mayfair Regent's concierge, has access to everything in New York.

The Mayflower Hotel
61st Street & Central Park West
New York, New York 10023
800/223-4164 (tollfree)
212/265-0060

Singles $95–$125
Doubles $110–$145
Suites $170–$185

The Mayflower Hotel is the best hotel on the Upper West Side, and offers one of the best values in the city. It's where the Metropolitan Opera stays, as well as executives and artists in the music and entertainment industries. At times the clientele is up to 70 percent theatrical.

More relaxed and with lower rates than its midtown counterparts, the Mayflower is undergoing a renovation that will make pleasant surroundings even better. The somewhat stereotypical lobby will receive a more unified look in shades of maroon; wallpaper and carpets will be replaced in the corridors, and the 377 rooms and suites will continue to be refurbished.

But even with the old rooms, the hotel has been used as the setting for a variety of motion pictures, starting with a Fred Astaire epic where the actor danced his way down the circular staircase of what is now the manager's duplex, to such films as *It's My Turn* and *Ghostbusters*.

In fact, 17G, a deluxe suite, was actually custom designed by actor Micky Rourke so he would feel comfortable during an extended stay. This suite features its own built-in sauna, in addition to two baths, a living room, a dining area, and a kitchen. The style is eclectic with a French provincial-style king-size bed in the bedroom, as well as lots of built-in drawers and closet space.

The living room features high ceilings, an eye-catching cabinet displaying Chinese plates, lots of mirrors, a marble coffee table, and a curved corner couch, part of which pulls out to form an armchair. A curtain opens to reveal a bird's eye view of Central Park—all the more striking because of the room's slate-gray walls.

A table in the dining area features four chairs, and the

suite has two color TVs and three telephones. Baths are of standard size, but tubs are more spacious than in new hotels.

It should be noted that the hotel does not provide cooking utensils, but all suites and many singles and doubles do have pantries.

The standard single, at $95, is as attractive as the single in hotels charging more than $50 more per night. Features include colonial-style furniture and a two-poster bed.

The bathroom has a tile floor, medicine cabinet and floral wallpaper on the ceiling. Special amenities include shampoo, body lotion, shoe shiner, and sewing kit.

The Conservatory, an in-hotel restaurant, provides surprisingly good service at breakfast, and lunch and dinner are also served. In the morning, classical music provides a nice accompaniment to breakfast. Room service operates between 7 A.M. and 11 P.M.

From large windows in the Conservatory, guests have a wonderful view of Central Park. This is especially appreciated during Macy's Thanksgiving Day parade, for which bookings are sometimes made a year in advance. The Mayflower is also close to Lincoln Center and Columbus Avenue.

Morgans
237 Madison Avenue
(at 37th Street)
New York, New York 10016
800/344-3408 (tollfree)
212/686-0300

Singles $130–$170
Doubles $150–$190
One-bedroom apartments $240–$350

Despite all the media hype about Morgans being the new in place to stay, the owners, who happen to be the former owners of the original Studio 54, have hatched a high-tech, high-quality establishment with the most innovative design in town.

Morgans is French interior designer Andree Putman's first hotel, and her credo that hoteliers shouldn't think guests so stupid as to be impressed by gilt should be chiseled into hotel school manuals. Before Putman and the owners remade the former Executive Hotel, they threw out everything they hated about hotels and started from scratch.

Located a block away from the Morgan Library (hence, the name), the building is devoid of any marking of name, but everyone from Brooke Shields to Boy George and buyers from the nearby garment district have found their way into the simple lobby.

In the lobby, shimmering, sanded-glass walls with shoji-like bronze mullions contrast with a granite harlequin floor pattern in black, white, and gray. Creating a trompe l'oeil effect, textured wool carpeting repeats the same pattern and colors.

Elevators have a checkerboard banding in black and white, which is later echoed in the bathroom. Corridors, inexplicably done in dim, cocktail-lounge lighting, lead to extremely inviting rooms that all follow a similar design pattern.

Mostly in black, white, and gray, with tones of beige, green, and melon, rooms are compact, but space is maximized. French-made units of richly grained gray bird's eye maple (also used for desks and doors) conceal shelves and drawers. Under windows covered with thin venetian blinds, a cushioned settee opens up for more storage space, and acts as a focal point. A built-in refrigerator is another space-saver.

Low queen-size beds are topped with duvets covered in pinstriped fabric from Brooks Brothers, which also covers headboards. Black and white buffalo-check blankets are folded at the foot of each bed.

Like hallways, the walls are finished with a spray-applied wall coating that gives the effect of speckled paint. Signed and numbered black and white photographs of flowers by Robert Mapplethorpe are the only wall adornment. Besides the single photograph, a real flower is placed in each room and bath.

Rooms also come with art deco–style lounge chairs covered in gray flannel suit fabric.

Each room also has a silver cube-shaped Sharp television

and stereo cassette player. VCRs can be requested, along with tapes and cassettes.

Special bath features in most rooms include black and white chessboard wall tiles, transparent glass shower doors from floor to ceiling, and curved metal sinks similar to those found on airplanes. Also included are white terry cloth robes, black Kleenex boxes, and Kiehls herbal shampoo from New York's oldest pharmacy. Most rooms have showers only.

Thirty percent of the rooms are suites, including a spectacular 10-room duplex penthouse with views of the Empire State Building. Six suites resemble the layout of a loft, the Cathedral Suite having a cathedral ceiling and bath in full view of the rest of the room.

Room service operates on and off throughout the day until 1 A.M., offering such unusual choices as new potatoes with caviar and oven-baked sandwiches. At other times, arrangements can be made with the front desk for outside delivery.

A complimentary continental breakfast is served in the breakfast room, and lunch and dinner are served in the basement restaurant owned and operated by Larry Forgione.

Morgans staff was chosen for looks and charisma, in keeping with the emphasis on the visual. What they might lack in experience is usually made up for in charm.

No. 1022
1022 Lexington Avenue
(at 73rd Street)
New York, New York 10021
212/628-5300

Atelier Suite $3800 monthly
Club Suite $4900 monthly
Terrace Suite $6700 monthly
Park Suite $7500 monthly

No. 1022, with only four guest accommodations, is New York's answer to the country inn, albeit an inn for the affluent. This is the best place to stay for total privacy and rooms that are hardly spacious, but elegant in an understated way.

Hotel management is most interested in reserving rooms for a minimum of a month, but sometimes exceptions are made. Daily rates approximate the cost of a deluxe room or small suite at a luxury hotel.

Most guests, who range from corporate leaders to Hollywood royalty, find out about 1022 through word of mouth, although one recently trimmed-down film giant found out about it through food of mouth. She inquired about what was upstairs while dining on spa cuisine at Jack's, the restaurant at 1022.

There are no outward signs that this 1870s townhouse is actually a hotel—no doorman, no lobby, no sign. Arriving guests proceed to the street level bar at Jack's, where innkeeper Michael Hopkins issues keys and assists with luggage.

The four suites include the studio-size Atelier Suite for one, with automatic skylight, bath, and pantry; one-bedroom Club Suite with either two twins or a queen-size bed, bath, and pantry; one-bedroom Terrace Suite with queen-size four-poster bed, wood-burning fireplace, bath, pantry, and terrace; and one-bedroom Park Suite, with queen-size four-poster, wood-burning fireplace, automatic skylight, bath, and small kitchen.

No. 1022's Park Suite is reached by climbing three flights of green-carpeted staircase (there is no elevator) past whimsical design elements—trompe l'oeil, vases jutting out from walls—provided by interior designer Georgina Fairholme.

The compact, English country-style living area is replete with chintz and handmade objects. Unusual colors, like sky blue, clear yellow, creamy peach, and apple green, provide a rarefied atmosphere.

Living room amenities add a homelike effect: decanters filled with liquors, magazines, flowers and a fruit basket, remote-control television, a stereo, and FM radio.

The tiny apple-green bedroom has little space for anything more than a lovely queen-size four-poster lushly decked out with swags in a floral pattern and covered with a delicate patchwork quilt. Hand-painted silk pillows grace the bed.

An elaborate curtain swept to one side covers the single window, and detailed white molding works its way around the ceiling. Other bedroom features include a telephone with automatic answering machine (all local calls are free) and a television.

The small bathroom has an extra-large wrap-around mirror with vanity lights, a hair dryer, and a Jacuzzi in a standard-size tub.

A small, utilitarian kitchen includes a microwave oven, toaster, coffeemaker, and other utensils. Each kitchen or pantry comes stocked with food for breakfast.

Daily room service is available from Jack's between noon and 3 P.M., and 6 P.M. and 11 P.M. Other services include daily housekeeping and one-day laundry service.

Guests can arrange for rooms to be stocked with specific items prior to their arrival.

Security is provided by a closed-circuit TV and buzzer system.

The Regency Hotel
540 Park Avenue
(at 61st Street)
New York, New York 10021
800/522-5455 (tollfree from within New York State)
800/223-0888 (tollfree from rest of U.S.)
212/759-4100

Singles $165–$215
Doubles $185–$235
Suites $295–$725

A room or suite at the Regency gains instant cachet for the business traveler. The power breakfast was born here —for more than a dozen years financiers, politicians, industrialists, and others have double-parked their limousines in the early morning hours at this Park Avenue address. Even Robert Tisch, president of Loews Hotels, of which this is the flagship, eats breakfast here. And of course, many CEOs sleep here, too.

The Regency gets its corporate image from an impeccable location, comfortable accommodations, a large number of suites (361 rooms, 111 suites), and highly professional service.

It's not so much what the hotel does—although the sky's the limit for concierge David Lopez and the rest of the staff—but the fact that in a city where not everything always works, most everything is done correctly here.

The lobby, in French Regency style, resembles the entrance of a newer Park Avenue co-op, with an Aubusson-style carpet over marble floors, an impressive wall tapestry, and several large chairs to wait for friends or associates. A lobby clock was rescued from a former Loews movie palace. Off the lobby, discreetly hidden, is a candy and newsstand.

Accommodations and hallways, which are being redecorated for completion in spring 1987, currently suffer from design overkill.

Features include king-size beds, ornate Italian provincial furniture, generous closet space, padded satin hangers, a small refrigerator, and a security safe for storing valuables.

Special room features are sachet in the drawers, HBO television and optional pay movies, a nightly turndown service, and a radio speaker and extra phone in the bath.

Bath mirrors have side extensions for views of the profile, in addition to a full complement of shampoos and body lotions. Guests may also arrange for a Monark exercise bike for use in their rooms, and private in-room massages. All guests are provided with complimentary terry cloth robes.

The difference between the standard and deluxe room is mainly size. All deluxe rooms and suites have a utility kitchen and five suites have terraces.

Guest services include 24-hour room service, a beauty salon and barber shop, and valet parking that provides access to the underground garage directly from the hotel.

On the ground floor, the Regency restaurant, newly christened 540 Park, is the scene of the power breakfast, lunch, and dinner. Tables are generously spaced for privacy. In addition to a continental menu, special spa selections are included, with caloric counts.

The adjacent Regency Lounge features nightly piano music, champagne and cocktails, and late-night supper.

The newest development at the Regency is a 2000-square-foot Fitness Center exclusively for guest use. Features include seven pieces of Nautilus equipment, a Universal Power Pak 300, free weights, a Versa climber, crosscountry ski machine, rowing machine, bike ergometers, and the ultimate in decadence—a section where guests can pedal an exercise bike while watching television with earphones.

Vista International Hotel
3 World Trade Center
New York, New York 10048
212/938-9100 or local Hilton Reservation Service

Singles $130–$185 ($205 on executive floors)
Doubles $160–$215 ($235 on executive floors)
Suites $335–$545

Lower Manhattan's last hotel was built at the turn of the century, so when this 829-room hostelry operated by Hilton International emerged between the twin towers of the World Trade Center in 1981, it was greeted with open arms. This is the best place to stay for travelers with a heavy round of appointments in and around Wall Street (the New York Stock Exchange is six blocks away), and time for little else besides a comfortable room, a good meal, and perhaps a swim or sauna.

Engulfed by New York's tallest buildings, the 22-story hotel retains its own architectural identity with horizontal strips of glass and aluminum panels that contrast with the twin towers' verticality.

The lobby level, which connects with the World Trade Center towers and concourse, is wrapped in dark wood paneling. An intimidating element, the roped-off check-in area (for forming lines), can be avoided with a new no-stop check out, allowing guests to receive their statement the night before, and drop their key off on the run.

Other lobby features are contemporary bronze sculptures, a branch of Brazil's H. Stern jewelers, car rental agency, magazine and tobacco store, concierge service, and the Tall Ships Bar with its 8-by-23-foot etched bronze mirror-glass mural depicting scenes of 19th-century ships in New York Harbor.

The major draw of the hotel is the American Harvest restaurant, which started saluting regional American cooking a few years before it became the current rage. The inventive prix fixe menus revolve around the month's harvest somewhere in the 50 states. So a well-prepared duck appears on the menu every month, but the recipe depends on what fruit or vegetable is in season.

In keeping with the American heritage theme, the restaurant loosely follows the design of a Federal townhouse, with additional glass vitrines containing art objects on loan from the Museum of American Folk Art. The restaurant has recently initiated a 60-minute lunch for the business traveler, as well as a "Healthy Alternative" menu with offerings low in calories, sodium, and cholesterol. American wines are also a specialty.

Rooms are almost uniform throughout the hotel, with size and location determining the price. Typical rooms contain a floral watercolor, dresser, luggage stands, and headboards of limed oak trimmed with cane panelings. More interesting than the room decors are the views, which provide a New Jersey sunset over the Hudson to the west and startling closeness to the twin towers to the east.

There is a nightly turndown service with customary chocolates, and rooms are stocked with complimentary Poland Springs water.

Two Executive Floors offer the same basic room, but extra frills are offered to justify the higher price. These include a more personalized check-in with a briefing by the assistant manager, a basket of seasonal fruit and long-stemmed flower in the room, ice delivered nightly, and complimentary early coffee or tea delivered to rooms.

Resembling the first-class lounge of an airline, the executive lounge is open from 6:30 A.M. to midnight, with a whole menu of complimentary perks for guests staying on Executive Floors, including continental breakfast, open bar, and snacks.

Other services of interest to business travelers (who make up the majority of the clientele during the week) are 24-hour room service, phones in the bath, on-premise offices available for rent, photocopiers, financial information available from computer terminals, one-hour pressing service, and flights from JFK, La Guardia, and Newark to the World Trade Center by New York Helicopter. One flight above the Executive Floors, the Executive Fitness Center (open to guests throughout the hotel) offers a cushioned jogging track (13 laps equal a mile), a 20-by-50-foot heated swimming pool in spacious indoor surroundings, two racquetball courts, sauna and steam rooms, and exercise equipment and aerobics classes (for a fee). Towels, shorts, socks, and T-shirts are provided free.

A booklet provided in rooms describes sites of historic and architectural interest along with a 4.9-mile Battery–Wall Street–Broadway jogging circuit.

Pleasure travelers might wish to partake of weekend packages that feature reduced rates, shuttle bus service uptown, and free walking tours to historic sites. In addition, the Vista is within walking distance of South Street Seaport, the Staten Island Ferry, and the Statue of Liberty (which can be seen from some parts of the hotel), and is close to Chinatown, TriBeCa, and SoHo.

Eighteen rooms have been set aside for the disabled.

The Wyndham
42 West 58th Street
(between Fifth Avenue and Avenue of the Americas)
New York, New York 10019
212/753-3500

Singles $85–$95
Doubles $95–$105
Suites $140–$170

The Wyndham is one of those great Manhattan finds—spacious accommodations just off Fifth Avenue at rates that are very reasonable for New York. Luminaries such as Laurence Olivier, Jessica Tandy, Mary Martin, and Lena Horne, who could probably afford to stay anywhere in town, choose the Wyndham.

Part of the appeal is that the hotel is little known—there is no brochure and no advertising—and family operated.

Also, there are no computers, and actual people operate the elevators—making for tight security.

Owner John Mados and his wife live in the hotel and Mrs. Mados oversees much of the interior design, purchasing most of the ubiquitous floral chintz at downtown sources.

The 75 rooms and 70 suites are large by New York standards and have lots of closet space and larger than normal bath tubs. Though they lack the sophisticated look of rooms done by a professional firm, they have a fresh charm that would appeal to many travelers.

No two rooms are alike, but in any room or suite the same pattern of chintz is used for draperies, chair, slipcovers, pillows, and even lamp shades and sometimes walls.

Room features include large Hollywood twin beds, a television, and in most cases a radio. Suites offer chaise lounges and curved couches taking up an entire corner of a room, in addition to extra telephones and televisions. Fireplaces do not work, and unfortunately the plants are plastic.

Although suites have cold pantries, the hotel does not offer room service.

The lobby is a pleasant hodgepodge of oriental rugs, live plants, marbleized mirrors, handsome wallpaper, chinese lamps, and more paintings.

A large restaurant and cocktail lounge is owned by the same management, and may be entered from the street or the lobby.

Front desk staff and elevator operators can perform some of the services of a concierge.

Across the street from the Plaza and Park Lane hotels, the Wyndham is near Central Park, Tiffany's and Fifth Avenue shopping, and everything that would attract a visitor to New York.

«OKLAHOMA CITY»

The Richmond Hotel
1600 Richmond Square
(Northwest Expressway at Blackwelder)
Oklahoma City, Oklahoma 73118
800/654-1440 (tollfree)
405/840-1440

Suites $85–$95, plus $10 per person
Boardroom suites $150 (no limit on number of occupants)

Just two years old, the Richmond is steadily earning a name as the discreet jewel of OKC's accommodations scene. The hotel is located 10 to 15 minutes north of downtown, a little out of the way and somewhat hard to locate. Look for an unimposing two-story building at the light before Northwest Expressway connects with Classen Boulevard, or hop on one of the hotel's stretch limos at the airport. The Richmond is small—just 53 beautifully appointed suites— and focuses its efforts on individuality, conscientious and professional staff, and vigilant attention to detail.

The building layout is fairly open. Some suites are a short outside walk from the reception area and adjacent dining room and bar. Suites are large, gracious, and comfortable, with many special touches. Bedspreads have extra-pretty patterns and fancy flounces; bathtubs are especially deep; two plush bathrobes hang in the walk-in dressing area; a wicker hamper of amenities provided to every suite holds wine (white and red), champagne, domestic and imported beer, juice, popcorn, and other treats.

Bedroom furniture includes king-size (with pullout sofa) or queen-size beds, elegant study table and chairs, and cable TV. All the nice big living rooms sport comfy sofas and easy chairs, classy butler's tables, and armoires with second TVs (also cable). Where layout permits, the living room opens onto a patio area complete with wrought-iron furniture, and corner suites have big bay windows.

Travelers requiring a small meeting space may want to request a Boardroom Suite, which has all the facilities of a regular suite as well as room for a small group to get together. In addition, the hotel maintains a central boardroom that holds 100 people for a meeting, or 40 for a sit-down dinner.

The hotel's Fairfax Dining Room is a favorite of city business people. The restaurant backs a respectable menu with a good wine list, and diners sit in comfy armchairs drawn up to tables with linen cloths and fresh flowers. The adjoining bar is overdecorated in a hunt theme—there are too many pheasant feathers and brass hunting horns around—but the bartenders' professional friendliness and easy banter seem just right. A pianist plays contemporary music every night except Sunday.

The Richmond's staff and management really take pride in catering to discerning visitors, and to that end provide any number of personal services. A stretch limo will take guests just about anywhere, including the International Fitness Center nearby (which substitutes for on-site fitness facilities). Full room service is offered from 6:30 A.M. to 11 P.M., and sandwich-type snacks are served 24 hours. A staff valet, concierge, and night porter can handle most special requests.

The Skirvin Plaza Hotel
One Park Avenue
(at Broadway)
Oklahoma City, Oklahoma 73102
800/323-7500 (tollfree)
405/232-4411

Singles, doubles $73–$97
Suites $135–$600

Seventy-five years ago the late Oklahoma oil man Bill Skirvin decided to build himself a fancy hotel in the center of town, and his Skirvin Plaza is still regarded by loyal Sooners as the classiest joint around. Home for a time to the magnate's socialite daughter, Pearl Mesta, then purchased in 1979 by a consortium of Oklahoma City businessmen, the Skirvin is the hotel of choice for OKC establishment folks. Its ballroom seats 1200, and the maitre d' has worked there for 36 years. On a display table on the mezzanine level lie heavy scrapbooks of clippings about the Skirvin and all the society functions held there; and just about everybody famous who comes to Oklahoma stays here.

Throughout the hotel—in its physical facility, management, and staff—the watchwords are style and elegance. Visitors enter a grand front lobby, replete with crystal chandeliers, carved oak pillars, and fancy ashcans where they stamp the hotel logo into the sand. Service is not the friendliest in the land, though staff are professional and competent.

The Skirvin was renovated in 1980, when its 365 rooms became 198 larger rooms and ten suites. In 1986 the Skirvin is planning another extensive renovation, this time to spruce up meeting and function spaces as well as give guest rooms a quick (though unnecessary) facelift.

There are two choices of accommodation—room or suite—but the variety of rooms is very great. Choices range from a somewhat cramped standard double to an executive king, which in another hotel might be called a suite: very large and comfortable, with a living-study area including sofa, easy chairs, coffee table, and desk.

The hotel is particularly proud of the fact that every room is decorated differently—a plus for frequent visitors. Furnishings, drapes, wall coverings, and spreads are tastefully chosen, and many rooms have live plants, another nice touch. Bathrooms are clean but undistinguished, with limited toiletries and small tubs. The Skirvin's ten suites are royal indeed; they consist of distinct kitchen and living-dining, bed, and bath rooms, the number of each varying from suite to suite. In addition to nice but standard hotel furniture, many suites are graced by lovingly finished an-

231

tiques or near-antiques. All rooms have remote-control color TV with 24-hour cable movie channels. Try to avoid the east side of the building, which faces the ugly Santa Fe railroad and downtown commercial parking lot (all rooms are soundproofed).

There are several dining possibilities. Adjoining the main lobby, the pleasant Palm Court serves breakfast and light afternoon fare, as well as evening drinks to the accompaniment of a piano player. The Park Avenue Room is the Skirvin's main restaurant, considered one of the best in the city, with an award-winning French chef and an elegant menu. Pinstripes is a pseudo–New York bar-cafe that offers drinks and deli-style lunches. Finally, there is a group of semi-ethnic fast-food stalls operated by the hotel in its basement (the basement connects to pedestrian tunnels that run underneath a fair bit of the downtown area); these hokey little eateries are depressing and best avoided. In addition, complete room service operates from 6 A.M. to 10 P.M.

The hotel offers a hair salon and valet service; there is no concierge as such, but the front desk staff are pretty helpful. Neither is there an in-house health club, though guests have free access to the YMCA six blocks away, which offers swimming, exercise and weight equipment, sauna, and racquetball (closed Sundays). The Skirvin's conference and meeting rooms offer a wide variety in size and decor; when renovations are completed this year they should look even better.

The Skirvin is very conveniently located in the center of town opposite the Myriad Convention Center. It's a 10- to 15-minute drive from the airport; the hotel limousine service ferries guests back and forth.

«ORLANDO»

Chalet Suzanne Country Inn
U.S. 27 North of Lake Wales
P.O. Drawer AC
Lake Wales, Florida 33859
813/676-6011

$60–$95 double occupancy (each additional person $6)

Excellent gourmet food is available at many central and gulf coast hotels and resorts, but a true epicure—a person devoted to luxurious living and a discriminating gratification of the senses, especially the senses of smell and taste—must savor the Chalet Suzanne experience.

Thirty miles southeast of Disney World, amid farms and endless rows of aromatic orange groves, Chalet Suzanne is an enchanting and unique country inn set on a 70-acre estate. The visitor first notes a colorful profusion of wacky buildings topped by green, blue, yellow, and pink turrets, minarets, spires, battlements, and towers. Then comes a balmy, gentle breeze blowing over glistening Lake Suzanne, carrying the scent of orange blossoms.

No matter the time of year, there are always baskets of fruit and candy in guest rooms. Each chalet guest room— there are 30 in all—is warm and uniquely furnished. Some of the floors tilt a bit, and nooks and corners are conveniently turned into blanket cupboards or miniclosets. All rooms offer the comforts of private bath, air conditioning, telephone, and color television. Amid these modern essentials you're liable to find Milanese pottery, wooden beds from

Norway, Irish linens, Japanese wickerwork, sinks made from ornamental bowls purchased in Portugal or Hong Kong, and deep but short bathtubs.

Started in 1931 by the late Bertha Hinshaw after her husband died and the family fortune was lost in the 1929 stock market crash, the chalet's attractions were Mrs. Hinshaw's gourmet cooking, the doodads, antiques, and other treasures she had collected from around the world, and the Alice-in-Wonderland flair of her buildings. The spirit of this busy, energetic, and imaginative woman is kept alive by her son, Carl, and his wife, Vita, both charming and intelligent people who are quick to personally welcome new guests and returning old friends.

That friendliness and Southern hospitality is echoed by their hotel and restaurant staff, who serve guests with class, but without a breath of snobbery.

And snobbery could have come very naturally: some very sophisticated and famous palates have savored Chalet Suzanne's food, from Susan Hayward, Dinah Shore, and Burt Reynolds, to Hugh Downs and Craig Claiborne, the *New York Times* food critic who gave it his highest rating. In fact, the restaurant's gastronomic glories have won dozens of awards.

The first course is broiled grapefruit with chicken liver, an exquisite combination and an invention of Vita's. This unusual combination was born of happenstance plus imagination. A dinner for food editors had hit a snag: Among the canapes to be served before dinner were chicken livers, but they were slow in getting done. By the time they were ready, the food editors had already sat down at the table. To prevent a total loss, Vita placed a chicken liver at the center of each cinnamon-broiled grapefruit, at that time the Chalet's standard first course. The food editors loved it, and the Chalet has been serving grapefruit and chicken liver ever since.

The next course is one of the Chalet's celebrated soups —its romaine is the most famous. The late Clementine Paddleford, food critic for the *New York Herald Tribune,* tasted some and wrote, "It's good! Good! Good!" Not to be outdone, *Gourmet* magazine called it "glorious, glorious!'' And it is. It was first whipped up by Bertha out of chicken broth, chopped spinach, mushrooms, carrots, chopped onions, and her own mysterious bouquet of herbs and seasonings after a trip to Rome—thus the name ''romaine,'' which means served in the Roman fashion. Son Carl has not only kept the magic flavor, but expanded the line of soups, even establishing a soup canning factory on the estate.

Among the main dinner selections is Chicken Suzanne, baked and basted many times in its own juices. It comes to the table sporting a high glaze, deep amber in color, with tender, moist meat that falls off the bone at the touch of a fork. Guests also rave about their lobster thermidor and Newburg, made with real Maine lobster, butter, and cream.

Besides the fine food, the surroundings have to be appreciated. One enters the restaurant through a long, split-level entrance hall decorated with showpiece antiques, 19th-century pianos, photographs of notables, and furniture from throughout the world. There are four separate dining rooms, each shaped and decorated differently. A favorite among honeymooners is the Balcony room. It offers a glass-enclosed dumbwaiter that can bring tasty nourishment directly to the newlyweds' hideaway without disturbing their privacy. In the main dining rooms, each table and chair also appears to be different and every table is set with its own china pattern from Royal Doulton to Wedgwood to rare plates from Portugal and Italy. Stemware varies from 9-inch goblets to tiny tulip-shaped glasses. There's an uncountable number of different styles of flatware. Nothing matches, but everything inexplicably fits.

The Hyatt Regency Grand Cypress
One Grand Cypress Boulevard
Orlando, Florida 32819
800/228-9000 (tollfree)
305/239-1234

Singles $120–$165
Regency Club rooms $195 single or double
Suites $250 and up

Spectacular is the only word that describes the 750-room Hyatt Regency Grand Cypress at Orlando. It's part of a 920-acre world-class resort that opened in 1984. Tropically lush grounds complemented by distinctive architecture and exotic art plus a courteous staff that offers impeccable service can't fail to impress even the most jaded traveler.

For the business traveler, the resort offers 57,000 square feet of meeting and exhibit space. There are 27 meeting rooms including the amazing 25,000-square-foot Grand Cypress Ballroom, which can be divided into nine separate rooms and accommodate 3500 people. In 1984, the $110 million hotel won a Gold Key Award for its meeting and convention facilities.

Recreational activities include a half-acre free-form swimming pool with 12 waterfalls, three Jacuzzis, a 45-foot water slide, and a grotto bar; a 21-acre lake with more than 1000 feet of white sand beach, a marina with sailboats, windsurfers, canoes, and pedalboats; and the Grand Cypress Racquet Club with 10 tennis courts, two racquetball and shuffleboard courts, a children's playground, and a fitness trail for walking or jogging. For golfers, there's an 18-hole, Jack Nicklaus signature golf course that features 40 sand bunkers and hazards and a nine-hole, three-par, Pitch 'n' Putt course.

And, of course, the resort is only three miles from Walt Disney World and EPCOT Center and is adjacent to Disney's Lake Buena Vista shopping area. The resort is less than a two-hour drive away from other Florida attractions including Sea World, Cypress Gardens, Silver Springs, Busch Gardens, and the Kennedy Space Center.

The 750 rooms include 75 suites: 42 executive suites, 14 VIP suites, five super VIP and deluxe multilevel suites that include sleeping loft, bar, and private spa with Jacuzzi, and others. The rooms and suites reflect a Florida feeling with wicker furniture, ceiling fans, shutters, wall-to-wall carpeting, and king-size or double beds. Each room has a dramatic view of either the sprawling recreational facilities or the elegantly landscaped entrance courtyard. Bathroom phones, track lighting spotlighting artwork, and hanging plants provide a feeling of refined elegance. Suites contain two color TVs featuring round-the-clock movies and a stereo complete with record player and tape deck. Each room is provided with a bar containing both hard and soft drinks and snacks ranging from crackers and macadamia nuts to pâté, brie, and caviar. The room account is billed for what is used. Ten rooms have been specifically designed to accommodate wheelchairs, with wider doorways, handrails in the bathrooms, and altered bath and closet arrangements for easy access.

The hotel offers the convenience of 24-hour room service plus four restaurants, and five bars and lounges, including a grotto bar and entertainment lounge. The restaurants provide excellent food of all types.

Don't miss luxuriating in the outdoor hot Jacuzzis on a cool evening and strolling across the gently swaying rope and board bridge suspended over the free-form pool. Admire the outdoor sculptures and the masterfully tended garden. Soar to the top of the 18-story hotel in one of Hyatt's patented glassfronted elevators and enjoy a sweeping view of the spacious interior lobby, which is filled with a goldfish pond and lush tropical greenery.

The Langford Hotel
300 East New England Avenue
Winter Park, Florida 32789
305/644-3400

Nov. 1–May 31: $50–$55 single, $60–$70 double
June 1–Oct. 31: $45–$50 single, $55–$60 double

The Langford Hotel is a distinguished downtown Winter Park hotel with reasonable prices that has hosted notables ranging from Lillian Gish to Mamie Eisenhower. Winter Park, an Orlando suburb, is convenient to all central Florida attractions including Disney World, EPCOT, Sea World, Cypress Gardens, and Circus World.

The hotel itself has a quiet atmosphere. Within walking distance, one can take a scenic boat ride or see unique art museums housing the largest collection of Tiffany glass in the world and a huge collection of rare and exotic seashells. Just a block away is swanky Park Avenue with 22 international-style restaurants and boutiques.

The dock for the boat tour is just two blocks away. The ride goes through tropical canals past gorgeous estates.

The hotel boasts an Olympic-size pool, tropical gardens, and waterfalls. A stroll through the tropical gardens, reveals authentic artifacts from Spanish galleons sunk off the Florida coast—cannon, dinnerware, coins—and a huge anchor that stands at the entrance to the hotel's delightful, informal Anchor Room Restaurant.

Fine dining, from steaks to seafood, is available at the hotel's exciting Empire Room Supper Club. Be prepared for an evening you won't forget, with meals like broiled pompano almondine and succulent roast prime rib, and exciting floor shows. Live entertainment, generally a spectacular song and dance revue, is presented Monday through Saturday. Intimate cheek-to-cheek dancing comes naturally with music provided by the Mickey Gioe band. Reservations are suggested.

Business meeting, banquet, or reception facilities are available, many featuring historic Spanish decor and overlooking the Langford's tropical gardens and pool. A new addition to the hotel's facilities is the Shangri La Health Spa, which features massages, facials, steam baths, sauna, and a Jacuzzi.

The hotel's 220 rooms are clean, airy, and spacious, often decorated with original art and sculpture. The Langford is an independent hotel founded, owned, and operated by Robert Langford. He is no absentee owner—it's obvious he gives the hotel his personal attention, and his staff responds by giving guests their personal best.

The Park Plaza Hotel
307 Park Avenue South
Winter Park, Florida 32789
305/647-1072

Deluxe rooms $50–$70 single, $60–$80 double
Balcony suites $90–$100

This charming little 27-room hotel offers distinctive lodg-ing on ritzy Park Avenue in Winter Park, a close-in Orlando suburb noted for its annual Winter Park Arts Festival.

Founded in 1924 and renovated in 1978, the Park Plaza projects a homey 1940s atmosphere. Two types of accom-modations are offered: deluxe single rooms and balcony room suites with a large king-size brass bed. In fact, each room features an old-fashioned, comfortable brass bed, white wicker chairs and sofa, hardwood floors, and ceiling-fans generating soothing breezes. Good-quality original water-color paintings grace the walls. The bathrooms all have skylights and inviting, old-fashioned, deep bathtubs.

Readers of *Central Florida* magazine recently picked the best hotels in the area and named the Park Plaza second only to the spectacular Hyatt Regency Grand Cypress. They also selected the Park Plaza Garden Restaurant—leased by the hotel to a private operator—as the best in central Florida for food and atmosphere.

Located on the corner of Park and New England, the hotel is right next to Central Park, and just one block from the beautiful Rollins College campus. Park Avenue offers fine boutiques, jewelry stores, and objets d'art for the serious shopper as well as for dedicated window shoppers.

One of the hotel's charms is its wide balcony. A com-plimentary continental breakfast is served on the balcony every morning. In the evening, committed people-watchers will enjoy sitting and watching—through a forest of con-cealing hanging plants—as college students gather in the park, teenagers cruise the streets, and couples stroll down Park Avenue hand in hand.

Watch your waistline while staying at the Park Plaza. Besides fine dining at the Park Plaza Garden Restaurant, the hotel lobby offers the Park Plaza Candy and Flower Shop, with fine imported Belgian chocolates, and next door is the East India Ice Cream Company, a gourmet's delight. Also within a five-minute walk are five other fine restau-rants.

Often it is the little extras that make one come back again and again to a hotel. Among the gracious gestures at the Park Plaza is the complimentary issue of the *Wall Street*

Journal delivered to guest rooms each morning, turndown service each evening, and Godiva chocolates placed on the bed each day.

The Park Plaza is central to many attractions and recreational opportunities. Winter Park itself is only minutes from downtown Orlando; less than an hour's drive west is Disney World, the EPCOT Center, Sea World, and other attractions; an hour's drive north brings one to Ocala's horse country and its famous Silver Springs; an hour south is Cypress Gardens, with its world-famous waterski shows; five minutes farther is picturesque Lake Wales with its beautiful Bok Tower Gardens and famous carillon concerts; an hour to the east brings one to the Atlantic Ocean, Daytona Beach, and its famous raceway; and an hour to the southeast is Cape Kennedy.

Don't miss the scenic boat tour that goes through the lakes and city-maintained canals that were used for logging many years ago. The boat dock is only three blocks away from the hotel.

«PHILADELPHIA»

---------------- BED AND BREAKFAST ----------------

Center City Bed and Breakfast
1804 Pine Street
Philadelphia, Pennsylvania 19103
215/735-1137

Bed and Breakfast of Philadelphia
P.O. Box 680
Devon, Pennsylvania 19333
215/688-1633

Society Hill Hotel
Third and Chestnut Streets
Philadelphia, Pennsylvania
215/925-1919

La Reserve
1804 Pine Street
Philadelphia, Pennsylvania 19103
215/735-1137

Bed and breakfast accommodations are a particularly appealing alternative in Philadelphia, where 18th-century streets are lined with charming brick-fronted townhouses of the same era.

Two bed and breakfast networks serve the city. Rates for this type of accommodation range from about $20 for some singles to $70 for some doubles, depending on location, facilities, and so on.

At least two establishments are in the style of bed and breakfast hotels, with several rooms and a domestic ambience. One is the Society Hill Hotel, with eight rooms, and the other is La Reserve, with five rooms.

B&B accommodations—whether one room in a house or a small hotel—can be charming and evocative of the spirit of a historic city's past. But guests should also be aware that certain services and amenities frequently desired by fast-moving business travelers are sometimes sacrificed to charm in these establishments. Particularly vulnerable are convenient telephone service (both message-taking and dialing long-distance from the room), daily housekeeping, room service, and security measures such as locks and safekeeping for valuables.

--------------------- HOTELS ---------------------

The Barclay Hotel
One Rittenhouse Square
237 South 18th Street
Philadelphia, Pennsylvania 19102
215/545-0300

Singles $75
Doubles $85
Suites $125

To contemplate a stay at the Barclay is to be reminded of the old saying that the three most important factors in a business's success are location, location, and location. That is not to say that there are not other reasons to stay at the Barclay. It's just that although one can find other hotels a stone's throw from this one, it's hard to imagine that the location on Rittenhouse Square could be beaten for convenience, prestige, or the views from the guest rooms facing the tree-lined historic square.

A step into the lobby from the outside daylight plunges the visitor into a dark, almost musty atmosphere. A closer look down the corridor, with its black and white diamond-patterned floors, reveals the architectural and design details of the cocktail lounge with its oriental screens.

This 1929 structure was considered one of the most elegant of its time. Its restaurant, cocktail lounge, and meeting rooms were gathering places for the Philadelphia aristocracy. About 10 percent of the 240 sleeping rooms in the hotel are actually residential condominiums.

The hotel sections house a mixture of renovated one-of-a-kind rooms where the occasional Jacuzzi sits anachronistically side by side with a gracefully sculpted, huge marble bathtub. Four-poster beds, oriental rugs, and a television set hidden in the mahogany armoire are some of the trappings awaiting the guest in the rooms.

The hotel advertises that it has a corporate lounge for the convenience of guests traveling on business. However the lounge—similar in ambience to a living room in which stacks of newspapers and magazines are available—is closed more than it's open. Breakfast and cocktails are served there, but at midday it becomes the hotel staff's private dining room. It's closed on weekends.

The Barclay offers 24-hour room service. The hotel houses a piano bar and Le Beau Lieu, a traditional continental restaurant. The only shop in the hotel is a small newsstand, although Center City boutiques, restaurants, and shops of all descriptions are within easy walking distance.

Four Seasons Hotel
One Logan Square
Philadelphia, Pennsylvania 19103
800/268-6282 (tollfree)
215/963-1500

Singles, doubles $147–$192
Bed and sitting room $197–$222
Suites $315 and up

Philadelphians—including many admirers in the hotel business—say that the Four Seasons Hotel is in a class by itself. This is a luxury hotel for luxury travelers.

Opened in July 1983, the Philadelphia representative of

the Canada-based chain of luxury hotels had to meet neighborhood design standards before it could be built on the edge of the tree-lined Benjamin Franklin Parkway, a location that gives guests easy access to City Hall in one direction and an impressive range of museums and cultural institutions in the other.

In winter, one is greeted by a doorman clad in a peaked fur hat and a brown overcoat trimmed with a bushy fur collar, thus setting the tone for the entire stay.

A traveling businessman who requests advice from the concierge on how to get to the airport in time to catch a flight to Bethlehem, Pennsylvania, is advised instead to hire a car with chauffeur to drive him to Bethlehem. He agrees. In two minutes, the concierge has reserved the car. The businessman never asks the price.

This hotel is so in that it does not have to put a mint on the guest's pillow and does not offer a selection of risque movies for viewing in the room.

The hotel lobby and other public areas are tastefully accented with the creative flower arrangements characteristic of the chain's hotels. Pink marble, crystal chandeliers, oriental rugs, and antique furniture create a feeling of quiet opulence.

The hotel, which has 377 rooms and suites, strives to create a residential atmosphere, reflected in rooms furnished with Federal period furniture and decorated in the deeper, richer colorings that reflect Philadelphia's Victorian heritage.

Each room contains a writing desk, television concealed in an armoire, and minibar stocked with drinks and snacks. A terry cloth bathrobe is provided for the use of each guest.

The hotel's premiere restaurant, the Fountain Room, has received a number of awards from local publications. Executive chef Jean-Marie Lacroix studied at Thonon Les Bains on Lake Geneva in France and worked at hotels and restaurants in the British Isles before serving as executive chef at the Four Seasons in Montreal.

In addition to the Fountain Room, which serves French food, the hotel offers the Swann Cafe and Swann Lounge and a summertime outdoor eatery, the Courtyard Cafe. Sunday brunch in the hotel's restaurants is a popular Philadelphia activity.

Special hotel facilities and services include a spa with swimming pool, whirlpool, and exercise machines; twice daily housekeeping; free overnight shoeshine service; and valet parking. The lobby contains a small newsstand–gift shop.

The concierge desk, staffed by several persons, assists guests with special needs ranging from babysitters to theater tickets.

Perhaps the only drawback to this hotel is that at times it may be too popular. During a busy holiday weekend the level of service can be somewhat marred by such small lapses of service as failure to relay a phone message to a guest, lack of available lockers for guests at the spa, and lack of hand towels in a public bathroom area.

Visitors who seek the experience of luxury at a more modest rate should look into the hotel's special weekend packages. They include a "revitalization weekend" featuring a physical exercise program in the spa; and a "freedom weekend" that focuses on visits to historic landmarks.

The Latham Hotel
17th and Walnut Streets
Philadelphia, Pennsylvania 19103
215/563-7474
Reservations: 800/228-0808 (tollfree)

Singles $95–$115
Doubles $115–$135
Suites $230–$400

"What can I do for you? How can I help you?"

The guest who spends a few minutes in the lobby of this small but efficient establishment will hear the words over and over again. They come from the porter, who will not allow guests to carry their own bags or pile them up on the luggage cart.

Old world European is how the management describes

this former apartment building. The small lobby sitting area is comfortably furnished with flowered sofas and a glass coffee table. On an end table stands a phone for the use of guests. From the sofa the view is of a huge vase of fresh flowers—one day the bouquet consisted of striking white lilies mixed in with pussy willows and tufty pink and purple blossoms.

Elevators with gleaming brass and mirrors take guests upstairs to their accommodations.

Furnishings in the 136 rooms are in traditional styles, including some antique reproductions, such as marble-topped night tables and a leather-topped, gracefully curved writing desk. Corner rooms offer an excellent view of the downtown area.

Special features in each room include two phones, a clock radio, a basket or bowl of toiletries, current magazines, and choice of complimentary newspapers. Some of the accommodations have make-up/shaving mirrors and hair dryers in the bathroom.

The management's concern for safety and security is reflected in the individual safes available in some rooms (as well as safekeeping arranged through the reception desk); and the presence of literature and diagrams showing what to do in case of fire or other emergency.

The wife of a former U.S. president was a hotel guest not long ago, and management is fond of pointing out that the hotel had to meet Secret Service standards in order for this to occur.

A restaurant, Bogart's, and a piano bar, Crickett, are located in the hotel. On the way down the hall to Bogart's, one passes a life-size poster of Bogey. Dining room decor might be described as quasi-Casablanca, featuring a ceiling of wooden slats punctuated with fans.

The Latham's downtown location is within walking distance of offices, stores, and restaurants—including a multi-restaurant complex consisting of the Commissary and other eating rooms known for reasonably priced food (of several ethnic flavors) in a casual setting, and Le Bec Fin, generally regarded as the city's premiere restaurant.

Latham guests are also offered temporary membership in a nearby health club and in Elan, a nightclub located in the Warwick Hotel a couple minutes' walk down the street.

The Palace Hotel
Benjamin Franklin Parkway at 18th Street
Philadelphia, Pennsylvania 19103
215/963-2222
Reservations: 800/223-5672 (tollfree)

Singles $95–$145
Doubles $110–$160

The style of the exterior is described by a hotel staff person as modern cylindrical. But once a guest is inside the Palace's 28-story round tower, the mood is set by elegant reproductions of period furniture, oriental rugs, and fresh flowers.

A former apartment building, the Palace is an all-suite hotel affiliated with the British Trusthouse Forte chain.

Shaped more or less like a pie wedge, each of the 244 one-bedroom and 41 two-bedroom suites has a living room with dining area, wet bar, and bathroom. There are also 41 studio rooms and a penthouse suite. Many of the suites have balconies.

For a guest who needs a place to settle in while on a long business trip or seeking a permanent home, the hotel will provide coffee pot, toaster, and other kitchen equipment free (except for a microwave oven, for which there is a charge).

The Palace's facilities include an outdoor swimming pool, sundeck, and sauna.

The Cafe Royal dining room pops up often on lists of Philadelphia's best hotel restaurants. It features what "our chef will grudgingly agree to (label) Country French Cuisine Moderne," says a hotel brochure.

Located at Logan Square, the hotel is within walking distance of City Hall and numerous cultural institutions—including the Rodin Museum and the Franklin Institute—yet convenient to Center City offices and shops.

Vacation and pleasure travelers are invited to special "mystery holiday weekends" in which guests are provided with costumes and clues and urged to track down fictional criminals.

The Warwick Hotel
17th at Locust Street
Philadelphia, Pennsylvania 19103
215/735-6000

Singles $99 and up
Doubles $114 and up
Suites $170 and up

One of the Warwick's biggest assets is the smiling welcome from concierge Betty George, the only concierge in the region who is a member of the international Clef d'Or society.

From her desk with full view of the hotel entrance, the concierge with a cap of curly red hair was one day nervously awaiting the arrival of a couple who were to be married in the hotel that night. It was snowing outside, traffic was slow, and a bottle of iced champagne was waiting in their room upstairs. George also handles more ordinary requests, such as booking flights and trains and theater tickets.

The Warwick is neither slick nor elegant, but it is spacious and comfortable and the staff is eager to please. The building feels larger than its 115 guests rooms and 15 suites, perhaps because it contains a selection of conference and meeting rooms, a ballroom, and large suites; and because it is a home to the residents of some 160 apartments.

The bedrooms, recently redone in what a spokesperson describes as French country decor, are a pleasant jumble of scallop-shell wallpaper, paisley printed curtains, and stenciled flower borders just below ceiling level. The accommodations are roomy and guests are provided with large, hooded terry cloth robes, a well-illustrated jogger's map of downtown, complimentary soaps and toiletries, and Home Box Office movies at no charge.

Guests may leave their shoes to be shined free of charge overnight. There's 24-hour room service and 24-hour meal service in the Brasserie cafe right off the lobby. Guests automatically have membership in the Elan disco and night-club, also off the lobby, and access to the facilities of a nearby health club. Also located in the building are a hair salon and pharmacy.

The Warwick's Center City location is close to shops and restaurants.

«PITTSBURGH»

Bigelow Apartment Hotel
Bigelow Square
Pittsburgh, Pennsylvania 15219
412/281-5800

Studios $70 single, $80 double
One-bedroom suites $90 single, $100 double
Two-bedroom suites $130 single, $140 double

The Bigelow Apartment Hotel, built in 1952, was a fore-runner of the currently proliferating all-suite hotels. As the industrial climate of Pittsburgh changed from blue-collar to white-collar workers in the last ten years, the hotel has changed to cater to a more upscale guest.

The Bigelow's 80 units offer comfort as well as convenience. Today, guests prefer to be able to relax for longer stays in a less commercial and more residential atmosphere. Executives are not the only ones who are enjoying the renaissance at the Bigelow. Many visitors find that for the price, the value cannot be beat. Many of the city's larger hotels are in the $90 and above range, and that does not include a complimentary breafast.

In the past two years, this hotel has been the single fastest-growing property in the city. Many of the apartments have been completely redone, and the lobby has just been renovated.

The new subway station at Steel Plaza is located just across from the entrance to the hotel, bringing guests within three minutes of any downtown location.

The lobby of the hotel, once rather inconspicuous and commercial in appearance, has been transformed into a chic oasis. Gone are the tired and worn furnishings and drab walls and in their place is a room with bright oak paneling and hunter green walls, decorated in the newest fabrics and furnishings.

A new green Italian marble reception desk that is totally computerized will aid in check in.

Units vary from studio, one-bedroom, and two-bedroom arrangements with two baths to an exclusive three-bedroom suite. Each is decorated and furnished in new styles and fabrics and includes both beds and sofa beds for added convenience. All have housekeeping once a week for long stays and daily for short stays. Full room service will be added as soon as the renovations are complete. Wake-up calls can be requested.

The biggest attraction of this hotel is its fine restaurant and lounge, the Ruddy Duck. This has a quiet, sporting, pub atmosphere. Continental dishes are served with style.

Guests also have the advantage of an in-house health club, including full Nautilus set-up, as well as indoor pool and saunas. Guests are provided a temporary membership.

Ligonier Country Inn
U.S. Route 30
Laughlintown, Pennsylvania 15655
412/238-3651

Singles, doubles $45–$70

The Ligonier Country Inn, located three miles from Ligonier, Pennsylvania, lies 30 minutes from downtown Pittsburgh.

Built in 1924 as the former Laurel Ridge Hotel, Ligonier Country Inn has the flavor of a colonial wayside stop. Operated for the last two years as a bed and breakfast by the Steitz family, the hotel is situated in the midst of the Laurel Highlands, a well-known vacation destination in western Pennsylvania.

The hotel's sixteen rooms vary in size and decor but all have a colonial flavor and varied furnishings. Each comes with a private bath. More like a country hotel, with a cozy, intimate atmosphere, the Ligonier Country Inn makes an excellent spot for a short stay.

Guests are treated to a hearty full farm breakfast on weekends and a continental breakfast on weekdays in the early American dining room, which is also noted for its fine traditional American cuisine.

All rooms are equipped with air conditioning, TV, phone, and sitting area. Bed arrangements include single, twin, queen-size, and one king-size bed.

Guests can enjoy a cocktail by the fireplace in the cozy lounge before dinner. Fresh foods are a specialty here and French dishes are served as specials on occasion.

Before the hotel was built, guests used to stop at the historic Compass Inn across the street. This area was always a wayside stop on the road from Philadelphia. Pittsburgh is a short drive away on Route 30, and many attractions surround the hotel in the Highlands.

Residence Inn—Pittsburgh/Greentree
700 Mansfield Avenue
Pittsburgh, Pennsylvania 15205
412/279-6300

Studio suites $82 single or double
Penthouse suites $98 single or double

Though the Residence Inn belongs to a nationwide chain, its management runs the hotel like an inn, with very personal service and careful attention to details.

Consisting of 152 units in 19 buildings, this hotel is arranged like a village around a central office and living room lounge with stone fireplace. Entrances are all private and each building has from three to five units.

Each building is designed with Tudor detailing of stucco and wood, and all are connected with a network of landscaped walks. Unlike more conventional hotels, this one is more like a grouping of townhouses or condominiums. As such, it is more like home and less commercial in appearance.

252

Another difference is the size of the units. Each unit, whether it be a simple studio or a more elaborate penthouse, is about the size of a normal apartment, with full-size kitchen facilities, including a dishwasher, and a stone fireplace that warms guests on cold nights.

Designed originally for business travelers, the inn is ideal for families or couples who want to stay in a more homey atmosphere. In fact, guests have enough room to entertain friends or associates.

Each unit comes with a fully equipped kitchen, dining area, and table settings for four people. Besides this, all the equipment necessary to cook a full meal is included and is of the finest quality. The interiors are contemporary in style, and furnishings have a comfortable look and feel. A unique part of the arrangement is the island kitchen with stools and coffeemaker and popcorn popper that come with each unit (also complimentary popcorn and coffee to start). Each unit also features a separate living area with sofa and chairs and color TV, as well as a bedroom with TV in the penthouse units.

Of the two kinds of units, the penthouse is the larger but no more luxurious than the studio. No expense was spared in decorating and outfitting the suites. The penthouse does have a separate loft bedroom, full bath, and separate dressing area upstairs, as well as a Murphy bed downstairs for extra sleeping room.

Though the hotel does not have a full-service restaurant, it provides a continental buffet in the central lounge for breakfast, which is included in the rate. This is not sparse by any means and includes homemade pastries and rolls as well as a selection of juices and other beverages and cereals.

A complimentary evening cocktail hour is held each day in the central Gatehouse lounge, and once a week, a complimentary barbecue or pizza party is held indoors or out depending on the season. The manager is the person who cooks the meat and serves the pizza. He also provides a great deal of help and information to guests.

For recreational purposes, the hotel has a small outdoor pool and sports court that can be used for racquetball, tennis, or badminton. There is also a whirlpool spa (outdoor) in summer and tables in the lounge for playing games on cold winter evenings.

The staff is especially skilled, having been trained in innkeeping rather than just hotel services. Just about anyone can give advice and information and all are encouraged to talk to guests.

Besides its accommodations, the inn is perfect for small seminars and meetings, offering state-of-the-art facilities. Convenient to the airport and only three minutes from downtown Pittsburgh, the inn provides a quiet place to come back to after a day of sightseeing or meetings.

The inn also provides rental cars to guests who may need them for short periods. Pets are allowed for an extra charge.

Westin William Penn Hotel
Mellon Square
Pittsburgh, Pennsylvania 15230
412/281-7100

Standard singles $100–$130
Standard doubles $120–$150
Crown floor luxury rooms $110–$140 single, $130–$160
   double

The William Penn Hotel has been a landmark in downtown Pittsburgh since its opening in 1916. The finest in accommodations have always been the norm, and the Westin outfit is now bestowing a $30 million renovation on the Penn.

Located on Mellon Square across from the new Bank Center shopping mall and also across from the new Light Rail Transit stop, the hotel features a beautiful regency interior that has managed to survive since its opening.

Once the renovations are complete, the hotel will have 595 rooms, rather than its present 800. There are two types of rooms available. The standard rooms feature conventional period reproduction furnishings set in contemporary decor. Featured is a marble bath with brass touches, Chippendale styling, and mirrored doors to expand space. As in all Westin hotels, luxury is the key, and guests will find soft and luxurious fabrics as well as color TVs with cable service.

The other style of room available is the crown room, located on the top two floors. All crown rooms were designed by the same firm that did the Century Plaza Hotel in Los Angeles. Each features luxurious carpeting, a terry cloth robe, a phone and speaker from the TV in bath, and free shoeshine. A central lounge with honor bar is also the place for continental breakfast. A complimentary wine and cheese cocktail hour is held every afternoon.

The most magnificient part of this hotel is the high-ceilinged lobby. In the elegant regency style, it features several large crystal chandeliers. A spacious lounge area offers piano entertainment in the afternoons and evenings. Balconies from the mezzanine area overlook the floor, where guests can partake of afternoon high tea in the English tradition.

The lobby itself and the restaurants will also be renovated. An expensive dining room is planned, with an entrance from the street. La Plume restaurant will feature French and continental dishes, and the present restaurant, the Terrace Room, will be reserved for weddings and the like. The lobby bar, a massive brass and mirrored affair at the far end, will be enlarged and some of the extra trim that has been added over the years will be removed, giving the lobby a more contemporary and elegant look.

Many staff members have been with the hotel for 20 years or more. Old world in manner, each staff member performs his or her duties with style and grace. They are especially helpful to guests new to the city.

As with other older hotels, corridors are wide and brightly lit. All rooms presently have high ceilings and smallish baths. When completed, all will have sitting areas and better heating systems. A wide variety of bed arrangements is available, and after renovation more king-size beds will be offered. Room service is available until 11 P.M. nightly.

A small coffeeshop has been opened on the lower mezzanine floor, serving breakfasts and light lunches until early afternoon. There are plenty of other places nearby for dining and shopping. A new subway system connects the hotel with various shopping and business districts of the city.

«PORTLAND MAINE»

The Chebeague Inn by-the-sea
Box 492
Chebeague Island, Maine 04017
207/846-5155

SEASON: $55–$80 double occupancy
OFF SEASON (MAY 24–JUNE 30. LABOR DAY–
 OCTOBER 1): $44–$64 double occupancy

The 21-room Chebeague Inn offers a great value and has recently been renovated from top to bottom. Located on Chebeague Island (the largest of over 250 islands in inner Casco Bay), it sits atop a small hill on the northeast tip, and has lovely views back to the mainland. It's accessible by passenger ferry from Yarmouth's Cousins Island, or by car ferry from Portland.

The living room is large, dominated by a massive stone fireplace, and furnished with old chairs upholstered with new bright fabrics. The view of the mainland from this room is the primary reason people like to gather here before dinner. During the day, or on warmer evenings, the wrap-around porch provides less obstructed views. The dining room, furnished with simple tables and chairs, serves good home-cooked food and fresh fish.

The views from the bedrooms that face out to sea are smashing; be sure to ask for one of these. New rugs have been laid, and the bathrooms are completely modern. The island itself is a getaway spot providing walks, biking, uncrowded beaches, and wonderful opportunities for picnics (which the kitchen at the inn is happy to put together). For a small greens fee golfers can use the course that surrounds the inn. The inn is open from late May to early October.

Homewood Inn
Drinkwater Point
P.O. Box 196
Yarmouth, Maine 04096
207/846-3351

SEASON: Suites and cottages $105–$206,
   rooms $44–$78
OFF SEASON: Suites and cottages $80–$180,
   rooms $34–$60

The inn is off the beaten track, yet not far from Portland. The innkeepers go out of their way to make guests feel at home. A variety of accommodations stand on water's edge. Many of the rooms have water views, and the best rooms are large enough to provide sitting areas and working fireplaces. Unlike many inns farther up the coast, Homewood does have telephones and television. Pleasant rooms are furnished mostly with antiques and some quality reproductions, and decorated in a sure-handed, homey style that is anything but intimidating. An otherwise beautiful view of a few of the 365 islands of Casco Bay is marred by an electric plant that was built in the very focal point of the inn's view a number of years ago.

Meals, served in the main lodge, are excellent. The emphasis is on seafood and lobster, but steak and chicken are also offered. Every Monday night there is a clambake. An antique shop is open in the lodge. Someone at the reception desk is always ready to provide information on activities in the area. Facilities at the inn include a freshwater pool, one tennis court, shuffleboard, croquet, saltwater bathing, and rental bicycles.

The Inn at ParkSpring
135 Spring Street
Portland, Maine 04101
207/774-1059

$60–$80 double occupancy

This classy addition to Portland's lodgings scene is a symbol of the new vigor of Maine's principal city. Opened in December 1983, the inn is styled as a guest-house cum executive lodging, and is very capably managed by Wendy Wickstrom. Flexible and creative service is the key to the inn's success. Guests are not shooed away at a rigid check-out time, and do not have to rush out of bed to enjoy the ample continental breakfast (included in the room rate). Many special provisions can be made for those here on business, including installing phone service, catering a lunch, and making sure that the meeting room is just so.

The townhouse, built in 1835, has been completely re-done. The decor is sophisticated and eclectic, from the entrance hall with coral-colored walls and oriental runners to the contemporary bath with cedar walls on the third floor. In the Park Room, guests can luxuriate in a four-poster bed and enjoy a marble fireplace and European-style bath. Third-floor bedrooms have skylights. Baths have luxurious toiletries and linens.

The inn can serve as a fine base for visiting Portland's West End and Old Port districts, the distinctive Portland Museum of Art, and all the shops and restaurants nearby.

«PORTLAND,»
«OREGON»

Alexis Hotel Portland
1510 Southwest Harbor Way
Portland, Oregon 97201
800/227-1333 (tollfree)
503/228-3233

Singles $95–$130
Doubles $115–$150
Suites $160–$400

Portland's splashy new waterfront hotel has been variously described by its builders as evoking the feel of a turn-of-the-century resort, an English manor lodge, and a New England yacht club. The brick and wood exterior, three rooftop rotundas, window flower boxes, and the marina setting all contribute to an ambience of quiet luxury, yet there is also an unmistakably informal and very regional atmosphere about the place.

Not to be confused with Portland's infamous Greek restaurant of the same name, this Alexis stands at one end of an esplanade in a newly created city neighborhood dubbed RiverPlace. Also part of the community is an arcade of retail shops (including, among other things, a yacht sales office), a 250-slip marina, pastel-colored condominium apartments, and Portland's waterfront park.

Handcrafted rugs and traditional-style furniture make for a comfortable, residential ambience in the hotel's public areas and private rooms alike. Guest rooms are decorated in warm blues and yellows. Wet bars, whirlpool baths, and wood-burning fireplaces are some of the extras that grace Alexis suites. Views are of the city skyline, water, park, or a landscaped courtyard. All rooms have movie channel and remote-control television.

Sister to the Seattle hotel of the same name, the Alexis Portland features many of the same amenities: complimentary sherry awaits guests upon arrival, complimentary continental breakfast is served each morning complete with newspaper (in bed on weekends), and plush terry cloth robes hang in all rooms for guest use. Glycerine and French milled soap, bath gel, and hand lotion are provided in all rooms. Down comforters may be requested.

Service is intentionally unstuffy. Overnight pressing, complimentary shoeshine, valet parking (at a lot underneath the hotel or in nearby surface lots), evening linen turndown service with pillow-side chocolates, 24-hour room service, assistance with tour or travel information, limousine service, and errand running are some of the services offered by the Alexis Portland staff. The unusual no-tipping policy (food and beverage service excepted) is intended to eliminate the outstretched palm on the part of personnel, and thus make guests feel more at ease.

Athletic guests have a choice between the waterfront jogging paths used by local runners and the RiverPlace state-of-the-art health and fitness center, which includes track, pool, weight room, sauna, and steam. There is also a spa and whirlpool inside the hotel.

Pacific Northwest seafood is the specialty of the neighborhood. Meals at the hotel's Esplanade Restaurant may be taken either in the elegant dining room with views of the waterfront, or in warm weather on a more casual patio with seating beside the river walkway. The teakwood and slate lounge is also a lovely spot for light lunch or dessert. The neighborhood also features a floating restaurant and pub at the end of the marina breakwater, and the popular Portland establishment of McCormick & Schmick's for dining and dancing.

The Alexis is located in south downtown, a bit of a walk

to Portland's major downtown streets. The hotel is accessible to the disabled.

Allenhouse
2606 Northwest Lovejoy Street
Portland, Oregon 97210
503/227-6841

$52–$57 single, $58–$63 double

Pecan waffles, freshly squeezed orange juice, homemade granola, fresh-baked fruit or nut muffins, coffee and tea, served in a sunroom overlooking the garden—it's no wonder that some of Barbara Allen's guests say they return just for the breakfast.

There are more attractions than the food (included in room rates) in this recently refurbished inn. The energetic owner delights in sharing her 1914-vintage home with guests who appreciate its spaciousness, period decor, and atmosphere of friendly informality. Amenities include a telephone line exclusively for guests, with jack outlets in all guestrooms; down duvets on the old-fashioned beds; and fresh flowers and a basket full of current magazines in each of the four guest rooms.

In the North Room, where the bed is canopied in green, exotically colored birds cover the wallpaper, and a white wicker peacock chair stands in one corner. The Master Room, with its four-poster bed, is largest, though the Suite has a side room, once a sunporch, for an extra guest. Each guest room is distinctively decorated with exquisite floral wallpaper, eyelet-edged linens, and a bright color scheme.

Allenhouse is located on a residential street within walking distance of many of Portland's most interesting shops and restaurants. It's popular with business travelers, and, since a major hospital is in the area, people in the medical field are also frequent guests. In the evenings, visitors enjoy relaxing by the fire in the large sitting room, perhaps joining Allen or another guest in a board game. And mornings bring a view of the little jewel of a garden, where camellias, a

261

flowering cherry tree, and tulips edge an enclosed, curving lawn.

Anne Hughes Guest House
2482 Northwest Marshall Street
Portland, Oregon 97210
503/227-4440

$35 double or single

Comfortable, unpretentious, and homey—Anne Hughe's gray-gabled guesthouse overflows with these qualities. Informality is the byword, and guests are treated like family (unless they prefer seclusion, and that wish is respected, too).

Hughes is a woman of eclectic interests, and most of them are on display in her home. Every inch of shelf space is crammed with books and sculpture, magazines and candles and fabric and whimsical art. Stick puppets from Thailand grace one wall; a colorful paper kite decorates a bedroom; a sequined sombrero hangs in a sitting room.

The three guest rooms, on the second floor, are simple and cozy, and sometimes have surprises—such as a closet lined with shelves of well-loved books, or a private balcony with wicker chairs and a view of Mount St. Helens.

There is no television, but other forms of entertainment abound, including dozens of games for children. The upstairs landing is a quiet nesting spot, while two sitting rooms with comfy couches on the ground floor offer additional space for sipping sherry or tea and getting acquainted with the host and other guests.

Breakfast, included in the room rates, is served at a communal table in the dining room. Guests enjoy hot muffins, granola, yogurt, fruit, and coffee or tea, and occasionally putter in the kitchen on their own when Hughes is busy with one of her favorite projects: running a coffee room in a local bookstore.

"I want people to relax and be comfortable here," Hughes says. She adds a quote from Carson McCullers: " 'The atmosphere of a proper cafe implies these qualities: fellowship, satisfaction of the belly, and a certain gaiety and grace of behavior.' " All are served with abundance and verve at Anne Hughes Guest House.

Corbett House
7533 Southwest Corbett Avenue
Portland, Oregon 97219
503/245-2580

Back room $35 single, $40 double; two front rooms $45 single, $50 double

Sylvia Malagamba, the owner of this blocky yellow house set high on a hill above the Willamette River is an artist. Evidence of her impeccable taste fills every corner of the early art deco inn. Both casual and sophisticated, Corbett House shows the touch of a sure artistic hand in its mingling of antiques and contemporary furnishings.

The inn is located in a pleasant residential area close to downtown Portland, and from its various windows guests catch glimpses of city lights, the river, Mount St. Helens, and Mount Hood.

In the three plant-filled rooms, guests find gracious extras such as sherry-filled decanters and alarm clocks with sleep-to-cassette features. A closetful of robes is available for guests' use, and a teddy bear, Nudge, may be rented for a nickel a night, Malagamba says with a straight face. Such bits of whimsy make this inn refreshingly different.

Many business travelers stop at the Corbett House, and Malagamba's breakfasts are one of the major attractions. Her previous experience as a caterer is a boon to guests; they are served homebaked breads, scones, muffins, and her specialty, Italian ices. Fresh fruits, cereals, juices, tea, and coffee are offered as well. Evening wine is served in the sitting room, where there's plenty of reading material and often a warming blaze in the fireplace.

The Heathman Hotel
Southwest Broadway at Salmon Street
Portland, Oregon 97205
800/551-0011 (tollfree)
503/241-4100

Singles $75–$125
Doubles $90–$140
Suites $175–$355

The original Heathman was Portland's grand Jazz Age hotel, but after it was converted to housing for soldiers and sailors during World War II, it never regained its stature. Since reopening in 1984, however, some of the Heathman's earliest guests have returned to recall the weddings and proms attended here, and to express heartfelt gratitude at the gracious revival.

The restored 1927 classical art deco exterior of terra-cotta brick and sandstone remains unchanged with the exception of a new white neon sign. The building is on the National Register of Historic Places. The Heathman's small lobby is marble and Burmese teak, the registration desk is black granite, and the elevators are paneled with blond and dark rosewood. Fresh or silk flower arrangements grace the public areas. The Heathman is accessible to the disabled.

The tea court, with its hand-rubbed eucalyptus-paneled walls, curving stairway, arched windows, and Steinway grand, is the one original room. Only the fireplace was added during renovation. This is the locale for the Heathman's afternoon tea ritual, which has been received with great fanfare by Portlanders. Complete with starched linen and silver tongs, it is an American Northwest version of high tea, with a menu that changes monthly (for example, rose hips tea is poured in June, in honor of the city's annual Rose Festival). Champagne and sherry are also on the menu, and overflow seating is at mezzanine tables with a view of the court.

The Heathman Restaurant across the lobby creates an entirely different ambience: three tiers of tables overlook Broadway (albeit through frosted, etched glass) in an airy setting. Coffered ceilings and marble tables lend a hint of the art deco style. Only the modern sculpture has been the subject of raised local eyebrows. The menu is seasonal Northwest fare, which means plenty of fresh seafood. The gelato is made on the premises.

The Heathman's truly eclectic art collection was exhibited

at a local gallery prior to the hotel's opening. Holdings range from the 18th-century oil paintings in the tea court to Andy Warhol's endangered species series in the restaurant. Guest rooms are hung with photographs, drawings, paintings, and prints by Northwest artists.

Upstairs, the Heathman is characterized by an elegant, residential feeling. Soft lighting, red-green carpet, and marble thresholds grace the corridors. Inside the 160 rooms, English chintz bedspreads match roman shades, and bamboo screens add a homey touch. Headboards are either rattan or hardwood, tables are travertine or brass, armoires are dark wood. All television sets are concealed within furniture. Baths are stocked with bath gel and Portuguese black soap as well as ordinary soap, shampoo, shoehorn, and shower-cap. Two thick terry cloth robes hang in all closets for guest use. All rooms have access to an enormous selection of in-room movies at no charge. One-third of the hotel's rooms are suites named for prominent Portland families. Even the smallest suites are quite spacious.

Hotel staff is above all resourceful. The concierge and housekeeping department will attend to car rental or card table set-up, bedboard or barbershop appointments, interpreters, manicures, and baggage repair, or just supply air-freshener. Linen turndown service comes with Godiva chocolates. Morning city papers are delivered to all rooms, and suites are furnished with copies of the fashionable Northwest magazine *Stepping Out*. The hotel gift shop delivers flowers. There is no charge for valet parking, and parking in the Heathman's garage is complimentary on weekends.

A runner's guide to the city is included in the room packet, but guests who would like more extensive fitness facilities can pay for privileges at either of two nearby health clubs. Alternatively, rowing and exercise machines will be delivered to guest rooms free of charge.

Square in downtown Portland, the Heathman shares its block with the city's newly renovated performing arts center (one banquet room, the Symphony, connects to the concert hall) and is a half block from two of the city's institutions: the literary Catbird Seat bookstore, and the fashionable and crowded eatery Metro on Broadway.

Mallory Motor Hotel
729 Southwest 15th Avenue
(at Yamhill Street)
Portland, Oregon 97205
503/223-6311

Singles $29–$50
Doubles $34–$60

Characterized by a certain faded elegance, the Mallory is a popular Portland hotel, and a fine bargain. This well-maintained hostelry is a favorite among Oregonians who come from elsewhere in the state to visit their big city.

The 1912 exterior is just a bit run-down, while the lobby is a mix of marble, crystal, and slightly worn carpet. The dining room, recently redone, offers a pleasant setting. Decor is eclectic; some of the 144 guest rooms are attractively appointed, others unexceptional.

The huge corner rooms are where the Mallory shines. Rooms on the upper floors feature great views of Mount Hood. Most have a shower and tub, others only a shower. Amenities in some rooms include a retractable clothesline in the bathtub on which to steam or dry clothes, and an embroidered pincushion and sewing kit for guest use. Linen is perfectly clean and adequate, though the towels could never be called fluffy.

There is only one guest elevator, but visitors enjoy friendly concierge and housekeeping services. The lobby newsstand carries the *New York Times* and the *Wall Street Journal* as well as Oregon papers and sundries. There are soft drink and ice machines on each floor. Parking is free.

The Mallory is located across the freeway from downtown proper—a walk of a few blocks. This location, however, puts one a bit closer to Portland's Washington Park, one of the city's most outstanding attractions.

Portland's White House
1914 Northeast 22nd Avenue
Portland, Oregon 97212
503/287-7131

$32–$55 single, $37–$60 double

In the heart of a quiet, tree-filled neighborhood stands one of Portland's most unusual homes: an ornate white mansion, complete with Greek columns, fountain, circular driveway and broad veranda. To enter the turn-of-the-century home, built by a wealthy lumber baron, is to step into the stately world of a bygone day. The walls of the entry hall are covered with landscape murals, the floors are of polished oak and inlaid Honduran mahogany, and crystal chandeliers hang from the ceiling. The only sounds are the tick of a grandfather clock and the song of a canary.

A wide central staircase leads to a landing where sunshine streams through the delicate pastels of antique stained-glass windows. Upstairs, the five guest rooms are furnished in a style befitting the period. There's a brass queen-size bed; lace curtains billow at oversized windows; clawfoot bathtubs are commodious.

In the spacious dining room, guests feast on scones and jam, mushroom omelettes, porridge, and fruit. Mary Hough, born in Dublin and raised in Coventry, serves an English breakfast as she learned it at her mother's boarding house. Breakfast is included in the room rates.

Every detail in the completely refurbished home, from the oriental carpets to the brass doorknobs, is given loving attention at Portland's White House. The resulting atmosphere combines an old-fashioned romantic elegance with warm hospitality.

Riverside Inn
50 Southwest Morrison Street
Portland, Oregon 97204
503/221-0711

Singles $49
Doubles $54–$58

From the outside, the Riverside resembles an unexceptional motel, and although all 138 rooms are nearly identical, the dark green carpet and green and white fabric with matching wallpaper in the bath, wicker chairs, card tables, photographs, and stocked bookshelves make this a more pleasant place to stay than the usual hotel room.

Some guest rooms have track lighting, some have balconies (unfortunately overlooking a parking lot, although at night the city sparkles beyond). Bookshelves hold an eclectic selection of hardbacks that the hotel purchased by the pound. At least a few in each room are literary. The flowerpots on either end of the shelves hold plastic flowers. Part of the hotel faces the Willamette River, and waterfront rooms have a pleasant view. Under clear skies, Mount Hood is visible.

The front desk will accommodate guests' standard needs such as dinner reservations or an ironing board. There are no health club privileges, though Waterfront Park is a popular jogger's route. Newspapers and tourist brochures are available in the lobby. Parking is free. Downstairs, the Riverside Cafe and Bar serves breakfast, lunch, and dinner and the coffeeshop serves breakfast and lunch only.

The Riverside has seen a wonderful neighborhood grow up around it within the last five years. Downtown First Avenue is the home of Yamhill Marketplace, a five-level atrium of produce and fresh fish vendors, gourmet candy and pasta, and a host of fashionable shops. Equally elegant shops, restaurants, and bars populate the surrounding blocks of renovated buildings. A stroll up the avenue brings one to Portland's "200 Block," home to art galleries, eateries, and more fine shops. Just beyond here is New Market Village, a restored marketplace in the heart of the city's historic Old Town district.

The Riverside Inn is where sailors stay during Portland's Rose Festival in June.

Westin-Benson Hotel
Southwest Broadway at Oak Street
Portland, Oregon 97205
800/228-3000 (tollfree) 503/228-9611

Singles $76–$109
Doubles $90–$124
Suites $250–$425

The twenty bronze drinking fountains that grace downtown Portland street corners were donated to the city by turn-of-the-century lumber baron Simon Benson, the same man responsible for this very elegant brick hotel.

The Benson's lobby is perhaps its grandest feature. The Circassian walnut paneling was shipped around the Horn from the forests of Russia, the silver-plated mirror at the head of the stairwell dates from the 1880s, the ceiling is classical coffered plaster, the railing along the veined white Italian marble staircase is cast iron, and the signature "B" is carved into the ashtray sand. Early risers are treated to coffee and tea in this setting, and complimentary hot beverages and a silver tray of sweets is served here weekday afternoons. The fireplace crackles in winter months.

The building is an Oregon historic landmark, and unlike many older hotels, the Benson has never witnessed a decline in status. But while the original French Baroque-style exterior with its unusual mansard roof still stands, the 1959 wing, which nearly doubled the number of rooms to the present 320, is much drabber.

In the Benson's early days, rooms came with grand pianos and circulating ice water, and guests were treated to hot clam nectar each morning. Today, the upstairs does not seem quite on par with the entryway. Elevator interiors are shabby, with framed Westin advertisements on display. Corridors are papered in unattractive black and gold, and decorated with poster-size advertisements for the dining room. Still, doors along the old wing are a rich mahogany with an inlaid "OH" signature (the hotel was built as the Oregon Hotel, but when Benson decided to manage it himself, he changed the name). Ceilings here are vaulted and stairwells are all marble, so it's worth a walk up or down. While the two wings are seamlessly joined, down to the graceful marble baseboard, the new doors are plainer wood with no embellishment, and ceilings are flat.

Guest rooms in the two wings do not differ markedly. Top of the line is the two-bedroom Crown Suite, but at the opposite end of the spectrum, the smallest rooms are very small indeed, some without room for a desk, and some with shower-only baths. In between, design varies from standard to above average.

Furnishings are either dark wood in modern Chinese Chippendale style, or light imitation French Provincial; some are locally crafted, and one room in the medium price range is actually appointed with antique furniture. Some guest room artwork is locally commissioned and documents regional history, while other pieces are on the attractive end of standard hotel oils.

All rooms come with nondigital clocks, and a small selection of movies available for a price. For an interesting change, some hotel linen is bright pink. All suites have refrigerators and all penthouse rooms have a wet bar as well.

The oak-paneled London Grill in the lobby is modeled after the English eatery frequented by Charles Dickens, and succeeds eminently in re-creating that atmosphere. Diners can sit at their tables in armchairs, and waiters will appear at the elbow to light a cigarette. Cuisine is continental with seasonal Northwest specialties, and an award-winning wine list. The Benson's extravagant Sunday champagne brunch is booked to capacity.

Services are rendered gracefully by the concierge who, in addition to the usual dinner or tour reservations, is also obliged to order flowers, have luggage repaired, and recommend local picnic spots. The housekeeping department, (which has its quarters inside the mansard roof), will supply a wide variety of articles including hot water bottles and cribs. Haircutting, manicure, pedicure, and shoeshine are available in the hotel's second-floor shop, and the lobby has a well-stocked gift shop cum newsstand. There are ice and soft drink machines on most floors. Guests returning in late evening will find their bed linens turned down, and although wake-up calls are computerized, guests can request that they be personally dialed. Overnight parking is at the hotel with no extra charge for valet service. A reasonable fee also entitles guests to use of nearby health club facilities. Room service operates 24 hours a day and includes daily newspaper on the menu.

In the early 1980s, when Western International formally changed the hotel's name to the Westin-Benson, there was an uproar on the city's editorial pages. The hotel willingly continues to answer to the name ''The Benson.''

«SACRAMENTO»

The Briggs House
2209 Capitol Avenue
Sacramento, California 95816
916/441-3214

Rooms, suites $50–$90

Standing regally on Capitol Avenue just a few blocks from the state capitol and the historic Sutter's Fort, the Briggs House is the oldest and most lavish of Sacramento's bed and breakfast inns. Built in 1901, this two-story, beige, cubical colonial served as the home of Dr. William Ellery Briggs, a well-known ear, nose, and throat specialist and respected conservationist. Briggs, whose grandson, C. K. McClatchy, is editor of the *Sacramento Bee*, lived here until his death in 1931. The home served for a time as a boarding house until it was purchased in the 1970s by a lawyer and interior decorator who undertook a major renovation task.

In June of 1981, the home was purchased by a group of educators, most of whom are employed by the state Department of Education, to be converted to a bed and breakfast inn. They added bathrooms, a new roof, furnishings, and accessories, including treasures and family heirlooms from their own homes. Shortly after opening, the entire Briggs House was rented by Andy Warhol and his entourage for a two-day stay.

The Briggs House can be best characterized by its atmosphere combining graciousness and elegance with homeyness. Turn-of-the-century Austrian, English, and

American antiques, oriental rugs, and delicate lace curtains grace spacious rooms of rich, dark wood paneling and shiny inlaid hardwood floors. In the evening, guests are treated to complimentary wine, fruit, and nuts, served in the cozy living room, where a blazing fire can be found during cool weather. The adjacent library has shelves of games and books with information on things to do in Northern California and Sacramento, including a notebook listing fine local restaurants. The living room also serves as the setting for a lavish breakfast served on heirloom china with sterling silver and lace tablecloths. Guests are served fresh-ground coffee and herb tea, juice, homemade bread, fresh fruit, and an egg dish or crustless quiche called Briggs House frittata. Breakfast may also be enjoyed in the guest rooms or on the garden patio in warm weather.

The Briggs House offers seven rooms, including five in the main house and two in a secluded cottage in the garden. In the main house, the only ground-floor room, located off the main hallway, is the Fireside Room, which features a massive Australian oak bed that converts from a king-size bed to two twin beds. A fireplace, Indian rug, and intimate dining corner give the room a cozy atmosphere. Upstairs, the Executive Room, decorated in blue and maroon, has a brass double bed, antique marble-top washstand, and Tiffany lamps. The Poster Room is so named for its four-poster bed covered with plush white comforters and eyelet pillows. The Executive and Poster rooms share a full bath, which includes a clawfoot tub. The Sunrise Room, with a private bath, features a private sunporch with wicker furniture overlooking the garden. The elegant Heritage Room features a French antique double bed and matching dresser. A spacious private bath with brass fixtures overlooks the garden.

Two suites popular with honeymooners are the Carriage House and Sleepy Hollow, located in the building that once housed Dr. Briggs's carriages. The second-story, ivy-covered Carriage House is whimsically decorated with teddy bears and features a hand-carved, heart motif oak bed, sitting room with country-style sofa bed, vintage kitchenette, and private bath. Downstairs is Sleepy Hollow, a cozy two-room suite with a sitting room that includes a fireplace and small refrigerator. The bedroom has a brass and white lacquer bed, a clawfoot tub in the open complete with rubber ducky and bubble bath, and a private bath.

It's the small touches at the Briggs House that make guests feel pampered. Fresh flower arrangements are found throughout the home and in all of the rooms, which also have bedside clocks, plenty of plush towels, kimonos and terry cloth robes, hand-embroidered handtowels, and small clothbound books where guests may record their thoughts on their visit.

The lush backyard features plenty of lounge chairs and tables, a hot tub and sauna, a hammock, and an old-fashioned swing hanging from a large orange tree. Bicycles are available for touring. During the summer, the garden is the site of outdoor concerts. In addition to concerts, a variety of events are held here during the year, including quilt and teddy bear shows and afternoon tea.

All rooms are air-conditioned and private phones are available by special arrangement. Young children and pets are not allowed, and smoking is confined to the living room and outdoors.

Hotel El Rancho Resort/Conference Center
1029 West Capitol Avenue
Sacramento, California 95691
800/952-5566 (tollfree) 916/371-6731

Rooms, suites $50–$95

Located in West Sacramento just three minutes from the state capitol, the Hotel El Rancho Resort/Conference Center offers some of the region's finest dining and fitness facilities. The 17-acre resort hotel is an unexpected tropical oasis on a strip of West Capitol Avenue characterized by fast-food restaurants, motels, and discount gas stations.

The 244-room hotel was built in 1940 in the California Spanish style, featuring primarily single-story bungalow buildings with hacienda-style red tile roofs, hand-crafted wood molding, and whitewashed adobe walls. The lush grounds are landscaped with brightly planted flower beds, shrubbery, eucalyptus, and more than 100 stately palm trees.

Notable guests over the years have included Ginger Rogers, Clark Gable, Robert Taylor, Rosalind Russell, and more recently, Danny Thomas, Joe Namath, and Clint Eastwood. The El Rancho recently underwent a massive facelift to recapture its original 1940s glamour.

One of the more outstanding features of the El Rancho is the Racquet and Fitness Center, available without charge to hotel guests. The Fitness Center features seven lighted tennis courts, six racquetball courts, a competition-size swimming pool, a complete weight training floor, spa and sauna, and a 1.2-mile Parcourse running trail with 18 exercise stations. Aerobics classes are offered, along with tennis and racquetball lessons, and massages are available by appointment. A unique feature of the center is the Environmental Capsule, a small, glass-enclosed space where the turn of a knob will create sunlight for tanning, jungle steam, a soft rain, and soft breezes. Music of your choice and complimentary champagne are provided. Bicycles, including a tandem, are available for an hourly rental.

The El Rancho is widely known throughout Sacramento for its superb Friday night seafood buffet and Sunday champagne brunch. On Friday nights in the El Condor dining room, diners may choose from among eight salads, a relish tray, cheese, clams casino, oysters Rockefeller, crab legs, baked salmon, shrimp, marinated herring, giant lobster tails, prime rib, vegetables, and a dessert table. Sunday brunch fare includes a variety of salads and fresh fruit, lox and bagels, a selection of fresh seafood, crepe and omelette carts, breakfast meats and prime rib, and a dessert table that includes eclairs, cream puffs, mousse, cheesecake, and pie. Breakfast, lunch, and dinner are served daily in the El Condor, which offers gourmet dining and flambé dinner entrees prepared at tableside. Although the decor is eclectic and somewhat busy, the dining room has a quiet and comfortable ambience, and service is polite, prompt, and friendly. In good weather visitors may dine outside in the La Paloma patio in a lush, tropical setting featuring an aviary with colorful birds and a koi pond. El Condor room service is available to guests.

Cabaret entertainment and dancing are offered nightly at

DQ's Windmill Cabaret, decorated in dark oak paneling, stained glass, brass, and blue and rust crushed velvet.

Single rooms and suites are available, many with wet bars and refrigerators and 20 with kitchenettes including a refrigerator, sink, and stove. A number of the rooms have Murphy beds, which are pulled down from the wall at bedtime. Adjoining rooms should be avoided, as the doors are quite thin and don't block noise very well. Although the decor is not outstanding, rooms are comfortable and quiet, and include climate control and cable TV. Because much of the hotel's business is geared toward conferences and meetings, a number of hospitality suites and break-out meeting rooms are available, as well as numerous meeting and banquet rooms, the largest of which can handle groups up to 750.

The friendly and hospitable staff will help guests arrange for sightseeing tours, babysitting, laundry and dry cleaning services. Pets are allowed and children receive special discounts. Many of the facilities are wheelchair-accessible. The El Rancho is 20 minutes from Metropolitan Airport and three minutes from downtown Sacramento. Guests may ride the Yolo Rolls, a restored 1938 White bus that previously served as a Yellowstone Park tour bus. The shuttle bus, which often appears in local parades, goes to various downtown locations.

«ST. LOUIS»

Chase–Park Plaza Hotel
212 North Kingshighway Boulevard
(at Lindell Boulevard)
St. Louis, Missouri 63108
800/325-8989 (tollfree)
314/361-2500

Singles $70–$110
Doubles $82–$122
Suites $150–$300

The Chase–Park Plaza, a monolith of red brick and white
stone anchored on the southwest corner of the trendy Central
West End, is the grande dame of hotels in St. Louis. The
western facade facing beautiful Forest Park opens onto a
vista of turn-of-the-century mansions with carriage houses
and stables.

No less opulent is the interior of the building, which
includes 385 single and double rooms, executive suites, 23
function rooms and 33,000 square feet of exhibit space. The
suites have a bedroom, sitting room, one or two baths, and
a bar. All the rooms have color TVs.

Upon entering the main lobby, one is aware of the luxury
and attention to details which are the hallmarks of the Chase.
Every convenience and service can be found on the premises: a pharmacy, florist, hair salon, and studio photogra-
pher, among others. Free parking is available.

Three dining rooms are located off the main lobby. For
a casual breakfast or lunch there is the Chase Cafe. Sunday

277

brunch is served from 10:30 to 2:30. The Hunt Room is open from 3 P.M. to midnight for dinner. The Tenderloin Room, famous for its steaks, seafood, and Senate-style bean soup, is a favorite dining spa for locals and travelers alike. Lounges include the Chase Cafe Bar, the Zodiac Bar, and the Tenderloin Bar.

The Chase–Park Plaza is located at the corner of two major thoroughfares in west St. Louis, less than a mile from Highway 40. Just down the block are Jewish and Barnes hospitals, while Washington and St. Louis universities are close by. The renowned St. Louis Cathedral is within walking distance, as are the shops, clubs, and bistros of the colorful Central West End.

With a dedication bordering on fanaticism, the manager and staff strive to make one's stay at the hotel pleasant and satisfying. To this end, everyone, including a concierge, works to satisfy the needs of every guest. A concierge will get theater tickets, a bellhop will have shoes shined, a desk clerk will help with reservations.

Service, comfort, and conviviality are the watch words at the Chase–Park Plaza Hotel.

Cheshire Inn and Lodge

6300 Clayton Road
Clayton, Missouri 63107
800/392-7378 (tollfree from within Missouri)
800/325-7378 (tollfree from rest of U.S.)
314/647-7300

Singles $65–$71
Doubles $75–$81

Once guests have experienced the luxury of oriental rugs underfoot, relaxed in the comfort of a four-poster bed, and savored the old world charm of antiques, they will return again and again to this quaint Jacobean-style hotel set at the corner of Clayton Road and Highway 40, 15 minutes from downtown St. Louis and five minutes from the heart of Clayton, St. Louis County's business center. Doctors, lawyers, businessmen, and, in increasing numbers, professional women appreciate the convenience and security of this 21-year-old landmark.

Management rightly emphasizes the quiet, reserved atmosphere of the lodge. The primary goal of all staff members seems to be to pamper the harried executive.

A typical evening for a guest might begin with a shower and short nap in one of the 108 rooms, each furnished with a mixture of antiques and newer pieces. Jumping into a pair of shorts, the relaxed individual joins like-minded enthusiasts in Ye Health Club, a co-ed gym equipped with the latest exercise machines, sauna, and soothing whirlpool.

Those who prefer to skip the exercise regime may decide to saunter into the Fox and Hounds, a charming replica of an old English hunt club, to sip a complimentary cocktail between 5 and 7 P.M., or down a yard of imported ale (half yards are available for the uninitiated). A board of assorted cheeses, nachos, and a fresh vegetable platter are provided. In the winter the large stone fireplace sheds warmth to the farthest corners of the club, and there is piano music six nights a week. Another piano bar is featured at the King's Arms, an intimate cocktail lounge that serves a full lunch and complimentary hors d'oeuvres from 5 to 7 P.M.

Three dining rooms serve a wondrous assortment of foods. For breakfast one might choose Mead Hall, where a buffet table groans under the weight of sausages, eggs, breads, fruits, and sweet rolls. Breakfast, lunch, and dinner are served in the Wassail Room, where succulent prime rib, steaks, and a variety of fresh fish make dining a memorable experience.

The tradition of fine gourmet dining continues in the Great Hall, which is situated between the Wassail Room and Mead Hall. A variety of French pastries and rich, elaborately concocted after-dinner drinks offer a grand finale to the meal.

The Cheshire meets the transportation needs of its guests with everything from an underground garage to an unusual fleet of vehicles. The inn features an English double-decker bus and a collection of horse-drawn carriages ranging from a two-seated surrey to the original *Hello Dolly* 42-passenger coach. Also available is a horse-drawn hearse, great if you want to be noticed arriving at a party, a wedding, or just riding around the neighborhood. The double-decker bus takes dinner guests to most sporting and theatrical events in the metropolitan area for the modest fee of $2. A chauffeur-driven 1962 Silver Cloud Rolls-Royce completes the set. Advanced reservations are required for all of these conveyances.

In the morning a wake-up call is accompanied by a complimentary cup of coffee and glass of orange juice. An airport limousine runs between the inn and Lambert–St. Louis International Airport.

The Clayton Inn
7750 Carondelet
Clayton, Missouri 63105
314/726-5400

Singles $68–$76
Doubles $78–$86
Suites $145–$245
Grand Suite $600

Within walking distance of the St. Louis County Courthouse and only a short distance from banks, real estate offices, and the headquarters of several companies, guests of the Clayton Inn may take advantage of the time they save on commuting and avail themselves of the many amenities offered for their enjoyment.

Two pools—one indoor, one out—allow guests to swim a few laps any time of day. A full-service health club features a Jacuzzi whirlpool tub, a sauna, steam room, exercise room, and men's and women's lounges. A masseuse is available by appointment.

After undergoing a complete renovation, the 212 rooms feature a blend of traditional and contemporary furnishings. Soft peach and green carpeting with coordinated spreads, draperies, upholstery, and accessories provide a restful setting for the blend of furniture which has a distinct art deco flavor. Remote-control TVs are in every room.

Parking is complimentary as is an airport limousine, which

is also available to take guests anywhere in the Clayton area. TWA and American airlines ticket offices are on the premises.

Two restaurants vie for honors in gourmet dining. The Velvet Turtle, a California garden-style dining room, is flush with flora in an open-air, contemporary setting. Fresh fish, salads, and a variety of meat dishes are served at breakfast, lunch, and dinner. Domestic and imported wines are available.

The Top of the Sevens is a traditional gourmet dining room, a favorite among guests and local diners alike. With a spectacular view of the city of St. Louis, the Sevens boasts great food in a romantic setting.

Lounges include Whispers, a New York–style nightclub that features nightly entertainment and a dance floor. The Wreck Bar has a shipwreck decor, a picture window facing the bottom of the outdoor pool and has nightly singalongs. The Top of the Sevens also has a piano bar, and the subdued background music adds much to the ease and intimacy of this popular lounge.

A variety of social and business functions can be accommodated in 11 rooms. There are four executive meeting rooms, a ballroom (three rooms open up to make one large banquet area), plus four more smaller meeting rooms. Three hundred people will fit easily into the triple suite.

At 27 years old, the Clayton Inn grew up with the Clayton business district. It is a familiar landmark to locals and out-of-towners, and one that they return to again and again, appreciating the location and services the hotel has to offer.

The Daniele Hotel
216 North Meramec
Clayton, Missouri 63105
800/325-8302 (tollfree from outside Missouri)
314/721-0101

Kings $95–$125
Doubles $95
Parlor Suites $150
One-bedroom suites $225–$275
Two-bedroom suites $325–$450

Quiet elegance in the old European tradition is the theme of the Daniele Hotel, situated in the heart of Clayton, Missouri. Although it is in the environs of the bustling, business-oriented seat of St. Louis County government, the tempo of the neighborhood is one of restrained affluence in an expensive suburban area.

Guests enter the lobby from a driveway on the south side of the building. Small and fashionably decorated, the hotel feels like a private home. There is no reservation desk (everyone pre-registers), contributing to the lobby's restrained elegance. There are limited-edition ceramics of birds and animals displayed in a glass cage beside the elevator, live plants, fresh flowers, and real leather upholstery. It is obvious, even to the casual observer, that there is nothing artificial on the premises.

Female bellhops assist guests to their rooms. There are 90 rooms in the Daniele, the majority having king-size beds, although rooms with two double beds are available. Traditional decor is prevalent on the lower floors, and the mellow richness of polished woods is highlighted by salmon, gray, and green shades dominant in the upholstery, carpeting, and wallcoverings.

On the fourth floor, however, the scene changes, and deep purple walls add visual excitement to the low-ceilinged corridors. Modern replaces traditional, and the suites are decorated in substantial cane furniture. Suites with one and two bedrooms are available. Some have kitchenettes, two baths, and a wet bar, and all have discreetly hidden color TVs.

"There are no microwaves on the premises," boasted the sales director when she described the hotel's dining facilities. Fresh fruit, fresh fish, fresh meat, and fresh pastries are the order of the day at the Restaurant, which caters to guests and local residents.

White tablecloths, sparkling crystal, and dark wood on the walls set the stage. For breakfast, one may choose French toast, cheese blintzes with strawberries, smoked trout, poached finnan haddie and, of course, freshly squeezed orange juice. At other meals, imported and domestic wines and beers accompany a varied menu of gourmet dishes.

Opposite the Restaurant is a small cocktail lounge where business deals may be discussed and gossip shared in an atmosphere of restrained intimacy.

A concierge is prepared to handle almost any situation to make a guest's stay as smooth as possible. Everything from calling a veterinarian (dogs are allowed in the hotel) to reserving tickets for sporting or theatrical events is considered part of a routine day.

Basement parking is available for people with their own transportation. The Daniele will supply a presidential limousine complete with a bar and television free of charge for use in the Clayton area. Airport service costs $25, or the limousine may be hired for $25 per hour (with a minimum charge of $37.50). Also available is a Rolls-Royce Spirit at $40 per hour, with a two hour minimum.

The owner boasts that the Daniele is a world-class hotel. Liberace, after staying at the Daniele for several nights, agreed. He spread the good word to other celebrities, and the Daniele has become increasingly popular with visiting luminaries.

The Forest Park Hotel
4910 West Pine Boulevard
(at Euclid Avenue)
St. Louis, Missouri 63108
314/361-3500

Singles, doubles $49
Suites $80–$125

In the midst of extensive renovation and restoration when visited, the Forest Park promises to offer distinctive lodgings in a fascinating neighborhood at reasonable rates. The 220-room hotel was built toward the end of St. Louis's heyday, in 1922. Now, thanks to its placement on the National Register of Historic Places, the hotel has been able to restore the style of its early life to all common areas—the lobby, meeting rooms, and cocktail lounge—and refurbish the guest rooms in an unobtrusive fashion.

The Forest Park excels primarily in its staff, many of whom have devoted decades to the hotel. Elevator operators, porters, check-in personnel, valets, housekeepers, and others are personable, not distant in the fashion cultivated by some hotels, and ready to smooth the way for newcomers and welcome back old acquaintances.

Three types of accommodations are offered: large guest rooms, small suites, and three-room suites. The rooms are pleasant and crisp, with only a hint of the generic hotel/motel look. Good-quality art prints adorn the walls and some rooms bear a distinctive border of wallpaper at the edges of the ceiling. The bathroom fixtures are brass, and a built-in hair dryer hangs near the washbasin. Next to the bed is an AM-FM clock radio. An electric shoe buffer stands at the ready. On the color TV (or TVs—there are two in the suites) guests can watch movies 24 hours a day. Also available 24 hours a day is full-menu room service from the deli downstairs. The small suites consist of a large combination living room and dining room with a small kitchen in one corner (separated by a bar with stools), and a bedroom. The large suites have an additional bedroom.

Hershel's Deli and Bakery, the first 24-hour restaurant in the Central West End, and a revamped cocktail lounge with live entertainment were also scheduled as part of the renovations. Other facilities available to guests are an outdoor pool and patio lounge, workout room with steam and sauna, and free parking.

The hotel also benefits from its location in the Central West End. Originally an elegant satellite of workaday downtown, then for a while depressed, the Central West End is now on the way to elegant again, but hasn't turned its back on its more humble, human side. Many spiffy restaurants and bars, book and record stores, boutiques, and antique stores, along with some of St. Louis's most lavish turn-of-the-century mansions, line Euclid Avenue and its side streets for several blocks in either direction of the hotel. The expansive Forest Park stretches away to the west (here are the old, sprawling St. Louis Zoo and the Art Museum, both built for the 1904 World's Fair), with Washington University and Clayton, the area's second business center, beyond the park. Downtown, to the east, and the airport, northwest of the city, are both convenient to the hotel.

«SAN ANTONIO»

───────── BED AND BREAKFAST ─────────

Bed and Breakfast Hosts of San Antonio
Laverne Campbell
166 Rockhill
San Antonio, Texas 78209
512/824-8036

Bed & Breakfast Society of Houston
Marguerite Swanson
921 Heights Boulevard
Houston, Texas 77008
713/868-4654

Bed & Breakfast Texas Style
Ruth Wilson
4224 West Red Bird Lane
Dallas, Texas 75237
214/298-5433 and 298-8586

    While bed and breakfast lodging in San Antonio is in its fledgling stages, these three organizations had a few listings at press time.

The Emily Morgan Hotel
705 East Houston Street
(across from the Alamo)
San Antonio, Texas 78205
800/356-5683 (tollfree from within Texas)
800/824-6674 (tollfree from rest of U.S.)
512/225-8486

Singles, doubles $70–$145
Sam Houston Suite $235

The Emily Morgan is anything but an ordinary hotel. It's upbeat, fun, refreshing. On the outside it's an eye-catching 12-story neo-Gothic structure shaped like a V, with a host of gargoyles peering down from its ledges. Inside, it's contemporary, decorated in cool blues and pinks with splashes of modern art.

The romantic hotel is named for "the yellow rose of Texas," a young mulatto indentured servant who was captured by Mexican general Santa Anna after his victory at the Alamo. Struck by Emily Morgan's beauty, the general took her as his personal traveling companion.

As the Mexican army marched toward the San Jacinto River, Emily—loyal to the Texans who were fighting against Mexico—sent another indentured servant to warn Sam Houston of Santa Anna's approach. Days later the Texas general attacked the Mexican forces while they were enjoying an afternoon siesta. The beautiful Emily is credited with occupying the Mexican leader's attention so completely that the Texas army made a surprise attack and won the battle. As a result of Sam Houston's victory, Texas became an independent republic.

Throughout the hotel are references to the heroine of Texas and her story, until recently ignored by historians. The hotel's logo is a yellow rose. And on the 12th floor, the Sam Houston Suite overlooks the Alamo.

Once the city's medical arts building, the 1920s building

opened as a hotel in 1985 after undergoing an $18 million conversion. Instead of regarding its odd-shaped rooms as a hindrance, the interior design team used the unusual configurations to their advantage, creating untraditional hotel units with individual style and flair.

The 176 guest rooms have a variety of designs, including those with one double, one queen-size, two double, or one king-size bed. Signature rooms, priced at $100 to $115, have single Jacuzzi tubs; plaza rooms and the Sam Houston Suite have double Jacuzzis.

The 73 Signature King rooms at $100 a night are the hotel's featured rooms. In addition to the Jacuzzi tub, they have refrigerators and a remote-control TV that can be viewed from the bed or tub. Especially spacious, they have comfortable seating areas.

The 12 Executive Kings, priced at $115, are particularly conducive for travelers who plan to work or entertain in their rooms. The seating area is separated from the bed, with a TV in both the seating and sleeping sections.

The Plaza rooms are a delight. Situated at the base of the V shape of the building, they have outstanding views of the Alamo and lots of space. Frosted sliding glass doors separate the three-sectioned bathroom from the sleeping area.

The rooms with double and queen-size beds are smaller but nice, and are especially good for single travelers who don't like being overwhelmed by a large room.

Decorated in light colors, all the rooms have an airy feel, accented with bird's eye maple veneer cabinetry, wooden miniblinds, soft-colored fabrics, and mirrored walls.

Amenities in the rooms are extensive: hair dryers, bathroom scales, shower massage, lighted makeup mirrors, digital clock radios, full-length mirrors. Best of all, complimentary breakfast is served in bed, with a choice of continental or full breakfast. Newspapers accompany the breakfast tray, which is delivered at the time each guest chooses.

The Emily Morgan has an attentive guest services staff, valet parking ($6 per night), and a complimentary wine social in the late afternoon. A hotel limousine is available for an added charge. Room service is offered from 11:30 A.M. to 10 P.M.

The hotel's exercise room is equipped with weights and exercise bikes as well as saunas in the men's and women's locker rooms. The adjoining outdoor deck has a small stainless steel pool and a hot tub.

Sarducci's restaurant serves northern Italian dishes (from scaloppine al Marsala to homemade amaretto cheesecake) and is open for lunch and dinner. For guests who prefer not to have breakfast in their rooms, continental breakfast is served in the lobby bar.

Equipped to handle meetings of up to 100, the hotel has four well-designed meeting rooms on the basement level.

The Alamo is just outside the hotel's doors, and the city's Riverwalk and central business district are within a few blocks, making the Emily Morgan convenient for travelers with or without cars.

Weekend packages that include such extras as barge rides on the Paseo del Rio and carriage rides through the streets of San Antonio are frequently offered.

Fairmount Hotel
401 South Alamo
(at Nueva Street)
San Antonio, Texas 78205
512/224-8800

Singles $125
Doubles $150
Suites $150–$350

San Antonio's first small luxury hotel, the 38-room Fairmount, is at the core of the city's tourist attractions and adjacent to the central business district. Although the lodging had not opened its doors by press time, it has outstanding promise.

Amid tremendous community support in a city that values its historic buildings, the Fairmount was saved from the wrecking ball by three business leaders who formed a company to restore and operate the hotel.

In spring 1985, the three-story masonry and wood building made world headlines when it was moved from an area being cleared for development to its new location six blocks away. Weighing more than three million pounds, the hotel broke records as the largest building ever moved in one piece on wheels, and the heaviest object ever transported over city streets.

Built in 1906, the Fairmount operated as a hotel until the late 1960s. In the intervening years the building was mostly deserted. Since it was never converted to other usage, it is unique in the strong retention of its original design. With an Italianate Victorian architectural style, it is richly ornamented, constructed of red brick with carved limestone. An addition that complements the original building in design houses the lobby as well as some of the guest rooms.

Projecting an image of refinement and sophistication, the Fairmount has antique furnishings in the lobby and period reproduction furniture in the guest rooms. Each room is distinctive in its decor and arrangement. Regular rooms have a choice of one or two queen-size beds. Suites are designated as parlor, executive, veranda, and master. In the executive suites, the bedroom has an attractive loft design. Veranda suites have private balconies.

Although plans for the hotel's restaurant were still being formulated at this writing, the owners intend it as a fine dining establishment. Adjoined by a Scotch bar, the restaurant is on the first floor of the original structure. Light meals and afternoon tea are served in the courtyard.

Meeting space includes a room accommodating up to 150 reception style, and another suited for groups of 15 to 20.

Basing its reputation on its service, the hotel has a concierge, 24-hour room service, valet parking, and limousine service.

Adjoining San Antonio's La Villita Historic District—a picturesque assortment of shops and restaurants in buildings ranging from simple adobe to Victorian—the Fairmount is across the street from the city's convention center and Hemisfair Plaza.

Four Seasons Hotel
555 South Alamo
(at Durango Street)
800/268-6282 (tollfree)
512/229-1000

Singles $92–$122
Doubles $112–$142
Suites $240–$460

A tranquil hacienda-like hotel spread over six acres, Four Seasons San Antonio reflects the city's Spanish heritage as well as its love of beauty. Guest rooms are arranged in two connecting wings—one with six floors and the other with four. Many of the rooms overlook the beautifully landscaped grounds, accented with fountains and a multilevel pool.

Despite the sense of being removed from the bustling city, the hotel is only a few blocks from the famed Riverwalk and one block from the Henry B. Gonzalez Convention Center and Hemisfair Plaza. The Alamo is five blocks away.

Throughout the hotel's grounds are touches of Mexico and Spain, from tiled floors in the lobby to exterior fountains and courtyards. Guests walk through a peaceful courtyard to enter the lobby. At the back of the hotel is its focal point: a tropical garden with Chinese pheasants, an arbor lounge, and three small historic houses, each representative of a different style of Texas architecture.

One of the houses has been converted into a well-equipped fitness center with exercise bikes, treadmill, weights, and saunas in the men's and women's locker rooms. The other two, dating from the 1840s, are used for meetings and private parties. The Diaz House is especially charming, with double fireplace and private patio. Showing the Alsace-Lorraine influence of the area, it has tufa wall construction, high ceilings, and hardwood floors.

Also on the grounds is the community's old German-American school—historic buildings with thick stone walls and large windows, and a courtyard with century-old trees. Four Seasons has converted the two low-lying buildings into a conference center with seven classroom-style meeting rooms.

The main hotel complex has additional group facilities, including a large ballroom and several meeting rooms.

Geared to the leisure as well as business traveler, Four Seasons has an array of recreational offerings—a heated outdoor pool with whirlpool, two lighted tennis courts, a putting green, and bicycles. Guests have golf privileges at Pecan Valley Golf Club.

The 250 guest rooms have two double beds or one king-size bed. Most rooms have balconies. Junior suites feature comfortable seating areas with televisions and an additional TV in the bedroom. The rooms have remote-control TV with cable reception (including a movie channel), hair dryers, terry cloth bathrobes, and full-length mirrors.

Staffed by a concierge, the hotel has 24-hour room service, serves complimentary coffee in the lobby every morning, offers free overnight shoeshine, and provides newspapers on request. A gift shop, also stocked with sundries, is near the lobby.

The Anaqua Restaurant, featuring an expansive overlook of the hotel's attractive gardens, serves regional American cuisine in a casually elegant setting. Open for three meals a day, the restaurant has a buffet brunch on Sundays. The Arbor, an outdoor eating area, serves light meals, and the Palm Terrace adjoining the lobby serves afternoon tea, drinks, and light fare.

Guests at the Four Seasons have a choice of valet or self-parking. For self-parking there is a fee of $1.50 each time the car leaves the lot.

La Mansion del Rio
112 College Street
San Antonio, Texas 78205
800/292-7300 (tollfree from within Texas)
800/531-7208 (tollfree from rest of U.S.)
512/225-2581

Singles $95–$140
Doubles $115–$160
Suites $275–$750

The Paseo del Rio, or Riverwalk, is the centerpiece of San Antonio, and the most charming hotel set along its banks is La Mansion del Rio, a quiet retreat from the fun-filled activity of the Riverwalk. The nucleus of the building dates back to 1852, when it was constructed as a Catholic school. In the 1920s the structure, which by then had been expanded, was converted into a law school.

La Mansion del Rio, a hotel since 1968, is a white Spanish colonial palace with classical arched entranceways, black wrought-iron railings, and red tile. At its cedar-shaded Riverwalk entrance, a profusion of greenery cascades from stone walls, and an arched bridge spans the Paseo del Rio.

Guests arrive at the hotel from the street entrance, driving into an attractive covered garage where attendants park their car or direct them to self-parking on a level adjoining their room.

The lobby—with its beamed ceiling, arches and columns, colorful tapestries, and greenery—conveys the hotel's Spanish theme. A multimillion-dollar renovation in 1985 has resulted in a sparklingly fresh interior, both in public areas and in guest rooms.

A rambling hotel due to the additions made to the structure over its years as a school, La Mansion del Rio has 338 guest rooms spread over seven floors. Many of the rooms overlook the river (a gentle waterway, flanked with boutiques and restaurants, which winds its way through the heart of San Antonio). Other rooms open onto two inner courtyards, one with a pool.

Guest rooms, Spanish in decor, have luxuriant bedspreads and plush new carpets. All have beamed ceilings and Spanish-style furnishings. While some rooms are small, all are comfortable and attractively designed. Some of the colorfully decorated bathrooms have separate vanity areas.

Designated as superior, deluxe, premier, and ambassador, rooms have two double beds, one queen-size, or one king-size bed. Superior and deluxe rooms overlook either the poolside or garden courtyard; premier and ambassador rooms have river views. All guest rooms have dry bars with refrigerators, digital clock radios, and remote-control televisions (most enclosed in armoires).

Ambassador rooms, at a rate of $140 single or $160 double, have such extras as express check-in and check-out, imported chocolates at check-in, complimentary coffee and danish offered through room service, free newspaper, and a bathrobe on request. Most of these accommodations have French doors opening onto private balconies.

Among the hotel's suites, the Navarro, priced at $375, is extremely spacious with a kitchenette in addition to living and sleeping areas. The Deluxe Hospitality Suite ($300 for one bedroom, $425 for two bedrooms) has a huge sitting area and overlooks the river.

The hotel's concierge, on duty from 7 A.M. to 11 P.M., fulfills guest requests from making hair appointments to arranging air transportation for their pets. Room service is available round the clock. Valet parking is free, a plus in a city where parking during peak seasons can be at a premium.

La Mansion del Rio's attractive pool courtyard, a focal point of the hotel, has outdoor poolside dining during appropriate times of the year. In addition to the hotel's pool, guests have access to the Downtown YMCA five blocks from the hotel, with a pool, racquetball and handball courts, indoor track, and weight room.

Restaurante Capistrano, overlooking the pool courtyard and gardens, serves Southwestern cuisine with an emphasis on authentic Mexican dishes. Las Canarias features continental cuisine, served in a romantic setting overlooking the river. In the evenings there is a flamenco dance show. El Colegio bar offers intimacy and quiet, with complimentary hors d'oeuvres.

From the hotel's lobby a spiral staircase leads to two floors of meeting space. Group rooms are well lit and pleasingly designed. The Iberian Ballroom can accommodate up to 500.

Another La Mansion hotel—La Mansion del Norte—is situated ten miles north of downtown near San Antonio

International Airport. A 306-room hotel, it has a classic Spanish colonial design with a central courtyard.

The Menger Hotel
204 Alamo Plaza
(across the street from the Alamo)
800/241-3848 (tollfree)
512/223-4361

Singles $50–$60
Doubles $63–$72
Suites $85–$144

When German brewer William Menger built a hotel in San Antonio in 1859, he had a practical purpose in mind: patrons of his brewery frequently needed a place to spend the night, and he was tired of converting his bar tables into makeshift beds. San Antonio was still a frontier town. The Alamo, next door to the new hotel, had fallen only 23 years earlier. Menger added a strong dose of refinement to the town, constructing a fine hostelry with beautiful furnishings.

Through the years the Menger has been at the center of Texas history. In its bar Teddy Roosevelt recruited his Rough Riders during the Spanish American War. As a lodging, the hotel was long popular with cattlemen when they came into town. The owner of the famed King Ranch, a crusty old gentleman, moved into the Menger during the latter part of his life and died there in 1865.

Proud of its history, the Menger claims to be the oldest continuously operating hotel west of the Mississippi. Its rotunda, with a stained-glass ceiling and two oval-shaped mezzanine floors overlooking the antique-studded lobby, is spectacular. Western art lines the walls—one massive prairie scene painting was used in the movie *Giant*.

Several one-of-a-kind suites, some decorated with antiques original to the hotel, open onto the mezzanines. Both the Devon Cattle Suite and the King Suite have a large carved bed with canopy, a parlor with lots of seating, and a step-up bathroom. (Why step-up? The hotel is of pre–indoor plumbing vintage, so when plumbing was installed the bathroom floors had to be elevated to conceal the pipes.)

At a nightly rate of only $80 to $85, guests step back into the days when cattle was king in Texas.

The Roy Rogers Room is named for the famed cowboy who stayed at the Menger during the Hemisfair in 1968. Redecorated to accommodate Roy Rogers and Dale Evans, the room is furnished with two twin beds and has rawhide and leather accents in its decor.

In the 1950s the Menger added a section to the hotel, and prior to the Hemisfair it added an adjoining motor inn. Today the entire complex with 300 guest rooms comprises a city block. Rooms in the motor inn have two double beds. Some have private balconies and overlook the pool or garden; others overlook the Alamo.

Rooms in the center section have two twin beds or one double bed and are well decorated. While most of the bathrooms are small (not all rooms have the same configuration), some have separate vanities with lavatories.

All rooms have color televisions with local channels and in-room movies. Unlike some older hotels, each room has individual thermostat controls.

For guests interested in savoring the essence of the hotel's history, it is recommended that they request one of the ten rooms in the original hotel furnished with antiques.

At the Menger's entrance is a spacious lobby, modern in design yet cognizant of the hotel's link to the past. Decorated with oriental rugs and plush couches, its focal point is the large courtyard garden visible through expansive floor-to-ceiling windows.

The Menger's pool is especially attractive, having an abundance of landscaping and several sitting and lounging areas.

The Patio restaurant is open for lunch and dinner; the coffeeshop serves breakfast and lunch. The Menger Bar—dark and cozy—is well worth visiting, and is decorated with photos of Teddy Roosevelt and the hotel's early years.

Meeting facilities include the Colonial Room, capable of accommodating up to 500 for receptions, the Minuet Room with a hardwood floor for dancing, and three smaller rooms.

Many of the hotel's personnel are long-time employees

who like to talk about the Menger's history. The staff will arrange such services as babysitters or tours upon request. Room service is available from 6:30 A.M. to 1:30 P.M. and 4 P.M to 10 P.M., and laundry and dry cleaning services are offered.

The hotel has a well-stocked drugstore and a beauty and barber shop. Valet parking costs $3.50 overnight. Bellmen will arrange limousine service between the hotel and the airport.

St. Anthony InterContinental
300 East Travis Street
San Antonio, Texas 78205
800/327-0200 (tollfree)
512/227-4392

Singles $85–$135
Doubles $100–$150
Suites $175–$450

A grand old hotel, the St. Anthony dates back to 1909. Owned for many years by a wealthy railroad builder and rancher, it became a showcase for the art objects and furnishings he collected in his extensive travels. After his death the property declined, but in 1983 it was beautifully restored by InterContinental Hotels, resulting in an exceptional luxury hotel with 360 guest rooms. Designated as both a Texas and National Historic Landmark, the elegant St. Anthony represents a side of San Antonio's personality often overlooked by visitors.

Decidedly European in flavor, the hotel has impressive treasures in its lobby: a custom-made rosewood and bronze Steinway piano, French regency couches that were once in the Russian Embassy in Paris, 19th-century bronze statues, and a wealth of paintings and mirrors. Hanging from the coffered ceiling are empire chandeliers. The Venetian mosaic tile floors are accented with area rugs, and puffed Austrian curtains frame the arched windows.

Across the street, and visible from the veranda-style lobby lounge, is Travis Park, a gem of green set in the city's downtown. The St. Anthony is four blocks from the Alamo, one block from the Majestic Theater, and has easy access to the Riverwalk.

Guest rooms are stylish, with traditional furniture and curtains and bedskirts of matching fabric. While no two rooms are decorated alike, each is cheerful as well as tasteful. The lighting is excellent, unlike that in some older hotels. Throughout the guest rooms there are accents of wood and brass. Doorbells add to the feeling of refinement. Bed choices include twin, double, queen, and king.

Suites range from executive suites (some with marble fireplaces) to the huge Presidential Suite, an exquisitely decorated apartment with art objects and festooned draperies. Some suites have chandeliers, wet bars, separate glass-enclosed shower stalls, and walk-in dressing rooms.

Every guest room has color cable television with a movie channel, radio, individual thermostat control, personal accessories such as soaps and sewing kits, and turndown service.

Hotel guests may dine at the St. Anthony Club, a prestigious private membership club that numbers nationally known politicians and entertainers in its list of members. Serving continental cuisine, the restaurant has a constantly changing menu.

The informal Brasserie is open all day, and Pete's Pub, serving light lunches, snacks, and cocktails in a speakeasy atmosphere, is open from 11 A.M. to 2 A.M.

Peacock Alley, a lounge adjoining the lobby, serves cocktails to the accompaniment of classical music. Sunday is a special day at the St. Anthony: The champagne brunch served in Peacock Alley is spectacular, with an array of delicious concoctions. Elaborate carved ice sculptures adorn the buffet table. A pianist on the Steinway and a violinist set the tone with classical music.

A hospitable hotel staff serves guest needs graciously. Chief concierge Dick Kinnally started working at the hotel as a bellman in 1943. Enraptured with the St. Anthony—its history and its romance—he enjoys telling guests about a multitude of celebrities who have stayed in the hotel. So popular are his stories that Kinnally hosts a Wednesday evening dinner in the Brasserie, and interested guests may request an invitation to sit at his table and enjoy his anecdotes.

The concierge fulfills such guest requests as arranging babysitters, secretarial services, tours, and theater tickets. The St. Anthony offers round-the-clock room service and same-day laundry and dry cleaning. Guests have a choice of valet parking at $7 or self-parking at the hotel's outdoor lot for $4.25. A sundry shop and newsstand is located off the lobby.

For recreation, the St. Anthony has a rooftop pool and lounge area, with outdoor food service during appropriate times of the year.

In keeping with its character, the hotel's meeting rooms are elegant and grand. The Anacacho ballroom, once used for entertaining the late Princess Grace and Prince Ranier, has a balcony encircling the two-story room. Reflecting the hotel's link to the cattlemen who dominated its guest register for many years, the Navarro Room has a huge painting depicting cowboys cooking on the open range.

«SAN DIEGO»

Britt House
406 Maple Street
San Diego, California 92103
619/234-2926

$80–$95 single or double

Charm is the keynote in this Queen Anne Victorian home, whose exterior is done in shades of caramel and butterscotch, so that it almost appears to be an edible confection. Inside, the lighthearted spirit continues in each room, all of which have permanent occupants—one or more stuffed animals like teddy bears or dolls, such as Raggedy Anns. All of these denizens of Britt House have names and are seated or lying about the guest rooms for the enjoyment of visitors. Two live cats—Maggie and Beaver—plus Sasha, a dog, have the run of the house. Rubber ducks are supplied in the bathrooms.

Britt House is rich with carved woods, bay windows, high ceilings, and stained-glass windows. A 97-year-old antique, the house has been nicely refurbished and has been a popular bed and breakfast favorite for seven years. Carefully tended flower gardens surround the building, which is located two blocks from San Diego's famed Balboa Park. Frequent bus transportation is available on two nearby streets.

An ample breakfast is served each morning (included in the cost of the room) and will be served in the guest room on request. Breakfast consists of home-baked breads, fresh juice, a variety of eggs, plus condiments. Afternoon tea service is also included. There is no alcohol service, but ice is available. Guests will find fruit and homemade cookies in rooms upon arrival. All rooms also have robes for the bath. A luxurious Finnish sauna is available for the use of all guests.

The management does not encourage children at Britt House, although they will be accommodated. Pets are not permitted, and cigar smoking is also prohibited indoors. There are no in-room telephones.

The staff at Britt House will assist in special requests, such as planning tours, preparing picnic lunches, and even catering an exquisite meal in your own room.

Check-in time is 4 P.M. to 10 P.M. Rooms can be shown by appointment between noon and 4 P.M. daily. Extra beds are available by prior arrangement and an additional charge will be made.

Hotel Del Coronado
1500 Orange Avenue
Coronado, California 92118
619/522-8000

Most rooms $99–$185
Lanai rooms with sitting area $170–$195
Suites $250–$395

One of the world's great examples of elegant Victorian architecture, the Hotel del Coronado will observe its centennial in 1988. Located on the Coronado Peninsula, the Del, as it is called by the local population, is reached from San Diego by a spectacular toll bridge. The Hotel del Coronado is one of the world's largest wooden structures, and has seen little outward change since it opened in 1888, although each of the original 399 rooms has been continually renovated to keep it as modern as any of its competitors.

The hotel has been designated a historic landmark by the U.S. Department of the Interior and by the state of California. It is located on 33 acres of pristine beachfront, and with the addition of a new complex, now has a total of 689 rooms and suites.

Inside and out, the decor may well be described as Brighton Beach, after the famed seaside resort on the southern coast of England. The surrounding grounds are a horticulturist's delight. The Del's main dining room, the Crown Room, has no interior supports, and its high domed ceiling, fashioned from sugar pine, is held together solely by wooden pegs. Breakfast, lunch, and dinner are offered here with a sumptuous Sunday buffet, served from 9 A.M. to 2 P.M., a great favorite with locals. The Prince of Wales Grill is traditional English with exceptional food and a fine wine list, serving dinner only, 6 to 10:30 P.M.

On the Ocean Terrace, which overlooks the beach and tennis courts, guests may enjoy an outdoor breakfast or lunch accompanied by the sound of the surf, and in the evening live music for dancing, with cocktail service. The Del Deli, open from 6 A.M. to 3 P.M., is a unique restaurant carved out of a huge cistern that once provided the hotel's fresh water.

Guest rooms and baths at the Del Coronado are spacious. Upholstery, wallcoverings, bedspreads, and linens are top quality and tasteful in design. Services are what might be expected from a great hotel, such as fast and elegant room service. There is a color TV and AM-FM radio in each room.

In addition to sunning and swimming on the beach, guests enjoy two large pools with sunning terraces, championship illuminated tennis courts, and physical fitness facilities in the hotel's health spa.

More than 20 specialty shops and service counters offer quality merchandise and every type of personal service necessary for vacation or business requirements.

One merely has to cross the bridge to enjoy charming San Diego, and Tijuana, Mexico, is a ten-minute drive from the hotel. Lindberg Field, the San Diego airport, lies 15 minutes away.

The U. S. Grant Hotel
326 Broadway
San Diego, California 92101
800/542-6082 (tollfree from within California)
800/854-2608 (tollfree from rest of continental U.S.)
800/854-6742 (tollfree from Canada)
619/236-1332

Singles $110–$130
Doubles $125–$145
Executive suites $150–$165
Deluxe suites $350–$1000

The U. S. Grant Hotel in downtown San Diego, on the occasion of its 75th birthday in 1985, reopened its doors after being closed for three years for renovation and restoration. The restorers of the Grant, which is on the National Register of Historic Places, have succeeded in preserving the old look of the stately hotel in spite of having spent millions of dollars to bring it up-to-date in every respect.

The hotel was built to honor the 18th president of the United States by his son, Ulysses S. Grant Jr. Royalty, politicians, and captains of industry have patronized the majestic landmark.

Guest rooms number 283, including 61 suites. Each suite boasts a built-in wet bar, fireplace, Jacuzzi bathtub, and luxurious chandeliers. All rooms have remote-control television, cable, and in-room movies. Furnishings include traditional reproduction mahogany pieces such as two- and four-poster beds, Queen Anne–style armoires, and wing-back chairs. Bathrooms are oversized, and feature Travertine marble and ceramic tile.

The U. S. Grant management has gone all out to provide attentive and courteous service at all levels of its operation, providing 24-hour valet service, as well as butlers and concierges who serve all guests.

The Grant Grill, once the place for the movers and builders of San Diego to wine and dine, has recaptured its former air of elegance, benefiting from the presence of women who, prior to 1969, were barred from patronizing the Grill until after 3 P.M. Featuring continental cuisine, the Grant Grill offers a setting of warm fabrics, brass, and rich woods. Another dining room is the Garden Room, spacious, comfortable, and elegant. Serving breakfast, lunch, and dinner, it features a mixture of California and continental cuisine. Cocktails are served in both restaurants and in the opulent lobby, and guests may also enjoy high tea in the lobby.

A symmetric garden of carefully selected plants and trees graces the rooftop of the 11-story Grant Hotel, creating a restful sight for hotel guests and nearby office workers, who look down from surrounding highrise office buildings.

Decor throughout the public spaces of the hotel was carefully planned to reflect a distinguished and opulent era: marble staircases, stately pillars made of mahogany and hand-shaped tiles, deep-pile carpets, hand-crafted ceilings with crystal and brass chandeliers, Chinese raised porcelain vases, damask wall coverings, beveled mirrors, and impressive fireplaces.

The U. S. Grant is located in the center of downtown San Diego, directly adjacent to the famed Westgate Hotel. It is one block from the new, colorful Horton Plaza shopping center, and a side entrance leads directly to the "Tijuana Trolley," a light-rail transit line that makes the 16-mile trip to the Mexican border at short intervals. All of San Diego's many attractions are within easy driving time of the Grant, as is Lindberg Field, the city's airport.

Vacation Village
1404 West Vacation Road
P.O. Box 9509 Mission Bay
San Diego, California 92109
800/542-6275 (tollfree)
619/274-4630

Singles $90–$110
Doubles $100–$120
Suites $195–$235
Full kitchen $20 extra

San Diego's Vacation Village is located on an island in beautiful Mission Bay, and is the closest thing to a Hawaiian island that can be found on the U.S. mainland. And while it is unquestionably the favorite retreat for family vacationing in San Diego, it is also popular with honeymooners and senior citizens.

Vacation Village is a series of one-story cottages set on a 43-acre private island covered with lush tropical greenery and blooming flowers of every hue. Blue lagoons and a mile-long white sand beach on the island's perimeter add to the illusion of a South Seas island.

Living quarters are set in 450 villas, including 95 suites, all of which are ground-level units facing either gardens, Mission Bay, or one of the lagoons. Each villa has separate dressing areas and vanities, private outdoor patio, refrigerator, color TV, clock radios, in-room coffee, and queen- or king-size beds. Parking is directly adjacent to each villa. Coin-operated laundromats are located on the grounds.

Recreation facilities at the resort are extravagant, with something outdoorsy for young and old. On the grounds are five outdoor swimming pools, two of them heated; eight tennis courts, four of which are lighted for night play; a marina with power, pedal, or sailing boats; a health spa; a bicycle center with singles, tandems and four-wheel cruisers; table tennis and shuffleboard; a children's playground and electronic game room; jogging paths for the health buff; and a wide expanse of beach front.

Dining facilities include the intimate Dockside Broiler, which seats only 90 persons and features continental specialties, delicate seafood, and broiled steaks. The Polynesian Princess restaurant adds to the exotic ambience of Vacation Village with South Sea island cuisine, dining on the outdoor patio, and a Sunday champagne brunch. The Bay Lounge offers cocktails, live music, and dancing.

While Vacation Village's setting is on Vacation Island, it is in fact connected to the mainland so that motor vehicles can be driven directly to the reception area and then to the assigned villa. Vacation Village is approximately ten minutes from San Diego's Lindberg Field, and is within easy driving distance of most of the area attractions.

La Valencia Hotel
1132 Prospect Street
La Jolla, California 92037
619/454-0771

Singles $88
Doubles $118
Suites $160–$225

Just 14 miles north of downtown San Diego, the town of
La Jolla straddles coves and bays of the sunny coastline,
out of sight of any interstate highway, and without such
benefits of civilization as billboards and garish neon. Fitting
perfectly into the ambience of this affluent enclave is a small
pink stucco hotel that exudes elegance.

This is La Valencia, which has only 100 guest rooms and
suites, most of them with sweeping views of the Pacific and
the La Jolla coastline. On the hotel's well-tended grounds
is a heart-shaped swimming pool and abundant tropical
greenery. Guests compare it to a Mediterranean villa typical
of the Spanish Costa Brava.

La Valencia plays host to a great many inconspicuous,
affluent visitors who could well afford more expensive quarters. Many of its guests have been regulars for decades,
some harking back to the early days of Hollywood, when
names on the guest register included Gregory Peck, Joan
Crawford, David Niven, Tennessee Williams, Greta Garbo,
and a great many other famous personalities—when they
could obtain reservations.

Between a dedicated clientele of devoted visitors and
appreciative locals, La Valencia's three restaurants are usually booked, due in great part to the congenial employees
who have set records for continuity on the job in an industry
not noted for the tenure of its workers.

The Whaling Bar & Grill is very British and while the
food is succulent, it is better known as a watering hole for
those who have done their turn playing tennis, golfing,
surfing, swimming, sunning, jogging, hiking, bicycling,
and engaging in other productive endeavors. Meat is king
in the Whaling Grill, featuring rack of lamb, choice Eastern
beef, and Wisconsin veal.

The Sky Room offers a luncheon buffet and a nightly prix fixe dinner menu of continental delicacies, along with ocean view. Al fresco dining takes place in the Mediterranean Room and Patio, which is somewhat like dining in a greenhouse, with all the plants and flowers surrounding the diners. Breakfast, lunch, and dinner are served on the patio outdoors or, if preferred, indoors, which is much the same because of large windows.

Temperate weather year round makes the use of room air conditioning superfluous but it's there if needed. For the same reason, the pool is heated. And there's a putting green, table tennis area, and shuffleboard. Alongside the pool is a small health spa and sauna.

Briefcases, name badges, three-piece suits, and neckties are not often seen at La Valencia, although modest facilities for small group meetings are available. Tennis shorts and skirts or golf attire are the uniform of the day except at dinner.

The Westgate Hotel
1055 Second Avenue
San Diego, California 92101
800/522-1564 (tollfree from within California)
800/221-3802 (tollfree from rest of U.S.)
619/238-1818

Singles $104–$124
Doubles $114–$134
Suites (one- and two-bedroom) $250–$550

Of the Westgate's 223 exquisitely furnished guest rooms, no two are alike. This is a hotel designed and operated like the European *palace de grand classe*, typical of those patronized by nobility and only the very rich commoner in the early part of the century.

Rooms at this regal establishment are furnished in the styles of Louis XV, Louis XVI, Georgian, and English regency. Every room is furnished with a king-size or two oversized double beds, carpeting is wall-to-wall, and appointments include original oil paintings, furniture made of exotic woods, and upholstery designed to order for the Westgate. Bathrooms are of Italian marble and have 14-karat gold and antique brass fixtures.

There are two impressive suites in the upper floors of the 20-story hotel, the Governor's and the Presidential, both having two bedrooms and two baths, plus a full kitchen and a large living room with a marble fireplace. Custom-designed furnishings and appointments are reflective of the Westgate's overall ambience, including priceless antiques.

Public spaces in the Westgate are no less impressive. The lobby is a re-creation of a Versailles anteroom with magnificently preserved furnishings and original artwork and statuary from 18th-century France. A parquet floor of solid oak is covered with Kerman rugs from Iran, while giant hand-cut Baccarat chandeliers sparkle above.

The French theme continues in the opulent Le Fontainebleu restaurant, where, not surprisingly, the gracious art of French haute cuisine is practiced to the accompaniment of unobtrusive live music for lunch and dinner. The Westgate Room is less pretentious, but the edibles are prepared with equal care. Continental and American fare is served from 6 A.M. to 11 P.M. Cocktail service is available in both dining rooms. The Plaza Bar is open from 10 A.M. to 2 A.M., with nightly entertainment beginning at 9.

"Lady Westgate" is the name of whichever efficient woman is staffing the concierge desk between 9 A.M. and 6 P.M. on business days, ready to meet the needs of the traveling tourist as well as the executive on a business trip.

While the Westgate has a small number of shops and services on its ground floor, guests need only step outdoors to find that they are in the bustling heart of San Diego's downtown, and are directly across the street from the city's new, imaginative Horton Plaza, a shopping center of unique design and riotous colors, with archways, trestles, and bridges to connect the several levels of the complex.

The Westgate provides complimentary limousine service between the hotel and the airport, and to many of the city's scenic attractions. The "Tijuana Trolley" line runs adjacent to the property.

«SAN FRANCISCO»

Amsterdam Hotel
749 Taylor Street
San Francisco, California 94108
415/673-3277 or 441-9014

Singles $30–$42
Doubles $35–$47

Sometimes the name of a hotel precisely describes its character—in the case of the Amsterdam Hotel, it certainly does. Though located just a few short blocks from San Francisco's Union Square, this narrow little establishment could easily be mistaken for that place you stayed in just off the canal in the Netherlands' principal city. Simple and unpretentious, the Amsterdam offers little in the way of amenities, but it does get the job done, providing clean and comfortable lodgings for weary travelers.

The Amsterdam does offer some things that other similarly priced hotels do not. There are TVs in every room, and some rooms come with private bath, while some others share one bath between two rooms (the remainder require a trip down the hall). There is also someone on duty at the desk 24 hours a day, a luxury at this price range. In addition, it offers proximity to the very heart of San Francisco, including almost immediate access to the Theatre District and fine Sutter Street shopping area.

Rooms are not large, but they are comfortable and pleasantly decorated, with brass beds supporting very firm mattresses. The walls have cheering, floral wallpaper, a wise move since only a few rooms get much light (a couple are in almost perpetual gloom); on the other hand, along with the absence of sun comes an absence of noise as well, a welcome relief in this congested part of town.

Although the rooms exhibit a minimum of character, the lobby and sitting room have a distinct, welcoming warmth. The long hall that leads to the concierge's desk is lined with bookshelves (whose books are available for guests' pleasure), and the sitting room resembles the parlor of, perhaps, a professor at an established East Coast university, one with traditional but homey taste. It feels very much like a room for leisurely reading, contemplation, and polite yet meaningful conversation. There is a comfortable sense of quiet and dependable civility.

Because the Amsterdam is small (26 rooms), the desk person can give guests a great deal of personal attention, including arranging tours, ordering tickets, recommending and making reservations at restaurants, and suggesting out-of-the-ordinary attractions. The owner lives on premises, though he relies on his young staff for most of the day-to-day operations.

Although no food is available, there is always complimentary coffee and tea on the main floor, and there are soda and ice machines on each floor. The hotel has no elevator, plus the street in front is quite steep, making it unsuitable for anyone with ambulatory limitations.

The Archbishop's Mansion
1000 Fulton Street
San Francisco, California 94117
415/563-7872

Rooms $95–$138
Suites $138–$175

Without question, the operant word for the Archbishop's Mansion is grand. Grand in size, grand in concept, and even grand in theme (each room is designed to represent a specific grand opera), this extravagantly ornate inn caters to a love of fantasy and luxurious splendor. Staying here is a bit like staying with royalty—except that one doesn't have to observe all that tedious protocol.

Built in 1904 for Archbishop Patrick Riordan, the 33,000-square-foot mansion has but 13 guest rooms, even the smallest of them large by hotel standards, with lavish touches at every turn. In fact, the decor and layout are so extraordinary that it's difficult to know where to begin describing things. Suffice it to say that the Archbishop's Mansion has it all: the finest antiques, oriental carpets, marble fireplaces by the dozen, crystal chandeliers, giant floral displays, and architectural embellishments guaranteed to knock your socks off.

Every guest room has its own flavor and eye-popping highlights. The Don Giovanni Room, for example, centers on an 18th-century canopied bed from a castle in southern France; its carved posts culminate in life-size cherubs. The bed in the La Traviata Suite sits beneath a silk tent-canopy, while the La Boheme features hand-embroidered linens and exquisite lamps.

Nine rooms have fireplaces, all very impressive and each one unique. All have private baths, again extravagant and again unique. In one suite, for instance, there is a choice between an antique clawfoot tub or a separate shower room with six shower heads positioned at different heights and angles. In the Carmen Suite, a beauty of a tub stands in the center of a large, carpeted room, facing the fireplace; a 19th-century tapestry screen hides the commode.

Rooms come with an assortment of luxury items, including French soaps and shampoo, bath gel, body cream, terry cloth robes, fine chocolates, and sherry. Beds have down comforters and pillows and the finest-quality sheets.

The sense of space and luxury extends to the inn's public spaces. The downstairs parlor features a hand-stenciled ceiling and massive marble fireplace. The central hall is immense, with a sweeping staircase guarded by two lifesize statues. A second-floor salon, on the grand scale like everything else, is open to guests or can be rented for private parties and receptions.

Rates include a large continental breakfast served in the breakfast room downstairs or delivered to your room in

French baskets. There is a chef and dining room available for catered dinners, and eventually the owners plan to serve a nightly meal only for guests and their friends or clients. The inn provides valet parking for up to six cars; additional space is generally available on the street out front.

The Archbishop's Mansion faces Alamo Square, a lovely swatch of green. The surrounding area is one of three officially designated historic districts in the city. It is, more generally bordered by a low-income neighborhood. While Civic Center lies less than a mile away, the passage, particularly at night, can be intimidating. The staff will gladly call a cab or arrange a limousine for those without cars.

The staff will assist in others matter as well, from getting documents duplicated to being sure pants get pressed or arranging a tour of the Napa Valley. They are especially eager to share their knowledge of the city's lesser known delights, such as small neighborhood restaurants of special distinction.

For all its extravagance, the Archbishop's Mansion never becomes too much. Owners Jonathan Shannon and Jeffrey Ross (who also operate the Spreckels Mansion, nearby) have managed to strike just the right balance between elegant fun and ostentation. While the hostelry is far too grandiose to take entirely seriously, it's all been executed with considerable aesthetic awareness. The result is a place of undeniable beauty, but one that never intimidates.

Argyle Hotel
146 McAllister Street
San Francisco, California 94102
415/552-7076

Junior suites $45–$72.50
One-bedroom suites $105–$115
Two-bedroom suites $125–$145

The casts and crews of touring Broadway shows often stay at the Argyle Hotel. With a kitchen provided in every room, a sundeck on the roof, and a weight room (soon to be replaced by a full line of Nautilus equipment and a sauna)—all for the price of an ordinary room in other establishments—it's easy to understand why members of the American Ballet Theatre and the companies of such shows as *Sweet Charity* and *My One and Only* call the Argyle home in the Bay Area.

Fortunately, one doesn't have to be in show business to stay here. Manager Clayton Brooks Hale and staff are eager to extend their hospitality to the rest of the public. The offer covers both daily rates and the lower weekly or monthly ones (approximately $300 per week, $1000 per month).

A typical room for two includes queen-size bed, dresser, upholstered easy chair, and color TV in the main room, plus a separate small kitchen with table for two, half-fridge, range and oven (either microwave or gas), sink, and a plentiful supply of cooking and eating utensils. Larger rooms also have a sofa, and some have two double beds rather than one queen. There are, in addition, three Queen Anne suites that feature full living room plus two bedrooms, one with a king-size bed and the other with two doubles. Baths are basic but clean, and all have fully refurbished clawfoot tubs that date back to the hotel's beginnings in 1903.

The spacious lobby favors a pleasantly understated decor, with a small comfortable seating area near the front. Colors are warm and muted, perhaps to quiet the nerves of often overexcited performers. When visited, the lobby was being expanded into adjacent store space to include either a public piano bar suitable for after-show gatherings and singalongs or a wine parlor open only to hotel guests. Eventual plans also include a restaurant.

One nice touch in the lobby is an old-fashioned telephone closet where guests can make calls in complete privacy. Those planning on a long stay should know that all rooms have jacks where a guest's own phone can be installed for a charge of about $12. Otherwise, expect to pay a service charge of 75 cents for every call made from the room.

The Argyle does not offer room service, but it does provide evening turndown complete with the now-common chocolate on the pillow. Valet laundry service is available, as is a basement laundromat. The desk will arrange tour bookings, restaurant reservations, theater tickets, and so on at your request.

Because of the hotel's show-business connection, the management from time to time promotes special theater packages that feature a room for two for two nights, dinner at a nearby restaurant, orchestra seats to a Broadway show, and a bottle of champagne on arrival for about $200. In addition, the staff often receive complimentary tickets to touring shows and will occasionally turn these over to guests. There is no guarantee of this, of course, but if you don't get to see a show for free, by staying at the Argyle you at least stand a good chance of meeting some of the cast.

Located in the Civic Center area, the Argyle lies just a short skip from BART and Muni-Metro trains. It is also within walking distance of City Hall, the symphony and ballet, and the Orpheum Theatre.

The Cartwright
524 Sutter Street
San Francisco, California 94102
800/652-1858 (tollfree from within California)
800/227-3844 (tollfree from rest of U.S.)
415/421-2865

Singles $58–$65
Doubles $68–$75
Rooms with twin beds $70–$78
Suites $100–$120

Family owned and operated, the Cartwright has attracted a legion of loyal patrons. Manager Dale Walwark, whose parents-in-law own this 114-room hotel very close to Union Square, has a file full of commendatory letters from satisfied guests. It's easy to see why visitors appreciate the Cartwright. The staff is friendly and knows regular guests by name, the rooms are homey and immaculately clean, and the public areas are comfortable and inviting. On top of that, rates are one-half to two-thirds those of the better-known establishments in the same area. How could you do better?

While there's nothing glossy about the Cartwright, there's no absence of taste and feeling. Every room has been individually decorated and furnished with an assortment of antique or near-antique furniture. The decor is not rigidly consistent. Instead, each room holds disparate pieces that blend together nicely, rather as in someone's home where comfortable furniture has been acquired over a period of time. The result is a very pleasant sense of coziness, emphasized by the placement of a small vase of flowers on the nightstand or dresser.

All rooms have private baths, direct-dial telephones, firm mattresses, and color TVs. On the dresser is a list of items that the hotel will supply, free of charge, for your use. Among the more than one dozen extras are iron and ironing board, reading pillow, crib, hair dryer, and shoe-care kit.

The downstairs lobby has a plant-filled sitting area, with sofas and easy chairs grouped around an oriental rug. Newspapers along with an array of current magazines are placed out every morning for leisurely reading.

The charming English-style restaurant behind the lobby serves breakfast, lunch, and tea, but is not open for dinner. There is no room service, so meals, which are not included in the room rate, must be eaten in the restaurant. Because so many guests have requested it, the management is considering adding a complimentary breakfast.

The hotel has no parking, but there are garages nearby. As for public transportation, the Powell Street cable car is half a block away, and several close parallel streets have bus lines. Shops, department stores, and theaters are within easy walking distance.

The Cartwright's sister hotel, the Savoy, has similar facilities and services. However, its lobby has a quite handsome bar, rather like a pub, that caters primarily to hotel clientele. Its low lighting, dark wood paneling, and brass fixtures make for a quietly romantic atmosphere.

The Casa Madrona
801 Bridgeway
Sausalito, California 94965
415/332-0502

Old Casa Madrona rooms $60 without bath, $75–$115
   with bath
Cottages $140–$160
New Casa Madrona rooms $100–$140
Three-room suite $275

For anyone torn between a visit to San Francisco or a
vacation in some romantic hideaway, the Casa Madrona is
the solution to the dilemma. Less than half an hour, by car
or ferry, from the heart of the city, this genuinely enrap-
turing hotel offers a setting and vista that can match almost
any resort in the world. Set on a steep hillside in the heart
of Sausalito, the rooms here provide a panoply of beguiling
views. Looking out across San Francisco Bay, to the north
you can see the Tiburon Peninsula, to the east Angel Island,
and to the south San Francisco itself. Directly before you
lies the Sausalito Yacht Harbor and Marina.

Were that all the Casa Madrona presented, it would probably prove sufficient; but, happily, the hotel itself is as fine
as the view. The hotel consists of several parts, each distinctive and each with its unique charms.

The oldest portion, an Italianate-style house built in 1885,
perches at the very top of the hill. Its 20 rooms (13 used
for guests) feature the extravagant carpentry and detailing
common to larger homes of its era. With its rustic front
garden and picket fence, the house has the feeling of a
country inn, and the rooms have been decorated and furnished to complement this impression.

Accompanying the house near the top of the hill are three
rather homespun cottages, with the kind of eccentric plain-
ness typical of early 20th-century structures in coastal towns.
Their decor wavers, pleasantly, somewhere between Victorian cozy and seaside shanty.

The third portion, constructed only in 1984, tumbles down
the hillside in a cascade of individually shaped projections.
While the earlier structures are undeniably charming, they
are not so unlike dozens of other similar inns in Northern
California. In this newer section, on the other hand, the
Casa Madrona really comes into its own. Not only is each

of the 16 new rooms individually shaped and placed at a slightly different point on the steep rise, but each one is also individually decorated by a different designer. While one suggests a place in the tropics through its use of wicker, plants, and gauzy fabrics, another has the soft colors and textures of a lovers' rendezvous. One room, with a high pitched ceiling, has been done as an artist's loft, complete with paints and canvas for guests to use. The Bridgeway to Hollywood room is awash in movie memorabilia and includes a VCR, while the Katmandu room has a high platform bed backed by a carved Nepalese screen and covered in jungle-patterned madras.

Fourteen of these 16 rooms have private terraces overlooking the Bay. They also all have color TVs, clock radios, small refrigerators with a replenishable supply of complimentary juices and mineral waters, and a basket of toiletries. Only one room in the original house has a private terrace, though there is a large terrace off the parlor for other guests. Two of the five rooms in the cottages have private terraces. In keeping with the Victorian spirit of the older structure, those rooms do not have TVs, and the bathroom fixtures are old-fashioned. Only two rooms, next to each other in the 1885 house, do not have private bath; they share one across the hall.

Rates at the Casa Madrona include a complimentary continental breakfast and early evening wine. The latter is served in the Victorian parlor, the former in the terrace restaurant built into the ground floor of the oldest structure. The restaurant, which specializes in French-accented California cuisine, is open for lunch Monday through Saturday and for high tea Monday through Friday; at these times, room service is also available.

Due to the Casa Madrona's unique geography, only four rooms are accessible to the handicapped. Anyone who finds climbing stairs either difficult or unappealing will also find the Casa Madrona of limited interest. But for others, this unique establishment should seem just one step short of heaven.

The Claremont Resort Hotel
P.O. Box 23363
Ashby and Domingo Avenues
Oakland, California 94623
415/843-3000

$125–$200 (special packages available)

For nearly 70 years, the castle-like Claremont Hotel has stood as a major landmark in the hills across the bay from San Francisco. Situated on the Oakland-Berkeley border, the hotel was built as a country retreat for well-to-do city dwellers. Such have times changed that the once long trip from San Francisco has now been pared to a mere 20 minutes and the once-idyllic location has been absorbed into the urban fabric of the Bay Area metropolis.

The bright side of this change in character means that the present-day traveler has the opportunity to combine urban business with rural pleasure or to turn one vacation into two by mixing the amenities of a resort with the excitement of a city.

The Claremont offers a full range of resort features: ten tennis courts, an outdoor Olympic-size swimming pool, a Parcourse, sauna and massage services, and 22 acres of gardenlike grounds. It also has a lavish restaurant serving the finest in contemporary California cuisine, with many herbs and vegetables grown in the hotel's own garden, as well as a coffeeshop for quick bites and a bar that offers a panoramic bay view and features live entertainment nightly. In addition, the vast East Bay regional park system, the largest urban-sited wilderness area in the U.S., begins immediately behind the hotel, with opportunities for everything from simple nature hikes to horseback riding and rock climbs.

Listed on the National Register of Historic Places, the Claremont went through a period of turbulence before a recent renovation and operations overhaul restored it to its former glory.

Rooms are unusually large, and many have stunning views

of the bay and San Francisco. Others look onto the natural landscape of the Claremont Canyon Preserve, while the rest face one of Berkeley's most exclusive residential areas. The decor is bright and cheerful, and furniture is quite distinctive, with such uncommon features as a contemporary chaise lounge rather than a couch and a Danish modern four-poster with upholstered banquette attached at the foot. Baths have many extras, including hair dryer, full range of toiletries, and gigantic bath towels.

The Claremont maintains a full line of business and conference services, including full catering, audiovisual equipment, and special events programming. The staff has, for example, arranged to greet attendees with a 100-piece marching band and to stage jugglers and dancing bears during cocktails. The hotel can handle banquets of more than 500. Many special corporate packages are available.

For the pleasure traveler, the Claremont offers weekend, tennis, honeymoon, and holiday specials. Contents of these packages, of course, vary considerably but can include such extras as champagne on arrival, free limousine service to and from the airport, tennis lessons, or meals.

For all guests, the hotel provides frequent complimentary shuttle service to a nearby BART station, from which trains whisk them into downtown Oakland, Berkeley, or San Francisco in a matter of minutes. The University of California lies 15 minutes away by bus. There is ample parking on the grounds to accommodate guests from all of the hotel's 300 rooms.

El Drisco Hotel
2901 Pacific Avenue
San Francisco, California 94115
415/346-2880

Rooms $50–$70
Suites $75–$90

In its heyday, the El Drisco regularly played host to Dwight Eisenhower. Anaïs Nin was for a time a month-to-month resident. For the rich and famous of surrounding

Pacific Heights, the El Drisco served as a spare bedroom when their own homes were filled to overflowing. Then came a period of decline in which the wonderful little hotel on the hill became something of an embarrassment to the neighborhood. Now under new proprietor Ronald Lockyer, the El Drisco is well on its way back to achieving a position of prominence.

Entering the El Drisco today seems very much like coming into a small, well-established hotel in London. The large hall, which also serves as the reception area and front desk, is lined in dark wood paneling and filled with architectural flourishes from an earlier time (the hotel opened in 1903). Wingback chairs and a davenport sit to one side beneath a large stained-glass window. The oriental rugs are comfortably worn, not pristine, attesting to their proud history. Off the hall, a wine parlor with easy chairs placed in small groupings has the feel of a private university club.

Because of its location at the crest of Pacific Heights, many rooms at the El Drisco have extraordinary views. A corner suite on the top floor offers a truly exceptional panorama that sweeps from the Golden Gate all the way to the Oakland-Bay Bridge. Rooms, especially suites, are generally quite large. Furnishings, however, vary greatly in quality—the legacy of neglect under previous management. Rather than undertake a massive and expensive one-time remodeling, Mr. Lockyer has chosen to proceed room by room, weeding out the admittedly dismal 1950s and '60s furniture and restoring the many beautifully crafted pieces that remain from earlier eras. By moving slowly he has been able to keep rates modest. Gradually, all the rooms will meet the standard already set in the public areas, and rates will still be affordable.

The hotel also has a dining room, open to the public, serving breakfast, lunch, and dinner. Like the hall and parlor, this room reflects a sense of tradition and comfort, with formally attired waiters, a dark-paneled room broken by columns, tables spaced widely for relaxed dining, and service on fine china. On weekend evenings, a harpist plays during the meal. This is the type of room where guests enjoy lingering over their meal for hours. Food, again modestly priced with entrees ranging from $8 to $12, tends toward the conservative (in keeping with the overall tenor of the hotel), eschewing both haute and nouvelle cuisine in favor of classic American cooking.

Ronald Lockyer's goal is to make the El Drisco a great American hotel, a place where guests feel as much at home as in their own house. The setting is elegant but not stuffy, gracious without being overbearing. Lockyer believes in the tradition of service and attention to personal needs and will attempt to honor guests' requests.

In 1986, the El Drisco will add a small shop on the main floor to provide newspapers and sundry items. It will also sell chocolates made especially for the hotel.

Hotel Beresford Arms

701 Post Street
San Francisco, California 94109
415/673-2600

Doubles $50
Small suites $70
Large suites $90

One might call the Beresford Arms a hotel for real people. There's no pretense here, and the wide variety of guests ranges from vacationing plumbers to bankers on business —and even Victor Borge, who stays here when in town. Friendliness may be a matter of policy at many hotels, but at the Beresford Arms the pervasive sense of good cheer seems so genuine it cannot possibly stem merely from corporate mandate. It's hard to imagine anyone save unregenerate fussbudgets or insufferable snobs not enjoying their stay here.

The lobby is spacious and relaxing. High ceilings with plaster friezes, large, arched windows, and intimately grouped furniture (including grandfather clock and writing desk) make it an ideal place to enjoy each morning's complimentary donuts and coffee. No matter that the carpet is a trifle too red and the furniture mediocre copies of elegant traditionals; everything comes together to produce a very salutary effect. Upstairs, corridors are broad, clean, and cheerful. Rooms range from typical hotel style to quite gracious.

The Beresford Arms was built in 1910 and originally had 45 suites. Remodeled several times since then, the hotel now has 96 rooms and suites. The basic room (done in typical hotel style) has either one double and one single bed or one queen-size bed, two easy chairs, a desk, and a bureau plus a private bath with a tub-shower combination.

For only $20 more, however, the accommodations take a big jump in quality. The Jacuzzi suites feature two queen-size beds, either a wet bar or full kitchen (including utensils and dining table), and a luxury bath complete with brass fixtures, two sinks, a bidet, and, as the name implies, a Jacuzzi in the tub. There is even a second phone in the bathroom.

By far the best bargain of all at the Beresford Arms are the queen suites, suitable for up to five people. These consist of two large rooms and a fully equipped kitchen (down to such minor accessories as coasters, placemats, and napkins). The bedroom holds a queen-size bed, is exceptionally large, and has two bay windows. The living room, equally large, has a graceful and comfortable seating area at one end set around built-in bookshelves and a handsome dining set at the other. A contemporary version of the Murphy bed pulls down from the living room wall, and a rollaway is available as well. The large baths are identical to those in the less expensive suites.

Queen suites can be combined with a neighboring basic room to form a very large suite joined by a private connecting hall.

All rooms have color TV and push-button phones (50 cents per outgoing call) as well as pickup bag for overnight laundry service. Refrigerators in the suites come stocked with wine, beer, and soda, paid for on an honor basis; a price list is posted in the room.

The hotel at present has no dining room, but guests can

charge meals at the White Horse Tavern in the nearby sister hotel, the Beresford. The garage next door offers a 25 percent discount to hotel patrons, with a resulting charge of $9.25 per day including in and out privileges.

Hotel Obrero
1208 Stockton Street
San Francisco, California 94133
415/589-3960

Singles $28
Doubles $35
Twins $45
Triples $45

A huge breakfast is included in the price of a room at the Hotel Obrero, but guests shouldn't expect to enjoy it over the morning paper. Owner and self-proclaimed mother hen Bambi MacDonald does not allow guests to hide behind the pages of the *San Francisco Chronicle* or *Wall Street Journal*. She wants people to talk to one another. It's also impossible to hide in the room watching the "Today" show —there's not a single TV on the premises. If you aren't sleeping, swallowing, or out, you'd better be talking up a blue streak.

"I expect my guests to make a contribution to the atmosphere," MacDonald unabashedly declares. "This is a meeting place, a melting pot, and anybody who's not comfortable with that—well, I won't say they're not welcome, but I don't hesitate to recommend other hotels if I feel someone's not going to like it here."

If MacDonald sounds a trifle formidable, the truth is she's warm and friendly. At the same time, she means what she says, and the joy of her hotel comes from a combination of her down-to-earth manner and her exuberance that pervades the whole place. Things don't get fancy at the Obrero, but they do get fun.

What the hotel offers are 12 simple, rigorously clean rooms, affordable prices, and an atmosphere of warmth and vitality. Each room has a bed, a dresser, a not-so-easy chair, and a lamp—and that's about it. Although there are towels in all the rooms, baths are down the hall. Located in the heart of Chinatown, the Obrero promises no respite from the teeming city. Rather, it throws you right into it. Open your window and you get the smell of fresh fish and sesame oil, the sound of traffic and Chinese, and the sight of hundreds of Asian merchants and shoppers. Open the door and you plunge into a rushing stream of very fast pedestrians.

Happily, before the plunge comes the aforementioned breakfast to build your strength. The complimentary morning table is a true feast—eggs, ham, cheese, and fruit plus all the homebaked bread and fresh-brewed coffee or tea you can handle. MacDonald means the meal to last all day, a gesture to budget-conscious travelers.

Those who make it back by 6:30 will be able to catch a second feast, this time a family-style Basque dinner. Before MacDonald took over the Obrero in 1978, the hotel served as a boarding house for Basque shepherds from California's Central Valley. She has chosen to carry on the tradition of nightly serving a hearty supper. Open to the public, dinner consists of two main courses (for example, shepherd's pie and Basque chicken), vegetables, salad, potatoes, bread, fruit, and all the wine you can drink for $9.50.

Just because it's cheap, however, don't think the Obrero is only for the economy-minded traveler. Regular guests include a Superior Court judge from New York, a BBC correspondent, the leader of a modern dance company, and a French museum director who stays at the Beverly Wilshire in L.A. and the Obrero in San Francisco.

Be forewarned: The Obrero is very easy to miss, even when you're looking for it. At street level, there is only a green door and a faded menu to signal the hotel's existence. There's no downstairs lobby. Nor an upstairs one, for that matter. The large dining room, ringed by a delightful mural painted by one of MacDonald's friends, handles all public functions.

Also be forewarned about arrival. Because she runs the place entirely on her own (except for one housecleaner), MacDonald closes the office between noon and 5 P.M. You cannot check in during that period. She will bend on many rules, but not on this one. And not on the morning paper.

The Huntington Hotel
1075 California Street
San Francisco, California 94108
800/652-1539 (tollfree from within California)
800/227-4683 (tollfree from rest of U.S.)
415/474-5400

Rooms $125–$180 single, $140–$195 double
One-bedroom suites $240–$500
Two-bedroom suites $360–$555

The Huntington Hotel is the type of place that still has an elevator operator—despite the fact that both elevators are now automatic. But Mary Frazier has been in the hotel's employ for so long (since 1946) that she has become a part of the establishment. Jimmy, the doorman, has been there 30 years, and many of the housekeeping and maintenance staff have been there nearly as long. Family-owned since it first opened in 1924, the Huntington thrives on tradition. And on excellence.

Luciano Pavarotti stays here when in San Francisco. And regardless of their professional rivalry, so does Placido Domingo. Other regular guests include Cary Grant, Robert Redford, and Henry Ford. The reasons for their choice are everywhere evident.

Situated at the top of Nob Hill, almost every room has a view, some of the city and bay, others of Grace Cathedral and Huntington Park, for which the hotel is named. With only 47 rooms and suites, the Huntington can offer both personal attention and discretion—autograph seekers cannot linger unnoticed in the elegant little lobby, and even the most aggressive guests are likely to find their manner tempered by the prevailing air of gentility.

Because the Huntington began its life as a residential hotel, switching to transient status only after World War II, most rooms are quite large. All have been individually decorated, the majority in what might be termed subtle luxury, with quality furnishings and fabrics designed to please without being overly dramatic. A few, however, do indeed exhibit a flair for the dramatic, with, for example, rich brocades or lacquered tables, but never carried to the extreme. And five suites were designed by Lee Radziwill with a rather more passionate touch, with a single color dominating. The furniture is primarily custom-made, accented by one or two choice antiques.

There are down pillows on every bed—and down cushions on every piece of cushioned furniture. Bathrooms are done all in white in the European fashion and provided with Irish linen towels made especially for the Huntington. There is also a full line of bath items, including glycerine soap, shampoo, and bath oil.

All the windows open, so guests can take advantage of San Francisco's generally accommodating climate. And housekeeping is provided twice a day.

The Huntington holds two restaurants, its own Big Four, a clublike room featuring historic memorabilia, and l'Etoile, a separately run French restaurant considered one of the premier restaurants in the city. The latter provides room service to hotel guests 24 hours a day.

From 7 A.M. until 11 P.M., there is a concierge in the lobby to take care of needs for tour arrangements, theater bookings, secretarial services, and babysitters. Guests are entitled to make full use of the facilities at the nearby Nob Hill Health Club, which offers a complete line of gymnasium and recreational services. Guests may also take advantage of valet parking and complimentary transportation to the Financial District in the hotel's Rolls-Royce.

All suites in the Huntington have either wet bars or pantries, and some have full kitchens. Should you wish to hold small receptions or business meetings, the concierge can arrange catering or serving assistance.

The Inn at the Opera
333 Fulton Street
San Francisco, California 94102
415/863-8400

Standard rooms $115
Deluxe rooms $135
Superior rooms and Junior suites $165
One-bedroom suites $195
Two-bedroom suites $225

Although San Francisco's Civic Center area has long been the cultural and government focus for the city, with the opera, symphony, Museum of Modern Art, and City Hall grouped closely together, the area has lacked a first-class hotel suitable for either patrons or performers. With the opening in the summer of 1985 of the Inn at the Opera, that picture has changed. Small and intimate, the inn's 48 rooms feature finely crafted furnishings created especially for the hotel, fine down comforters and pillows, color TV, direct-dial phones, wet bar, refrigerator and microwave oven, and terry cloth robes inside the handsome armoire that graces each room or suite. The emphasis throughout is on the sedate and elegant.

The small size allows the staff to attend to the personal needs of each guest. Services include a chilled bottle of wine on arrival, linen turndown at night, continental breakfast and choice of newspaper delivered to guest rooms each morning, call screening and call forwarding, ticket booking, and 24-hour room service. At check-in, guests receive a form to fill in requesting additional services and preserving their preferences for future stays.

The inn operates a fine restaurant, the Act IV, behind the lobby which serves from breakfast until 2 A.M., an unusually late hour for San Francisco, where few restaurants serve after 11 P.M. Like the rest of the hotel, the Act IV is small and intimate, with a pianist in the evening and a low-key bar that draws many after-show concertgoers. The restaurant has proved especially popular with women traveling alone, since it is the kind of room where they do not feel conspicuous or out of place. Service is formal and attentive, and the menu is inventive.

The inn is located less than half a block from the Opera House, and, depending on which direction you head, a walk one block farther will take you to the symphony, the museum, and City Hall, or the clubs and restaurants that have sprung up along Hayes Street. The inn's classy entrance and small, handsome lobby make a welcome contribution to the area's character.

The Mansion Hotel
2220 Sacramento Street
San Francisco, California 94115
415/929-9444

$74–$150 single, $89–$200 double

It's safe to assume that a hotelier who writes books, collects sculpture (he has a major Bufano collection), keeps a parrot in the living room, and plays the musical saw is not going to run an ordinary hotel. And the Mansion, a twin-turreted Queen Anne Victorian, is definitely not ordinary. Robert C. Pritikin's taste and boundless energy make that certain.

A few of his hotel's more unusual features include a ghost named Claudia, who plays piano concerts; a billiard room with a wall-sized mural of pigs; caged white doves; priceless Joseph Turner and Joshua Reynolds paintings; and a staff in full Victorian costume. One of the world's largest examples of stained glass stands in the dining room. The mural, originally created for a villa in Spain, is nine feet high and stretches for 32 feet in a continuous scene of color and design.

The 21 guest rooms, not surprisingly, are sumptuous in the Victorian manner, with four-posters, potted palms, and elaborately trimmed wardrobes. They also include piped-in classical music, fresh flowers and candy, velvet quilts, and red carpets. All rooms have private baths. Continental breakfast is included in the room rates.

There's nothing understated about the Mansion. Yet, with all its glitter and opulence, the hotel has a lighthearted atmosphere. This step back into another century is meant to be fun. Even the ghost seems to have a good time, concluding her evening concerts with a rousing march or ragtime tune, while bubbles float to the ceiling.

The Orchard Hotel

562 Sutter Street
San Francisco, California 94102
800/433-4434 (tollfree from within California)
800/433-4343 (tollfree from rest of U.S.)
415/433-4434

Rooms $85–$105
Suites $170

All the furniture for the lobby and 94 rooms of the Orchard Hotel was imported from Europe. The notion, devised by Bent Severin, the hotel's architect, was that the Orchard would have an old world style. As personal architect for both the queen of Denmark and the queen of England, Severin clearly knew what he was up to. Looking into the small, narrow reception lobby from Sutter Street, it's quite easy to momentarily imagine yourself in some European country. Everything appears so understated—stylish, well-to-do, even elegant, but definitely reserved. The decor is neither old-fashioned nor contemporary, but carefully classic.

Farther in, the lobby expands somewhat to accommodate a seating area that serves both as "parlor" and cocktail lounge, chairs and sofas grouped in formal but comfortable arrangements near a piano. In the evening, the pianist provides appropriate cocktail music from 6 until 11.

Upstairs, the rooms reflect the same sensibility, though with distinctly American touches. Most beds, for example, are king-size, with a few in the very smallest rooms only queen. And there is a TV in every room, including both rooms of a suite. Bathrooms are quite large, with two sinks each, and an extra half bath in the suites.

All rooms have mini refrigerators stocked with wine, juice, soda, and mineral water—use of which is charged to your bill. The hotel stocks its own soaps and shampoos in the bathrooms. And suites include terry cloth robes.

Rooms have mahogany chairs, armoires, and cabinets, with damask upholstering on easy chairs and sofas. These latter tend to be somewhat stiff and formal, more for "proper" upright sitting than lazing or lounging. The living rooms in the suites, for instance, would be suitable for meetings, informed conversations, or perhaps even teas, but not the kind of rooms where you would be inclined to kick off your shoes and curl up with a good book. For reading, however, the beds come with four pillows each (down-filled, on request) and bedside lamps.

Off the lobby, Anabel's serves fine continental cuisine at lunch and dinner. In the morning, the hotel uses the same space to serve light breakfasts; breakfasts are convenient but fairly high-priced considering their quality. All meals can be charged to your room.

The Orchard, which has a sister hotel of the same name in Perth, Australia, is located less than a block from the Powell Street cable car and surrounded by some of the city's most fashionable shops, including Laura Ashley, the Maxwell Galleries, and Williams-Sonoma.

There is a separate concierge desk in the lobby, and the hotel can provide small amenities such as umbrellas when it's raining. Parking in a nearby garage costs $13 a day; a chit from the hotel permits in-and-out privileges not ordinarily allowed.

Pensione San Francisco
1668 Market Street
San Francisco, California 94102
415/864-1271

Singles $29–$32
Doubles $35–$38

Sandy Darlington and his partner patterned the Pensione San Francisco after the kind of modest hostelry they had encountered throughout Europe, the type of place where you can get a basic sleeping room that is clean, safe, and comfortable without paying an arm and a leg. As in Europe, rooms do not have private baths, phones, TVs, or other nonessentials—just a bed, a chair, a desk or bureau, an armoire, and a basin.

But unlike its generally conservative continental counterparts, the pensione in true San Francisco fashion displays the slightly whimsical outlook of its creators. Each room has its own peculiar touch to dispel any possibility of anonymity. One room, for example, has an actual kayak hitched to the wall, while another features an old band uniform and a trombone. In another bit of whimsy, to enliven the rather pedestrian view from side windows, Darlington is setting up a field of plywood cows on an adjoining roof. While the bucolic conceit certainly won't deceive a single soul into believing they're at a country inn, it will at least lend some color to a generally lackluster setting.

Surprisingly, though staring directly onto Market Street, San Francisco's main thoroughfare, the pensione's front rooms truly do have a slight bucolic feel. Large, leafy trees planted at the sidewalk's edge all but block out the decidedly urban streetscape.

Rooms here do not come with breakfast, but you do get a morning espresso or cappuccino at the pensione's very popular and trendy restaurant, Cafe Pensione. While the hotel's decor, apart from its touches of humor, runs to natural colors typical of the '70s (when it first opened), the cafe is '80s new wave—hot colors and sharp angles. The centerpiece (if you don't count the display of homemade-looking pastries at the entrance) is a sofa upholstered in a wild assortment of tea towels—somewhat hideous but appealing in a brash sort of way. The food, with dinner entrees in the $10–$12 range, tends also to an '80s-style nouvelle California cuisine.

Located close to major transit lines, the pensione is also convenient to the cultural activities of the city's Civic Center. It's a five-minute walk to the opera and symphony. Darlington maintains a free telephone line from the airport, so you can try for last-minute reservations or get transportation information with ease on arrival.

Although all rooms are at least one flight up, the pensione has a small elevator, and the surrounding district is relatively flat. The neighborhood is up and coming, and it would be wise to stick to the main thoroughfares if you don't consider yourself streetwise. It's not truly a dangerous area, but the side streets can seem lonely after dark.

The Sausalito Hotel
16 El Portal
Sausalito, California 94965
415/332-4155

Rooms $50–$120
Suites $125–$150

Immediately across the Golden Gate Bridge from San Francisco, Sausalito has become something like the ultimate tourist town. Small and compact, its steep, hilly terrain filled with picturesque houses squeezes the shop-filled downtown right up against the bay. Once a true working sailors' town, it is now more akin to a stage set. But if it is a set, it's a lovely one, and its location so close to a major city makes it all the more attractive.

Right in the heart of Sausalito, lying on the thin strip of flat land that makes a commercial district feasible, the Sausalito Hotel entertains guests in a Mission Revival structure that harks back to the town's more robust past. Occupying the second floor of a thriving commercial building, the hotel originally served vacationers who came from San Francisco on the ferry and businessmen having connections to the area's fishing or shipbuilding industries.

For many years, it served as a residential hotel, but in the mid-seventies new owners transformed it into one of the metropolitan region's first bed and breakfast inns. It was carefully restored to its original character, and authentic Victorian and Edwardian furnishings were installed to emphasize its history. That the interior styles derive more from ''Upstairs Downstairs'' (including room names like Prince Albert and Princess Alice) than from the Spanish-influenced Mission Revival detracts from its authenticity but not from its charm. All the froufrous and excesses of Victoriana serve to counteract the sterility of modernism in comforting ways that mission oak generally would not.

In a gesture to Americana, the Marquis of Queensbury Room holds the bed of Ulysses S. Grant, an appropriately solid-looking and imposing piece of furniture with a truly massive headboard. A matching dresser with near full-length mirror sits across the room beside the hotel's only fireplace.

Most rooms are small, with coziness rather than space as the principal draw. Of the inn's 15 rooms, ten have private baths and five share three hall bathrooms. A basket of Crabtree & Evelyn soaps, shampoos, and bath gels sits on the bureau. Rooms also have a range of live plants and fresh flowers to give them extra cheer.

There are no private phones, but each room does have a black and white TV. All are bright and sunny, and most have either a bay or park view (looking toward the Tiburon Peninsula, farther into Marin County, rather than toward San Francisco); a few look onto the bustle of the Bridgeway, Sausalito's main street.

The ferry to San Francisco docks directly across from the hotel, and there are restaurants for every palate within a few blocks. Validated parking is provided in the nearby city lot.

The Sherman House
2160 Green Street
San Francisco, California 94123
415/563-3600

Rooms $170–$300
Suites $300–$475
Executive suites $500–$600

There is a world apart from the one most of us inhabit, a world of ease and privilege that seems, if not beyond imagination, at least beyond ordinary expectation. Luxury in this other world is not merely a pleasant interlude in an otherwise unexceptional existence, but rather the foundation on which all else is built. Personal service is not simply provided—it is assumed.

The Sherman House, an intimate hotel in one of San Francisco's most fashionable districts, is very much a part of this special world. Owner Manouchehr Mobedshahi, an Iranian-born economist, acquired the French-Italianate structure (originally built in 1876 by the founder of the Sherman Clay Music Company) in 1981 and transformed it into a more-than-elegant hostelry for more-than-discrimi-nating clientele.

With interiors by the late world-class designer Billy Gay-lord, the rooms adhere primarily to a French second empire design, with a few in a Biedermeier or Jacobean motif. Furnishings are either antique or custom-made. The rooms give a sense of solidity and permanence, as if they and everything in them had been and will be around forever. Expensive carpets, draped beds, marble counters, brass fix-tures, crystal chandeliers, original art—all this and more combine to create a rather princely enclave.

The Sherman House, however, is definitely not for everyone—that is, not even for everyone who can afford it. The level of service can become somewhat discomfiting to anyone not used to extreme deference. Maids (in tradi-tional black uniforms with white aprons and caps), garden-ers, and housekeepers tend to melt into the background, backing into doorways and standing nearly at attention to let you by. There is no desk clerk, but rather a well-dressed employee who personally greets guests and escorts them to their rooms. Once there, someone else offers to unpack and hang one's clothes. For some people, such attention from staff is expected; for others, it's a welcome change; for still others, it's awkward and embarrassing.

If you happen to fall into the first two categories, the Sherman House can hardly be topped. What could one pos-sibly want that it doesn't offer? Fine food? The hotel main-tains a fine French chef and staff to cook meals solely for the inn's clientele and their invited guests; there is a six-course *menu gastronomique* at $55 or a seven-course set menu at $75. Perhaps you just cannot live without a TV in your bathroom; you'll have it here, as well as another in the bedroom and one in the living room if you rent a suite. One suite, incidentally, comes with its own private 800-square-foot garden with deck and arbor.

In the salon, complete with palatial bird cages and grand piano, wine is served in the afternoon, and there is some-times a special wine tasting. At night, there are often small recitals, continuing a tradition that dates back to the time when Caruso performed for small groups here.

Needless to say, the staff will attend to all needs, from arranging secretarial services to getting shoes repaired or lining up a special tour. The inn's Rolls is ready to chauffeur guests from the airport into town.

Spreckels Mansion and Guest House
737 Buena Vista West
San Francisco, California 94117
415/861-3008

Doubles $88–$125
Suites $134–$190

This elegant San Francisco landmark was built in 1887 as a country estate for one of the city's leading families. Nearly a century later, after several changes of ownership, the present owners (who also run the Archbishop's Mansion) bought it to prevent its conversion to condominiums. They decided to use their expertise in historical restoration and design to bring the mansion's glory days to life again. Combining traditional Victoriana with modern comforts, they achieved their desired effect: a warm, charming, luxurious home reminiscent of old San Francisco.

Spreckels is actually two inns with a total of ten rooms and suites; one is the mansion itself and the other is the Guest House next door, also a three-story Victorian home with similar amenities. Guest rooms and suites are spacious and comfortable, and each has a distinctive personality. The Sunset Suite, in shades of gold and rose, has two canopied double beds, antique etched windows, and French furnishings. In the Sugar Baron Suite, the carpeted bathroom is larger than most hotel rooms and includes a working fireplace, ceiling-high fan windows, and an old-fashioned free-standing tub.

The mansion's former ballroom is now the San Francisco Suite, which covers the entire third floor and can accommodate two couples (for $260). Its views of the ocean, bay, and city skyline are stunning. But for cozy romance, the Valentine Room is the place to be, with its collection of antique valentines adding a tender touch to the French furniture and canopied, queen-size bed.

Guests enjoy a complimentary continental breakfast and, in the evenings, wine in the library. There the innkeeper and staff gladly share their knowledge of the fabled city's restaurants and highlights.

Both Spreckels Mansion and the Guest House have been carefully renovated and lavishly redecorated. Today they convey the flavor of the time when it was a country home, rather than part of a hillside residential area just a few minutes from downtown San Francisco.

Victorian Inn On The Park
301 Lyon Street
San Francisco, California 94117
415/931-1830

Rooms $75–$115
Rooms with fireplace $105–$115
Suites $115–$200

Senator Thomas Cluny built his family manse on the Panhandle leading to Golden Gate Park in 1897. He lived there until his death, and current owners Lisa and William Benau like to believe his friendly ghost still haunts the premises. If it does, the senator should be pleased with what the Benaus have done since acquiring the house and turning it into an inn in 1981.

This is perhaps the most perfect example of the San Francisco bed and breakfast inn—intimate, friendly, decorated in period furniture, and true to the spirit of its historic character. The decor is properly beautiful and luxurious, but the proprietors are so down to earth that the atmosphere is always relaxed and easy. Lisa, whose parents are co-owners, was a lawyer and William a teamster before they opened the inn, and they don't go in for affectations and pretense.

Lisa and her mother, Mrs. Paul Weber, decorated each of the 12 rooms themselves, relying primarily on century furniture and accessories from the 19th and early 20th centuries, acquired at auctions, estate sales, and antique stores. They gave each room an individual feel that accents its particular architectural design. One room has an outdoor terrace in one of only two open-air belvedere towers remaining in San Francisco. Another has a wall consisting entirely of small-paned windows. Yet another has a Persian-style sitting room with overlapping layers of carpeting, mounds of cushions, and tentlike drapings. The wallpapers throughout the house were designed by a local craftsman and fitted to the character of each room.

All rooms save one have queen-size beds; the exception has twin beds. They come with thick comforters, exquisite handmade spreads, and piles of fancy pillows. There are welcome brass reading lamps above the bed and a clock radio beside it. All rooms have private baths, which are particularly handsome and come with a variety of French soaps and shampoo. Some baths have large sunken tubs and french doors; all have expensive tile floors, wood trim, and brass fixtures. There is also a decanter of sherry in each room.

Furnishings vary from room to room, but all rooms have ample closet and bureau space. There are up to a half dozen lamps per room, all period pieces, as well as contemporary fixtures where needed. Rooms do not have televisions, but the Benaus will provide one on request. Rooms have telephone jacks, so private phones can be arranged. Otherwise, local calls are free from phones in the hall and library.

A large continental breakfast is served in the morning. In addition to a plate of fruit and cheese and a fresh croissant, William bakes something special each day. Coffee, tea, and juice are also offered.

Breakfast is served in the charming oak-paneled dining room. A large parlor off the entrance hall serves as the site for afternoon wine, where the Benaus chat with their guests around the fireplace and offer suggestions on what to see and do in town. Next to the parlor, a small library has a large assortment of guidebooks and general reading material for guests' use, along with menus from more than 200 local restaurants.

The inn has no private parking, but there is generally no problem finding a spot on the street. Two bus lines run within one or two blocks, leading either downtown or to the Marina District near the Golden Gate Bridge. Golden

Gate Park is within walking distance, and the connecting green strip of the Panhandle facing the inn allows runners to trot without interruption all the way to the ocean.

Vintage Court Hotel
650 Bush Street
San Francisco, California 94108
800/654-7266 (tollfree from within California)
800/654-1100 (tollfree from rest of U.S.)
415/392-4666

$79 single or double

In August of 1985, San Francisco's newest giant chain hotel had a miserable 15 percent occupancy rate. By contrast, the Vintage Court, a small (106 rooms) locally owned hotel set between Chinatown and Union Square, rented out 92 percent of its rooms during the same period, the highest rate in the city.

The key to the Vintage Court's success lies in a combination of personal service, attractive and comfortable design, and reasonable rates.

When you enter the lobby, you step down into a relaxing, low-key space marked by comfortable, contemporary furniture ringed around a working fireplace. Although totally remodeled in 1982, the building dates back to the early 1900s, and the lobby features the coffered ceiling and carved columns of the earlier era.

Rooms are large by local center-city standards, though only medium-size by suburban standards. Each room has either a king or queen bed, and 60 percent have bay windows with built-in window seats. Because there is no room service, each room also has an honor bar—a small refrigerator stocked with champagne, wine, beer, and soda to be paid for on check-out according to use. Baths offer standard tub-shower combos but are made fairly cheerful by use of patterned wallpaper rather than paint. This paper complements that of the room, which in turn carries over the gardenlike pattern from the comforter covers and drapes. In keeping with the hotel's name, burgundies and wines predominate.

Every few months, the hotel dedicates one of its rooms

337

to a particular California wine, staging a wine tasting, free to registered guests, for the occasion. There is, in addition, complimentary wine service each afternoon from 3:30 to 6 in the main lobby. (Complimentary coffee and tea are available at all hours.) Fashion and gift shows, also free to guests, are scheduled intermittently.

While the Vintage Court does not have its own dining room, Masa's, one of the finest restaurants in the city, occupies a portion of the ground floor. The hotel uses the space for a buffet breakfast ($4.50 per person), but dinner, for which reservations must be made at least four weeks in advance, is out of its province. However, the hotel staff can often arrange tables very early in the evening or for guests to fill in for last-minute cancellations. Meals (which run around $160–$200 for two) are renowned for the exquisite preparation and presentation.

The bar at Masa's is always open to hotel guests and features a Cruvinet system for providing individual glasses of distinctive wines that would ordinarily be available only by the bottle. Both the bar and the lobby are popular with women traveling alone because of their low-key, nonhassle atmospheres.

The Vintage Court has special attractions for business travelers, including free limousine service to the Financial District. It offers corporate discounts and has a skylighted conference room (seating up to 15, with audiovisual equipment) available for $100 per day. For regular corporate visitors, the Vintage Reserve Club throws in breakfast, the morning paper, and guaranteed reservations at the discount rate.

In the off season, the hotel offers special discount packages for noncorporate customers. With a two-night minimum, these also include breakfast and the morning paper, plus a free drink at Masa's.

The Vintage Court also has three sister hotels in the Union Square area. The Juliana, just up the block, has similar features and services but also has suites. The somewhat more sumptuous Galleria Park (all rooms $89, suites $125) has a running track and rooftop terrace plus whirlpool tubs. The Bedford, near the theaters, is a restored art deco hotel.

—————————— UNION SQUARE INNS ——————————

Small inns of considerable charm are rarely found right downtown in American cities. Yet San Francisco can boast three of them smack in the heart of Union Square, the city's prime shopping and entertainment district. Though independently owned, each offers similar accommodations and services including complimentary breakfast, wine or tea in the afternoon, and turndown service at night. Each also offers highly personalized attention to its guests.

At all of these inns, the owner or manager will see to tour and dining arrangements, provide advice and recommendations, arrange for secretarial or transportation needs, and, if possible, cater to personal whims of their guests. You will also find umbrellas provided for that sudden afternoon shower and other small touches that most establishments would not think of.

Emperor Norton Inn
615 Post Street
San Francisco, California 94109
415/775-2567

Double rooms $60–$85
Connecting rooms $145
Emperor's Suite $120

With only ten rooms, the Emperor Norton Inn strongly reflects the personality of manager Penelope MacInnis, an outgoing Scotswoman whose hearty manner could warm up the chilliest San Francisco day. While the inn is named for a colorful figure from the city's rather eccentric history, the decor is decidedly contemporary—light woods, beiges, and grays accented by soft mauves. Also contemporary are the televisions, mini refrigerators, AM-FM radios, and direct-dial telephones. The four lowest-priced rooms share a bath; all others have their own restored clawfoot tubs with brass fixtures.

The Emperor's Suite has a full kitchen, and the larger rooms have a small sitting alcove with loveseat and tea or breakfast table. Other rooms have two easy chairs, and all have large, decoratively curtained windows that let in lots of light.

La Petite Auberge
863 Bush Street
San Francisco, California 94108
415/928-6000

Queen rooms $95
Fireplace rooms $125–$145
Suite $185

La Petite Auberge has 26 rooms, all with private baths or showers. Eighteen of the rooms also have working fireplaces. Billing itself as "French country inn," the Auberge features rather high-style rustic furniture, down comforters, and baskets of fresh fruit and dried flowers. Breakfast, served in a lounge that opens onto a garden, is more filling than most continental-style repasts, with homemade breads and pastries, cereal, fresh fruit, and coffee or tea all available.

Some rooms are fairly dark, but there is a definite touch of whimsy that lightens up the whole place. A carousel horse graces the entry hall, and a collection of teddy bears lines the stairway to the lounge.

The Inn At Union Square
440 Post Street
San Francisco, California 94102
415/397-3510

Rooms $80–$150
Suites $110–$250
Penthouse $300

The Inn at Union Square is considerably more urban in style. Its small ground-floor entry resembles the library of a Boston or Philadelphia townhouse, all dark woods and low lighting. The truth is, with the 30-story St. Francis Hotel directly across the street, there's not a lot of light to be had; owners Nan and Norman Rosenblatt have wisely opted to build on the urban setting rather than counter it.

Rooms, too, tend toward the urban handsome instead of the country lovely. At the same time, the Georgian furniture, goosedown pillows, and carefully selected fabrics do not stint on comfort.

Breakfast—croissants, juice, coffee—is served on the lobby of each floor, where you can also sit for an afternoon tea of cucumber sandwiches and cakes. The inn has 30 rooms, including a penthouse suite, all with private bath.

«SAN JUAN»

Caribe Hilton International
Puerta de Tierra
San Juan, Puerto Rico 00903
1-800/932-3322

Singles $91–$110
Doubles $120–$150
Rates lower in summer

The Caribe Hilton, the first hotel in the Hilton International group, built more than 30 years ago, is still one of the finest in San Juan. Incorporating part of old Fort San Jeronimo, it sits on a point of land overlooking both the lagoon and the ocean.

Even though it is part of a chain, this hotel manages to retain a cordial Latin character and warm hospitality that comes from loyal staff members, many of whom have been with the hotel nearly 20 years or more.

It is one of the most convenient to Old San Juan and yet is a complete resort. Everything guests might desire is available here, from beautiful views to spacious public areas and a dramatic pool area along the ocean. The Caribe maintains a classy air that comes from a good management and hard-working staff. Service is excellent and all parts of the hotel are kept in top shape.

Accommodations are in a variety of rooms. The older ten-story building and newer 20-story tower are connected by walkways. Those rooms in the main hotel are the largest, with plush appointments and furnishings. These have the traditional two double beds, color cable TV, beautiful tile baths, and good views from upper floors.

The rooms in the new tower are smaller in size and are the most plush of all. They have the same layout and amenities as the older ones but better fabrics and more modern decor are used. For those who prefer more tropical rooms, then the garden wing would be better. These rooms, built in 1963, have a tropical flavor, with rattan furnishings, large tile baths, tile floors, and large windows with views of the pool area and garden.

Four restaurants provide excellent cuisine. A special feature is the theme night, offered all year round. These are special dinners prepared from recipes of Hiltons all over the world and are dramatically presented, usually outside on the terrace.

The Rotisserie is the top restaurant and offers elegant dining on continental fare. Reservations are always needed and a dress code is adhered to. Less formal is the air-cooled coffeeshop and a cafeteria-style terrace that serves breakfast and lunch only. For dinner the terrace is transformed into a romantic candlelit dining area with a reasonably priced menu.

For after hours, the hotel has several bars and a nightclub with a floor show. In addition, there is a casino (very formal) and an exclusive disco. Dress wear should be packed for a visit to this hotel.

Activities run the gamut from swimming in a free-form pool under a three-story atrium to fishing along the reefs to games and lessons of all sorts by the pool. Tennis is very popular and the courts are almost never empty. The six courts are lighted for night play, which is expensive. There are also lessons and a pro shop.

The Hilton has a complete health club (for men only) and an aquacenter for watersports. There is a scuba course, with one hour of pool time and diving included.

This resort caters to families. Activities are available for children as well as a babysitting service for younger ones. This and its popularity with the locals may make this hotel not as quiet as some others.

GranHotel El Convento Hotel
Cristo Street
Old San Juan, Puerto Rico 00902
1-800/223-0888

Singles $75–$90
Doubles $120–$150

El Convento Hotel, housed in a former Carmelite convent built in 1651, is located in the heart of Old San Juan. While not a hotel for beach buffs, it is perfect for those who prefer history to the sun.

In this very European hotel, rooms, service, and dining are all styled after a Spanish hacienda and remind guests of paradors in Spain, rather than a modern hotel in San Juan. The boutiques and museums of the old city are just a short stroll away on cobbled streets. Romance is very much a part of this hostelry.

While other hotels on the strip east of the old section are flashy, active, and often noisy, this hotel is quiet, calm, and intimate. More than any other hotel in Puerto Rico, it brings Caribbean life forward and honors it in its menus and service.

Accommodations are in contemporary, spacious rooms with old world Spanish decor and furnishings using lots of heavy wood. All rooms open onto the arcaded courtyard, part of which is covered to protect diners from the rain in the early afternoons.

Guests may dine in either courtyard or a plush Spanish colonial dining room. Gourmet cooking prevails and Spanish specialties are quite popular.

Rooms also have all modern amenities, including color cable TV, air conditioning, beautiful tile baths with marble vanities, and plush carpeting. More rooms have recently been added and are smaller, but with many of the same features.

Service, while good, is very slow. Guests should not expect the same swiftness that is found at other hotels on the beaches. Free transportation is provided up to the beaches in the Condado district as well as to tennis courts at other hotels.

Dorado Beach Hotel
Dorado, Puerto Rico 00646
800/228-9000 (tollfree)

Singles, doubles $190–$300

A short flight from San Juan Airport will bring travelers to one of the island's best hotels. Set on a 1700-acre former coconut plantation along a two-mile stretch of powdery beach, the Dorado Beach Hotel originally belonged to Dr. Alfred Livingston, who grew grapefruits with the coconuts. His original plantation house is the centerpiece of an elegant resort managed by Hyatt.

The former home is known as Su Casa, and the three-tiered restaurant of the same name is known throughout the world. Fame does have its price. Everything here is costly, from rooms to services to food. This is a place where guests come to impress someone—many corporations send their top salespeople here to cater to clients, especially on the resorts well-groomed golf courses.

The hotel features its own private airstrip, as well as a casino (next door at sister hotel Cerromar Beach), two pools with spacious patios and cocktail service. The main building contains an open-air lounge and terrace for tropical drinks in a romantic setting next to a covered bar for those rainy afternoons.

Rooms are in a variety of arrangements, running from luxurious ocean-view accommodations to private and expensive *casitas* (little houses) set in lush gardens and along the fairways of the two 18-hole golf courses.

Each room features cool floor tiles, a large furnished terrace, tropical decor and furnishings, and a very small bath. Some have balconies and overlook the pool or beach.

Casitas are set along the powdery sand beach. Each features a skylighted shower in the bath, terraces leading directly to the beach, refrigerators, and air-conditioning.

Service is not always as fast as back on the mainland. Because of the prices, some guests feel that they should be getting more for their money. The recent change to Hyatt management may make a difference.

Transportation is provided by shuttle buses around the grounds and to Cerromar Beach Hotel adjacent. The Cerromar is mostly used for large groups, but all of its facilities are available for use by Dorado's guests.

«SANTA BARBARA»

El Encanto Hotel & Garden Villas
1900 Lasuen Road
Santa Barbara, California 93103
805/687-5000

Guest rooms $100–$180 single or double
Villas $200–$300 single or double

In the hills above gemlike Santa Barbara lies El Encanto Hotel, with a generous view of the city and its coastline. The 100 detached units, with their attractive Spanish-Mediterranean design, sprawl over ten beautifully landscaped acres, which are a delight for those who appreciate a spectrum of flora. Geraniums, hibiscus, and bougainvillea, plus shimmering eucalyptus and sycamore trees are part of the lush growth surrounding the cottages. Also on the grounds are fish ponds, fountains, a wishing well, tennis courts, and a swimming pool.

El Encanto was constructed in 1915 and has been restored and the interiors beautifully decorated with a French country decor. Handsome polished woods are plentiful in cabinets and trim, while brass and crystal highlight the living quarters. The dining room features a panoramic view of Santa Barbara and also boasts some fine California cuisine with a French flair, prepared under the practiced hand of executive chef Renaud Defond, who owned his own successful restaurants in his native France.

An unobtrusive lounge features casual entertainment in the evenings. There is no disco on the property. While children are welcome at El Encanto, it appears to be a retreat preferred primarily by adults.

El Encanto was and is a hideaway for the famous from the world of sports, entertainment, and politics. It is located only a half mile from the famed Santa Barbara Mission and is near beaches and sightseeing in nearby communities.

Santa Barbara is 90 miles north of Los Angeles via U.S. Highway 101 and is also served by United Airlines as well as five regional and commuter airlines.

San Ysidro Ranch
900 San Ysidro Lane
Montecito, California 93108
805/969-5046

Rates quoted are for two persons European Plan:
Cottage rooms and studios $135–$195
Cottage suites $200–$230
Individual cottages $230 and up
Cottages with Jacuzzi $300 and up

The city of Montecito, neighbor to Santa Barbara, is the locale of the famed San Ysidro Ranch, soon to observe its one-hundredth birthday. Formerly a way station for Franciscan monks, it was acquired by two men in the 1920s, one of whom was the late film star Ronald Colman. San Ysidro became a hideaway for the likes of Somerset Maugham, Sinclair Lewis, and Winston Churchill, all of whom worked on manuscripts in the quiet of the Santa Ynez Mountains. Movie stars retreated to the ranch (and still do) to get away from the Hollywood grind.

A wooded hillside comprised of 550 acres holds only 14 single units and 24 suites, nine of which have private Jacuzzis. Some units have kitchens, and each one is furnished differently from the others. All have a living room, bedroom and fireplace. Most of the accommodations are private buildings separated by cobbled walkways, rose bushes, and oleander shrubs. Guests find that their names have been carved on a wooden shingle that hangs in front of their reserved cottages. Instead of numbers, the cottages bear names like Creek, Jasmine, Willow, Lilac, Pine, Geranium, and Magnolia.

There are no TV sets at San Ysidro, except for one in the main hacienda, where there is also an honor bar. San Ysidro is quaint and outdoorsy, with a stable of fine riding horses (horses are stabled on the American plan for $20 daily), heated swimming pool, tennis courts (extra charge), and miles of hiking trails. There is a kennel where pets can be kept ($6 fee) while owners are out on the town.

A big drawing card for ranch guests and local patrons at San Ysidro is its fine restaurant. Dishes like sauteed Wisconsin veal with Dubonnet, or fresh artichoke hearts with prawns in mustard sauce are typical of the elegant fare to be found on the daily menu. A frequent patron is Julia Child. The same restaurant is used for all meals. The Plow and Angel, a cellar where the Franciscans used to make wine, is now an evening watering hole for casual entertainment and dancing.

San Ysidro's present owners have thus far spent in excess of $1 million in refurbishing and improvements and are still spending.

«SANTA FE»

Santa Fe's bed and breakfasts, all in homes dating back 100 years or more, are liberally furnished with antiques, fine reproductions and a generous helping of Southwestern charm. All have some rooms with private bath and some with shared bath, and include breakfasts with fresh fruit and juice, homemade breads, and preserves. Off-street parking is provided.

Sociable types who enjoy meeting strangers, and who are relatively indifferent to amenities like room service (or even a private bath) will find that these B & Bs have much to offer. They are equal in charm to a city that many find the most charming in the nation.

The Preston House
106 Faithway Street
Santa Fe, New Mexico 87501
505/982-3465

$45–$98

The Preston House, a 100-year-old Queen Anne residence two blocks from the Plaza on a quiet, tree-lined street, offers six rooms, each with a welcoming carafe of Sherry. Artist Signe Berman, who restored the residence in 1981, or her manager is always available with friendly suggestions on current Santa Fe activities. It's also possible to spend some quiet hours reading in the old parlor or looking out on the well-kept lawn.

Grant Corner Inn
122 Grant Avenue
Santa Fe, New Mexico 87501
505/983-6678

$45–$100

Three blocks from the Plaza, at the opposite end from the Preston House and on a busier street, the Grant Corner Inn has furnished its 11 rooms with four-posters and brass beds, old quilts, tile stoves, and antique sinks. Halls are decorated with the owner's collection of fine old Indian blankets and baskets. All rooms have private phone and TV. A full breakfast—very popular with local residents, too—is served in two charming downstairs parlors, and, in good weather, on the covered porch outside.

El Paradero
220 West Manhattan
Santa Fe, New Mexico 87501
505/988-1177

$35–$95

Less central, El Paradero, near the State Capitol, has nine rooms, including budget-priced (and-sized) doubles at $35 to $65, sharply discounted from that low price in the winter. They are clean and simple, with shared baths in the hall. More spacious rooms are available, as well.

——————————— HOTELS ———————————

La Fonda
100 East San Francisco Street
Santa Fe, New Mexico 87501
505/982-5511

Double rooms $70–$90
Minisuites $95
Suites $150 and up
Off-season (Jan. 15–June 15) rates $10–$15 lower

There has been an inn (*fonda* in Spanish) on Santa Fe's Plaza since the city was founded in 1610. The present hotel, built in 1919, was owned by the Atchison, Topeka and Santa Fe Railroad, and operated by the Fred Harvey organization until 1968, when it was sold to private investors.

The hotel continues to attract guests because of its Plaza location, still the center of Santa Fe life, because the management has been careful to maintain the look of an old-fashioned Western Harvey House, and because the hotel understands that some are unwilling to forgo conveniences like air conditioning, color TV, and direct-dial telephones for the sake of nostalgia.

The lobby is clearly like no other in the United States. Huge leather and wood chairs are occupied by guests, locals, and Indians patiently waiting for customers for the turquoise and silver they hold on their laps. The paintings on the wall by Santa Fe artist Gerald Cassidy are the originals for the famed Santa Fe Railroad posters of the twenties.

Lobby, mezzanine, and a below-lobby arcade are lined with gift shops, are galleries, beauty parlors, and boutiques. Guests can buy Indian jewelry, antique carpets, piñon nut candy, or 100-year-old photographs without leaving the hotel.

A restaurant, La Plazuela, occupies the center patio, and a cocktail lounge is just off the lobby. In the summer, drinks are also served on a fifth-floor terrace with a spectacular sunset view of the town and the Jemez Mountains. A new indoor garage with room for more than 200 cars and a rooftop patio and bar is scheduled for completion in November 1986.

About 100 of the 160 rooms have been refurbished, with new carpet and drapes and remodeled bathrooms. Old furniture and tiles have been kept when possible; reproductions are hand-painted by resident artist Ernesto, who has been decorating the hotel's bedsteads, chests, light fixtures, and halls with flowers, birds, and abstract patterns in soft Southwestern colors for more than thirty years. Many of the rooms have original Indian art on the walls.

Rooms are not struck from a mold. Some have fireplaces, some balconies. Newer rooms, from an expansion in the forties, are rather small, with closet space unsatisfactory for a longish stay. There are spacious suites with bedrooms, parlors, and huge terraces overlooking the city. There are also minisuites with separate sitting areas. When requesting reservations, be sure to state your preference. La Fonda understands service, does its best to provide it, and will honor your request, if they can.

«SEATTLE»

Alexis Hotel
1007 First Avenue
Seattle, Washington 98104
800/426-7033 (tollfree)
206/624-4844

Singles, doubles $110–$150
Suites $150–$240

This buff-colored brick edifice occupies a corner of Seattle's Waterfront Place, a renovated mixed-use neighborhood in downtown. Built at the turn of the century and now listed on the National Register of Historic Places, the building actually housed a parking garage before the Alexis opened its doors in 1982.

Inside, a casual sort of luxury is evident in the combination of art deco and antiques. Peach, rose, and blue tones warm both the lobby and the hotel's 54 guest rooms. A grand piano sits beneath the lobby skylight, and fresh flowers are in view as elevator doors open on the upper floors. Though layout, size, and furnishings vary, services are, for the most part, offered across the board. These include a welcoming glass of sherry upon check-in, complimentary weekend continental breakfast in bed (served in the dining room on weekdays), complimentary shoeshine and morning newspaper, use of Pierre Cardin terry cloth robes, free local calls, turndown service with bedside chocolates, a telephone extension in the bathroom, and movie channel and cable news network. The hotel is wheelchair accessible. A clothesline pulls out from the wall inside the tub to steam or dry clothes, and a basket of soaps and lotions also holds a shoehorn, mending kit, and nail file set.

Almost all rooms have one piece of functional antique furniture—perhaps a large desk, a secretary, or an armoire. Local artwork (including works by Northwest Indians) is displayed tastefully in each room, and the marble-topped surfaces in all the baths were regenerated from torn-down Seattle buildings. The 12 suites feature a wet bar, a small refrigerator stocked with juice, sparkling cider, mineral water, and soft drinks, and Jacuzzi jets in the bathtub. Top of the line are the fireplace suites. The hotel's two meeting rooms, both with fireplaces, are ideal for small weddings or private dinners.

One of the most unusual practices at the Alexis is its no-tipping policy (food and beverage service excepted). Management claims this eliminates the palm-out attitude on the part of personnel and thus makes guests more comfortable.

Anyone at the reservation desk will serve as concierge, making tour arrangements or calling a cab. Private steam room sessions are available, rooftop tennis courts at a nearby garage may be used free of charge, and guests can pay for passes to either of two area health clubs. Parking is available at the hotel's underground garage (valet parking is also offered) or stickers will be given out for a nearby lot.

Locally grown ingredients are featured at the hotel's small restaurant, notable for its reasonably priced seafood. The fireplace in the adjoining bar crackles twelve hours a day in winter. Guests and locals alike partake of the eminently civilized late-night cognac happy hour. In addition, the hotel is about to purchase the corner pub, a place with a reading-room atmosphere where patrons can linger over ale and wonderful homemade soft pretzels.

Fudge, furniture, high tech products, shoe repair, and a host of other goods and services are available within the six-block Waterfront Place complex. At the elegant bookshop that adjoins the hotel lobby, browsers can delight in a selection of fine periodicals or purchase local preserves and smoked salmon.

The College Inn Guest House
4000 University Way, N.E.
(at 40th Street)
Seattle, Washington 98105
206/633-4441

Singles $30–$32
Doubles $37–$44
Triples $48

The innkeeper's touch is what makes a stay at the College Inn special. Hospitality and personal attentiveness to guests' requests is skillfully combined with respect for privacy. Guests ring the bell of this restored Tudor-style mansion to enter a small foyer where the exposed brick wall is lined with photographs of early Seattle. Up the stairs, two floors hold 27 rooms, all decorated with rose-colored carpet, floral print bedspreads, and Levelor blinds. Owner Gladys Fred combed Washington State's antique stores to find a collection of dressers, desks, night tables, lamps, mirrors, sideboards, hall trees, armoires, brass pots, and firescreens with which to furnish her hotel. Some of the loveliest are hand-hewn early American. Even the smallest single is a beautiful room.

The fourth-floor attic serves as combination breakfast nook, sitting room, library, music room, and office. Continental breakfast (included in the price of the room) is served from 7 to 9 A.M. along with the morning paper, and coffee and tea is available all day for a quarter a cup. The long wooden tables with their oak or mahogany chairs are also perfect for letter writing. Paperbacks left by guests, stacks of *National Geographics*, tourist brochures, and area restaurant menus fill the shelves of the bookcases. Guests are also free to play the grand piano in the corner.

The College Inn's prices are as low as they are due to the lack of frills: each room has a washbasin, towels, glasses, and soap; men's and women's bathrooms—gleaming and modern—are down the hall on each floor. Custom-made brass clothes racks replace closets, and a telephone room on the top floor stands in for private lines. The office will take messages for guests. To preserve the atmosphere of the European inn, there are intentionally no televisions or radios in guest rooms. Linen is changed every third or fourth day for ongoing guests (more often if requested) and those who stay on for several days may also request room service for breakfast.

The College Inn is also special for its location: Seattle's University District is in many ways more colorful and interesting than downtown. Excellent second-hand book and record stores, the university bookstore, lively cafes, and the University of Washington campus are at the inn's doorstep. Downtown is a short way by car, and half a dozen buses travel between the two areas. Parking at the university garage one block away is reasonably priced, or there is metered street parking. The inn's building also houses a very pleasant 24-hour corner cafe, a grocery-delicatessen, and a pub.

Now on the National Register of Historic Places, the College Inn was Seattle's first bed and breakfast. Its doors first opened in 1909 for visitors to the Alaska-Yukon-Pacific Exposition; the inn opened under current management in 1980. As a member of the nonprofit Seattle Bed and Breakfast Inn Association, the innkeeper will gladly recommend a sister institution if all rooms are booked.

Four Seasons Olympic Hotel
411 University Street
Seattle, Washington 98101
800/828-1188 (tollfree)
206/621-1700

Singles $130–$180
Doubles $150–$200
Suites $205–$825

The opening of the original Olympic Hotel in 1924 meant that Seattle's upper classes no longer had to travel to San Francisco to go dancing. Built to serve the city's civic-minded citizens, the Olympic was called "the parlour, the front room of this great metropolis of the Northwest," and was once compared to the great cathedrals of Europe. Indeed, standing on the mezzanine today, one can well imagine throngs of costumed women and their dapper escorts gathered to attend a debutante ball or cotillion.

The Italian Renaissance–style building occupies an entire city block in downtown Seattle. Opened as part of the Four Seasons chain in 1982 (which also includes the New York Pierre and the Chicago Ritz-Carlton) this restored landmark offers commodious comfort as well as a good measure of splendor.

The hotel's inner lobby still serves as something of a social club: Hand-burnished oak, marble- and glass-topped tables, and finely upholstered chairs and couches are arranged to form so many sitting rooms. Vaulted ceilings, carved arches, curved stairways, grillwork, and oak-paneled elevators complete the setting. Arcade shops offer luxury goods and services of both regional and international repute. The hotel is accessible to the disabled; wheelchairs and escorts are available.

In contrast to the activity downstairs, upstairs is hushed as a library. Rooms are spacious (the hotel's original 750 rooms were remodeled to form 450), and all have a separate sitting room or area. Drapes are wonderfully heavy chintz or linen. Over half the rooms in the hotel are Four Seasons suites, featuring curtained french doors to close off the bedroom.

The style throughout is residential. Furniture is mostly dark wood, fashioned by Hendredon (makers of home, not hotel furniture), bureaus and desks are free-standing, and wallpaper patterns are small prints. Baths have marble vanity sinks, a telephone extension, an assortment of toiletries including a jar of cotton balls and unwrapped soap, and luxurious terry cloth robes.

Hotel services are naturally extensive. In addition to the usual taxi-hailing and sightseeing information, guests can also call upon the concierge for a baby stroller, typewriter, or umbrella. Housekeeping will likewise provide heating pad, bed board, or clothes brush as well as the usual iron or extra blanket. Mending service, one-hour pressing, and complimentary shoeshines are also available. Linen turndown service includes chocolates, and room service is on call 24 hours. Facials, manicures, pedicures, haircutting, and flowers are all available within the hotel. Valet parking is available. Service throughout is attentive yet not intrusive.

In addition to use of the second-floor terrace atrium pool, exercise room, Jacuzzi, sauna, and sundecks, guests may pay extra for access to nearby gym facilities. Massage is available by appointment.

High tea, cocktails, and meals are served in several settings, including the Georgian Room, with its original antique chandelier and silk-upholstered chairs, the Garden Court with a wall of two-story Palladian windows, and a seafood restaurant that resembles a turn-of-the-century corner alehouse with the addition of outdoor tables. This last was at one time a men's clothing store; the original dark wood is ornately carved and where two tiers of suits once hung there is now recessed seating. All hotel menus are notable for their alternative selections low in calories, cholesterol, and sodium. At breakfast this may mean a bran-carrot muffin with apple butter; for dinner, perhaps an entree of broiled sturgeon with grapefruit-ginger sauce.

Inn at the Market
86 Pine Street
(at First Avenue)
Seattle, Washington 98101
800/446-4484 (tollfree)
206/443-3600

Singles $63–$110
Doubles $78–$125
Suites $133–$200

The name of Seattle's newest hotel supplies a perfect description: a bed and breakfast inn at the doorstep of Pike Place Market, the city's waterfront array of food stalls, shops, and restaurants. The new red-brick building was constructed around a 50-year-old cherry tree; watercolor prints of the wooden building that formerly occupied the site hang in all guest rooms. The building's unusual design—different sides are of varying heights in a stair-step configuration on a sloping site—means that guest rooms are exceptionally sunny and almost all of the 65 have views of water and mountains. Those that look over the center atrium see a small fountain with potted plants and flowers. Glass bricks make the hallways, with their flowered carpet and off-white walls, bright and warm. Elevators are brass-railed and wallpapered.

Interior decoration is country French style: cotton floral prints and soft green, mauve, or beige tones. Two special suites are done in blue and yellow. All room furnishings are light pine reproductions. All rooms have a small refrigerator, and a percolator that comes complete with a sample of coffee from a local merchant, and glass cups and saucers. Outer shower curtains are heavy cotton, and there are phones in all baths. Glycerine almond-honey soap, aloe and comfrey lotion, and bath crystals are some of the treats that fill a basket in each bath. When linen is turned down in the evening, a fresh flower is left on the pillow. Most rooms have sliding floor-to-ceiling doors and many have bay windows. Many are also furnished with bar, sink, and cupboard space, and some also have a chaise, a windowseat, or a small balcony.

Free continental breakfast with pastries from several local bakeries is served up daily with the morning paper. Guests may seat themselves either in the comfortable lobby or at the tables on the fifth-floor roofdeck which overlooks the waterfront. In the evening, this area serves as a picnic spot where guests can bring food from the nearby market stalls. On sunny summer days, sunbathers gather here.

A limousine will bring guests anywhere downtown for free (including to the airport shuttle). Front desk personnel will arrange childcare as well as the usual tourist services of dinner and theater reservations. Housekeeping is on call for room amenities and extras. Parking is available, though there is no valet service.

A jogging map of the area is left in each guestroom, or for a fee, guests are entitled to take advantage of the facilities at a nearby health club. The downstairs restaurant will supply either take-out or room service for hotel patrons.

Three floors of shops and eateries help make the inn a part of historic Pike Place. Among these are a fine bookstore, a juice bar, and a new Dilettante Chocolates, the latter a Seattle institution.

Mayflower Park Hotel
405 Olive Way
Seattle, Washington 98101
800/562-4504 (tollfree from within Washington)
800/426-5100 (tollfree from rest of U.S.)
206/623-8700

Singles $48–$60
Doubles $56–$68
Suites $90–$125

The pineapples carved into the exterior of this 1927 building are an old European symbol of hospitality, and while the Mayflower's decor is not on the whole old world, the hotel retains a traditional touch with its proliferation of brass (which is polished daily throughout the hotel), original crystal chandeliers, and fresh flower arrangements.

Modern additions include sound-insulated windows, ice and soda machines, and fairly standard furnishings in the 200 rooms. All upper-floor rooms provide city views, and all baths have original hexagon floor tile. Guest rooms are decorated in beige and rust tones with plenty of brass, except for the nine executive parlor suites, which are individually appointed. The suites, some of which served as permanent quarters in the hotel's early days, are especially nice, with some combination of dressing area, track lighting, wet bar, refrigerator, and digital clock. Those staying in suites (as well as frequent guests) are also treated to turned-down linens in the evening, in addition to a bucket of ice, soft drinks, and seltzer.

Although no shops are housed in the hotel, newspapers, stamp machines, maps and tourist brochures, snack machines, and cigarettes can be found in the lobby. Parking is free, and upon request a bellperson will park for guests. Privileges at a nearby athletic club can be purchased for a fee. The Mayflower's front desk and bellpersons will make dinner or theater reservations, and housekeeping will take in minor sewing jobs, find a babysitter, and furnish cribs, rollaway beds, or wheelchairs as well as the usual iron, blanket, or pillow.

The Mayflower's two restaurants are reasonably priced. Clipper's, a cheery dining room, serves up Northwest fare. Oliver's is a popular lunch spot well known and loved for its cheese-filled quiche. Large windows make for a fine streetside view here. The marble table tops were pulled from an old Seattle building. The hotel's bakery is on the premises, and its products are excellent. An attractive mezzanine-level sitting area (with original stained glass) is a good place to meet either friends or business colleagues.

Pacific Plaza Hotel
Fourth Avenue at Spring Street
Seattle, Washington 98104
800/732-1235 (tollfree from within Washington)
800/426-1165 (tollfree from rest of U.S.)
206/623-3900

Singles, doubles $44–$62
Suites $85–$132

The Pacific Plaza caters to young business travelers on a budget. A shy English bulldog has been crowned the hotel's mascot—the sign out front is stamped with her face, room keys are large, nicely carved dog bones, and the private guest lounge has been dubbed the Top Dog.

The 160-room hotel was renovated and reopened as a historic landmark in 1981. The original 1929 hardwood doors, brass knobs, porcelain faucet fixtures, and marble thresholds remain intact, complemented by more modern fabrics and furniture. For example, traditional curved headboards are upholstered with a contemporary print.

Rooms are decidedly small, though arranged tastefully, and the private lounge (opened by room keys) is accessible at all times to add some space. The smallest studio rooms include a couch that folds out to a twin bed. The 14 corner rooms with king-size beds are the largest. All baths have mosaic tile floors, and those without a tub make up for it with the addition of a marble wall. Some rooms also have ceiling fans and old-fashioned bottle openers with cork-screws mounted to the walls. All are decorated with black and white drawings of Seattle and the Puget Sound done by a local artist.

Front desk personnel and bellpersons take care of tour arrangements and reservations. Linen will be turned down in the evening upon request. Guests can park at one of two nearby garages. Although the hotel has no health club af-filiate, Seattle's YMCA and YWCA are both nearby and offer full gym facilities.

The Red Robin restaurant, which opens into the hotel lobby, takes care of room service and allows guests to charge to their room tab. Much nicer though is City Picnics, the small, New York–style deli and bakery that also serves breakfast, lunch, and dinner. The sandwich board is exten-sive, and diners can take their food to the hotel's intimate upper lobby. Continental breakfast is served in the guest lounge, where there are also drink and snack machines, telephones, and tourist brochures.

Sorrento Hotel
900 Madison Street
Seattle, Washington 98104
206/622-6400

Singles, doubles $95–$110
Suites $120–$725

The Honduran mahogany–paneled walls in the Sorrento's lobby are hand-oiled every few months. Afternoon tea in the Fireside Room—also mahogany-paneled with an un-covered Rookwood fireplace—includes scones with double cream, and the hotel's meticulous brewing method is de-scribed on the menu. The managing director doubles as the hotel florist, which means exquisite fresh flower arrange-ments throughout. The Sorrento is truly a master among small deluxe hotels.

Built on what was once a bluff in Seattle's First Hill neigh-borhood, several blocks up from downtown, guests enter the Italian Renaissance building (modeled after a castle in Sorrento, Italy) by way of a circular carriage drive styled after a Mediterranean forecourt. The Hunt Club, the hotel's small restaurant, serves excellent seafood, and as its name suggests, is reminiscent of a rather exclusive gathering place. Continental breakfast and cocktails are served in the Fireside Room.

Muted browns, dark reds, greys, greens, and blues are used to decorate guest rooms, all of which are appointed with dark wood furniture. Because the hotel's original 150 rooms now form only 76, some have idiosyncratic alcoves or angles, enhancing the residential atmosphere. All have a separate sitting room or sitting area. The *Wall Street Journal* is delivered to all doors in the morning; other papers are for sale at the front desk. In addition, rooms are supplied with copies of such periodicals as *Architectural Digest, Fortune,* and the *New Yorker*. All suites have a refrigerator and a dressing area, and most have stereo components.

The Sorrento prides itself on personal yet unobtrusive service. The concierge will supply not only travel information, but also courier, translation, babysitting, and secretarial services, or can even charter an aircraft. Housekeeping will provide guests with such extras as cribs and bedboards; shoeshines are complimentary, and clothing can be pressed or repaired as well as laundered and dry cleaned. Pillowside mints accompany turned down linen in the evening.

Complimentary limousine service in quite an attractive car operates in the downtown area, or to the airport for slightly less than the cost of a taxi. Guests may pay to use a nearby athletic club, and a Seattle jogging map is left in each room. There is parking at the hotel with valet service.

The Sorrento, which was built in 1909 for the Alaska-Pacific-Yukon Exposition, witnessed considerable decline, and reopened as a luxury hotel in 1981. Staff like to speak of the hotel as a home. Indeed, in days bygone, prominent city families resided here, and the style of quiet luxury living has been re-created with impressive authenticity.

Stouffer Madison Hotel
515 Madison Street
Seattle, Washington 98104
800/468-3571 (tollfree)
206/583-0300

Singles $105–$145
Doubles $115–$155
Suites $350–$700

The Madison is a large hotel in downtown Seattle that aims to conduct itself as a small one—and succeeds with a well-tailored combination of luxury and hospitality. Best evidence of this is the complimentary morning paper and coffee or tea that accompanies personal wake-up calls (with just the right amount of time between the ringing phone and the knock at the door). Continental breakfast comes with the more expensive rooms. Those who prefer no intrusions may set the AM-FM clock radio provided in all rooms and pour themselves free coffee from the large silver urns in the lobby, available all morning. After an evening out, guests can return to turned down linens and before-bed chocolates.

In between, services are plentiful. The concierge will make the usual theater or dining reservations as well as arranging for interpreters, babysitters, and Mailgrams. The bell captain will arrange a complimentary shoeshine, and room service is available 24 hours. Courteous and unobtrusive best describe the way hotel personnel go about their duties.

A rooftop health club consists of a lovely, if small, heated indoor pool (with large windows providing fine city views), a Jacuzzi, and small exercise room. Massage and hydrotherapy are arranged by appointment. The hotel also houses a beauty shop for men and women, and a florist, as well as a newsstand-giftshop. Parking is available at the hotel.

Though a concrete highrise, the building's elegant green awnings presage its interior: clean lines and neutral and dark green tones make for both warmth and elegance. Several beautiful 19th-century silk-embroidered tapestries hang in the public areas.

The narrow tower structure allows impressive views in many rooms. The building's four sides overlook the Puget Sound, the port of Seattle, downtown, and the mountains. All rooms include a marble-top dressing or writing table, a walnut armoire, and complimentary cable channel. Over half also have a separate sitting room or area.

Hotel dining and drinking take place in four spots: a quiet bar, a casual restaurant with an American menu, a more formal 28th-floor restaurant (waiters are clad in bow ties and aprons) serving northern Italian cuisine, and a rooftop lounge with dance floor. Views from these last two establishments are sweeping.

Recent renovations include the addition of outdoor tables to a lobby bar and two club floors. The hotel is accessible to the disabled.

«TAMPA»
«ST. PETERSBURG»

The Don CeSar
3400 Gulf Boulevard
St. Petersburg Beach, Florida 33706
800/237-8987 (tollfree)
813/360-1881 collect

Fall and Winter: Rooms $100–$135, suites $140–$300,
   penthouses $500
Spring: Rooms $90–$115, suites $130–$250, penthouses
   $500
Summer: Rooms $80–$100, suites $115–$250,
   penthouses $500

In the midst of an extensive $5 million renovation, the
Don CeSar Beach Resort, one of the oldest and best-known
hotels on Florida's gulf beaches, still offers old-time splendor.

The focus of most of the remodeling effort is the Don's
272 guest rooms, which are being redone floor by floor in
Italian marble, new wallpaper, curtains, and wall-to-wall
carpeting. However, the neo-Spanish decor and a blend of
Mediterranean and Moorish ambience will be maintained.
The gulf waters are still blue, the palms are green and the
exterior of the hotel remains the patented Don CeSar pink.

The Mighty Don, or the Pink Palace as it is known, was
built in the mid-1920s and it was built to last with two-foot-
thick reinforced concrete by millionaire real estate specu-
lator Thomas J. Rowe. The ornate complex has withstood

hurricanes and disasters such as the Great Depression and was recently registered in the government's Register of Historic American Buildings.

This palatial, historic landmark has always been a haven for notables: Clarence Darrow, Babe Ruth, and F. Scott Fitzgerald are among the many famous individuals who have stayed here. Today's visitor with a taste for reasonably priced opulence still finds it a romantic hideaway with towering ceilings, ornate moldings, and antique furnishings.

For all its tradition, the Don doesn't lack modern amenities, including 11 elegant, multipurpose meeting rooms that can hold groups from ten to 500. The Grand Ballroom is the showpiece of the hotel. High ceilings, arched windows, and a combination of plush carpeting and highly polished wood flooring provide a feeling of grandeur. On the fifth floor of the hotel are more meeting rooms highlighted by a spectacular fountain and two-story windows that overlook the Gulf of Mexico.

The Don's beachfront location is ideal for watersport enthusiasts, who can slowly sail the smooth gulf waters on the hotel's 41-foot ketch or thrill to exciting jet skiing or parasailing.

Back on land, guests enjoy sunning and swimming in the Don's large pool with adjacent Jacuzzi. Tennis enthusiasts can volley and rally to their heart's content on lighted all-weather courts and golfers can play on immaculate greens of a nearby championship course. Fitness buffs can enjoy the Health Club, work out in the exercise room, and relax with a massage or in a sauna or whirlpool.

The Don's gracious accommodations are outdone only by the wonders of nature. Depending on the location of your room, you can wake to promising sunrises over sailboat-studded Boca Ciega Bay or retire to equally majestic sunsets over the Gulf of Mexico.

The Don is reasonably close to area attractions such as the Salvador Dali Museum, Tampa's Busch Gardens, and Sarasota's Ringling Museum. It's also within a two-hour drive of Walt Disney World, EPCOT Center, and other Orlando attractions.

Saddlebrook, The Golf and Tennis Resort
One mile east of I-75 on County Road 54 (exit 58)
Wesley Chapel (Tampa), Florida 34249
800/282-4654 (tollfree from within Florida)
800/237-7519 (tollfree from rest of U.S.)

Special golf, tennis, and spa package rates available; typical rates (honeymoon and anniversary package) follow.

Jan. 6–April 3: Deluxe rooms $251 per couple, extra nights $116; one-bedroom suites $287 per couple, extra nights $134

May 1–June 14: Deluxe rooms $203 per couple, extra nights $92; one-bedroom suites $239, extra nights $110

June 15–Sept. 14: Deluxe rooms $139 per couple, extra nights $60; one-bedroom suites $157, extra nights $69

Saddlebrook Golf and Tennis Resort depicts a side of Florida many tourists have yet to experience. Just a few minutes after exiting I-75, guests drive past horses grazing on verdant pastures and are admitted through a guardhouse gate to a resort surrounded by tall cypress and pine trees.

A winding, tree-lined drive passes blue lakes before reaching Saddlebrook's Walking Village, a cluster of conveniently placed two-story condominium units laid out and designed to preserve Florida's country atmosphere. The condominium suites are surrounded by lush tropical landscaping that attracts many varieties of birds including herons such as the gray neck egret. Central parking, located an easy, soothing walk from the suites, assures that no bird song is interrupted by automobile noise.

Located in Wesley Chapel, a Tampa suburb just 25 minutes north of Tampa International Airport, Saddlebrook offers tourists a location central to top-rated attractions. Gulf beaches and deep-sea fishing are less than an hour away.

But it's when the tourist is tired of touring and needs a breather that Saddlebrook comes into its own. It's an excellent place to relax. One can enjoy the sun while playing golf or tennis, or while lounging next to Saddlebrook's immense pool.

The golf course's 36 holes were designed by Arnold Palmer and Dean Refram and have been rated as among the finest in the state. Since Saddlebrook is headquarters for the U.S. Professional Tennis Association, the tennis complex, with its 11 Har-Tru and four Laykold tennis courts, is just as well planned as the golf courses. Luxurious one-, two-, or three-bedroom condominium-style suites—each with a splendid view of golf course or lake—are clustered within steps of the spectacular pool and within easy walking distance of the golf courses and tennis courts. Meandering through the center of the Walking Village, the 270-foot-long pool allows plenty of room for water volleyball and basketball; 25-meter swimming lanes, a diving area, heated whirlpools, a supervised children's pool and play area, cocktail bar, and snack shack.

At one end of the pool is the Centre Club. Built primarily of stone, glass, and natural wood, with luxurious marble accents, the Centre Club overlooks a nine-hole golf course. Under one roof is the Cypress Dining Room, the Gourmet Room, Polo Lounge, a gift shop, the Pegasus Ballroom, Jockey Club Spa, and meeting rooms for conferences large and small. The Cypress Dining Room is known for its Sunday brunch. Award-winning French haute cuisine is served by white-gloved waiters in the ornate Gourmet Room. This dining room is decorated with pure silk wall and seat coverings, and hand-sewn woven English wool carpeting.

Calories put on by gourmet cooking can be worked off through exercise. Saddlebrook's Jockey Club Spa offers guests a complete physical fitness center with separate facilities for men and women. Guests can enjoy working out on their own with the latest exercise equipment or participate in individualized exercise classes. After exercise, they can reward themselves by taking advantage of heated whirlpools, saunas, steam rooms, or a massage.

Visitors rave about the fishing in Saddlebrook's many ponds and streams—freshwater bass and bream abound—and the exotic plants that can be seen during a nature walk along the 480 acres of woodland, gardens, and rolling hills.

Besides natural beauty, little touches make staying at Saddlebrook special. There's a basket of personal toiletries in every bath, and a sampler of coffee and tea in each kitchen, along with several electric appliances, including a blender. Decor and furnishings are lavish, including original art and brass accessories. The beds are triple-sheeted and the color-coordinated bed linen is ironed every morning. In addition, a terry cloth robe is provided each guest for trips to and from the pool.

«WASHINGTON,» «D.C.»

Adams Inn
1744 Lanier Place, N.W.
Washington, D.C. 20009
202/745-3600

Rooms $25–$45

The Adams Inn is irresistibly tiny. With only ten rooms, plus an efficiency apartment in the carriage house, this bed and breakfast establishment is amply cared for by one housekeeper and one manager. The owners, who live across the street, fill in whenever and wherever necessary, even opening their home to guests who find they need to stay an extra night.

In many ways the inn is reminiscent of an English B&B. An unprepossessing turn-of-the-century townhouse on a residential street, it was renovated in 1983 to capture the growing market for European-style lodgings. The first floor holds a comfortable sitting room, furnished with easy chairs, bookshelves, an oriental rug, and a gas fire; the dining room, where continental breakfast is served at one large, solid table, and where guests may work at any hour; and a small kitchen. The brick patio in back has room for a small gathering. One feels at home despite the presence of a pay phone in a corner of the dining room.

The bedrooms are little more than that; five have private bathrooms with shower stalls, six do not. The rooms without baths are equipped with sinks, European-style. There are no phones or TVs, but a writing table can be borrowed if necessary. The main building is centrally heated and air-conditioned. An extra blanket is included in the closet. The carriage house, which is separately heated, contains two double beds, a bath, and a kitchenette.

Proximity to several large convention hotels attracts many business travelers, and the inn's owners claim most of its guests are of the early-to-bed, early-to-rise variety. All are advised, however, to take taxis if they return after dark, to avoid walking on unfamiliar back streets. The inn provides limited parking—six spaces in two separate garages.

Lanier Place is just minutes away from Adams Morgan, one of the liveliest areas of Washington. Ethiopian and Latin American restaurants abound, as do antique shops and international shops of all kinds.

No smoking is allowed in the inn, and guest rooms are not wheelchair accessible.

The Adams Inn is affiliated with several bed and breakfast agencies. Reservations should be made two to three weeks in advance.

The Capitol Hill Hotel
201 C Street, S.E.
Washington, D.C. 20003
202/543-6000

Suites $95–$135

The Capitol Hill Hotel opened in 1982 to serve the needs of the corporate business traveler. Just four blocks from the Capitol and across the street from many other government buildings, it is the ideal location for the corporate lobbyist or anyone else in Washington on government or quasi-government business.

The philosophy of the hotel reflects its target market. It offers peace, quiet, and security rather than entertainment and ostentation. All 153 suites are equipped with a queen-size bed, a convertible sofa, a fully outfitted kitchen, and a standard bathroom. Prices vary according to the size and layout of the rooms. The premiere suites have a separate living room with dining area, while the smaller guest suites have sitting areas at one end of the bedroom and an ell for the dining table. The very smallest suites combine sitting, dining, and sleeping areas in one long room.

With either a light blue or a lavender-gray color scheme, each room is subtle and homey. On the walls hang framed and very attractive posters from special art exhibits and retrospectives. Both the bedroom and the living room (when separate) contain remote-control color television sets. For other entertainment, guests are invited to select books from the shelves in the lobby, and easy chairs are provided for comfort.

Taking care of guests means, at the Capitol Hill, providing them with plenty of room to conduct business and putting them at ease. Each traveler receives complimentary wine and cheese and a luxurious bathrobe for the length of the visit, and the *Washington Post* delivered to the door each morning. Those who don't have time to shop for their groceries may leave a list with the front desk. And all guests receive discounts at the nearby Capitol Hill Squash Club.

The hotel encompasses two buildings. In the second building's Executive Salon, complimentary breakfast is provided for special guests, as well as sherry in the evening. Room service is available anywhere in the hotel from 7 to 9 A.M. and 6 to 10 P.M. Guests also have check-signing privileges at Yolanda's Restaurant, reached by the canopied entrance between the hotel's two buildings.

Parking is limited, and travelers are urged to inquire about availability in advance. There is an overnight fee of $7.

Although not equipped with handbars or large bathrooms for wheelchairs, the hotel should be accessible to the semi-ambulatory. The entrance is at ground level, corridors are wide, and both buildings have elevators.

The Capitol Hill can accommodate small boards or executive committee meetings in any of three board rooms. Its one conference hall holds 45. Complimentary Perrier is provided for all meetings, and catering services can be supplied on request.

Nearby Pennsylvania Avenue offers bright lights and a variety of restaurants. The rest of Washington is accessible from the Metro station just a block from the hotel. Most guests prefer to go out to play, and come home to the Capitol Hill for rest and contemplation.

The Embassy Row
2015 Massachusetts Avenue, N.W.
Washington, D.C. 20036
202/265-1600

Singles $130–$165
Doubles $145–$185
Suites $200–$550

With a third of its clients foreign and U.S. diplomats, the Embassy Row is used to serving dignitaries. It is one of Washington's newer luxury hotels, built in 1971 by a local dentist with big dreams. Yet it has already undergone a major renovation. Owned and managed by the Lincoln Hotel Group, the Embassy Row is a member of Preferred Hotels Worldwide.

The hotel benefits immensely from its location. Not one full block from Dupont Circle, a cultural and entertainment center for the city, the hotel offers a quiet retreat and convenient home base. It marks the start of the stretch of Massachusetts Avenue that supports many of the major foreign embassies in Washington. It is also just minutes from Rock Creek Park, a fine area for jogging or picnicking, and from Georgetown.

All of the hotel's rooms face either front or back. The view over Massachusetts Avenue is nothing to sneeze at, but that at the back, over the roofs of northwest Washington and on up to the Washington Cathedral, is perhaps the most elegant feature of the hotel. Enormous plate-glass windows allow the fortunate guests to survey fully this superb panorama, which gives Washington the look of continental Europe.

Inside, the rooms are decorated tastefully in muted pinks, grays, and greens. The standard furniture in the guest rooms makes up in comfort what it lacks in distinction, and the beds—all queen- or king-size—are luxurious. All of the rooms, with or without sitting area, are spacious and plush.

Amenities include a rich, heavy cream-colored robe with the Embassy Row seal on the breast. Larger rooms and suites include a wet bar and refrigerator, and every room has its own safe.

The staff of the hotel is carefully selected, and takes its work extraordinarily seriously. Though the bellperson may be garrulous and able to converse in several languages, there is a line of respect between servant and guest that is not crossed. The traveler's comfort and safety is of primary concern; in addition to its basic staff, the Embassy Row hires retired D.C. police officers to stand guard 24 hours a day.

The three dining and entertainment areas on the mezzanine offer three very different styles. The Bar, a windowless room paneled in light wood, seats about 25 persons in small groups under paintings of soldiers and gentlemen. Across the way, the Winter Garden atrium gives a bright, open atmosphere to breakfast, lunch, or evening cocktails. And for formal dining, the Ambassador Grill presents a dark, mirrored interior with a balcony open in summer. Food is serious business here, from the delicious sourdough bread to the continental and new American entrees.

Monday through Friday evenings, pianist John Eaton provides music in the lobby between the three rooms.

The conveniences of the Embassy Row go beyond amenities to personal attention. The hotel's seamstress stands ready to mend a torn shirt or popped button, while valet parking service costs $10 for 24 hours no matter how many times it is necessary to pull in and out. Room service also extends round the clock, and the menu includes a short wine list. For groups, four meeting rooms accommodate up to 200 persons, and all rooms are equipped for audiovisual presentations. Finally, the hotel's concierge can help with any needs that aren't covered in the extensive service directory.

Topping it all off is a rooftop pool open Memorial Day to Labor Day. Available for private receptions as well as for general relaxation, the pool overlooks Georgetown and the embassies directly, and, of course, much of Washington besides.

The Georgetown Dutch Inn
1075 Thomas Jefferson Street, N.W.
Washington, D.C. 20007
202/337-0900

Singles $95
Doubles $105
Penthouses $200

The 46-suite Dutch Inn in Georgetown is one of hundreds of hotels nationwide that claim to possess European charm and flavor. Unlike many of the others, though, the Dutch Inn can support its claim with some figures. Some 83 percent of its clients are Europeans, from single business travelers who stay for a night to relocating families who stay for weeks.

Tucked off busy M Street, the inn presents an unremarkable brick front. Its underground garage might be mistaken for public parking, were it not for the subtle yet explicit sign above its entrance. On the inside, however, the hotel cannot be mistaken. The lobby area, a few steps below street level, is cozily if modestly furnished, and surveyed 24 hours a day by one of several outgoing staff members at the reception desk. Continental breakfast, included in the room rate, is served in the lobby from 7 to 11 A.M.

Lisa Goldman, the Dutch Inn's charismatic manager, is responsible for the hotel's philosophy. Trained on the European model, Goldman takes pride in establishing ongoing relationships with her guests. Informality is the rule—the inn isn't out to capture the luxury hotel market, or imitate its style. Instead, Goldman boasts about the advantages of not being a grand hotel: the low staff turnover rate and the ability to meet individual needs. This she is willing to do even over prices. If you're staying over a week, or have another special circumstance, Goldman says, "Let's make a deal."

All of the guest rooms are suites with fully equipped kitchens. There are 39 one-bedroom suites, furnished with twin, double, or king-size beds, plus a pullout couch in the living room. The walk-in closets are large enough to be— and are sometimes used as—nurseries. Each suite has a push-button phone in the bedroom, bathroom, and living room. The living rooms include a wingback chair, coffee table, dining table with chairs, writing desk, and color television. Notable are the Chinese painted screens that decorate the walls. The full drapes and red wall-to-wall carpeting make the suites feel like home. The kitchen, however, is better than home—utensils and dishes, available on request, will be washed by the housekeepers if it's too much effort to turn on the dishwasher.

But the seven duplex penthouse suites are Lisa Goldman's pet projects. Varying in size and shape, each one has a kitchen, living room, and half bath on one floor, and two bedrooms and full bath upstairs. Every room has its own thermostat for the comfort of the guests. The basic contents are the same as in the smaller suites, but Goldman is replacing the standard hotel furniture, piece by piece, with antiques she picks up on weekends in Maryland and Virginia.

The penthouse suites double as the hotel's meeting rooms. If a member of a group stays in the hotel, Goldman points out, the meeting room comes free of charge. She will set up a room not according to the number of people, but the style of the conference. Again she advises, "You tell me what you want, and I'll show you what I can do for you," from a circle of wingbacks for an informal meeting to 50 chairs arranged theater-style for a presentation.

The icing on top of the Dutch Inn's cake consists of room service from 11 A.M. to 11 P.M. and a rooftop pool open from Memorial Day to Labor Day. The pool is tiny—12 by eight feet—but there is plenty of deck space. Goldman plans to beat the Georgetown market by opening its first rooftop cocktail lounge for use from early spring through late autumn.

Leo & Linda's Restaurant, in the basement, is leased out, and thus avoids providing mere hotel restaurant food. The pink and white dining area seats 60 at tables of four. A glass door at the back lets onto Georgetown's C & O Canal Park, and tables are moved out in the summer months.

The Dutch Inn is a find you may want to share with friends and family. Goldman makes it easy, by offering low rates for extra persons. Up to two children under 16 stay free with their parents. In the one-bedroom suites, it's $10 for each additional person; in the penthouse suites, the rate is fixed no matter how many people share the space.

Lisa Goldman lives on the premises, so there's never a delay in response to a pressing situation. She has cheerily resigned herself to seeing a limited number of new faces. After all, 58 percent of her guests are returning to the fold.

The Hotel Washington
15th Street and Pennsylvania Avenue, N.W.
Washington, D.C. 20004
800/424-9540 (tollfree)
202/638-5900

Singles $84–$99
Doubles $96–$111
Suites $220 and up

Despite its 350 guest rooms, the Hotel Washington considers itself a small hotel. It has been owned by one corporation since the 1940s, and is run as a family operation. The hotel management boasts principally of the longevity of its staff, many of whom have given over 30 years of service. Similarly, the same business and government groups return to this home near the White House year after year.

The hotel is a national landmark, and when visited was in the process of a multimillion-dollar restoration scheduled to be completed by June 1987. The lobby is dominated by soaring arches with decorative friezes, and contains original furniture from the hotel's opening in 1918. Oriental rugs cover the marble-tiled floor, and nine marble urns, from an original set of ten, are displayed about the lounge area. When completed, the Two Continents restaurant will feature three murals uncovered during restoration, as well as its original fireplace.

The Hotel Washington capitalizes on its proximity to the White House and the monuments in several ways. During the summer, dinner is served in a glassed-in rooftop restaurant. Lunch, cocktails, and weekend brunch are offered at the open-air Skywalk Cafe from the last weekend in April through November. Both offer sweeping views of monumental Washington. For the future, the hotel has plans to open a sidewalk cafe on its F Street corner during the summer, allowing up to 200 persons to overlook the East Lawn of the White House on the one hand, and on the other, the hotel's impressive external friezes depicting American heroes and presidents.

All guest rooms have full-view windows, bringing a fair chunk of the capital city into focus. Prices vary according to which chunk one gets. Two color schemes—blue and dusty rose—differentiate the decor of one room from the next. Though the single and double rooms are not large, the furniture—bed, writing desk, armchair, standing lamp, and cabinet (containing remote-control TV with alarm clock)—is particularly tasteful, as are the silk flowers on the bedside table. The bathroom features a marble bath, a clothes line over the tub, a built-in hair dryer, and a second phone. The hotel has received an award for the packaging of its amenities—shampoo, soap, hand cream, and sewing supplies are tucked neatly into a cardboard replica of the Washington Monument.

A doorbell outside each room assures that guests won't miss callers, whose knocks might be absorbed by the solid walnut doors.

Many of the hotel's clients are part of groups of varying sizes. Ten meeting rooms, including the ballroom, are available to accommodate meeting and banquet needs, as is the in-house catering staff. The hotel offers special rates also to tour groups during the summer and winter months and on weekends.

A full complement of services is available, including Talbert Ticket Agency, for theater tickets, in the lobby. The hotel has no garage, but public parking is available on F Street and G Street for a competitive fee.

The Kalorama Guest House
1854 Mintwood Place, N.W.
Washington, D.C. 20009
202/667-6369

also at
2700 Cathedral Avenue, N.W.
Washington, D.C. 20008
202/328-0860

Singles $25–$70
Doubles $35–$75
Suites $60–$95

Designated by only a tiny brass sign beside the door, the Kalorama Guest House snuggles inconspicuously between the other townhouses on Mintwood Place. The guest house encompasses three buildings on Mintwood—1854, 1852, and, across the street, 1859—and another two on Cathedral Avenue, for a total of 42 guest rooms. A certain nonchalance characterizes the operation of the hotel, making the Kalorama a home not only for the managers who live on the premises, but for its guests. The latter are encouraged to rummage around in the chest of drawers in the hall for extra towels and sheets and for first aid supplies. In summer, guests make use of the backyard tables and grill for their own barbecues.

Each of the Kalorama's properties provides similar services and considerations. Continental breakfast, included in the overnight price, is served every morning; at 1854, it's in a low-ceilinged basement nook with pink placemats and ice cream parlor tables. Coffee is left on all day, and there's a television near the dining area. From 5 P.M. on, sherry is served in the hotel's parlor, encouraging guests to congregate and converse.

The charm of the guesthouse is enhanced by its furnishings. The front desk is just that—a desk in the richly appointed front parlor. A varied collection of Victorian furniture rests on a warm oriental rug at 1854 Mintwood, and a fire burns on the hearth through the winter.

Aside from a brass bed with a firm mattress and an alarm clock beside it, no two guest rooms share the same furniture. The hotel has been outfitted almost entirely with antiques. However, each bedroom is provided with a writing area of some sort, with ample closet or wardrobe space, and with wall-to-wall carpeting.

There is a wide variety of rooming options at the Kalorama. A few rooms have private baths, but most have just a sink in the bedroom and share a bath. The Mintwood Place property offers two suites and one efficiency apartment, including kitchenette. Prices vary with size, number of beds, and position within the hotel. (Guests pay slightly more for a view of the street or Kalorama Park.) Although the guest rooms do not have telephones, guests are urged to use the house phone—one is located in each of the separate buildings. Each guest room includes a pamphlet explaining the ways of the hotel and what to do in an emergency. Televisions are available for rent.

All of the townhouses, both on Mintwood Place and on Cathedral Avenue, have laundry facilities, including an ironing board. Because only one of the buildings is air-conditioned, each room has its own air-conditioning unit to ward off the summer's heat waves.

Both properties are close to many Washington attractions, including the National Zoo, the Connecticut Avenue–Dupont Circle shopping area, Adams Morgan, and the embassy area. Both are also within walking distance of bus and subway stops. Plenty of area maps and service directories are available to aid with planning activities and expeditions. Parking is extremely limited. A public lot on nearby 18th Street charges $6 for 24 hours.

The Kalorama Guest House fills up from March through November, and reservations should be made at least three weeks in advance. To make winter stays more attractive, in 1985 the guest house initiated a "Culture-in-Residence" program, through which those with expertise in a particular area of the arts stay free in the hotel in exchange for an evening's lecture or reading in one of the front parlors.

The Kalorama Guest House requires prepayment in full. Refunds are made only with two weeks' notice of cancellation or if canceled rooms are filled; credit is given when refunds cannot be made.

The Mayflower Hotel
1127 Connecticut Avenue, N.W.
Washington, D.C. 20036
800/468-3571 (tollfree)
202/347-3000

Singles $165–$225
Doubles $185–$245
Suites $350

Accommodations at the Mayflower begin at deluxe and go up from there. It is impossible to avoid or to ignore the elegance of this giant, whether one views its double-towered, gold brick facade from across Connecticut Avenue, strolls beneath the Promenade's nine chandeliers stretching from the lobby to the 17th Street doors, or simply sits back in any of 680 guest rooms with a drink from the prestocked refrigerator. It is just as impossible to challenge the authenticity of this opulence. The lobby's floors are marble, its column caps 22-karat gold leaf, and the bronze statues at the entrance to the waiting area originals from the Vanderbilt Collection.

All this—and a ballroom, too—could easily overwhelm the visitor. Yet the Mayflower creates an atmosphere of welcome, without intimidating. The generous staff (575 in all) is chatty, cheerful, and earnest—they want to be good at what they do. Chairs and tables are grouped in small, intimate clusters, bringing elegance from the grand to a more human scale.

The Mayflower has earned its status as a District of Columbia landmark. Washington's first luxury hotel, it opened on February 18, 1925, and hosted Calvin Coolidge's inaugural ball less than a month later. The hotel has hosted an inaugural ball for every president elected since Coolidge, and has housed countless American and foreign dignitaries for months at a time. John P. Marquand's novel *B.F.'s Daughter,* written while the author was in residence, depicts hotel life during the Second World War, when skylights were covered and the hotel prepared to convert its barber shop into a hospital if necessary. When diplomatic relations with the People's Republic of China were reopened in 1973, the entire Chinese ambassadorial delegation lived and worked at the Mayflower for seven months, pending the establishment of permanent diplomatic offices. A $100 million restoration of the hotel was begun in 1982, not long after the Stouffer Company took over management of the hotel, and in 1983 the Mayflower was listed on the National Register of Historic Places.

Guest rooms fall into three categories: deluxe, deluxe with sitting area, and suite. The basics include firm king- or twin-size beds with headboard, writing desk with protective glass top, easy chair, large closet, and standing cabinet that opens to reveal a color television with HBO. (The cabinet also has drawers for clothing.) The deluxe with sitting area adds a second chair and table with lamp, a loveseat, and a butler table. Suites have the standard bedroom furniture plus large sitting rooms with sofa, secretary, and fireplace with original 1925 mantelpiece. Each suite also includes a pantry with a fully stocked wet bar, and connecting doors make it possible to create two-bedroom suites.

Perhaps even more than the bed and sitting rooms, with their rich fabrics and dark wood, the bathrooms establish the Mayflower as a luxury hotel. Marbletop sink and brass fittings on basin and tub are reflected in an enormous over-sink mirror and a full-length mirror on the back of the door. There's a pull-out clothesline over the tub, and a hair dryer on the wall beside the sink. Guests need not pack soap, shampoo, shower cap, or shoehorn—or even bathrobe—as all are provided by the hotel.

One might get carried away by the abundance, were it not for the extra costs that the high admission price doesn't cover. The prestocked minibars are inventoried daily, and charges for the expensive drinks and snacks added to the room bill. Room service is pricey here as elsewhere, and to open your room to an added guest costs a hefty $30.

The amenities at the Mayflower do however seem endless. Not one but three touch-tone phones grace the rooms, at bedside, on the desk, and in the bathroom. The computerized pass cards that serve as room keys can be replaced instantly. Guests needn't wake up to order breakfast, as a tag is provided on which the order (including choice of newspaper) can be checked, then left on the doorknob before midnight. Literature on the desk includes the extensive menu for 24-hour room service and those for all in-house restaurants as well as a comprehensive directory of services. Best of all, checkout time isn't until 2 P.M.

On the first floor, in addition to the ballroom and several meeting rooms for the groups that make up one-half of the clientele, are a newsstand, florist, Cartier jewelry shop, and several entertainment areas. The Cafe Promenade, where breakfast and lunch are served seven days a week, is lit by an enormous domed skylight, and contains two murals painted by WPA artist Edward Laning in the 1950s. The musician's gallery is functional—a harpist presides over Sunday brunch. Behind the reception desk, the Nicholas Restaurant is open for dinner every night and for lunch on weekdays. Operated independently, the Nicholas has earned a name for itself among Washington restaurants for its new American cuisine. The Town & Country Lounge, tucked into the Connecticut Avenue and DeSales Street corner, is dark and intimate, providing live music Monday through Saturday evenings.

Below stairs, a shoeshine stand and beauty salon–barber shop complete the hotel's services. Parking is available in a garage behind the hotel on DeSales Street, at $11 a night.

It wouldn't be difficult to confine oneself to the Mayflower for weeks at a time with minimal cravings for the world outside. But the neighbors also beckon. The hotel sits between the White House and Dupont Circle, just above the K Street Corridor, one of Washington's busiest commercial areas. Restaurants and bars abound, and the streets are crowded with vendors. In short, whether inside or out, a guest of the Mayflower Hotel is at the heart of Washington's good life.

The Normandy Inn
2118 Wyoming Avenue, N.W.
Washington, D.C. 20008
202/483-1350

Singles $70
Doubles $80
Suites $160

It's almost impossible to keep a steady conversation going with Jeanette Weir, the Normandy Inn's vivacious general manager—she keeps turning to greet another guest, ask after family news, or introduce neighbors at breakfast. But she always turns back and picks up where she left off, with a smile. She is in the hotel business because she loves people, and she is a success because people love her.

The homey tea room beyond the lobby is the center of the inn. Large mirrors in dark wood frames give a sparkling quality to this oddly shaped corner, which encourages intimacy. Continental breakfast is served here every morning for $3.50, and complimentary tea and coffee are left out from 11 A.M. to midnight, with cookies served at 3 P.M. As a consequence, a handful of guests can be found chatting relaxedly at almost any hour, in French or English. On Tuesday evenings, Weir puts on a wine and cheese affair to make it easier for guests to meet each other. The cheese may run out, but Weir promises that the wine will not as long as guests are enjoying themselves.

The 74 guest rooms are moderate in size and modest in decor. Oranges and light browns in the fabrics, coupled with limited views (mostly of other buildings), make the bedrooms a tad drab. But the beds are taut as drums, and each room has two velvet-covered wingback reading chairs with a standing lamp between, as well as a color television. Closet space is ample. Continental breakfast will be served in the rooms from 7 to 11 A.M. at no extra charge.

Guest bathrooms are exceptionally clean and bright—and ready to put travelers in the same condition. A choice of two soaps is laid out on the Formica counter, and one can bathe and shampoo with the multipurpose Eurobath soft soap in the dispenser above the tub. The plain white towels are noticeably softer than the average hotel linens.

The inn has four suites, each of which has a sitting room with sofa that converts to a queen-size bed, two easy chairs, a desk, and a coffee table. For families, the inn offers separate corner rooms that share a common entrance. (Children under 12 stay free in the same room with their parents. There is a $10 fee for a cot.)

Security has never been a problem. The front door closes at 11:30, and guests use a phone to gain entry. The only other entrance is through the garage, and that door is controlled by the front desk. Safety deposit boxes are available at the reception desk.

Special services of the inn include bus tours (limousines are hired to transport the disabled), same-day dry cleaning, foreign language assistance, and luggage storage for those who find the noon checkout time inconvenient. Parking in the underground garage is free for guests. The inn has one meeting room, which holds up to 50 persons.

The Normandy Inn lies halfway between Dupont Circle and Adams Morgan, both centers for dining, shopping, and entertainment. The ethnic restaurants in Adams Morgan are some of the best in Washington. The inn's service directory includes a select list of local businesses and eating establishments.

Old Town Holiday Inn
480 King Street
Alexandria, Virginia 22314
800/368-5047 (tollfree)
703/549-6080

Singles $88–$100
Doubles $91–$106
Courtyard rooms $94–$106
King leisure rooms $97–$109

For the traveler who has visited Washington before and wearied of its monumental aspect, the Old Town Holiday Inn may represent a welcome retreat. It's not so much the hotel that soothes as the locale—Old Town Alexandria is a charmingly restored colonial seaport. Like Georgetown, this part of Alexandria is built to a smaller scale, and its treasures are the fine 18th-century homes and narrow streets. Unlike Georgetown, it is not overrun by noisy youngsters in search of entertainment. The crowds pursue the more muted pleasures of fine dining, window-shopping, and strolls by the Potomac, where the schooner *Alexandria* is lit up at night.

Alexandria was George Washington's boyhood home, and Old Town is filled with reminders. The George Washington Masonic National Memorial dominates King Street, the main drag, and most of the sights of the historic district bear some relation to the man who wouldn't be king. There are also a few commemorative plaques to Confederate soldiers and supporters—the site of the Holiday Inn is where the "first martyr to Southern Independence" is said to have fallen. But though the Ramsay House Visitors Center can direct you to plenty of "official" sights, none deserves undue attention in and of itself. Old Town must be taken as a whole to be appreciated. Most buildings on King Street are not original, though built to seem it. The best finds are on the streets that parallel King to the north and south. The little alleys and courtyards off Cameron Street offer a multitude of painted brick and wooden houses, almost every one designated by a "Historic Alexandria Foundation" plaque, and Prince Street preserves one block of cobblestone close to the river. Horse-and-buggy tours leave from the waterfront park, and may be an entertaining alternative to walking.

The Holiday Inn occupies a key spot on King Street about four blocks from the waterfront. This red brick, imitation colonial building faces King Street's shops and fountain plaza on one side, a quiet side street on another. The hotel's prized inner rooms have balconies that open onto its own courtyard, where in summer the outdoor GW's Tavern serves lunch at midday, and drinks and light snacks into the evening.

Though it bills itself as a luxury hotel and is independently franchised, this Holiday Inn is much like any other Holiday Inn. Muzak greets the ear as one enters the lobby. Furniture in the guest rooms recalls suburban bedroom sets—solid, but uninspired.

The rooms do have many conveniences: color television with HBO, controlled from the bedside alarm clock; two sinks, one within and one without the bathroom door; and a safe deposit box. The beds are firm, the pillows soft, and the standard amenities adorn the bathroom. Room service is available from 7 A.M. to 10:30 P.M. In addition, the hotel has a number of nonsmoking rooms, and three rooms fully equipped for the disabled.

The hotel's indoor swimming pool and sauna, open year round, are appealing features.

About 20 percent of the Holiday Inn's guests are with groups, and the hotel hosts banquets and wedding parties as well. The fifth floor has meeting rooms and a separate kitchen to take care of these functions; unfortunately for guests in the nearby rooms, the banquet rooms are not fully soundproof.

Concierge service includes morning coffee (6:30–8 A.M.) and afternoon tea (3–5 P.M.) on weekdays in the lobby. The concierge, whose desk is near the reception area, can provide information and literature on both Virginia and the District.

Old Town lies about ten minutes distant from Washington's National Airport. Parking underneath the hotel is complimentary to guests. Those without cars can take advantage of the free courtesy van to and from Washington National, which offers complete morning coffee service (in the afternoons, it's Perrier).

Clearly, the distinction of the Old Town Holiday Inn lies in the first half of its name. But the hotel's conveniences, including special weekend rates, may tip the balance in favor of staying on a few extra days.

The Tabard Inn
1739 N Street, N.W.
Washington, D.C. 20036
202/785-1277

Singles $39–$85
Doubles $59–$105

The Tabard Inn is easily the most romantic spot in Washington. On entering one seems transported to the 18th century in old England, or, more accurately, in the young republic. No attempt has been made to match walls to floor or chair to table—everything in the inn is just old. Dark wood, framed mirrors, and a collection of furniture that defines eclecticism give each of the public areas and guest rooms its own flavor.

Consisting of three adjoining buildings that have been connected at various points, the Tabard is a labyrinth of stairways and corridors. Some of the landings toward the front are furnished with an overstuffed loveseat or two; scenes of horsemanship and the hunt adorn the walls. Since the buildings were once individual homes, the rooms vary in size and shape according to the original function of each. Rates vary with the rooms—one pays more for the front parlor than for the servants' quarters.

There is no way to categorize the bedrooms. All 40 have polished wood floors and each contains at least one bed, bureau, writing table, easy chair, and push button phone. But there the resemblances end. In one of the front rooms, the traveler will find a brass bed, an enormous mirrored wardrobe, a fireplace with ornamental mantel seasonally decorated, a tiny private bath, and a stand-up piano. Another room has a double and a single bed, a plain fireplace, wainscoting halfway up the wall, and a slightly larger bath. And in a smaller room, a single bed stands against one wall with a secretary scrunched between bed and window opposite a large chest of drawers, and there is no bath at all.

The public areas of the hotel are equally various. Of the two lounges, the first has seven sofas and couches that divide the room into four or five intimate areas, a huge fireplace (the inn's only working one) where the fires roar in winter, bookcases, and sketches of Revolutionary figures on the walls. The second lounge, above the restaurant, is smaller, and decorated in a fairly consistent Asian motif—except for the piano. The restaurant looks spare in comparison, with its black-and-white tile floor and small tables. Continental breakfast is served here for guests every morning, 7–10 on weekdays and 8–10:30 on weekends. The restaurant is open to the public for lunch and dinner, and drinks from the bar can be carried to either lounge. In summer, tables are put outside on the patio.

The disadvantages of the Tabard are the disadvantages of any small inn. There are no ramps or elevators, making access for the disabled difficult if not impossible. There is no parking to speak of, and luggage storage is haphazard —under the stairs or in the basement. Yet those who are unaffected by these inconveniences will find the Tabard Inn to be, like its namesake in Chaucer's *Canterbury Tales*, a pleasant and hospitable resting place for wandering pilgrims.

«Index»

393

FOR YOUR INFORMATION

The Harvard Common Press is located in Boston, Massachusetts. We publish practical guides to small business, careers, family matters, and cooking. We specialize in travel guides. We have listed below a few of the titles that we thought might interest readers of this book. If you'd like more information or a copy of our catalog, or if you would like to order directly from us, please write: The Harvard Common Press, 535 Albany Street, Boston, Massachusetts 02118. All of our books are also available at local bookstores.

You may also wish to obtain a copy of our *Best Places to Stay in New England*, the only accommodation guide that caters to your particular interests. It includes family resorts, farms, gilded cottages, getaways—gourmet, island, and romantic—spas, and much, much more. We would be happy to give you a 10 percent discount off the list price of $9.95. If you would like a copy, send a check for $10.96 (includes $2 postage and handling) to the address above. Be sure to tell us that you read about *Best Places to Stay in New England* here.

Our other travel guides:

How to Take Great Trips with Your Kids
The Portable Pet: How to Travel Anywhere with Your Dog or Cat
Exploring Our National Parks and Monuments
A Traveler's Guide to the Smokey Mountains Region
The Carefree Getaway Guide for New Yorkers
The Best Things in New York Are Free
Inside Outlets: The Best Bargain Shopping in New England
Paradores of Spain: Unique Lodgings in State-owned Castles, Convents, Mansions, and Hotels
Pousadas of Portugal: Unique Lodgings in State-owned Castles, Palaces, Mansions, and Hotels
The Best Things in New York Are Free
Inside Outlets: The Best Bargain Shopping in New England

Paradores of Spain: Unique Lodgings in State-owned Castles, Convents, Mansions, and Hotels

Pousadas of Portugal: Unique Lodgings in State-owned Castles, Palaces, Mansions, and Hotels

«BEST PLACES REPORT»

We appreciate any information you can supply about the quality of the lodging. Detailed information about the building, furniture, service, food, and setting is most important. Describe as many rooms as you can, including living rooms, dining rooms, other common rooms, and of course bedrooms. A note about activities and nearby sights would be wonderful. Finally, how did you hear about the place, and how long have you been going there?

We will be happy to send you a free copy of the next edition of the book if we use your suggestion.

To: Bruce Shaw
      Best Places to Stay in America's Cities
      The Harvard Common Press
      535 Albany Street
      Boston, Massachusetts 02118

Hotel: _____

Address: _____

_____ Zip: _____

Telephone: _____

Description: _____

_____

_____

_____

_____

_____

_____

_____

Your name: _____ Telephone: _____

Address: _____

_____ Zip: _____

«BEST PLACES REPORT»

We appreciate any information you can supply about the quality of the lodging. Detailed information about the building, furniture, service, food, and setting is most important. Describe as many rooms as you can, including living rooms, dining rooms, other common rooms, and of course bedrooms. A note about activities and nearby sights would be wonderful. Finally, how did you hear about the place, and how long have you been going there?

We will be happy to send you a free copy of the next edition of the book if we use your suggestion.

To: Bruce Shaw
     Best Places to Stay in America's Cities
     The Harvard Common Press
     535 Albany Street
     Boston, Massachusetts 02118

Hotel: _____

Address: _____

_____ Zip: _____

Telephone: _____

Description: _____

_____

_____

_____

_____

_____

_____

_____

Your name: _____ Telephone: _____

Address: _____

_____ Zip: _____

«BEST PLACES REPORT»

We appreciate any information you can supply about the quality of the lodging. Detailed information about the building, furniture, service, food, and setting is most important. Describe as many rooms as you can, including living rooms, dining rooms, other common rooms, and of course bedrooms. A note about activities and nearby sights would be wonderful. Finally, how did you hear about the place, and how long have you been going there?

We will be happy to send you a free copy of the next edition of the book if we use your suggestion.

To: Bruce Shaw
   Best Places to Stay in America's Cities
   The Harvard Common Press
   535 Albany Street
   Boston, Massachusetts 02118

Hotel: _____

Address: _____

_____ Zip: _____

Telephone: _____

Description: _____

_____

_____

_____

_____

_____

_____

_____

Your name: _____ Telephone: _____

Address: _____

_____ Zip: _____

«BEST PLACES REPORT»

We appreciate any information you can supply about the quality of the lodging. Detailed information about the building, furniture, service, food, and setting is most important. Describe as many rooms as you can, including living rooms, dining rooms, other common rooms, and of course bedrooms. A note about activities and nearby sights would be wonderful. Finally, how did you hear about the place, and how long have you been going there?

We will be happy to send you a free copy of the next edition of the book if we use your suggestion.

To: Bruce Shaw
      Best Places to Stay in America's Cities
      The Harvard Common Press
      535 Albany Street
      Boston, Massachusetts 02118

Hotel: _____

Address: _____

_____ Zip: _____

Telephone: _____

Description: _____

_____

_____

_____

_____

_____

_____

_____

Your name: _____ Telephone: _____

Address: _____

_____ Zip: _____

«BEST PLACES REPORT»

We appreciate any information you can supply about the quality of the lodging. Detailed information about the building, furniture, service, food, and setting is most important. Describe as many rooms as you can, including living rooms, dining rooms, other common rooms, and of course bedrooms. A note about activities and nearby sights would be wonderful. Finally, how did you hear about the place, and how long have you been going there?

We will be happy to send you a free copy of the next edition of the book if we use your suggestion.

To: Bruce Shaw
       Best Places to Stay in America's Cities
       The Harvard Common Press
       535 Albany Street
       Boston, Massachusetts 02118

Hotel: _____

Address: _____

_____ Zip: _____

Telephone: _____

Description: _____

_____

_____

_____

_____

_____

_____

_____

Your name: _____ Telephone: _____

Address: _____

_____ Zip: _____

«BEST PLACES REPORT»

We appreciate any information you can supply about the quality of the lodging. Detailed information about the building, furniture, service, food, and setting is most important. Describe as many rooms as you can, including living rooms, dining rooms, other common rooms, and of course bedrooms. A note about activities and nearby sights would be wonderful. Finally, how did you hear about the place, and how long have you been going there?

We will be happy to send you a free copy of the next edition of the book if we use your suggestion.

To: Bruce Shaw
      Best Places to Stay in America's Cities
      The Harvard Common Press
      535 Albany Street
      Boston, Massachusetts 02118

Hotel: _____

Address: _____

_____ Zip: _____

Telephone: _____

Description: _____

_____

_____

_____

_____

_____

_____

_____

Your name: _____ Telephone: _____

Address: _____

_____ Zip: _____

404